VARIATION IN THE INPUT

STUDIES IN THEORETICAL PSYCHOLINGUISTICS

VOLUME 39

For further volumes:
http://www.springer.com/series/6555

VARIATION IN THE INPUT

Studies in the Acquisition of Word Order

Edited by

MERETE ANDERSSEN
University of Tromsø, Tromsø, Norway

KRISTINE BENTZEN
University of Tromsø, Tromsø, Norway

MARIT WESTERGAARD
University of Tromsø, Tromsø, Norway

Editors
Merete Anderssen
University of Tromsø
Center for Advanced Study in Theoretical Linguistics (CASTL)
9037 Tromsø
Breivika
Norway
merete.anderssen@uit.no

Kristine Bentzen
University of Tromsø
Center for Advanced Study in Theoretical Linguistics (CASTL)
9037 Tromsø
Breivika
Norway
kristine.bentzen@uit.no

Marit Westergaard
University of Tromsø
Center for Advanced Study in Theoretical Linguistics (CASTL)
9037 Tromsø
Breivika
Norway
marit.westergaard@uit.no

ISSN 1873-0043
ISBN 978-90-481-9206-9 e-ISBN 978-90-481-9207-6
DOI 10.1007/978-90-481-9207-6
Springer Dordrecht Heidelberg London New York

Library of Congress Control Number: 2010933509

Printed on acid-free paper

Springer is part of Springer Science + Business Media (www.springer.com)

Contents

The Acquisition of (Word Order) Variation 1
Merete Anderssen, Kristine Bentzen, and Marit Westergaard

Optional Illusions 17
Andrea Gualmini

'Optional' Doubly-Filled COMPs (DFCs) in Wh-Complements in Child and Adult Swiss German 33
Manuela Schönenberger

The Acquisition of Adjectival Ordering in Italian 65
Anna Cardinaletti and Giuliana Giusti

Input Factors in Early Verb Acquisition: Do Word Frequency and Word Order Variability of Verbs Matter? 95
Anja Kieburg and Petra Schulz

Word Order in the Development of Dative Constructions: A Comparison of Cantonese and English 129
Chloe C. Gu

Using Early ASL Word Order to Shed Light on Word Order Variability in Sign Language 157
Deborah Chen Pichler

Variable Word Order in Child Greek 179
Konstantia Kapetangianni

Optional Scrambling Is Not Random: Evidence from English-Ukrainian Acquisition 207
Roksolana Mykhaylyk and Heejeong Ko

The Acquisition of Apparent Optionality: Word Order in Subject and Object Shift Constructions in Norwegian 241
Merete Anderssen, Kristine Bentzen, Yulia Rodina, and Marit Westergaard

Index 271

Contributors

Merete Anderssen University of Tromsø, Tromsø, Norway, merete.anderssen@uit.no

Kristine Bentzen University of Tromsø, Tromsø, Norway, kristine.bentzen@uit.no

Anna Cardinaletti Università Ca' Foscari di Venezia, Venice, Italy, cardin@unive.it

Deborah Chen Pichler Gallaudet University, Washington, DC, USA, deborah.chen.pichler@gallaudet.edu

Giuliana Giusti Università Ca' Foscari di Venezia, Venice, Italy, giusti@unive.it

Chloe C. Gu University of Massachusetts Amherst, Amherst, MA, USA, cgu@linguist.umass.edu

Andrea Gualmini Utrecht University, Utrecht, The Netherlands, a.gualmini@uu.nl

Konstantia Kapetangianni University of Michigan, Ann Arbor, MI, USA, kapetang@umich.edu

Anja Kieburg Johann Wolfgang Goethe-University Frankfurt, D-60323 Frankfurt am Main, Germany, kieburg@em.uni-frankfurt.de

Heejeong Ko Seoul National University, Seoul, South Korea, heejeong@alum.mit.edu

Roksolana Mykhaylyk Stony Brook University, Stony Brook, NY, USA, rmykhayl@ic.sunysb.edu

Yulia Rodina University of Tromsø, Tromsø, Norway, yulia.rodina@uit.no

Manuela Schönenberger University of Oldenburg, Oldenburg, Germany, iris.schoenenberger@uni-oldenburg.de

Petra Schulz Johann Wolfgang Goethe-University Frankfurt, D-60323 Frankfurt am Main, Germany, P.Schulz@em.uni-frankfurt.de

Marit Westergaard University of Tromsø, Tromsø, Norway, marit.westergaard@uit.no

The Acquisition of (Word Order) Variation

Merete Anderssen, Kristine Bentzen, and Marit Westergaard

1 Introduction

This book contains chapters that investigate children's acquisition of different types of variation in the primary linguistic data (PLD) that they are exposed to. Natural languages often display word order variation that may at first sight seem like instances of optionality. An example of this is the word order alternation in particle verb constructions in Norwegian, where the particle may precede or follow the direct object DP, illustrated in (1a, b):

(1) a. Han kastet **ut** **hunden**.
he threw out dog-the
'He threw out the dog.'
b. Han kastet **hunden ut**.
he threw dog-the out
'He threw the dog out.'

Language-internal optionality has represented and continues to represent a challenge for any linguistic theory that is based on economy principles, since generally one of the options should be more economical than the other and thus constitute the only grammatical one. What does it mean for one and the same speaker to find both word orders in (1) grammatical? One possibility is that the speaker is entertaining two different grammars (or parameter settings) simultaneously. This hypothesis is supported by the fact that only (1a) is possible in Swedish, while Danish only uses (1b). So does a speaker of Norwegian who alternates between (1a) and (1b) access two parallel grammars with respect to particle shift, one corresponding to the Swedish pattern

M. Anderssen (✉)
University of Tromsø, Tromsø, Norway
e-mail: merete.anderssen@uit.no

M. Anderssen et al. (eds.), *Variation in the Input*, Studies in Theoretical Psycholinguistics 39, DOI 10.1007/978-90-481-9207-6_1,

and one corresponding to the Danish one? Approaches to word order variation along these lines have been proposed for both adult and child language by for example the Theoretical Bilingualism Hypothesis of Roeper (1999) or Yang's (2002, 2004) Variational Learning Model.

However, in recent years it has become increasingly clear that there is very little true optionality in language; rather, instances of apparent language-internal optionality tend to be governed by (often subtle) interpretive nuances, generally related to information structure. We have already seen one such example in (1) from Norwegian. This particle shift alternation is also found in English: *I can't pull* ***down my sleeve*** vs. *I can't pull* ***my sleeve down***. A further example of word order optionality from English is the double object construction: *She gave* ***Peter some wine*** vs. *She gave* ***some wine to Peter***. The word order choice in these cases is not random, but dependent on the type of object, pronouns being impossible in the unshifted position or as a direct object in the DP + DP construction. According to Bresnan et al. (2007), when the syntax allows two word orders, the choice of the two may be predicted by a variety of pragmatic factors, such as discourse accessibility, length, definiteness, etc.

While optionality represents a challenge for the description and analysis of adult languages, it appears to be a defining characteristic of child language. For example, child languages typically exhibit a great deal of optionality as far as the inclusion of various elements is concerned. Well-studied examples of this are Optional Infinitives as well as Null Subjects in non-null-subject languages, cf. e.g. Wexler (1994, 1999) and Rizzi (1993/1994, 1994, 2000). Thus, optionality has received much attention in language acquisition studies. But so far relatively little has been done on how children treat optionality in the input.

This book aims to bridge this gap in the study of language acquisition by focusing on questions such as: What kind of optionality and variation are children exposed to and what are the relevant distinctions in the adult language? How do children deal with this variation in the PLD? Do they exhibit any preferences in such cases and if so, what kinds of considerations influence their choices? How early and to what extent are children sensitive to prosodic cues and the small nuances in syntax and information structure that govern adult grammars in cases of variation? What is the role of input frequency? And what can the study of language acquisition reveal about the nature of the variation that is permitted in the adult language?

It is in many ways surprising that children's behaviour with respect to variation in the input has not been studied more extensively, since natural languages exhibit numerous examples of these phenomena. The reason why these ideas have been neglected in child language studies is presumably due to a common idea within generative theory that, in order to be learnable, grammars should only consist of major parameters. In fact, the main rationale behind the parametric approach has been to explain the ease and speed of language acquisition, and despite the common claim found in the acquisition literature that children are so-called 'conservative learners', it has also been assumed that some aspects of a parameter may fall into place with very little or perhaps no exposure to the relevant structures in the input.

To our knowledge, there exist relatively few studies addressing word order optionality in the input. Important examples are Zuckerman (2001) and Zuckerman and Hulk (2001), who investigate the acquisition of French *wh*-questions, where the *wh*-element may either move or stay in situ in the adult language. They find that French children have a preference for the *wh*-in-situ option at the early stages, even though these occur with a lower frequency in the input. This lack of movement in child language is argued to be the result of what is referred to as economy-based markedness, and is taken to be the result of an acquisition strategy rather than the reflection of a defect in the children's grammars.

The acquisition group at the University of Tromsø has recently established a project addressing word order optionality: VIA – Variation in the Input in Acquisition. This is based on some work that has already been carried out by the Tromsø group, and much more is in the planning. While most of the early publications have analysed spontaneous production data from a corpus of Norwegian (Tromsø dialect), see e.g. Anderssen (2006), the more recent work is based on experiments carried out in an acquisition lab that was established a couple of years back. Some examples of the linguistic phenomena that have been addressed so far by the Tromsø acquisition group are outlined here.

Westergaard (2003) discusses the acquisition of the well-known micro-variation with respect to V2 and non-V2 in *wh*-questions found in many Norwegian dialects (see e.g. Vangsnes 2005). In The Tromsø dialect, this variation is dependent on the type of *wh*-element, V2 being required with disyllabic *wh*-words, while either word order may be used in questions with monosyllabic *wh*-elements. In the latter case, the two word orders are distinguished by information structure, non-V2 being used with informationally given subjects (typically pronouns) and V2 with informationally new or focused subjects, as illustrated in (2a, b).

(2)	a.	Ka **hete** **han der** **typen** **der**? *what is-called that there guy-the there* 'What is that guy called?'	V2
	b.	Ka **han** **gjør** her? *what he does here* 'What is he doing here?'	Non-V2

Westergaard (2003) shows that children produce both word orders from early on, and furthermore, that they seem to be sensitive to the subtle distinctions in information structure. In Westergaard (2009a, b, c) it is shown that the syntactic micro-variation related to the type of *wh*-element is also acquired early.

A further example of variable word order relates to verb placement in embedded clauses in Norwegian, where the standard language generally requires the verb to follow adverbs or negation, as shown in (3). Recent work on certain Northern dialects (Bentzen 2005, 2007) shows that there is a considerable degree of dialect variation with respect to embedded clause word order, indicating that the input to children is not as straightforward as previously assumed.

(3) Det fins studenter som **aldri drikker** vin / *som **drikker aldri** vin.
there exist students who never drink wine / who drink never wine
'There are students who never drink wine.'

The word order of children's embedded clauses is discussed in Westergaard and Bentzen (2007), which is based on both spontaneous and experimental data from Norwegian. It is shown that children produce non-target-consistent word order with verb movement across negation or aderbs for an extended period of time (at least until age 6), and the findings are discussed in terms of issues such as frequency, syntactic complexity, and economy. Similar findings are attested for Swiss German child language (Schönenberger 2001), suggesting an interesting area for comparative work in the VIA project.

Another example of word order variation concerns the placement of objects in relation to negation and sentence adverbials in the Scandinavian languages, so-called Object Shift. This construction involves obligatory leftward movement of unstressed pronominal objects, illustrated in (4b), while the full DP object in (4a) must appear following the adverbial.

(4) a. Jon spiser **aldri sopp**.
Jon eats never mushrooms
'Jon never eats mushrooms.'

b. Jon spiser **det aldri**.
Jon eats it never
'Jon never eats it.'

A number of studies on the acquisition of Object Shift and Object Scrambling in Dutch and German have been carried out (Schaeffer 2000, Barbier 2000), generally concluding that there is a certain delay in children's production of these constructions. In a study of Object Shift in child Swedish, Josefsson (1996) shows that this is infrequent in spontaneous child data, and an elicitation test indicates that children up to the age of five avoid the construction and frequently fail to shift pronominal objects. In the present book, Anderssen, Bentzen, Rodina and Westergaard address this phenomenon in Norwegian, comparing it to the acquisition of two different subject positions.

The two subject positions in Norwegian are found in non-subject-initial V2 clauses, one preceding and one following adverbs or negation, illustrated in (5a, b).

(5) a. Denne vinen vil **ikke studentene** drikke.
this wine will not the students drink
'This wine the students won't drink.'

b. Denne vinen vil **de ikke** drikke.
this wine will they not drink
'This wine they won't drink.'

This is sometimes called Subject Shift, and in Westergaard and Vangsnes (2005) it is argued that the high position is reserved for informationally given subjects (often pronouns) while the low position is preferred for subjects conveying new or focused information; see also Bentzen (2009). With respect to the acquisition of this Subject Shift construction, Westergaard (2008) shows that there is a consistent preference for the unshifted position in early Norwegian child language, but that the construction becomes target-consistent as early as around age 2;6–3;0.

Finally, word order variation is not only found in the clausal domain. A relevant example of apparent word order optionality found in the nominal domain in many languages is related to the position of demonstratives. In languages such as Greek, Hebrew, Romanian and Spanish, the demonstrative may either precede or follow the head noun. This is illustrated by the Spanish examples in (6) (from Brugè 2002: 15). A similar situation can be observed for the Scandinavian languages with regard to the position of so-called reinforcers in demonstrative noun phrases, illustrated for Norwegian in (7).

(6) **este** libro / il libro **este**
this book / the book this
'This book.'

(7) **den der** bok -a / **den** bok -a **der**
that there book-the / that book-the there
'That book.'

Possessive structures also often exhibit word order variability. Many languages, including several varieties of Norwegian, allow both pre- and post-nominal possessors, as illustrated in (8).

(8) **Bil-en min** er på verksted. / **Min bil** er på verksted.
car-the.mas my.mas is on garage / my.mas car is on garage
'My car is at the garage.'

In the adult Norwegian varieties that permit both structures, these two noun phrases do not receive the same interpretation. When the possessive precedes the noun, this yields a contrastive interpretation, stressing the fact that the reference is to *my* car as opposed to some other car. When the possessive pronoun is post-nominal, the possessive relationship is more parenthetical. This interpretive distinction between the two possessive noun phrases in (8) is also signalled prosodically; the possessor is most prominent when it precedes the noun, while the noun is more prominent when the possessor is post-nominal (Anderssen 2006). The acquisition of the variable placement of possessors is addressed in Anderssen and Westergaard (2010), and the study reveals that children start out with a higher proportion of prenominal possessors as compared to adults. Thus, the acquisition of possessives represents a case where children *do* prefer one word order over another and where this order is not the most frequent one in the adult language.

So far the Tromsø group has mainly focused on the acquisition of variable word order in Norwegian. One notable exception is Diakonova (2003). She shows that both OV and VO word orders, which are possible in adult Russian subject to certain discourse factors, are attested extremely early in Russian child language, with the exception of a slight delay in the scrambling of pronominal objects. Optionality in the input is also addressed in Rodina (2008), which focuses on the acquisition of gender in Russian in cases where the target language displays both optionality and a mismatch between morphological and semantic cues. And in Westergaard (2009b), the findings from word order studies in Norwegian are compared to the acquisition of inverted word order in *wh*-questions in English child language.

Regarding variation in the input, it is clear that there are different kinds of conditions under which this applies, and the types of elements involved also vary somewhat. This means that there is in fact no or very little true optionality in the input. The findings so far indicate that some word order variation is target-consistent in child language from early on, while some constructions are slightly delayed and others severely delayed. These results open up a host of further questions about children's linguistic behaviour when exposed to different kinds of word order variation and also suggest many areas where comparative work will be relevant. This book addresses some of these interesting questions.

2 The Articles in This Book

Six of the chapters in this book were presented at a workshop on language acquisition at GLOW XXX in Tromsø in April 2007, while three chapters have been added later (Gu, Chen Pichler, and Anderssen et al.). The GLOW workshop was organized as part of the VIA project at the University of Tromsø, thus focussing on variation in the input. The articles presented here address a number of relevant issues for this topic from many perspectives and from a variety of languages. We thus feel that the present book aptly reflects the diversity of the project.

The first chapter, by Andrea Gualmini, addresses variability concerning scopal relations. Gualmini discusses an experimental study investigating how adults and children resolve and interpret scopally ambiguous sentences containing negation in English and Dutch. The main focus of the chapter concerns whether occasional inconsistent behaviour is the result of selection of different grammars at different trials or of one grammar that licenses ambiguities. It is argued that adults and children resolve scopal ambiguities in more or less the same way. More specifically, the claim is that variable behaviour by both adults and children is due to the selection of one grammar that allows ambiguity. The context of the sentence in question plays a significant role when determining which reading to adopt in each case. Thus, the selection of a specific reading for a specific sentence is not a random process, neither in adult nor in child language. However, in accordance with Yang's (2002, 2004) Variational Learning Model, optionality is predicted to be involved when children initially select one grammar over one of the other grammars possible within UG.

The next chapter, by Manuela Schönenberger, focusses on variability in the left periphery of embedded *wh*-complements, more specifically the use of 'doubly-filled COMPs' (DFCs) in adult and child Swiss German. Schönenberger examines adult data from St. Galler German (SG) and child and adult data from Lucernese (LU), and demonstrates that there are dialectal differences between SG and LU with respect to the distribution of DFCs. In SG there is a correlation between the use of DFCs and the length of the *wh*-phrase, in the sense that DFCs are obligatory with *wh*-phrases of two syllables or more, but rarely occur with *wh*-phrases of only one syllable. In LU, on the other hand, DFCs are obligatorily included whenever the *wh*-phrase, for prosodic reasons, cannot host a subject clitic. In all other contexts they are optional in LU. Both spontaneous speech and elicited production from child LU are discussed, and in both conditions, DFCs are preferred with bisyllabic *wh*-phrases, although they appear to be optional. However, DFCs are hardly ever used with monosyllabic *wh*-phrases. The children thus seem to apply a system that in one sense resembles adult LU and in another sense resembles adult SG.

In the chapter by Anna Cardinaletti and Giuliana Giusti we move to variability inside the DP. Their chapter addresses the acquisition of adjectival ordering in Italian NPs, where adjectives may appear in a variety of positions with respect to other elements (nouns, determiners, etc.) depending on the type of adjective as well as a number of syntactic and interpretive factors. This is an understudied phenomenon, presumably due to the fact that adjectives are rare in child language corpora. Adjectives mainly appear in isolation in early child data, while a study of their ordering obviously requires adjectives to occur with other elements such as nouns, determiners, and other adjectives. The chapter uses current theoretical research on the syntax of adjectival ordering in adult languages (e.g. Cinque 2005) in order to formulate hypotheses about the acquisition of adjectives, which are then tested against individual utterances by children. The authors show that the children's production mirrors the attested variation in a fully competent way from early on, with an interesting timing in the first appearance of certain orders, reflecting their frequency in a corpus of spoken adult Italian.

The chapter by Anja Kieburg and Petra Schulz investigates the influence of several input factors on the acquisition of different verb types. More specifically, Kieburg and Schulz compare the acquisition of simplex verbs, particle verbs and verb particles to the occurrence of these elements in the input. German-speaking children have been shown to start using verb particles at a very early age, even before they start using simplex verbs, and the authors investigate to what extent this developmental order can be explained in terms of the word frequency and/or the word order variability of these elements in the adult language. If early acquisition is the result of a high input rate, we would expect mothers to use more particle verbs than simplex verbs. If, on the other hand, early acquisition is an effect of word order variability, we would expect particle verbs, which are acquired earlier, to exhibit less variable word order in the input. In order to test this, Kieburg and Schulz analyse utterances from three mothers in eight 1-h sessions recorded when the children were 14, 16, 18 and 20 months old. Their results reveal that the early acquisition of verb particles by these children cannot be due to simple input frequency, as measured in terms of type frequency, token frequency, and type-token frequency; the mothers do not produce more particle verbs than simplex verbs in any of these measures. However, the results show that verb particles predominantly appear in what the authors refer to as the right sentence bracket (verb-final position) in the mothers' production, while simplex verbs are more variable in their placement. This suggests that the early acquisition of verb particles cannot be explained by simple input frequency; instead this appears to be the result of word order variability, or rather the lack of it. The fact that these elements more stably occur in the same position the input seems to aid their early acquisition.

The topic of the next chapter in this volume, by Chloe C. Gu, stays within the VP/vP domain and considers the acquisition of double object constructions by English-Cantonese bilinguals as well as English and Cantonese monolinguals. Gu's study confirms the results from Snyder and Stromswold (1997) that English children start out by using the double object dative, while the prepositional dative is delayed. According to Snyder and Stromswold, the reason for this delay is that the acquisition of the double object construction (as well as some other constructions, including the verb particle construction) is dependent on two parametric properties; one of these properties generates double object datives (and V-NP-particle constructions), while both properties are required to produce prepositional datives (and V-particle-NP constructions). Gu argues against the view that the acquisition of the double object dative and the V-NP-particle order are associated with the same parameter, as the two are not acquired simultaneously by all children. Gu also discusses the compositional approach to double object constructions promoted by Viau (2006). According to Viau, the developmental lag of the prepositional dative can be attributed to late development of the primitive GO, assumed to be a part of the prepositional dative, as compared to the primitive HAVE, which is taken to be involved in the double object dative. Gu shows that English children are not delayed in the acquisition of the primitive GO in dyadic constructions, thus indicating that late acquisition of this primitive cannot be the cause of the delay of prepositional datives. Instead, she proposes that the delay is related to the ambiguity of the prepositions involved in the prepositional dative, *to* and *for*, and especially the distinction between the prepositional dative *to* and the triadic directional *to*, which may both occur with the same verbs. The study reveals that children who acquire the use of both triadic directional *to* and triadic dative *to* within a short period of time, and who are thus aware of the different meanings of *to* in these contexts, progress from the double object dative more quickly than children who take longer to acquire the distinction between these prepositions.

The next two chapters address variation in the position of arguments with respect to the verb. First, Deborah Chen Pichler discusses the acquisition of the VO/OV alternation in American Sign Language (ASL). The canonical word order in ASL is SVO, but the order OV is also used to some extent, mainly in two contexts: topicalization, which is accompanied by brow raise, head tilt, and an intonational break, and when expressing modification on the verb (aspectual, locational, or instrumental), so-called *reordering morphology*. The study observed four deaf children (of deaf parents) acquiring ASL, at the age of 20–30 months. The children used the VO and OV orders at almost the same frequency, indicating that they might not have set the Head Parameter at this stage. However, on closer investigation, Chen Pichler finds that for three of the children, almost all OV orders contain reordering morphology. The fourth child, ABY, did not include such morphology on her OV orders, but more than half of these orders involve a prosodic break between the object and the verb. Chen Pichler analyses these constructions as early topicalization structures. Thus, she argues that the children *have* set the Head Parameter correctly, and furthermore, that they have acquired some of the pragmatic, morphological, and syntactic features at play in the language.

In the second chapter on argument placement relative to verbs, Dina Kapetangianni investigates the acquisition of word order in Greek, focussing on the position of subjects and verbs in different clause types. Greek is a null subject language, and when the subject is overt, three different word orders are found in the adult language: SV, VS and OV(S). The word order chosen in a particular case is dependent on both syntactic and pragmatic or discourse factors. More specifically, preverbal subjects may be associated with a topic interpretation in the TopP. Alternatively, they may be interpreted as new information and appear either in the FocP (if focused) or in the IP domain. Postverbal subjects, on the other hand, are always associated with new information and appear in the vP. Using production data from three monolingual Greek-speaking children, Kapetangianni shows that overt DP subjects and variable word order are attested in child Greek at the earliest stages of linguistic development. Based on a detailed investigation of the grammatical properties of the word order produced by the three children, evidence is presented that the

Null Subject parameter is set early and that the children have an early knowledge of the syntactic, semantic, and pragmatic principles that govern subject-verb word order in the adult grammar.

The final two chapters discuss the acquisition of scrambling phenomena. In the first one of these, Roksolana Mykhaylyk and Heejeong Ko investigate the acquisition of object scrambling in Ukrainian by English-Ukrainian bilingual children. They argue that object scrambling in adult Ukrainian is optional with specific objects, but not acceptable with non-specific objects. Consequently, specific objects may or may not scramble, while non-specific objects must remain in situ. The child language study reveals that English-Ukrainian bilingual children scramble objects less frequently than adult speakers, which is consistent with the results from Schaeffer's (2000) study of the acquisition of scrambling in Dutch. However, unlike Schaeffer, Mykhaylyk and Ko argue against a pragmatic account of the lower rate of scrambling in child language. This is based on the observation that, while the children do not scramble specific objects as often as adult speakers, they never illegitimately scramble non-specific objects, which would be expected if the underlying problem were pragmatic in nature. Instead, Mykhaylyk and Ko suggest that the under-application of scrambling is the expression of a failure to consistently associate a syntactic EPP feature with the semantic notion of specificity.

Finally, the chapter by Merete Anderssen, Kristine Bentzen, Yulia Rodina, and Marit Westergaard discusses the acquisition of subject and object placement in Norwegian, cf. examples (4) and (5) in the previous section. In the target language, pronominal subjects and objects must 'shift' across negation and other adverbs, while full DP subjects and objects remain below such elements. Anderssen et al. show that children at an early stage make mistakes with both Subject and Object Shift, leaving pronominal elements in a position following negation. However, whereas Subject Shift appears to fall into place fairly early, by the age of 3, Object Shift is substantially delayed and is not acquired until around the age of 5. Various types of explanations of these findings are considered: pragmatic principles, prosody, syntactic economy, and frequency effects. It is argued that the acquisition patterns follow from an interaction between syntactic economy and input frequency. Whereas economy principles may lead children to initially leave pronouns in non-shifted positions, the authors suggest that the persistence of this non-target behaviour in Object Shift constructions compared to Subject Shift is related to input frequency, as the former construction is considerably less frequent in the input than the latter.

3 Variation in the Input

What can we learn from the VIA project and the chapters in this book? As mentioned at the end of Section 1, the main findings of the work discussed here indicate that there is very little true optionality in language. The variation investigated is dependent on many different linguistic factors, often related to fine distinctions in either syntax or information structure (or both). For example, the position of the subject in Greek is dependent on whether this element is given vs. new information and whether it is focused or non-focused, these distinctions corresponding to four different positions in the syntactic structure. The position of the object in Ukrainian, on the other hand, is dependent on specificity, non-specific objects always appearing in postverbal position while specific objects optionally scramble to a position to the left of the verb. Thus, the factors involved in the word order variation that is discussed in this book are quite subtle and display a high level of complexity.

For this reason it might be expected that this variation would constitute a major challenge for the language-learning child and cause severe delays in the acquisition process. Other possible (and not unlikely) findings could be that children make a high number of mistakes, showing a preference for one of the possible word orders in all contexts for an extended period of time. However, most of the chapters in this volume present data showing that children's production is more or less target-consistent from early on.

The chapters consider variation from different perspectives. For example, Gualmini shows that children (basically) use the same strategies as adults when resolving scopal ambiguities. The chapter by Kieburg and Schulz discusses whether order of acquisition can be predicted by simple input frequencies or by variability in word placement. They find that early acquisition of particles (as compared to simplex verbs) can be explained by the fact that these elements stably occur in clause final-position in the input. Thus, lack of variation in word placement is found to affect the order of acquisition. In Gu's chapter, on the other hand, the order of acquisition of the two dative constructions in English is related to children's difficulty with the multiple interpretations of the preposition *to*. Along a similar vein, Schönenberger shows that children acquiring Lucernese Swiss German obligatorily use doubly filled COMPs in contexts where they are optional in the target language. Thus, the children seem to strive to regularize a pattern that is variable in the input.

The other chapters in this volume address the acquisition of word order variation more directly. For example, Anderssen et al., Mykhaylyk and Ko, and Chen Pichler consider the acquisition of the variable placement of objects, while Kapetangianni and also Anderssen et al. consider the acquisition of the variable placement of subjects. Cardinaletti and Giusti study how the different positions of attributive adjectives in the NP are acquired. In all of these cases, children are found to display the relevant variation from an early age, and in Kapetangianni's work on child Greek and Cardinaletti and Giusti's chapter on child Italian, the children's behaviour is found to be target-like from early on. But in the other studies, the children seem to behave slightly differently from adult speakers. For example, even though Norwegian children shift both subjects and objects at a relatively early stage, they do so less than adult speakers. Similarly, English-Ukrainian bilinguals scramble objects less often than adult monolinguals. Anderssen et al. attribute the non-target-like behaviour of Norwegian children to an economy principle causing the relevant movements to be avoided, while Mykhaylyk and Ko argue that the bilingual children they studied scramble less due to an unstable mapping between a syntactic EPP feature and the semantic feature specificity. Chen Pichler, on the other hand, finds that children acquiring ASL use the canonical VO order inconsistently, and produce more OV orders than adult signers. This situation appears to be somewhat different from what was found in the other two studies: On some theoretical accounts (e.g. Kayne 1994), this would suggest an over-application of a movement operation, rather than under-application, as in the case of Norwegian and Ukrainian-English child language. A finding such as this one seems to be less common in acquisition studies and possibly also incompatible with an economy approach (but see Westergaard and Bentzen 2007).

Nevertheless, it appears that, overall, in structures displaying word order (and other) variation, the production of the children investigated in these studies is close to target-like. In cases where the children differ from adults, this seems to be due to the relevant constructions not being attested in child language yet (in the case of certain adjective orderings in Italian) or to general principles that are not part of narrow syntax, e.g. economy (in the case of Norwegian subject and object shift) or instability in the mapping between syntax and semantics (in the case of Ukrainian object scrambling). Based on the child data investigated, we may thus argue that early child grammars are not substantially different from adult grammars. This is of course nothing new, as this has been argued for extensively within the continuity approach to language acquisition (e.g. Hyams 1992, Verrips and Weissenborn 1992, Poeppel and Wexler 1993, Platzack 1996, Borer and Rohrbacher 2002). But the findings in this volume show that children's generally target-consistent behaviour cannot simply be due to the existence of prewired UG principles, as the variation discussed here must be learned from the input. Thus we may conclude that children must be endowed with an ability to make fine distinctions in syntax and information structure from early on. This conclusion seems to be incompatible with the view that children learn the syntax of their particular language by setting major word order parameters.

The child data discussed in this book resonate with previous findings in the acquisition of syntax, showing that young children's errors are typically errors of omission rather than errors of commission. This has led to the common view that children are so-called conservative learners, sometimes interpreted as an argument against a UG-based model of language acquisition. A recent discussion of this concept may be found in Snyder (2007), who adopts a parametric approach that takes syntactic variation into account. This issue is also considered in Westergaard (2009a) within a cue-based model of acquisition, according to which children are sensitive to micro-cues in the input. However, there are also some exceptions to this notion of conservative learners, as illustrated by the obligatorily doubly filled COMP in Lucernese Swiss German child language and the overuse of the OV construction in ASL. This suggests that more research is needed to establish all the potential outcomes of the acquisition process when word order (and other) variation is involved. However, these studies, as well as the other contributions in this book, show that not only are children sensitive to micro-variation in syntax and information structure at an early age, but also that the acquisition process proceeds in a principled and rule-governed way.

References

Anderssen, Merete. 2006. *The acquisition of compositional definiteness in Norwegian*. Doctoral Dissertation, University of Tromsø.

Anderssen, Merete and Marit Westergaard. 2010. Frequency and economy in the acquisition of variable word order. *Lingua*, doi: 10.1016/j.lingua.2010.06.006.

Barbier, Isabella. 2000. An experimental study of scrambling and object shift in the acquisition of Dutch. In *The acquisition of scrambling and cliticization*, eds. Susan Mary Powers and Cornelia Hamann, 41–69. Dordrecht: Kluwer Academic Publishers.

Bentzen, Kristine. 2005. What's the better move? On verb placement in Standard and Northern Norwegian. *Nordic Journal of Linguistics* 28(2): 153–188.

Bentzen, Kristine. 2007. The degree of verb movement in embedded clauses in three varieties of Norwegian. *Nordlyd 34: Scandinavian Dialect Syntax 2005*, University of Tromsø. 127–146.

Bentzen, Kristine. 2009. Subject positions and their interaction with verb movement. *Studia Linguistica* 63(3): 1–31.

Borer, Hagit, and Bernhard Rohrbacher. 2002. Minding the absent: Arguments for the full competence hypothesis. *Language Acquisition* 10(2): 123–175.

Bresnan, Joan, Anna Cueni, Tatiana Nikitina, and Harald Baayen. 2007. Predicting the dative alternation. In *Cognitive foundations of interpretation*, eds. Gerlof Bouma, Irene Krämer and Joost Zwarts, 69–94. Amsterdam: Royal Netherlands Academy of Science.

Brugè, Laura. 2002. The positions of demonstratives in the extended nominal projection. In *Functional structure in DP and IP: The cartography of syntactic structures*, ed. Guglielmo Cinque, vol. 1, 15–53. New York: Oxford University Press.

Cinque, Guglielmo. 2005. Deriving Greenberg's Universal 20 and its exceptions. *Linguistic Inquiry* 36: 315–332.

Diakonova, Marina. 2003. *The acquisition of word order in English and Russian*. MA thesis, University of Tromsø.

Hyams, Nina. 1992. The genesis of clausal structure. In *The acquisition of verb placement: functional categories and V2 phenomena in language acquisition*, ed. Jürgen Meisel, 371–400. Dordrecht: Kluwer.

Josefsson, Gunlög. 1996. The acquisition of object shift in Swedish child language. In *Children's language* 9, eds. Carolyn E. Johnson and John H. V. Gilbert, 153–165. Mahwah: Lawrence Erlbaum.

Kayne, Richard. 1994. *The anti-symmetry of syntax*. Cambridge: MIT Press.

Platzack, Christer. 1996. The initial hypothesis of syntax: A minimalist perspective on language acquisition and attrition. In *Generative perspectives on language acquisition*, ed. Harald Clahsen, 369–414. Amsterdam and Philadelphia: John Benjamins.

Poeppel, David, and Kenneth Wexler. 1993. The full competence hypothesis of clause structure in Early German. *Language* 69(1): 1–33.

Rizzi, Luigi. 1993/1994. Some notes on linguistic theory and language development: The case of root infinitives. *Language Acquisition* 3(4): 371–393.

Rizzi, Luigi. 1994. Early null subjects and root null subjects. In *Language acquisition studies in generative grammar*, eds. Teun Hoekstra and Bonnie D. Schwartz, 151–176. Amsterdam and Philadelphia: John Benjamins.

Rizzi, Luigi. 2000. Remarks on early null subjects. In *The acquisition of syntax: Studies in comparative developmental linguistics*, eds. Marc-Ariel Friedemann and Luigi Rizzi, 269–292. Harlow: Longman.

Rodina, Yulia. 2008. *Semantics and morphology: The acquisition of grammatical gender in Russian*. Ph.D. dissertation, University of Tromsø.

Roeper, Thomas. 1999. Universal bilingualism. *Bilingualism: Language and Cognition* 2: 169–185.

Schaeffer, Jeanette. 2000. *The acquisition of direct object scrambling and clitic placement: Syntax and pragmatics*. Amsterdam and Philadelphia: John Benjamins.

Schönenberger, Manuela. 2001. *Embedded V-to-C in child grammar: The acquisition of verb placement in Swiss German*. Studies in Theoretical Psycholinguistics. Dordrecht: Kluwer.

Snyder, William. 2007. *Child language: The parametric approach*. Oxford/New York: Oxford University Press.

Snyder, William, and Karin Stromswold. 1997. The structure and acquisition of English dative constructions. *Linguistic Inquiry* 28: 281–317.

Vangsnes, Øystein A. 2005. Microparameters for Norwegian *wh*-grammars. *Linguistic Variation Yearbook* 5, 187–226. Amsterdam and Philadelphia: John Benjamins.

Verrips, Maaike, and Jürgen Weissenborn. 1992. Routes to verb placement in early German and French: The independence of finiteness and agreement. In *The acquisition of verb placement: Functional categories and V2 phenomena in language acquisition*, ed. Jürgen Meisel, 283–331. Dordrecht: Kluwer.

Viau, Joshua. 2006. Give = CAUSE + HAVE/GO: Evidence for early semantic decomposition of dative verbs in English child corpora. In *Proceedings of the 30th annual Boston University Conference on Language Development*, eds. David Bamman, Tatiana Magnitskaia and Colleen Zaller, 665–676. Somerville: Cascadilla Press.

Westergaard, Marit R. 2003. Word order in *wh*-questions in a North Norwegian dialect: Some evidence from an acquisition study. *Nordic Journal of Linguistics* 26(1): 81–109.

Westergaard, Marit. 2008. Verb movement and subject placement in the acquisition of word order: Pragmatics or structural economy? In *First language acquisition of morphology and syntax: Perspectives across languages and learners* [Language Acquisition and Language Disorders], eds. Pedro Guijarro-Fuentes, Pilar Larranaga and John Clibbens, 61–86. Amsterdam: John Benjamins.

Westergaard, Marit. 2009a. *The acquisition of word order: Micro-cues, information structure and economy*. Amsterdam: John Benjamins.

Westergaard, Marit. 2009b. Usage-based vs. rule-based learning: The acquisition of word order in *Wh*-questions in English and Norwegian. *Journal of Child Language* 36(5): 1023–1051.

Westergaard, Marit. 2009c. Microvariation as diachrony: A view from acquisition. *Journal of Comparative Germanic Linguistics* 12(1): 49–79.

Westergaard, Marit R., and Øystein A. Vangsnes. 2005. *Wh*-questions, V2, and the left periphery of three Norwegian dialects. *Journal of Comparative Germanic Linguistics* 8: 117–158.

Westergaard, Marit, and Kristine Bentzen. 2007. The (non-) effect of input frequency on the acquisition of word order in Norwegian embedded clauses. In *Frequency effects in language acquisition: Defining the limits of frequency as an explanatory concept* [Studies on Language Acquisition], eds. Insa Gülzow and Natalia Gagarina, 271–306. Berlin/New York: Mouton de Gruyter.

Wexler, Kenneth. 1994. Optional infinitives, head movement and the economy of derivation. In *Verb movement*, eds. David Lightfoot and Norbert Hornstein, 305–350. Cambridge: Cambridge University Press.

Wexler, Kenneth. 1999. Very early parameter setting and the unique checking constraint: A new explanation of the optional infinitive stage. In *Language acquisition: Knowledge representation and processing*, special issue of *Lingua*, eds. Antonella Sorace, Caroline Heycock and Richard Shillock, 23–79. Amsterdam: Elsevier.

Yang, Charles. 2002. *Knowledge and learning in natural language*. Oxford: Oxford University Press.

Yang, Charles. 2004. Universal grammar, statistics or both? *Trends in cognitive sciences* 8: 451–456.

Zuckerman, Shalom. 2001. *The acquisition of "optional" movement*. Ph.D. dissertation, Groningen University.

Zuckerman, Shalom, and Aafke Hulk. 2001. Acquiring optionality in French *wh*-questions: An experimental study. *Revue québécoise de linguistique* 30(2): 71–97.

Optional Illusions

Andrea Gualmini

Abstract This chapter reviews recent psycholinguistic studies on adults' and children's resolution of scope ambiguities. Against this background, we discuss two different types of optionality that could in principle be found. First, we consider the possibility that children's behavior, as documented in some experiments, reveals the selection of different grammars on different trials. Second, we focus on stages in which children's hypothesis space mostly consists of one grammar which licenses an ambiguity. We will offer two claims. First, one can expect optionality when it comes to children's selection of one grammar out of the ones that are available in the hypothesis space defined by Universal Grammar (UG) (see Yang, *Knowledge and Learning in Natural Language*, 2003, Yang, *Trends in Cognitive Sciences* 8: 451–456, 2004). Second, optionality is not to be expected when it comes to children's selection of a specific reading out of the ones that are licensed in the grammar they happen to draw upon to analyze a specific piece of input.

Keywords Language acquisition · Sentence processing · Semantics · Pragmatics · Ambiguity · Negation

1 The Pattern of Scope Resolution in Child Language

Scope ambiguities have proven a fruitful domain for psycholinguistic investigations. In recent years, a debate has taken place trying to determine which factors enter into children's (and adults') resolution of scope ambiguities (see Musolino and Lidz 2006, Gualmini 2004, Hulsey et al. 2004). In this chapter, we put aside the issue of how children and adults differ and how those differences should be explained (or described), but rather highlight how we should go about determining whether the occasional inconsistencies in children's or adults' behavior

A. Gualmini (✉)
Utrecht University, Utrecht, The Netherlands
e-mail: a.gualmini@uu.nl

M. Anderssen et al. (eds.), *Variation in the Input*, Studies in Theoretical Psycholinguistics 39, DOI 10.1007/978-90-481-9207-6_2,

depend on their selection of different grammars across trials or rather their selection of different interpretive options (from the same grammar).

The starting point for current investigations of scope ambiguities in child language is Musolino (1998). This study reports the results of several experiments investigating children's and adults' interpretation of scopally ambiguous sentences containing negation. We can start our discussion with Experiment 3 from Musolino (1998), which focused on children's interpretation of the indefinite *some* in object position.

In order to investigate children's interpretation of the positive polarity item *some* in negative sentences, Musolino (1998) conducted a Truth Value Judgment task using sentences like (1). In a Truth Value Judgment task, the child is asked to evaluate whether or not the target sentence correctly describes the outcome of a short story (see Crain and McKee 1985, Crain and Thornton 1998). In Musolino's study, sentences like (1) were presented as a description of a context in which the detective had found two of the four guys participating in the story.

(1) The detective didn't find some guys.

The context employed by Musolino (1998) was designed to make (1) true on its adult inverse scope interpretation (i.e., the interpretation paraphrased in (2)), and false on its non-adult surface scope interpretation (i.e., the interpretation paraphrased in (3)).[1]

(2) There are some guys that the detective didn't find.
(3) It is not the case that the detective found some guys.

The finding was that children as old as 5;9 rejected the target sentence 50% of the time, whereas the adult controls consistently accepted it. In particular, many of the children interviewed by Musolino (1998) pointed out that (1) was incorrect because the detective had indeed found some guys. Apparently, children's rejection of (1) follows from the interpretation in (3), an interpretation that is unavailable in the adult grammar.

At first glance, the group results documented by Musolino (1998) lend themselves to several interpretations. First, it is possible that each individual child is behaving at chance. Second, it is possible that the 50% acceptance rate results from two groups of children who consistently draw upon different grammars. A third possibility is that all children draw upon identical (or at least overlapping) grammars, but they differ in how they choose among the interpretations that are made available by those grammars. Of course, a

[1] Together with Ladusaw (1979), we assume that *some* is a positive polarity item in adult English (see also Szabolcsi 2004).

combination of any of these patterns of behavior is instantiated in the data. For any given experiment, it seems crucial to determine whether the attested pattern is a true instantiation of chance behavior or rather consistent individual differences (see Grodzinsky and Reinhart 1993, Reinhart 2006 for discussion). The question then is how we determine what scenario we are dealing with.

To answer this question we will consider the way the data collected by Musolino (1998) were viewed in the original study and in a further analysis by Gualmini (2004). As we just saw, Musolino (1998) reports that 30 children (age 3;10–6;6) unexpectedly rejected the target sentences 50% of the time. Each subject was presented with four target trials and the relevant data are plotted in Graph 1.

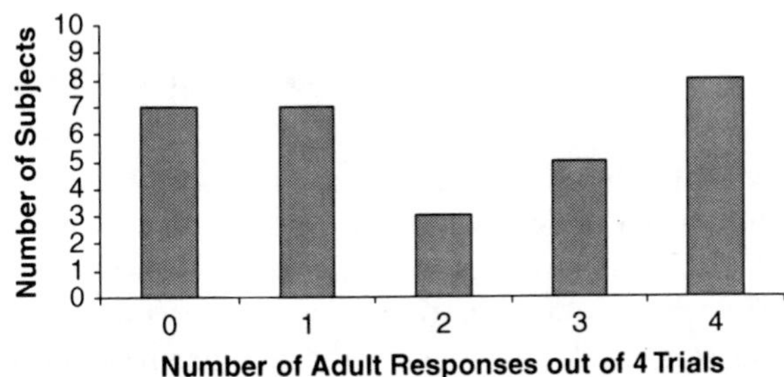

Graph 1 Individual responses in Experiment 3 from Musolino (1998)

As can be seen from the graph above, the individual responses do not really seem to fit the pattern that would be predicted by chance, since only three subjects out of thirty gave an equal number of adult and non-adult responses. The claim offered by Musolino (1998) is that the data result from two groups of children. To illustrate, one could classify children on the basis of the responses that they gave on most trials. Thus, children who give an adult-response on all or most of the trials could be described as children whose hypothesis space is mostly occupied by the target grammar. By contrast, the children who gave non-adult responses on all or most of the trials could be seen as children whose hypothesis space mostly consists of a non-adult grammar which still needs to be specified. In particular, according to Musolino (1998), children's non-adult behavior results in the occasional selection of a grammar in which the inverse scope interpretation of (1) is not available On this view, the data are taken to yield a bimodal distribution, and the occasional inconsistencies are treated as cases in which children happened to select two different grammars across different trials. In other words, the data would suggest that children's hypothesis space could be represented as in (4) and their development should be viewed as the gradual 'growth' of G_2 at the expense of G_1.

(4)	G_1	G_2
	*Some>not	some>not
	Not>some	*not>some

The question is whether this is an accurate characterization of children's underlying development. In particular, the question is whether children's hypothesis space should include a third grammar which we will call G_3 which licenses the interpretations that are licensed by G_1 and the ones licensed by G_2. Under this scenario, children's development would entail the selection of the target grammar at the expense of two non-target grammars. In particular, it might be possible to identify three stages in children's linguistic development, where each stage is defined by which grammar more accurately characterizes the child's linguistic competence.

(5)	G_1	G_3	G_2
	*Some>not	some>not	some>not
	Not>some	not>some	*not>some

Determining whether children's hypothesis space resembles the one in (4) or the one in (5) is crucial because it determines what data the child needs in order to attain the target grammar. Nevertheless, settling this issue is far from easy. The answer to this question is even harder if we consider that the transition from one stage of development to the next one need not be abrupt (see Yang 2003).

Let us review one of the main features of the Variational Learning Model proposed by Yang (2003). Simplifying somewhat, Yang (2003) assumes that children can initially draw upon any grammar made available by Universal Grammar (UG). On this view, the process of language acquisition starts off as a random walk. In principle, the child is free to select any grammar that is made available by UG according to the probability associated with that grammar. In the long run, successful acquisition is ensured by the fact that whenever the child selects the grammar of the local community, he can analyze any piece of input he might be exposed to. By contrast, for any grammar other than the target grammar, the child will at some point encounter data that are un-analyzable on that grammar and give grounds for 'punishing' the particular non-target grammar that the child happened to select. On this view, like on many others, failures are crucial and assuming that children select grammars at random ensures that failures can occur.

Going back to the example we started with, consider the case of a child who gives a response indicative of the *some>not* interpretation. This behavior could be obtained in two ways. First, the child might have randomly drawn upon G_2 to analyze the relevant piece of input. As a second possibility, the child might have randomly selected G_3 to analyze the relevant piece of input and then might have been led by the psychological parser to select the *some>not* interpretation (for instance because only that interpretation makes the sentence true in the context).[2] Similarly, consider the case of a child who provides both a *not>some*

---

[2] Throughout the chapter, we will focus on one of the tasks of the psychological parser, namely ambiguity resolution (see Crain and Steedman 1985).

and a *some>not* interpretation (across two different trials). The question is whether this child's behavior follows from the selection of G_1 and G_2 across different trials or rather the selection of G_3, coupled with a difference in the way the ambiguity is resolved in the two cases.

As a first step into resolving this issue, Gualmini (2004) set off to determine whether the responses of children who show some sort of inconsistency appear to be random. A cursory look at the data reported by Musolino (1998) shows that this is not the case. In fact, four of the five subjects who only provided one non-adult response did so on the same experimental trial, namely the fourth one. Moreover, one can observe that none of the seven subjects who provided one adult-like response ever did so on the fourth experimental trial. This cannot be an accident and invites us to scrutinize this particular trial further. We can illustrate our point by considering two trials from Experiment 3 in Musolino (1998) in further detail. On the fourth trial in this experiment, children were told a story about five friends at a barbecue. When the barbecue was over, one man decided to mow the lawn. While he was mowing the lawn, he accidentally hurt two of his guests, though two other men were unscathed. At the end of the story, children were presented with the sentence in (6).

(6) The old man didn't hurt some guys.

This trial can be contrasted with the trial in which the story was about a detective playing hide-and-seek with his four friends. As we saw above, the detective found two guys, but he failed to find the other two. Children were asked to evaluate sentence (1), repeated below:

(1) The detective didn't find some guys.

Despite their similarity, the two trials yielded a different response pattern from children. In particular, the 30 children interviewed by Musolino (1998) accepted the target sentences in (6) 10 times (33%) and the sentence in (1) 18 times (60%). Among all the trials of the experiment, (1) gave rise to the lowest number of non-adult responses, whereas (6) yielded the highest number of non-adult responses.

According to Gualmini (2004), this pattern calls for further consideration. Whenever such patterns arise, the research strategy should be to put forward a hypothesis about what factor is responsible for the particular reading that is accessed in each experimental trial. The next step is then to design an experiment in which that factor is controlled for.

The particular hypothesis that Gualmini (2004) put forward is that the difference in children's interpretation of (1) and (6) was related to a feature of negative sentences discussed by Wason 1965 (see also Wason 1972, Horn 1989, De Villiers and Tager-Flusberg 1975, Glenberg et al. 1999), namely the fact that negative sentences are felicitous when they point out that something which could be expected to happen didn't happen (see Hulsey et al. 2004 for a different view). Under this hypothesis, the difference in children's responses to (1) and (6) might be due to the fact that some children find it easier to 'accommodate' the expected outcome required by (1) than the one required by (6). The next step is to design an experiment that controls for the expected outcome entertained by each subject. This is what Gualmini (2004) did. In Gualmini's experiment, children were told stories in which a character had a task to carry out. To take one example, children were told a story in which Grover orders four pizzas from the Troll. The Troll is supposed to deliver all four of them, but loses two pizzas on the way. According to Gualmini (2004), the story sets up an expectation, namely that the Troll should deliver all of the pizzas. The puppet then utters either (7), whose surface scope and inverse scope interpretations are paraphrased in (8a) and (8b), respectively, or (9), whose surface and inverse scope interpretations are paraphrased in (10a) and (10b), respectively.

(7) The Troll didn't deliver some pizzas.
(8) a. The Troll didn't deliver any pizzas.
b. There are some pizzas that the Troll didn't deliver.
(9) The Troll didn't lose some pizzas.
(10) a. The Troll didn't lose any pizzas.
b. There are some pizzas that the Troll didn't lose.

According to Gualmini (2004), the difference between sentences (7) and (9) in the context of the pizza story parallels the difference between (1) and (6) in Musolino's experiment. In particular, Gualmini (2004) argues that (7) is felicitous in the present context because it points out the discrepancy between what was expected to happen, i.e., that the Troll would deliver all of the pizzas, and what actually happened. Sentence (9) on the other hand, does not point out this discrepancy. Thus, in the present context, (9) does not meet the felicity requirements for sentences containing negation. Gualmini (2004) found that children accepted (7) at a much higher rate than (9). Fifteen children, ranging in age from 4;1 to 5;6 (mean 4;10), accepted (7) and similar sentences 90% of the time (54/60). A different group of 15 children, ranging in age from 4;2 to 5;8 (mean 4;11), accepted (9) and similar sentences only 50% of the time (30/60).

To summarize, we have reviewed some data provided by Musolino (1998) and have considered how many and which kind of grammars we need to postulate to explain children's behavioral patterns. We then looked at some data by Gualmini (2004), which suggest that indeed some of the responses that initially looked like children's selection of two non-overlapping grammars are dictated by the context. Let us now concentrate on this last issue, namely the change in children's behavior as a function of the context in which the relevant target sentences are presented. Logically speaking, there are at least two possibilities.

Under the assumption that *some* is a positive polarity item in the adult grammar, then the data are to be explained by the fact that some children have already reached the adult stage, while others are still lagging behind. The question is whether this is all there is to the data. Under this hypothesis, Gualmini's (2004) data would be quite surprising. What is surprising isn't the fact that some children seem capable of both surface and inverse scope interpretations, but rather the fact that these children select the surface or inverse scope interpretation of the target sentence as a result of the context. On the assumption that grammar selection is a random process, an assumption that seems crucial for models of language acquisition like the one proposed by Yang (2003), this suggests that the parser is involved. In particular, the data suggest that we should try to explain why the same context seems to lead subjects to resolve the ambiguity involving negation and the indefinite *some* differently in (7) and (9), an issue that we will address in the next section.[3]

We would like to end this section by reviewing some more recent data, due to Unsworth and Gualmini (2007), which provides us with another application of the strategy outlined above. Unsworth and Gualmini (2007) attempted to explain Dutch-speaking children's non-adult interpretation of scrambled indefinites in negative sentences in the same way English-speaking children's behavior has been explained. In particular, these authors turned to some findings documented by Krämer (2000). That study included an experiment on children's interpretation of sentences like (11).

(11) De jongen heeft een vis niet gevangen.
the boy has a fish not caught
'There is a fish the boy hasn't caught.'

The result of an experiment with 38 Dutch-speaking children from 4;0 to 7;7 was that children very often rejected (11) as a description of a story in which a boy had caught two fish out of the three fish available in the context, whereas adults always accepted it (see also Unsworth 2005). Children, unlike adults, apparently interpreted the indefinite *een vis* ('one fish') in the scope of negation, which corresponds to the inverse scope interpretation of (11).

Drawing upon the work with English-speaking children documented above, Unsworth and Gualmini (2007) put forward the hypothesis that Dutch-speaking children would go through a stage in which their hypothesis space would mostly consist of a grammar licensing an ambiguity, to be resolved by the parser in the same systematic way discussed above. In particular, Unsworth and Gualmini (2007) set off to determine whether Dutch-speaking children go through a stage

[3] We will speculate on why ambiguity resolution – differently from the selection of one grammar out of the child's hypothesis space – cannot be assumed to be a random process in the concluding section of the chapter.

during which sentences like (11) are ambiguous between a surface scope and an inverse scope interpretation. To answer this question, they conducted a version of Krämer's original experiment that also took into account the work by Gualmini (2004). To illustrate, children were told a story about a boy who was supposed to catch all the fish. Given the findings of Gualmini (2004), the prediction was that children would accept the sentence in (11) to a higher extent than (12).

(12) De jongen heeft een vis niet laten zwemmen.
the boy has a fish not leave swim
'There is a fish the boy didn't leave swimming.'

Children accepted (11) 71% (57/80) of the time whereas they only accepted (12) 45% (38/85) of the time. Taken together, the findings from experiments with Dutch-speaking children offer us a picture that is quite similar to the one represented in (5). Initially, children's hypothesis space seems to consist mostly of one non-target grammar in which scrambled indefinites must be interpreted in their base position. In a later stage, the (non-target) grammar which dictates the majority of children's responses licenses an ambiguity: scrambled indefinites may be interpreted in their surface position or in their base position. Notably, at this stage, context seems to play a crucial role in determining which reading children ultimately select. Finally, children exposed to Dutch reach the adult state, in which their hypothesis space is occupied by a grammar requiring scrambled indefinites to be interpreted in their surface position.

To sum up, this section focused on child language. We have drawn upon recent experimental work to highlight one difference between grammar selection and ambiguity resolution. Along with Yang (2003), we have assumed that grammar selection is a random process, and we have argued that ambiguity resolution is not.

2 The Pattern of Scope Resolution in Adult Language

In this section we focus on adult speakers' interpretation of scopally ambiguous sentences containing negation. As we saw in the previous section, a great deal of research has investigated children's comprehension of the same sentences. The question that we would like to address here is whether the same systematic pattern suggested by ambiguity resolution in children can be found in the system that provides most of the input to children, namely the adult system.

In order to properly characterize the input to which children are exposed, one would like to have a good description of adults' production. In the case of scopally ambiguous sentences containing negation, an attempt to characterize adults' production is due to Gennari and MacDonald (2005/2006). These authors turned to adults' production to explain children's behavior with sentences like the following (see Musolino 1998, Gualmini et al. 2005).

(13) Every horse didn't jump over the fence.
(14) The detective didn't find two guys.

In particular, Gennari and MacDonald (2005/2006) asked adult speakers of English to provide a description of the same stories that had been used by Musolino (1998) and much subsequent work. The finding by Gennari and MacDonald (2005/2006) was that adult speakers tend to use sentences that do not include negation (e.g., *The detective only found two guys, some of the horses jumped over the fence* etc.). This finding seems to be particularly robust in the case of pictures that would make (13) or (14) true on their inverse scope interpretation.

The relevance of the study by Gennari and MacDonald (2005/2006) for child language has already been discussed by Gualmini (2005/2006). For present purposes, we would like to add that the experimental data confirm what has been noted since the work of Wason (1965) and Wason (1972) (see also Horn 1989), namely that negative sentences are somewhat marked. Unfortunately, this finding does not answer the question of whether the surface and inverse scope interpretations are equally available in the input to children. If Gennari and MacDonald (2005/2006) are correct in claiming that adult speakers refrain from using scopally ambiguous sentences even in experimentally controlled situations, our next option of tapping into their competence is by resorting to comprehension studies.

This brings us to a study by Musolino et al. (2000). These authors decided to assess adult speakers' preferred interpretation of sentences like (13), by asking them to come up with a context that would make such sentences true. The result was that subjects typically came up with contexts that only made the sentence true on its inverse scope interpretation (i.e., contexts in which some horses jumped over the fence, but others didn't). The conclusion that Musolino et al. (2000) reach is that adult speakers have a preference for the inverse scope interpretation of sentences like (13).

A different kind of sentence was investigated by Musolino and Lidz (2003). Among others, this study reports the results of a series of experiments assessing adults' interpretation of sentences such as (15).

(15) Two frogs didn't jump over the rock.

The relevant finding comes from Experiment 2 by Musolino and Lidz (2003). In this experiment, they asked adult speakers of English to evaluate sentences like (15) in contexts that made the target sentence true on its surface scope interpretation as well as contexts that made the target sentence true on its inverse scope interpretation. The result was that adult speakers of English accepted the target sentence in the former condition significantly more often than in the latter condition. In particular, Musolino and Lidz (2003) found that in a context in which only the inverse scope reading makes the sentence true (i.e., one frog jumps over the rock and one frog stays behind), adults accepted sentences like (15) only 27.5% of the time. In turn, they took this finding to reflect a default preference for surface scope interpretations.

Taking stock, the picture emerging from comprehension studies with adults is not very clear. Of course, one could object to Musolino et al. (2000) that the result of their experiment might simply denote a preference for a given context, rather than a preference for the reading that goes with it (see Crain and Steedman 1985). Furthermore, one could object to Musolino and Lidz (2003) on grounds that the context they used might favor a specific reading of the indefinite (see Gualmini 2007a). Nevertheless, these objections would not bring us any closer to determining what adults' preference is.

In the remainder of this chapter, we would like to pursue a different strategy. In particular, we would like to explore the hypothesis that adult speakers do not display a preference for either reading of a scopally ambiguous sentence. In a sense, this is consistent with Labov (1972), which started from the individual variation emphasized by Carden (1973) and reached the conclusion that almost all subjects can select either reading of the sentences we are concerned with, "when we control the context effectively" (p. 194). The next step is to attempt to formalize how the context can be controlled. One possible way of doing so is suggested by recent work by Hulsey et al. (2004). Although the focus of Hulsey et al. was child language, their model could also be extended to adults. Thus, we recall the main features of this proposal.

The study reported in Hulsey et al. (2004) developed a new model of scope resolution that makes reference to independently motivated principles of communication. According to this model, which Hulsey et al. (2004) call the Question-Answer requirement (QAR), children privilege the scope assignment which entails an answer to the Question under Discussion (QUD). According to this model, what is relevant in the pizza story used by Gualmini (2004) is the troll's task. At the end of the story, one wants to know whether the troll has carried out his task or not. This amounts to asking the 'yes/no' question *Did the troll deliver all the pizzas?* Notice that either scope assignment of (7), repeated below as (16), entails an answer to that question.

(16) The troll didn't deliver some pizzas.

Thus, either scope assignment is viable as far as the Question-Answer requirement is concerned. Since the Question-Answer requirement is satisfied, children can make use of the Maxim of Charity, instructing them to select the interpretation that makes the target sentence true. This will lead them to select the inverse scope interpretation (i.e., *There are some pizzas that the troll didn't deliver*), which makes the sentence true in the context because indeed there are some pizzas that the troll didn't deliver.

By contrast, consider (9) repeated below as (17).

(17) The troll didn't lose some pizzas.

In this case, only the surface scope interpretation entails an answer to the Question under Discussion. To illustrate, if some pizzas were not lost (i.e., the state of affairs described by the inverse scope interpretation of (17) holds), then it follows that some pizzas were delivered, but it does not follow that all pizzas were. By contrast, assuming that delivering and losing pizzas are the contextually relevant alternatives, if we know that no pizza was lost (i.e., the state of affairs described by the surface scope interpretation of (17) holds), then we know that all pizzas were delivered: we do have an answer to the question *Did the troll deliver all the pizzas?* Given that only one interpretation satisfies the Question-Answer requirement, that interpretation is selected. The inverse scope interpretation is not selected – even though it would make the target sentence true – because it does not entail an answer to the Question under Discussion.

Let us take stock. We have illustrated one proposal about how the context can be used in resolving scope ambiguities. This model was motivated by the observed differences in children's behavior across contexts. A recent study by Zondervan et al. (2009) attempted to determine whether the QAR model can also explain the putative inconsistencies that can be observed in adults. Zondervan et al. (2009) conducted an experiment using the Truth Value Judgment task. In the experiment, adults were told stories modeled after the ones employed by Gualmini (2004) with children. The stories were acted out in front of the subjects using props and toys. Each subject was presented with four trials, interspersed with fillers. At the end of each story, one experimenter solicited the target sentence by means of a question. The puppet manipulated by the second experimenter always answered using a sentence containing negation and the universal quantifier *all*. For example, subjects were told a story about a man who was delivering some hot-dogs to Wonder Woman. The hot-dog delivery guy had four hot-dogs in the car, and he delivered two out of these four hot-dogs. At this point, the puppet was either asked the question in (18) or the question in (19), depending on which experimental condition subjects had been assigned to. In both experimental conditions, the puppet answered as in (20), and this is the statement that subjects were asked to classify as either 'right' or 'wrong.' In both conditions, the target sentence was uttered with stress on *all*, destressed *not*, and rising intonation on *delivered*.

(18) Were all the hot-dogs delivered?
(19) Were some hot-dogs delivered?
(20) I think all the hot-dogs were not delivered.

The prediction of the QAR account is that the interpretation selected by adults would be influenced by the preceding question. In particular, the prediction is that adults should select the inverse scope interpretation of the target sentence when that sentence is presented as an answer to the question in (18), since the inverse scope interpretation entails an answer to that question and makes the sentence true. By contrast, adults are expected to select the surface scope interpretation of the target sentence when that sentence is presented as an answer to the question in (19), since only the surface scope interpretation entails an answer to that question. This is exactly what happened. Fifteen subjects accepted a sentence like (20) 98.3% of the time (59/60) when it followed a question like (18), but sixteen subjects only accepted it 23.4% of the time (15/64) when it followed a question like (19). Moreover, when subjects rejected the target sentence in the latter condition, they consistently pointed out that the puppet was wrong because some hot-dogs had indeed been delivered. This indicates that they had selected the surface scope interpretation of (20) (i.e., for all the hot-dogs, it is not the case that they were delivered).

These results show that adults' interpretation is influenced by the Question under Discussion (which Zondervan et al. (2009) chose to present overtly following Gualmini (2007c)), as predicted by the QAR model. When both interpretations address the Question under Discussion, adult speakers make use of the Maxim of Charity. When only one interpretation entails an answer to the Question under Discussion, however, adult speakers select that interpretation even if this ultimately results in the violation of the Maxim of Charity.

From a methodological point of view, the relevance of these results goes well beyond the debate on scope resolution. Since the work of Crain and Steedman (1985), we know how crucial it is to control the context. In this respect, there seems to be no way to tap into subjects' judgments without providing them with a context in which each interpretation of the target sentence receives a truth value (see Gil (1982) for a study on sentences that do not involve negation). However, we now know that the context does not simply mean the set of characters and objects that are available, but also the plot that revolves around them and the set of assumptions that the subject may bring to the task.

It is time to sum up. When it comes to scopally ambiguous sentences containing negation, our understanding of the adult system is somewhat partial, due to the difficulty of eliciting these sentences (see Gennari and MacDonald 2005/2006). Nevertheless, if we look at comprehension, we see that adults can access both readings of scopally ambiguous sentences and that once contextual factors are controlled for, their behavior is quite systematic.

3 Conclusion

This chapter examined recent psycholinguistic studies on children's and adults' interpretation of scopally ambiguous sentences containing negation. We placed our discussion against the background provided by the Variational Learning

Model proposed by Yang (2003). One of the issues addressed by this model is the fact that children's development seems to be more gradual than the Principles and Parameters framework can explain (see Chomsky 1981). According to Yang's model, one of the reasons why target grammars rise gradually is that children have access to multiple grammars, out of which they select randomly. We have considered a scenario in which one grammar is equivalent to the union of the competing grammars (see (5)). On the surface, the selection between two non-overlapping grammars or the selection among the options specified by a grammar that is equivalent to their union seem indistinguishable. Nevertheless, whereas the first process is random, the second isn't. In this respect, the language acquisition device (LAD) seems to have very different properties than the parser (see also Crain et al. 1994). Empirical support aside, we would like to end with a speculation about why we should stick to the assumption that true optionality is a feature of grammar selection unknown to the parser.

Let us start with the claim that grammar selection, when available, is a random process. If we adopt Yang's model, the reason is clear. On this model, language acquisition succeeds if the learner has the possibility of encountering evidence that leads to the reward of the target grammar as well as evidence that leads to the punishment of its competitors. If the learner could 'choose' one grammar out of his hypothesis space in the same way as a he would choose the intended reading of an ambiguous sentence, that is according to the same criteria, then the occasions for failure would disappear. For instance, if we could invoke charity to justify the selection of a grammar that makes true the sentence we're confronted with, then there would be no occasion to punish any grammar that makes the input false, as that grammar would never be selected to analyze an input that makes it false.

Let us now turn to the claim that optionality is unknown to the parser, the main claim of the present chapter. The conceptual motivation for this claim has to do with learnability considerations. To illustrate our point, we need to recall a recent proposal by Gualmini and Schwarz (2009). These authors took children's interpretation of the indefinite *some* as a case study. In particular, they focused on the task of children who have to move away from the grammar that licenses an ambiguity (i.e., G_3 in (5)). Under the assumption that adults can't interpret *some* in the scope of negation (see Ladusaw 1979), children may be facing a learnability problem. The solution by Gualmini and Schwarz (2009) is to enlarge the set of events that would count as failure of a given grammar. To illustrate, consider the dialogue below.

(21) Speaker A: Some pizzas were not lost.
Speaker B: Well, no pizza was lost!

As far as Speaker B knows, no pizza was lost. Furthermore, Speaker B's utterance signals that Speaker A's utterance does not count as a cooperative contribution to the conversation. If *some* receives wide scope over negation in

Speaker A's utterance, then we know why his utterance is uncooperative: the proposition that some pizzas were not lost triggers the implicature that some pizzas were indeed lost, but this implicature is not met in the context, since no pizza was lost. If *some* could receive narrow scope below negation, however, Speaker A's utterance would be true and cooperative, as it would express the same proposition expressed by Speaker B, namely that no pizza was lost. The question for anybody witnessing the dialogue above then would be: why can't Speaker B be charitable to Speaker A and interpret Speaker A's utterance on the meaning that would make the sentence true and felicitous in the context? A plausible answer is the following: because Speaker B cannot access that meaning. In other words, Speaker B's contribution signals that Speaker B has no choice but to access the interpretation that gives rise to such an implicature, i.e., the surface scope interpretation of Speaker A's utterance. Gualmini (2007b) referred to this mechanism as pragmatic bootstrapping (see Gleitman (1990) and Pinker (1984) for classic work on syntactic and semantic bootstrapping respectively). We leave to future research the task of determining whether this mechanism is empirically plausible. For present purposes, however, we would like to point out that the argument relies on the assumption that children assume that conversational participants follow the same principles in ambiguity resolution. If ambiguity resolution was a random process, the child would never be able to draw any consequence from the fact that an adult fails in selecting a specific reading, as this could simply be a matter of chance. However, as we have just suggested, it seems necessary for the child to use adults' failures in order to expunge non-adult readings from their grammar. When presenting Yang's Variational Learning model, we recalled how the Language Acquisition Device must allow the child to select grammars randomly: this ensures that failures will occur, thereby triggering a change in the child's hypothesis space. This assumes that the child does not discount these failures on other grounds. If, as we argued in this chapter, children and adults resolve ambiguities in the same systematic way, then the child will not be able to chalk upon any failures to differences in how identical grammars are put to use, and will be forced to conclude that different grammars are involved.

Acknowledgments I would like to thank Gillian Ramchand for discussion and for directing my attention to Labov's work. Many thanks also to Charles Yang for many stimulating discussions. Many thanks also to Merete Anderssen, Kristine Bentzen, Luisa Meroni, Michelle St-Amour and Marit Westergaard for comments on previous versions of the paper. This work was supported in part by a Standard Research Grant from the Social Sciences & Humanities Research Council of Canada (SSHRC) and a VIDI grant from the Netherlands Organization for Scientific Research (NWO) and Utrecht University.

References

Carden, Guy. 1973. *English quantifiers: Logical structure and linguistic variation*. Tokyo: The Taishukan Publishing Company.

Chomsky, Noam. 1981. *Lectures on government and binding*. Dordrecht: Foris

Crain, Stephen, Laura Conway, and Weijia Ni. 1994. Learning, parsing, and modularity. In *Perspectives on sentence processing*, eds. Charles Clifton, Lyn Frazier, and Keith Rayner, 443–467. Hillsdale: Lawrence Erlbaum Associate.

Crain, Stephen, and Cecile McKee. 1985. The acquisition of structural restrictions on anaphora. *Proceedings of NELS 15*, 94–110. University of Massachusetts

Crain, Stephen, and Mark Steedman. 1985. On not being led down the garden path: The use of context by the psychological parser. In *Natural language parsing: Psychological, computational and theoretical perspectives*, eds. by David Dowty, Lauri Karttunen, and Arnold Zwicky, 320–354. Cambridge: Cambridge University Press.

Crain, Stephen, and Rosalind Thornton. 1998. *Investigations in universal grammar: A guide to experiments on the acquisition of syntax and semantics*. Cambridge: MIT Press.

De Villiers, Jill G., and Helen Tager-Flusberg. 1975. Some facts one simply cannot deny. *Journal of Child Language* 2: 279–286.

Gennari, Silvia, and Maryellen MacDonald. 2005/2006. Acquisition of negation and quantification: Insights from adult production and comprehension. *Language Acquisition* 13: 125–168.

Gil, David. 1982. Quantifier scope and linguistic variation. *Linguistics and Philosophy* 5: 421–472.

Gleitman, Lila. 1990. The structural sources of verb meanings. *Language Acquisition* 1: 3–55.

Glenberg, Athus, David Robertson, Jennifer Jansen, and Mina Johnson-Glenberg. 1999. Not propositions. *Journal of Cognitive Science Systems Research* 1: 19–33.

Grodzinsky, Yosef, and Tanya Reinhart. 1993. The innateness of binding and coreference *Linguistic Inquiry* 24: 69–102.

Gualmini, Andrea. 2004. *The ups and downs of child language: Experimental studies in children's knowledge of entailment relationships and polarity phenomena.* New York: Routledge.

Gualmini, Andrea. 2005/2006. Some facts about quantification and negation one simply cannot deny: A reply to Gennari and MacDonald (2005) *Language Acquisition* 13: 363–370.

Gualmini, Andrea. 2007a. And now for some facts about adults' interpretation of ambiguous sentences. *Proceedings of the Fifth Semantics in the Netherlands day*, 1–11. The Netherlands: Groningen University.

Gualmini, Andrea. 2007b. Scope ambiguity in child language: Old and new problems. *Proceedings of On Linguistic Interfaces (ONLI)*, available at http://www.socsci.ulster.ac.uk/comms/onli/program.html

Gualmini, Andrea. 2007c. Scope resolution and overt questions: A test for the QAR. *Proceedings of the Eighth Tokyo Conference on Psycholinguistics*, 121–135. Tokyo.

Gualmini, Andrea, and Bernhard Schwarz. 2009. Solving learnability problems in the acquisition of semantics. *Journal of Semantics* 26: 185–215.

Gualmini, Andrea, Sarah Hulsey, Valentine Hacquard, and Danny Fox. 2005. *Overcoming isomorphism*. Paper presented at the Annual Meeting of the Linguistic Society of America, January 6–9, San Francisco, CA.

Horn, Laurence R. 1989. *A natural history of negation*. Chicago: University of Chicago Press.

Hulsey, Sarah, Valentine Hacquard, Danny Fox, and Andrea Gualmini. 2004. The question-answer requirement and scope assignment. In *Plato's problem: Problems in language acquisition*, eds. Aniko Csirmaz, Andrea Gualmini and Andrew Nevins, 71–90. Cambridge: MITWPL.

Krämer, Irene. 2000. *Interpreting indefinites*. Ph.D. Dissertation, Utrecht University.

Labov, William. 1972. *Sociolinguistic patterns*. Philadelphia: University of Pennsylvania Press.

Ladusaw, William. 1979. *Polarity sensitivity as inherent scope relations*. Ph.D. Dissertation, University of Texas.

Musolino, Julien. 1998. *Universal Grammar and the acquisition of semantic knowledge: An experimental investigation into the acquisition of quantifier-negation interaction in English.* PhD Dissertation, University of Maryland.

Musolino, Julien, Stephen Crain, and Rosalind Thornton. 2000. Navigating negative quantificational space. *Linguistics* 38: 1–32.

Musolino, Julien, and Jeffrey Lidz. 2003. The scope of isomorphism: Turning adults into children. *Language Acquisition* 11: 277–291.

Musolino, Julien, and Jeffrey Lidz. 2006. Why children aren't universally successful with quantification. *Linguistics* 44: 817–852.

Pinker, Steven. 1984. *Language learnability and language development*. Cambridge: Harvard University Press.

Reinhart, Tanya. 2006. *Interface strategies: Reference-set computation*. Cambridge: MIT Press.

Szabolcsi, Anna. 2004. Positive polarity-negative polarity. *Natural Language & Linguistic Theory* 22: 409–452.

Unsworth, Sharon. 2005. *Child l2, adult l2, child l1: Differences and similarities. A study on the acquisition of direct object scrambling in Dutch*. Utrecht: LOT Dissertation Series.

Unsworth, Sharon, and Andrea Gualmini. 2007. *Uncovering the pattern of children's interpretation of negation and indefinites*. Paper presented at the Boston University Conference on Language Development, November 2–4, Boston, MA.

Wason, Peter. 1965. The context of plausible denial. *Journal of verbal learning and verbal behavior* 4: 7–11.

Wason, Peter. 1972. In real life negatives are false. *Logique et Analyse* 15: 17–38.

Yang, Charles D. 2003. *Knowledge and learning in natural language*. Oxford: Oxford University Press.

Yang, Charles D. 2004. Universal grammar, statistics or both? *Trends in Cognitive Sciences* 8: 451–456.

Zondervan, Arjen, Luisa Meroni, and Andrea Gualmini. 2009. Experiments on the role of the question under discussion for ambiguity resolution and implicature Computation in Adults. *Proceedings of SALT XVIII*, 765–777. Ithca, NY

'Optional' Doubly-Filled COMPs (DFCs) in Wh-Complements in Child and Adult Swiss German

Manuela Schönenberger

Abstract Data from two children are examined to determine at what stage in their linguistic development they start to use 'doubly-filled COMPs' (DFCs) and in which contexts they use them. The term DFC refers to a configuration in which a phrasal element (e.g. a wh-phrase) co-occurs with a complementizer (e.g. *that*) in COMP. The focus is on DFCs in wh-complements of Swiss German. The distribution of DFCs in samples of adult data from two dialects is compared to extract the contexts in which DFCs are used. While in both dialects DFCs are excluded in wh-complements with monosyllabic wh-phrases, they are obligatory with non-monosyllabic wh-phrases in one dialect, but somewhat optional in the other. It has been shown that Swiss-German children acquire DFCs around age 5. This is also true of the children discussed here. However, the question of how children deal with the variable distribution of DFCs has not been addressed before. It will be shown that while DFCs seem somewhat optional in the input one of the children is exposed to, this optionality is not visible in the child data. This is taken to reflect the child's striving to regularize a seemingly irregular pattern.

Keywords Clitic · Doubly-filled COMP (DFC) · Monosyllabic wh-phrase · Non-monosyllabic wh-phrase · Optional verb movement · Prosodic unit

1 Introduction

The term 'doubly-filled COMP' (DFC) dates back to a pre-Barriers framework (Chomsky 1986), in which transformational grammarians distinguished between S' and S (rather than CP and IP) and the position preceding a sentence S was referred to as COMP. COMP could host various constituents, e.g. a wh-phrase (1a), a complementizer (1b), or it could be doubly-filled, as in the Swiss-German example in (1c), where both the wh-phrase and the complementizer occupy COMP.

M. Schönenberger (✉)
University of Oldenburg, Oldenburg, Germany
e-mail: iris.schoenenberger@uni-oldenburg.de

M. Anderssen et al. (eds.), *Variation in the Input*, Studies in Theoretical Psycholinguistics 39, DOI 10.1007/978-90-481-9207-6_3,

(1) a. I wonder [why he came].
b. I wonder [if she really likes him].
c. Chunt drufaa [wie frisch dass de Teig grad isch].
depends on how fresh that the dough GRAD is
'It depends on how fresh the dough is.'

I shall refer to the wh-constituent as the wh-phrase, independent of whether it consists of one word (*why*) or more than one word (*for what reason*).

DFCs are not a recent phenomenon, since they are also attested in earlier stages of e.g. German and English, as in (2). DFCs also occur in other Indo-European languages besides Germanic (see a.o. Haegeman (1992) for DFCs in West Flemish, Henry (1995) for DFCs in Belfast English, Taraldsen (1986) for DFCs in Norwegian), as e.g. in Romance in (3), as well as in non-Indo-European languages (see Penner and Bader (1995) for DFCs in Hebrew, and Shlonsky (1991) for DFCs in Palestinian Arabic).

(2) a. nu hoert [wa daz er mir lougent niht aller mîner leide]
'now listen how much of my pain he denies'
(Middle High German, Bayer 2004)
b. men shal wel knowe [who that I am]
'one shall know who I am'
(Middle English, Bayer 2004)

(3) non so [quando che Maria arriverà]
not know1sg when that Maria will.arrive
'I don't know when Maria will arrive'
(Variety of Italian, Bayer 2004)

The examples above show DFCs in wh-complements in which the wh-phrase co-occurs with a complementizer corresponding to *that*, but this is only one of the typical combinations. Wh-phrases can also be combined with *of* 'if', as in (4). DFCs are also found in other embedded contexts, as e.g. in relative clauses (5a) and in adverbial clauses (5b). Moreover, they are not necessarily restricted to embedded clauses, but can also occur in root contexts, as in (6).

(4) Ze vroeg [wie of het boek gelezen had].
she asked who if the book read had
'She asked who had read the book.'
(Variety of Dutch, Hoekstra 1992)

(5) a. dea Hund [dea wo gestern d'Katz bissn hot]
the dog the *wo* yesterday the-cat bitten has
'the dog that bit the cat yesterday'
(Bavarian, Bayer 1984)

b. I tue-s no schnell ufschribe [bevor dass-mer-s vergässet].
I do-it still quickly down.write before that-we-it forget
'I'll quickly write it down before we forget it.'
(St. Galler German, Schönenberger 2005)

(6) Quoi que Jean veut?
what that Jean wants
'What does Jean want?'
(Quebec French, Levevre 1985)

In this chapter I concentrate on the distribution of DFCs in wh-complements of child and adult Swiss German. The focus is on what governs the distribution of DFCs rather than the technicalities of whether the wh-phrase and *dass* occur in the same projection or in different projections in the C-domain. The two children of my study are exposed to a dialect in which DFCs appear to be optional to a certain extent. Moreover, some optionality is also found in the word order of wh-complements, which besides the verb-final pattern also allow verb movement (in certain contexts). There is an interaction between verb placement and the occurrence of a DFC. However, while DFCs never occur in wh-complements with verb movement, they do not always appear in wh-complements without verb movement. The occurrence of a DFC not only depends on the absence of verb movement, but also on the prosody of the wh-phrase and the constituent following it. The degree of optionality with respect to verb placement and the distribution of DFCs in the input may complicate the learning task for the child. The child has to discover that (i) wh-complements allow two verb-placement patterns and (ii) that DFCs only occur with one of these. Furthermore, she has to discover that (iii) the distribution of DFCs also depends on prosody and (iv) identify the constituents whose prosodic structure matters. Finally, she has to discover (v) in which contexts DFCs are obligatory and in which they are optional.

The chapter is organized as follows. Section 2 describes the corpora of adult and child speech used for the analysis. It also contains a brief note on verb placement in wh-complements and its interaction with the distribution of DFCs. In Section 3 the adult data are examined to extract the context in which DFCs are found, since there is no detailed description of DFCs in Swiss German, and there may be dialectal variation as well. The adult samples from two dialects are compared to determine whether there is dialectal variation. There indeed seems to be. In both dialects DFCs are excluded with monosyllabic wh-phrases, but in one dialect DFCs seem obligatory with non-monosyllabic wh-phrases, while in the other DFCs seem to be somewhat optional. Two hypotheses about the distribution of DFCs in related dialects are evaluated, but ultimately not adopted since they are incompatible with the data. Finally, a parallel between optional verb movement in wh-questions of Norwegian dialects and the optional distribution of DFCs in Swiss German is drawn. Section 4 investigates at which stage in their language development the children acquire DFCs in the dialect with optional DFCs. Based on an examination of the production data of one of the children it is shown that the acquisition of DFCs happens around age 5. Nothing conclusive can be said about the other child, who produces few spontaneous examples of the relevant type. Elicitation data will also be included in the discussion. The optionality found in the adult data is not visible in the child data, which may be interpreted as the children's striving to regularize a seemingly irregular pattern. Some support for this hypothesis can be seen in the children's adoption of generalized verb movement in embedded contexts before age 5. Section 5 contains the conclusions.

2 A Note on the Adult and Child Corpora of Swiss German

The corpora I prepared for this study contain adult data from St. Galler German, henceforth abbreviated as SG, and adult and child data from Lucernese. To obtain the SG sample I recorded and transcribed several hours of conversations between three adults who grew up in the same town and therefore speak the same variety of SG. The Lucernese data come from a longitudinal study of two children, called Moira and Eliza, and were extracted from audio recordings made by Moira's mother. Moira was recorded while interacting with other members of her family, and the two children were recorded while playing together. The 150 h of recorded data cover Moira's ages from 3;10 to 8;01 (147 h) and some late data, age 8;02–9;08 (3 h). Moira's corpus consists of over 5,500 embedded clauses produced spontaneously and several hundred elicited embedded clauses. Eliza's corpus is much smaller, but still contains over 600 spontaneous embedded clauses and several hundred elicited embedded clauses. I also transcribed excerpts of the recordings in which adults interacted with Moira, in order to better understand the input to which Moira was exposed. Most of the adult data come from her mother, who speaks a mixed dialect since she grew up in Zurich but moved to Lucerne as a young adult. I shall nonetheless refer to her dialect as Lucernese.

The word orders used in the wh-complements produced by the adults are described here, since word order interacts with the occurrence of DFCs. Wh-complements generally display the verb-final pattern, but verb movement resulting in V2 is not categorically excluded. There are many examples in which the wh-complement shows matrix clause word order, as in the examples from Lucernese, abbreviated as LU, in (7). It is difficult to pin down exactly which variables render V2 acceptable in this context. But it is clear that at least the matrix predicate (e.g. *frooge* 'ask' vs. *säge* 'say'), the mood in the matrix clause (e.g. the occurrence of a modal), and negation (e.g. *nöd wüsse* 'not know' vs. *wüsse* 'know') function like this.

(7) a. Ich ha ned gwüsst [was lauft zersch]. (LU)
I have not known what runs first
'I didn't know what they would show first (at the cinema).'

b. De mue-n-er vo obenabe go luege [wo hät s öppis]. (LU)
then must-he from upstairs go look where has it something
'Then he has to look from upstairs where there's something.'

c. Etz ha-n-ich de Teckel gsuecht und lueg [wo liit-er]. (LU)
now have-I the lid looked for and look where lies it
'I've been looking for the lid and look where it is.'

Many of the wh-complements with V2 are selected by *weisch*, which is the 2nd person singular present tense of *wüsse* 'know', illustrated in (8). Native speakers generally agree that V2 sounds perfectly acceptable in this context. Another context where V2 is readily accepted by speakers is in medial wh-constructions, as in (9). These two contexts account for 63 of the 78 wh-complements with the V2 pattern in the adult data.

(8) Weisch [worum isch das Blüemli do ine]? (LU)
know2sg why is that flower.Dim there in
'Do you know why that little flower is in here?'

(9) a. Was meinsch [was isch do drunder]? (LU)
what mean2sg what is there under
'What do you think is under this?'

b. Was tenksch [wie fühlt dä sich so im Flugzüg ine]? (LU)
what think2sg how feels this self so in-the plane in
'How do you think he feels in the plane?'

Sometimes it is impossible to tell whether verb movement has applied or not. There are contexts in which the word order in the wh-complement could be confused with V2, i.e. in certain wh-complements in which the wh-phrase is the subject, as in the examples in (10). The word order in these examples is truly ambiguous. Example (10a) could be derived either by verb movement to the left (as in matrix clauses) or by extraposing the constituent selected by the auxiliary verb *tuet* to the right, which would be an instance of Verb-Projection Raising (cf. a.o. Haegeman and Van Riemsdijk 1986, Haegeman 1992, Schönenberger 1995). Similarly, in example (10b) the finite verb *fehlt* has either undergone movement to the left or the adjunct PP *bi der* has been extraposed to the right. The embedded clause in example (10c) consists only of the subject wh-phrase and a finite verb.

(10) a. denn wett ich luege [wär tuet mini Perlechetti schtäle] (LU)
then want I look who does my pearl necklace steal
'then I'd like to see who will steal my pearl necklace'

b. Muesch luege [was fehlt bi der]. (LU)
must2sg look what lacks by you
'You should check what is missing from your deck of cards.'

c. Lueg etz [was passiert]. (LU)
look now what happens
'Now see what is happening.'

The verb-placement patterns in the wh-complements of Lucernese produced by the adults are summarized in Table 1, those of SG in Table 2. Since there is an interaction between verb placement and the distribution of DFCs, the distribution of the latter is shown in relation to the verb-placement patterns used. As can be seen from these tables, DFCs are only found in wh-complements that do not involve verb movement. Hence independent of what exactly governs the distribution of DFCs in wh-complements, the child has to discover that (i) V2 as well as the verb-final pattern are possible in wh-complements of Swiss German, and (ii) that only in the latter can DFCs possibly occur.

Table 1 Interaction between DFCs and word order in wh-complements (LU)

DFC	V2	Ambiguous	Not V2
−DFC	75	11	485
+DFC	0	0	72
Total	75	11	557

Table 2 Interaction between DFCs and word order in wh-complements (SG)

DFC	V2	Ambiguous	Not V2
−DFC	3	0	115
+DFC	0	0	28
Total	3	0	143

Although DFCs are only found in verb-final wh-complements, not every verb-final wh-complement contains a DFC. Thus the verb-final pattern is a necessary but not a sufficient condition. Based on the two adult samples, other factors which may be relevant to the distribution of DFCs are examined in the next section.

3 The Distribution of DFCs in Adult Swiss German

Based on the dialect corpora of SG and Lucernese I try to determine the context in which adult speakers use DFCs in spontaneous speech and whether there is dialectal variation. In Section 3.1 a published description of the distribution of DFCs in Bernese Swiss German is discussed and evaluated against the spontaneous production data from the other two dialects. It will be shown that the description of Bernese, which is not based on an examination of actual data, is vague and partially contradictory. Moreover, there is variation between the two dialects examined here: There is a clear correlation between the occurrence of a DFC and the length of the wh-phrase in St. Galler German, but whether such a correlation exists in Lucernese is far from clear. Prosody, although relevant in both dialects, may play a key role in the latter. In Sections 3.2 and 3.3 the context surrounding a DFC, i.e. the predicate selecting the wh-complement as well as the constituent following the wh-phrase (or the DFC), is studied. The prosody of the constituent following the wh-phrase combined with that of the wh-phrase itself seems to be relevant, while the predicate selecting the wh-complement does not. In Section 3.4 a recent syntactic approach to the distribution of DFCs, based on a questionnaire study on two German dialects is summarized, but not adopted, since it is not compatible with my empirical findings. In Section 3.5 a comparison is drawn between the variable distribution of DFCs in Swiss German and the optionality of verb movement in matrix wh-questions of some Norwegian dialects.

3.1 Do DFCs Depend on the Weight of the Wh-Phrase?

In a description of Bernese (BE), Penner and Bader (1995:128) note that a DFC is 'generally preferred' with simple wh-phrases and 'strongly preferred' with complex wh-phrases. They give *wo* 'where' in (11a) as an example of a simple wh-phrase and *i welem Huus* 'in which house' in (11b) as an example of a complex 'wh-phrase'. Although the difference between *wo* and *i welem Huus* may be intuitively clear in the examples in (11), it is not made precise. For instance, to which category would a wh-phrase like *wie luut* 'how loud' or *werum* 'why' belong? Penner (1996:65), on the other hand, observes that DFCs in Bernese are 'optional' with light wh-phrases, but 'obligatory' with heavy wh-phrases. The labels 'light' and 'heavy' are not defined. I assume that 'heaviness' may be dependent on the number of syllables (rather than morphemes), but it is again unclear whether e.g. bisyllabic wh-phrases are subsumed under light or heavy wh-phrases. Penner's observation is similar, but not equivalent, to that of Penner and Bader. In both a difference between two classes of wh-phrases is appealed to, without clarifying what makes a wh-phrase belong to one class rather than the other. But while Penner assumes that DFCs are optional with one class of wh-phrases, Penner and Bader assume that they are generally preferred with that class.

(11) a. I ha ne gfragt [wo (dass) er wohnt]. (BE)
I have him asked where that he lives
'I asked him where he lives.'

b. I ha ne gfragt [i welem Huus ?*(dass) er wohnt]. (BE)
I have him asked in which house that he lives
'I asked him in which house he lives.'

(Penner and Bader 1995:128)

I have tried to evaluate whether either of these observations on Bernese extends to my dialect corpora by classifying the wh-phrases into number of syllables. Wh-phrases consisting of one syllable, two syllables, or more than two syllables were distinguished and only wh-complements that were unambiguously verb-final were considered. The data are summarized in Tables 3 and 4.

Table 3 Interrelation between DFC and weight of wh-phrase in syllables (LU)

DFC	One syllable	Two syllables	More than two syllables
−DFC	439	39	7
+DFC	2	40	30
Total	441	79	37

Table 4 Interrelation between DFC and weight of wh-phrase in syllables (SG)

DFC	One syllable	Two syllables	More than two syllables
−DFC	115	0	0
+DFC	1	21	6
Total	116	21	6

As can be deduced from these tables, the two dialects do not behave alike, and neither shows the pattern observed by Bader and Penner (1988) or Penner (1996) for Bernese. In both Lucernese and SG monosyllabic wh-phrases are generally construed without a DFC. Thus a DFC with monosyllabic wh-phrases in these two dialects is clearly neither generally preferred nor optional. If DFCs were truly optional in wh-complements with monosyllabic wh-phrases, such an asymmetric distribution would not emerge. Moreover, DFCs in Lucernese do not appear to be obligatory, independent of the weight of the wh-phrase. Although they occur proportionally more often with longer wh-phrases than with wh-phrases with two syllables, they are not obligatory in either context, as shown in (12). The wh-phrase in (12a) consists of two syllables and that in (12b) consists of five syllables.

(12) a. Glaubsch ned [wivil du scho uf s Bändli
believe2sg not how much you already on the tape.Dim
gredt häsch]. (LU)
spoken have
'You won't believe how much you've spoken on the tape.'

b. Si wett no lose [was föres Gschichtli mer hüt
she wants still listen what kind of a story.Dim we today
am Morge verzellt händ]. (LU)
in-the morning told have
'She'd like to know what kind of fairy tale we told this morning.'

The distribution of DFCs in SG is much clearer. DFCs seem to be obligatory with wh-phrases of two or more syllables, as illustrated in (13).

(13) a. Weisch no [för wa dass-mer di aagmolde händ]? (SG)
know2sg still for what that-we you up-signed have
'Do you still remember what we signed you up for?'
b. und denn ha-n-i verzellt [wivil Räum dass-mer hand] (SG)
and then have-I told how many rooms that-we have
'and then I mentioned how many rooms we have'

Neither of the observations for Bernese captures the distribution in my dialect data. DFCs are not generally preferred or optional with monosyllabic wh-phrases, which may consist of more than one morpheme (*wär* 'who.Nom/Acc' vs. *wäm* 'who.Dat'), in either dialect, and they are not obligatory with long wh-phrases in Lucernese. Moreover, in SG they seem to be obligatory with all non-monosyllabic wh-phrases, even if these consist of only two syllables, as e.g. *worum* 'why'.[1]

To summarize, the length of a wh-phrase measured in syllables has an impact on whether or not a DFC is used: monosyllabic wh-phrases generally occur without a DFC. Wh-phrases consisting of two or more syllables occur with a DFC in SG and can optionally occur with a DFC in Lucernese. A difference between these two dialects seems to exist. But so far only the wh-phrase itself was examined, not the predicate selecting the wh-complement or the constituent following the wh-phrase. These are examined next.

3.2 Do DFCs Depend on the Predicate Selecting the Wh-Complement

Most of the wh-complements in the Lucernese data are selected by *wüsse* 'know', *luege* 'look', *lose* 'listen', *säge* 'say', *gseh* 'see', and *zeige* 'show'. I shall concentrate on *wüsse*, since it is the predicate most often used. As mentioned above, *weisch* – the 2nd person singular present tense of *wüsse* 'know' – selects a wh-complement which can either show V2 or the verb-final pattern, as in (14a)

[1] In his chapter on D-linking, Pesetsky notes that '*which*-phrases are discourse-linked (D-linked), whereas *who* and *what* are normally not D-linked...' (1987:107f.). Because monosyllabic wh-phrases are not D-linked and do not occur with a DFC in my data, and longer wh-phrases often contain *weli* 'which', one could be tempted to interpret *dass* as signalling a D-linked wh-phrase in Swiss German. However, Pesetsky also observes that 'it is cross-linguistically extremely difficult to D-link the word that means *why*' (1987:127, Footnote 31). There are 42 examples of wh-complements in which the wh-phrase is *worum*/*wiso* 'why' and many of these occur with a DFC, even in the Lucernese data. I conclude that there is no evidence that DFCs have anything to do with D-linking.

and (14b) respectively. Sometimes a wh-complement selected by *weisch* occurs with a DFC, as in (15a), and sometimes it does not, as in (15b).

(14) a. Weisch [a was erinneret mich das]? (LU)
know2sg of what reminds me this
'Do you know what this reminds me of?'
b. Weisch [wo s Gschpenscht isch]? (LU)
know2sg where the ghost is
'Do you know where the ghost is?'

(15) a. Weisch [wie schpoot dass' isch]? (LU)
know2sg how late that-it is
'Do you know how late it is?'
b. Weisch [wivil 20 isch]? (LU)
know2sg how much 20 is
'Do you know how much 20 is?'

In the examples in (16) and (17) the matrix clauses are identical. While the wh-complement has a DFC in (16a) and (17a), it does not in (16b) and (17b).

(16) a. Weisch du [weles dass Camembert isch]? (LU)
know you which that Camembert is
'Do you know which one is the Camembert?'
b. Weisch du [worum t'Rahel fort isch]? (LU)
know you why the-Rahel away is
'Do you know why Rahel went away?'

(17) a. Ich weiss nöd [wie wiit dass si scho glueget hät]. (LU)
I know not how far that she already looked has
'I don't know how far she has already watched the film.'
b. Ich weiss nöd [weli du meinsch]. (LU)
I know not which you mean
'I don't know which one you mean.'

Based on this brief discussion I conclude that the occurrence of a DFC cannot be solely dependent on the matrix predicate selecting the wh-complement. In fact, the matrix predicate may even be irrelevant to the occurrence of a DFC in its complement (see also Section 4.1 on the occurrence of DFCs in non-selected clauses). Whether the constituent following the wh-phrase (or *dass* in the case of a DFC) influences the distribution of DFCs is examined in the next section.

3.3 Is the Occurrence of a DFC Dependent on the Constituent Following the Wh-Phrase?

The answer to whether the constituent following the wh-phrase influences the occurrence of a DFC will be 'yes, partially'. In the following paragraphs I try to show that in both dialects the prosody of the constituent following the wh-phrase as well as that of the wh-phrase itself influence the occurrence of a DFC. The following generalizations will be derived: (i) If the wh-phrase and the following constituent form a prosodic unit – a trochaic foot – a DFC is excluded. (ii) If the constituent following the wh-phrase is a clitic that cannot be integrated into the prosodic structure of the wh-phrase, a DFC must be inserted. (*N*-insertion in intervocalic contexts is taken to signal whether or not the wh-phrase and the following constituent form a prosodic unit.) (iii) In all other contexts, DFC may be optional in Lucernese, while in SG they are obligatory with all non-monosyllabic wh-phrases. To derive these generalizations, I first concentrate on the constituent immediately following the wh-phrase (or the DFC) and then consider the prosody of the wh-phrase.

The constituent immediately following the wh-phrase (or the DFC) is typically the subject. In general, unstressed pronouns are more restricted in distribution than stressed pronouns or nominal DPs. In the case of pronominal subjects, unstressed subject pronouns must be adjacent to either the finite verb in a V2 configuration or to the subordinator in an embedded clause. Moreover, an unstressed subject pronoun that is a clitic needs to undergo cliticization, i.e. it needs to attach to, e.g., the complementizer *dass* in an embedded clause introduced by this complementizer.

Since wh-complements with a monosyllabic wh-phrase generally do not occur with a DFC, but often contain unstressed subject pronouns which are clitics, the occurrence of the latter does not require the presence of a DFC. That is, subject clitics can undergo cliticization to a monosyllabic wh-phrase. In an intervocalic context, i.e. when the wh-phrase ends in a vowel and the following word starts with a vowel, as in (18), an intrusive *n* is inserted to prevent a hiatus. This *n* is called intrusive because it is not present in the underlying phonemic representation. The pronouns in (18) are subject clitics, but *n* is also inserted in an intervocalic context when the subject pronoun receives stress, as in (19). Note in passing that the *n* in 'cha-n-i' in (19b) is a linking *n*, which is present in the underlying phonemic representation. The form *chan* sometimes surfaces in clause-final position. This is also true of other examples in which *n* surfaces if a finite verb occurs in C°, and both ends in a vowel and precedes a constituent with an initial vowel.

(18) a. Chasch der-en vorschtelle [wie-n-er usgseht]. (LU)
can2sg you-him imagine how-he out.looks
'You can imagine what he looks like.'

b. Die hät gwüsst [wo-n-er isch]. (LU)
this has known where-he is
'This one knew where he is.'

c. Weisch [wa-n-i amel ha müese]? (SG)
know2sg what-I sometimes have must
'Do you know what I had to do sometimes?'

(19) a. Aber am Aafang … händ-er müese säge
but at-the beginning have-you.pl must say
[wie-n-eer heisset]. (LU)
how YOU.pl called
'But at the beginning you had to tell them what YOU are called.'

b. Denn cha-n-i verzelle [wie-n-eer eu troffe händ]. (SG)
then can I tell how YOU.pl met have
'Then I can tell other people how YOU two met.'

Intrusive *n* is excluded in (20), although the wh-phrase ends in a vowel and the following word starts with a vowel. The pronouns in (20) are possessive pronouns rather than subject pronouns and they are bisyllabic with stress on the first syllable. What exactly governs the distribution of *n*-insertion is not clear to me.[2] There are also dialectal differences (see e.g. Kabak and Schiering 2006).

(20) a. Etz weiss ich nüm [wie-*n-ires Meitli heisst]. (LU)
now know I no.longer how-your daughter calls
'I don't know what her daughter is called.'

[2] The fact that the possessive pronouns in the text examples in (20) are bisyllabic cannot be the reason why intrusive *n* is excluded, since *n*-insertion is obligatory in an intervocalic context involving a bisyllabic object clitic, as in (i). Stress itself cannot be the determining factor either, since the stressed object pronoun in (ii) is incompatible with *n*-insertion, while a stressed subject pronoun is compatible with it, as in the text examples in (19). This seems to imply that the grammatical function of the pronoun, i.e. subject vs. non-subject, may be relevant rather than stress alone or the number of syllables of the pronoun.

(i) Si cha sich nüme erinnere [wo-n-ere da scho mol passiert isch] (SG)
she can self no longer remember where-her this already once happened is
'She can no longer remember where this happened to her before.'

(ii) Si weiss aber [wo EM da passiert isch]. (SG)
she knows but where HIM this happened is
'But she remembers where this happened to HIM.'

b. Ich weiss nöd [wie-*n-eri Usbildig isch]. (SG)
I know not how-her education is
'I don't know what kind of education she has.'

Even in a context in which the wh-phrase ends in a vowel and the following constituent is a subject pronoun starting with a vowel, *n*-insertion is not always possible, as shown by the contrast between (21a) and (21b). Both wh-phrases end in a vowel, but *wo* in (21a) is monosyllabic and *wiso* in (21b) is not. I interpret the impossibility of *n*-insertion in (21b) to reflect the fact that the subject pronoun and the non-monosyllabic wh-phrase do not form a prosodic unit. In the case of subject clitics this means that they do not cliticize onto the wh-phrase. Since clitics cannot form a prosodic unit by themselves, I suggest that *dass* is inserted, as in (21c), to function as a host for the clitic. A phonological constraint may therefore require the use of a DFC to prevent clitics from stranding.

(21) a. Weisch [wo-n-er wohnt]?
know2sg where-he lives
'Do you know where he lives?'
b.* Weisch [wiso-*n-er chunt]?
know2sg why-he comes
'Do you know why he's coming?'
c. Weisch [wiso dass-er chunt]?
know2sg why that-he comes

Is it possible that this phonological constraint can account for the distribution of DFCs in both dialects? For this to be the case all wh-complements with a DFC would have to contain clitics that need to be hosted by *dass*. There are no examples in the data in which a clitic is left dangling, i.e. a subject clitic cliticizes onto the wh-phrase if possible and otherwise it cliticizes onto *dass*. On the other hand, there are also wh-complements in both Lucernese and SG that contain non-pronominal subjects, but which co-occur with *dass*, as in (22). Moreover, these examples do not contain object clitics that might require the presence of *dass* as a host for cliticization. There are 12 such examples in Lucernese and 11 in SG. Therefore the phonological constraint that *dass* is inserted only when a clitic cannot be hosted by the wh-phrase fails to account for all instances of DFCs.

(22) a. Muesch de Manuela säge [wiso dass t'Rhea s Lämpli
must2sg the.Dat Manuela say why that the-Rhea the lamp.Dim
mues usetue]. (LU)
must out.do
'You have to tell Manuela why Rhea has to put the lantern outside.'

b. und lueget eifach [wie müed dass s ander usgseht] (SG)
and looks simply how tired that the other out.looks
'and one simply looks how tired the other (person) looks'

The use of a DFC may sometimes be preferred for purely prosodic reasons, since *dass* can provide an unstressed syllable. In (23) the second syllable of *wiso* is stressed as is the first syllable of the nominal *s Bebe*, and *dass* provides an unstressed syllable between two stressed ones. In (24a) *dass* is used although the wh-phrase is monosyllabic, but there is heavy stress on *dää* (see also Footnote 3). The same holds for the Bernese example in (24b), in which *dää* is also heavily stressed (and the wh-phrase is monosyllabic).

(23) Denn isch si go luege [wiso dass s Bebe brüelet]. (LU)
then is she go look why that the baby cries
'Then she checked why the baby was crying.'

(24) a. sonig wo gfrogt händ [wäm dass dää Garte ghör] (SG)
those who asked have who.Dat that this garden belongs
'those who asked who that garden belongs to'
b. Wo dass dää scho überau isch gsi! (BE)
where that he already everywhere is been
'(It's amazing, unbelievable) Where he has been!'
(Penner and Bader 1995:128)

The example in (25) differs from those in (24) in that the monosyllabic wh-phrase itself receives heavy stress. Since the wh-phrase ends in a vowel and the subject clitic starts with a vowel, *n*-insertion would signal that these two elements form a prosodic unit. However, *n*-insertion is not possible when a monosyllabic wh-phrase is heavily stressed. Again *dass* is inserted to host the subject clitic.

(25) Me händ-m-s gseit [WIE dass-er da söll handhabe].
we have-him-it said HOW that-he this should handle
'We told him how he should deal with it.' (Köbi Kuhn, 3.4.07)

The examples in (26) from my Lucernese corpus may support the assumption that DFCs are sometimes used for purely prosodic reasons. In (26a) the subject pronoun *ich* receives contrastive stress, whereas in (26b) it does not. In the latter a DFC is used.

(26) a. Weisch du [worum ICH en Schwanz mach]? (LU)
know you why I a pigtail make
'Do you know why I make a pigtail?'
b. Weisch du [worum dass ich das mach]? (LU)
know you why that I this make
'Do you know why I'm doing this?'

My data sample of SG may be too small to draw strong conclusions. I tentatively conclude that in SG all non-monosyllabic wh-phrases must be combined with *dass* independent of the type of constituent following it. There seems to be a genuine difference between the two dialects: In SG the occurrence of a DFC is obligatory with non-monosyllabic wh-phrases, while in Lucernese it is not. In both dialects DFCs are obligatory whenever the wh-phrase cannot host a clitic following it, but in all other contexts they may be optional in Lucernese.

The prosodic unit 'trochaic foot' seems to play an important role. According to Kabak and Schiering (2006), the combination of two function words in German dialects results in a trochaic foot, as, e.g., in the combination of a complementizer and a weak pronoun or a preposition with a determiner. Based on this observation, I suggest that the insertion of *dass* would destroy this unit, which may explain why DFCs are generally dispreferred with monosyllabic wh-phrases. Focus on a monosyllabic wh-phrase changes the weight of the syllable and may turn it into a prosodic word to which an unstressed syllable cannot be suffixed. If a DFC is used, *dass* and an unstressed syllable can form a trochaic foot. The prosodic structure of non-monosyllabic wh-phrases does not seem to be relevant in SG: Independent of where the word stress falls, a DFC is used. For instance, in the bisyllabic wh-phrases *worum*, *wiso*, *för wa* 'what for', word stress falls on the second syllable, while in the bisyllabic wh-phrase *weli* 'which one' it falls on the first syllable. In the case of Lucernese, prosody does seem to be relevant to whether or not a DFC is used with non-monosyllabic wh-phrases.

To summarize, the prosody of the wh-phrase as well as the following constituent can influence the occurrence of a DFC. The organization of linguistic material into prosodic units of trochaic feet seems to be preferred in Swiss German. The combination of a wh-phrase and a pronoun into a prosodic unit is signalled by n-insertion in intervocalic contexts. Based on these observations the following generalizations were derived:

- If the wh-phrase and the following constituent form a prosodic unit – a trochaic foot – DFCs are excluded.
- If the constituent following the wh-phrase is a clitic, which cannot be integrated into the prosodic structure of the wh-phrase, a DFC must be inserted. The clitic and *dass* form a trochaic foot.
- In all other contexts, DFC may be optional in Lucernese, while in SG they are obligatory with all non-monosyllabic wh-phrases.

A number of caveats should be noted. While the SG data are taken from a conversation between adults, the Lucernese data arise from adults interacting with a child. Moreover, most of the adult data in the Lucernese sample come from a single speaker, the mother, who speaks a mixed dialect. It is also noticeable that she often speaks particularly clearly when addressing the child, which might subtly distort the data. If prosody is indeed relevant to the occurrence of DFCs then clear speech might influence the overall prosodic structure. Tables 5 (for Lucernese) and 6 (for SG) summarize the use of DFCs by the individual speakers within the respective data samples. The '+' and '–' symbols in the tables mark the presence and the absence of a DFC respectively.

Table 5 DFC and weight of wh-phrase in syllables per speaker (LU)

Speaker	One syllable	Two syllables	More than two syllables
Mother	396(–)/1(+)	39(–)/36(+)	7(–)/26(+)
Father	16(–)/1(+)	–	2(+)
Sister	27(–)	4(+)	2(+)
Total	439(–)/2(+)	39(–)/40(+)	7(–)/30(+)

Table 6 DFC and weight of wh-phrase in syllables per speaker (SG)

Speaker	One syllable	Two syllables	More than two syllables
AS	39(–)/1(+)	8(+)	2(+)
KS	20(–)	1(+)	1(+)
MS	56(–)	12(+)	3(+)
Total	115(–)/1(+)	21(+)	6(+)

Before turning to the Swiss-German child data in Section 4, I discuss a recent syntactic approach to DFCs, developed for two German dialects, in Section 3.4, and point out parallels between the occurrence of DFCs in Swiss German and verb movement in matrix questions in some Norwegian dialects in Section 3.5. Neither the analysis of DFC in the German dialects nor the syntactic account of verb movement in questions of Norwegian dialects can be extended to the Swiss-German situation.

3.4 *Are Monosyllabic Wh-Phrases Complementizers in Disguise?*

Bayer and Brandner (2008a, b) investigated the distribution of DFCs in Alemannic and Bavarian. Their data pertain to judgement and hence are quite different from my natural speech data. Informants were asked to rate sentences containing DFCs which were read to them on a scale from 1 ('I would use such a sentence in my dialect') to 6 ('I would never use such a sentence in my dialect'). The findings are similar to mine: monosyllabic wh-phrases with a DFC were generally rejected, while full wh-phrases with a DFC were generally accepted. One of the problems with these judgement data, as noted by Bayer and Brandner, is that all of these dialect speakers are also native speakers of Standard German, which may have influenced their grammaticality judgements since DFCs are not used in Standard German. The attitude towards dialects in Germany also appears to be quite different from that in the Swiss-German part of Switzerland. Native speakers of Swiss German are primarily dialect speakers. They also know Standard German, but may not use it regularly in day-to-day interactions.

Bayer and Brandner propose that short wh-items and overt complementizers compete for the same syntactic position because short wh-items have a hybrid status in that they can function as wh-operators and complementizers at the same time. Wh-items like *warum* 'why', *wieviel* 'how much' and *wem* 'who.Dat', which is monosyllabic but bears a Case-feature, are acceptable with a DFC and are said to involve phrasal structure just like full wh-phrases. They arrange the various types of wh-phrases along a scale, given in (27), ranging from what they consider a short wh-phrase in (27a) to what they consider a long wh-phrase in (27c). The longer or more complex the wh-phrase is the more acceptable it is with a DFC.[3]

(27) a. *wer* 'who', *wen* 'who.Acc', *was* 'what', *wie* 'how', *wo* 'where'
b. *warum* 'why', *wieviel* 'how much', *wem* 'who.Dat'
c. wh-DPs, Wh-PPs

(cf. Bayer and Brandner 2008a:89)

The hybrid status of certain short wh-phrases can straightforwardly account for why they are incompatible with a DFC in wh-complements. Bayer and Brander suggest that clauses in general need to be typed as <interrogative>, <declarative>, etc. Thus at some point in the derivation the wh-phrase merges with TP to endow the clause with an interrogative feature. In an embedded context, a short wh-phrase can activate a latent C-feature, blocking the insertion of *dass* for economy reasons. In a matrix context, a short wh-phrase does not need to discharge its C-feature since it is latent, and therefore the C-feature can be spelled out by the finite verb. In fact, verb movement to C forces the short wh-phrase to merge as a maximal projection. Certain technical details may be problematic, e.g., the insertion of *dass* after a wh-phrase without a latent C-feature has been merged with TP. However, the core idea that certain short

---

[3] The text example (24a) in which the wh-phrase is *wäm* 'who.Dat' would qualify as a possible candidate for *dass*-insertion given Bayer and Brandner's scale. Although *wäm* is monosyllabic it is structurally more complex than *wär* 'who' because of the feature <Dative>. There are a few examples in my corpora in which *wäm* is preceded by a preposition, thus qualifying as wh-PPs, but (24a) is the only example in which the wh-phrase is simply *wäm*.

wh-phrases are potential complementizers is appealing. Bayer and Brandner convincingly show that in a number of languages some short wh-phrases have been grammaticalized as complementizers (e.g. in North Eastern Italian dialects *che* 'what' functions as a complementizer).

From a psycholinguistic perspective it is not clear how to interpret the scale in (27). If the occurrence of a DFC solely depends on whether or not the wh-phrase has a latent C-feature, then one would expect that the same wh-phrase is always treated in the same way by a given speaker, since he/she presumably stores a lexical item, here a wh-phrase with its feature matrix, in the mental lexicon. Turning to a concrete example in my data set: there are 33 examples in which Moira's mother uses a wh-complement that is introduced by *worum* 'why'. In 21 of these she does not use a DFC and in 12 she does. The optional use of a DFC with *worum* implies that she either has two lexical entries for *worum* or that for her *worum* is underspecified for the latent C-feature. Neither of these solutions seems attractive.

3.5 *Optional Verb Movement in Wh-Questions in Norwegian Dialects*

There are certain parallels between the occurrence of DFCs in Swiss-German wh-complements and verb movement in matrix wh-questions in dialects of Norwegian. Properties of the wh-phrase seem to interact with both phenomena.

Norwegian dialects usually display V2 in matrix clauses. In contrast to Standard Norwegian, in some of these dialects verb movement in matrix questions with monosyllabic wh-phrases is ruled out, according to Rice and Svenonius (1998) (see Vangsnes (2005) for a detailed discussion of various Norwegian dialects and also Westergaard (2003, 2005)). This is shown in the examples in (28), in which the finite verb is underlined. However, if a monosyllabic wh-phrase is focussed, as in (29a), or the wh-phrase is not monosyllabic, as in (29b), verb movement must apply. Rice and Svenonius (1998:9) note that 'the prosody of the wh-phrase' matters, but that 'the prosodic size of the verb or of the subject are not relevant'. They develop an account in terms of prosody couched in an Optimality-theoretic framework.

(28) a.% Ka <u>sa</u> ho?
what says she
'What does she say?'

a′. Ka ho <u>sa</u>?

b.% Kor <u>bor</u> du?
where live you
'Where do you live?'

b′. Kor du <u>bor</u>?

(29) a. KA <u>sa</u> han Ola?
what said she Ola
'What did Ola say?'
a′.* KA han Ola <u>sa</u>?
b. Koffor <u>skrev</u> han?
Why writes he
'Why does he write?'
b′.* Koffor han <u>skrev</u>?

Westergaard (2003, 2005) and Westergaard and Vangsnes (2005) observe that the information structure of the subject does matter and that in non-V2 structures 'the subject is virtually always familiar or given information'. These authors note that there are dialects of Norwegian in which verb movement is not triggered even if the wh-phrase is not monosyllabic.

The following parallels between the Norwegian dialects and Swiss German seem to hold:

- Monosyllabic wh-phrases are special: they do not trigger V2 in certain Norwegian dialects and they do not occur with DFCs in Swiss German.
- If these monosyllabic wh-phrases receive stress they lose their special status: V2 is triggered and DFCs are possible.
- There is dialectal variation concerning non-monosyllabic wh-phrases and non-V2 in Norwegian dialects and the occurrence of a DFC in Swiss-German dialects.
- The subject type may be relevant to the application of verb movement and to the occurrence of DFCs in at least some of the dialects of Norwegian and of Swiss German.

In contrast to Bayer and Brandner (2008a, b), Westergaard and Vangsnes use a Split-CP framework (cf. Rizzi 1997). In their analysis verb movement can target different heads in matrix questions, dependent on the projection properties of wh-phrases as well as the information status of the subject.

Despite the parallels between the Norwegian dialects and Swiss German, listed above, there are also crucial differences, making an account along similar lines unlikely. As shown by Westergaard and Vangsnes verb movement in matrix questions with monosyllabic wh-phrases interacts with the information status of the subject. In contrast, monosyllabic wh-phrases in Swiss German generally do not occur with a DFC independent of whether the subject conveys new or old information. An appealing feature of Westergaard and Vangsnes's analysis is that although verb movement in matrix questions looks alike, different heads are targeted by the verb depending on the type of wh-phrase. It may well be the case that *dass* and verb movement in Swiss-German questions do not involve the same head either, i.e. C° in Bayer and Brandner's analysis. Still, as I have tried to argue in Section 3.3, there seems to be a strong interaction between prosody and the use of DFCs in Swiss German, which may be difficult or even impossible to capture in a purely syntactic account. Thus it is also not quite clear why stress on a monosyllabic wh-phrase in Norwegian would interact with projection properties in Int(errogative)P, as suggested by Westergaard and Vangsnes (2005:135).

4 The Distribution of DFCs in Child Swiss German

In this section I study at what stage Lucernese-speaking children start to use DFCs and in which contexts these appear. Can the variable distribution of DFCs in the input also be seen in the child data?

To learn the distribution of DFCs in Lucernese, the child has to pay close attention to verb placement in wh-complements, and to the prosody of the wh-phrase as well as the constituent following it. In particular, she has to discover the following:

- Some wh-complements are compatible with verb movement, while others are not.
- DFCs never occur in wh-complements with verb movement, but they can occur in wh-complements without verb movement.
- The prosody of the wh-phrase matters: DFCs are generally not found in wh-complements with monosyllabic wh-phrases, but they can be found in those with non-monosyllabic wh-phrases.
- The prosody of the constituent following the wh-phrase also matters: DFCs are obligatory if this constituent is (a) a clitic and (b) cannot form a prosodic unit with the wh-phrase.
- DFCs are optional in all other contexts.

Presumably a child cannot produce a DFC-configuration before she has started to produce wh-complements and clauses introduced by the complementizer *dass*. The Lucernese children Moira and Eliza use wh-complements in the first recordings at age 3;10, but the first recorded utterance in which Moira produced an embedded clause with *dass* is at age 4;01, and for Eliza at age 4;10. Since Eliza has not been recorded as regularly as Moira, the late occurrence of *dass* may just be a sampling discrepancy (see also Rothweiler (1993) and Grimm (1973) for the late occurrence of the complementizer *dass* in some German child data).

Penner (1996) notes that Bernese-speaking children acquire DFCs around the age of 5. In several elicitation tasks, child J. did not succeed in repeating a DFC at age 4, shown in (30). In a later elicitation task, carried out when the child was 4;10, J. managed to successfully produce DFCs, as in (31). J. started to produce the first DFCs spontaneously about 2 weeks later, as in (32).

(30) a. target: Weisch [werum dass ds Nomi so truurig isch]?
know2sg why that the Naomi so sad is
'Do you know why Naomi is so sad?'
a′. elicitation: Was het's di gfraagt?
'What did it (a toy duck) ask you?'
b. child: dass ds Nomi so truurig isch (J:3;11,29)
that the Naomi so sad is
'that Naomi is so sad'
(Penner 1996:66)

(31) a. target: I weiss nid [i welem Dorf dass dr Andi wohnt].
I know not in which village that the Andi lives
'I don't know in which village Andi lives.'
a′. elicitation: Was weiss i nid?
'What don't I know?'
b. child: [i welem Dorf dass dr Andi wohnt] (J:4;09,30)
in which village that the Andi lives
'in which village Andi lives'
(Penner 1996:66)

(32) a. lue mau [wi längi Finger dass i ha] (J:4;10,12)
look once how long fingers that I have
'look how long my fingers are'
b. i wott wüsse [wi lang dass mis Mami tuet (dusche)] (J:4;10,13)
I want know how long that my mother does (take a shower)
'I want to know how long Mummy will take a shower'
(Penner 1996:67)

The two children of my study, Moira and Eliza (who is 1 week younger than Moira) speak Lucernese. Before age 4;11 they generalize verb movement in embedded clauses and do not use the verb-final pattern (cf. Schönenberger 2001). They also apply verb movement in wh-complements, giving rise to V2 in this context. The likelihood of a DFC surfacing in wh-complements with verb movement is small if *dass* and the finite verb compete for the same position. Although Moira and Eliza are slow to acquire the verb-final pattern, the acquisition of DFCs does not seem to be delayed.

Eliza's corpus contains 140 wh-complements and only 58 do not show the V2 pattern. All of these are produced after age 5. In 55 of these 58 wh-complements the wh-phrase is monosyllabic. Only one of these occurs with a DFC. In the remaining three the wh-phrase is bisyllabic: two occur with a DFC (the following element is an unstressed pronoun), and one occurs without a DFC (the following element is not a pronoun). The sample of her production data is small, but there is no conflict with the target grammar.

Moira's corpus contains 828 wh-complements of which 551 do not show the V2 pattern. The first DFC-like structures are produced by Moira before age 5, shown in (33). All of these involve non-target-like verb movement, but the diacritic in (33) is used to mark the impossibility of a DFC rather than that of verb movement. In (33a) and (33b) a DFC would be excluded in the target grammar, since DFCs are disallowed in adverbial clauses introduced by *wenn* 'when, if' and in relative clauses introduced by *wo*. In (33c) and (33d) a DFC is possible in the target grammar.

(33) a.% Dä ghört's nid [wenn dess chunt öpper eifach is
this hears-it not when that comes somebody simply in-the
Schloss]. (M:4;06)
castle
'He doesn't hear it when somebody simply walks up to the castle.'

b.% es Ross [wo dass gseht uus wie a de Rahel eri Hoor] (M:4;07)
a horse which that looks out like to the Rahel her hair
'a horse which looks like Rahel's hair'

c. Chasch au säge [weles Tier dass nimmsch du au no]. (M:4;10)
can2sg also say which animal that take you also not
'You can also tell me which animal you are also going to take.'

d. [Bevor dass gönd-mer] de tue-mer … (M:4;10)
before that go-we then do-we
'Before we go we …'

Table 7 summarizes the data from Moira. All wh-complements that are not V2 are included in this table. The wh-phrases in these complements are classified according to the number of syllables. The examples produced after age 8;01 are added in brackets. These 'late' examples are set apart in the discussion, because after age 8;01 there are few recordings of Moira, which were taken at very irregular intervals (see Section 2).

Table 7 Moira's DFCs in wh-complements without V2

DFC	One syllable	Two syllables	More than two syllables
−DFC	451 (+32)	8	8
+DFC	2	19 (+3)	26 (+2)
Total	485	30	36

Once Moira starts to produce the verb-final pattern in wh-complements, the distribution of DFCs appears to be adult-like. Except for two examples, in which she uses a DFC with a monosyllabic wh-phrase, she produces them with non-monosyllabic wh-phrases.

When the constituent which would follow the non-monosyllabic wh-phrase is a clitic, Moira always uses a DFC. This is an obligatory context for DFCs in the target grammar. In other contexts in which DFCs seem optional in the target grammar, i.e. when the constituent following the wh-phrase is not a clitic, she sometimes uses a DFC. In both (34a) and (34b) the wh-phrase is bisyllabic and the subject is non-pronominal. In (34a) the wh-complement occurs without a DFC while in (34b) it occurs with a DFC.

(34) a. Ich weiss [weles s Zwei isch]. (M:5;04)
I know which the two is
'I know which one is (number) 2.'
b. Weiss gar nid [wie groos dass Luzern isch]. (M:5;10)
know1sg at.all not how big that Lucerne is
'I don't know how big Lucerne is.'

Although the optionality of DFCs with non-monosyllabic wh-phrases is apparent in the child data in Table 7, it is not clear whether Moira has indeed converged on optional DFCs. Figure 1 shows Moira's production of wh-complements in which the wh-phrase is not monosyllabic and there is no verb movement. The contexts in which the target grammar requires the use of a DFC (obligatory context) are distinguished from those in which it does not (optional context). As shown in this figure the first obligatory context for a DFC occurs at age 5;10; before that age there are only optional contexts for DFCs.[4] Before age

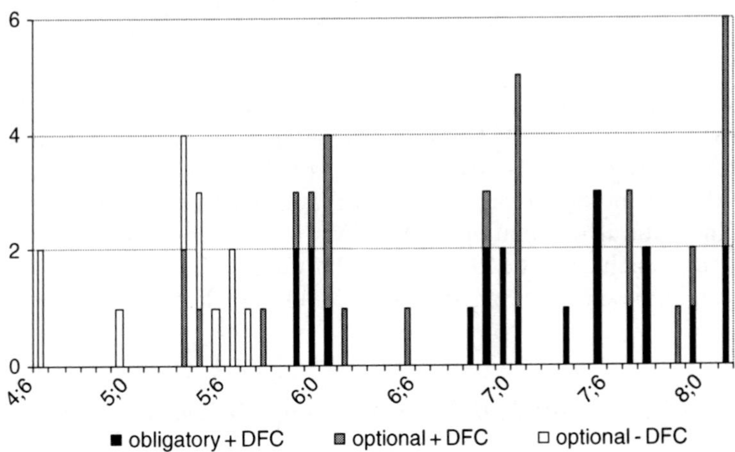

Fig. 1 DFCs in Moira's wh-complements (with non-monosyllabic wh-phrases and without V2) (age: 4;06–8;01)

[4] For reasons of space the data before age 4;06 are not included in the figure. There were 5 optional contexts for DFCs, in which Moira did not use a DFC. Thus it appears that before age 5;07 Moira generally prefers not to use a DFC, while after that age she generally prefers to use one.

5;03 there are three examples in the child data in which her mother would optionally use a DFC and in which Moira does not, labelled 'optional-DFC'. Between ages 5;04 and 5;07 she sometimes produces a DFC in an optional context, labelled 'optional + DFC'. And after age 5;07 she produces DFCs in all optional as well as obligatory contexts.

Example (35a′), produced at age 6;05, is excluded from Fig. 1 since it is unclear whether verb movement has occurred or not. Moira optionally uses Verb Raising with auxiliaries selecting a participle, and so does Eliza (see Schönenberger 2008). This is an option which is disallowed in Lucernese, but possible in e.g. Bernese. Thus in Moira's grammar, the word order in (35a') could have been derived by either extraposing the participle to the right of the finite auxiliary or by moving the finite auxiliary to the left. In adult Lucernese the word order in (35a') would be a case of V2, since the word order could only have been derived by moving the finite auxiliary. As mentioned above, the use of a DFC is not possible in a wh-complement displaying the V2 pattern. If (35a') does not involve verb movement, then a DFC would be possible and hence would run counter to Moira's general tendency of using a DFC even in optional contexts after age 5:07.

(35) a. mother: Was isch si go luege?
'What did she check?'
a′. child: [wivil Mane sind cho] (M:6;05)
how many men are come
'how many men came'

It seems that Moira has adopted the pattern consistent with SG rather than Lucernese, i.e. she uses DFCs in all wh-complements with non-monosyllabic wh-phrases after age 5;07. However most of the adult Lucernese data come from Moira's mother, as summarized in Table 5, and it is therefore not clear what the natural distribution is of DFCs in the local Lucernese dialect. I tentatively conclude that Moira's use of DFCs is different from her mother's, but I cannot be sure it is consistent with the local dialect.[5]

4.1 Multiply-Headed DFCs in Adverbial Adjuncts

The distribution of DFCs in other contexts, e.g. in temporal adjuncts introduced by *bevor* 'before', *nochdäm* 'after', or *bis* 'until', which can co-occur with *dass*, might shed light on the issue of whether DFCs are optional in Moira's grammar. According to Penner and Bader (1995:145) DFCs are optional in these temporal

[5] Mills (1985) notes that some German-speaking children produce *die wo* in relative clauses (cf. example (5a)), although they are not exposed to this sequence in the input.

adjuncts and are referred to as 'multiply-headed' DFCs, involving two heads – a preposition and a complementizer – rather than a phrase and a head.

In the Lucernese adult data there are 28 examples of adverbial clauses introduced by *bevor*. All are produced by Moira's mother and none shows a DFC. As shown in (36), a clitic can encliticize onto *bevor*, although *bevor* is bisyllabic.

(36) a. aber nöd am morge [bevor't in Chindi gosch] (LU)
but not in-the morning before-you to kindergarten go
'but not in the morning before you go to kindergarten'
b. und das häsch du gwüsst [bevor's du serviert häsch] (LU)
and this have you known before-it you served has
'and you knew this before you served it'

Moira produces 17 *bevor*-clauses. In 16 of these she uses a DFC (3 of these are produced after age 8;01), as in (37). The only exception is (38), in which the diacritic % marks the non-target-consistent verb placement. Eliza does not produce any *bevor*-clauses.

(37) a. Ich wett lieber achli [bevor dass ich dusse bi]. (M:7;09)
I want dearer some before that I outside am
'I'd rather have some before I'm outside.'
b. [bevor dass t'Eliza am Nomitag vom Chindi (M:6;08)
before that the-Eliza in-the afternoon from kindergarten
heichunt]
home comes
'before Eliza returns from kindergarten'

(38) % Da ha-n-i chöne [bevor-i i't Schuel bi cho]. (M:7;07)
this have-I could before-I to-the school been come
'I could do this before I started going to school.'

In the SG data there are 7 examples with *bevor* and in only one of these does a DFC occur. Thus Moira does not adhere to a pattern used in either Lucernese or SG. For Moira, DFCs seem to be obligatory with *bevor*, while in the adult samples DFCs seem to be dispreferred in this context.

There are very few examples of adverbial clauses introduced by *nochdäm* 'after'. There are 5 examples in the adult data (1 in Lucernese and 4 in SG), and 1 example in the child data. In all the adult examples *nochdäm* co-occurs with *dass*, as in (39a). Moira produces one example, in which she does not use *dass*, shown in (39b).

(39) a. [nochdäm dass-mer bis R. gsi sind] (LU)
after that-we at R. been be
'after we visited R.'
b. [nochdäm ich jo fertig gsi bi] (Moira:7;07)
after I JO finished been be
'after I'd finished'

Another context in which the occurrence of *dass* is said to be optional is in clauses introduced by *bis* 'until'. In German the co-occurrence of *bis* with *dass* is not possible. Still, in church marriage services the saying in (40) is common. This may be archaic, as is its English counterpart, in which the object pronoun precedes the verb as in Old English, rather than follows it as in present-day English.

(40) bis dass der Tod euch scheidet
until that the death you part
'till death us do part'

In the Lucernese adult sample there are 32 examples with adverbial *bis* and in none is a DFC used. There are 29 produced by Moira's mother, 1 by Moira's father and 2 by Moira's sister. The SG sample contains 9 *bis*-examples and in none a DFC used.

Moira produces 63 *bis*-clauses, of which 3 are produced after age 8;01. The first 12 examples, produced between the ages of 3;10 and 4;11, show the sequence *bis n* or *bis wenn* 'until when', as well as verb movement, as in (41a). In her grammar, *wenn* does not seem to function as a placeholder for *dass*, which first appears in the recorded data at age 4;01. The complementizer *wenn* is not used instead of *dass* before age 4;01, nor is the sequence *bis n* or *bis wenn* replaced by *bis dass* after Moira starts to productively use *dass* in clauses introduced by a complementizer. Only in one of the remaining 51 *bis*-clauses does Moira use *bis dass*, shown in (41b), which may involve another non-target-consistent instance of Verb Raising, indicated by the diacritic %.

(41) a.% Hät gwartet [bis'n sind's wider heicho]. (M:4;01)
has waited until when are-they again home come
'He waited until they came home again.'
b.% [bis dass' isch nur no Erde gsi] (M:7;02)
until that-it is only still earth been
'until it was only earth'

Just as in the adult data, Moira does not use *bis dass*, except for one instance. Eliza produces 6 examples with *bis*. Four of these show the sequence *bis n* and verb movement.

The occurrence of DFCs in Moira's adverbial clauses is not the same as in the adults' adverbial clauses. In contrast to the adults, she generally uses *bevor dass*, and before age 4;11 she combines *bis* with *(wen)n*, a combination not used by the adults. Not enough data are available to study the distribution of DFCs in adverbial clauses introduced by *nochdäm*.

4.2 Elicitation of DFCs in a Sentence-Repetition Task

A few weeks before Moira's 5th birthday, I asked Moira's mother to elicit data for me. This was the start of a series of elicitation sessions carried out over several months. At first these sessions were rather informal and improvised. I told her what kind of sentences I was interested in and sent a few examples from which she constructed her own and used them while playing with the children. During this game – referred to as the parrot-game – the children were asked to repeat a sentence produced by the mother. These sentences contained embedded clauses introduced by either a complementizer or a wh-phrase with the verb-final pattern, patterns not used by the children up to this age. Some of the wh-complements also contained DFCs. My original examples were based on Penner and Bader's description of Bernese, shown in (42):

(42) a. Weisch [i welem Huus dass s Grosmami wohnt]?
know2sg in which house that the grandmother lives
'Do you know in which house granny lives?'

b. Weisch [wo dass s Grosmami wohnt]?
know2sg where that the grandmother lives
'Do you know where granny lives?'

Although, with hindsight, examples with wh-complements in which a monosyllabic wh-phrase is combined with *dass*, as in (42b), are not ideal, they provoked an interesting comment from Moira's mother. After constructing several examples of the type in (42b) in an early session, she commented 'Ich säg im Fall nie "weisch wo dass-mer Zucker chauft". Ich säge "weisch wommer Zucker chauft"' (By the way, I don't say 'Do you know where that one buys sugar?' I say 'Do you know where one buys sugar?'). Her observation is correct, since she indeed does not use DFCs in wh-complements with monosyllabic wh-phrases.

A target sentence of the type in (43) could be repeated by Moira in any of the ways shown in (44). In (44a) the finite verb is doubled, in (44b) the finite verb has undergone movement resulting in V2, and (44c) the word order is the same as in the target sentence, but a DFC is not necessarily used by the child.

(43) Target sentence:
Ich weiss ned [wie schnell dass en Papegei cha flüge].
I know not how fast that a parrot can fly
'I don't know how fast a parrot can fly.'

(44) Moira's repetition:
a. ...[wie schnell cha en Papegei cha flüge]
how fast can a parrot can fly
b. ...[wie schnell cha en Papegei flüge]
how fast can a parrot fly
c. ...[wie schnell (dass) en Papegei cha flüge]
how fast that a parrot can fly

In the early sessions around Moira's 5th birthday, Moira rarely repeats a target sentence with a DFC. Instead of producing a DFC, she often omits *dass* and doubles the finite verb. In later sessions, shown in Fig. 2, she usually uses the verb-final pattern and only occasionally doubles the finite verb or moves it to the left, resulting in V2. In contrast to the early sessions, she often succeeds in repeating the target sentence with a DFC. Most of the examples with Verb Doubling and V2 are produced at age 5;05. In the examples in which Moira uses the verb-final pattern at this age, she fails to repeat a DFC used in the target sentence in 12 cases. All contain non-monosyllabic wh-phrases. Between ages 5;06 and 5;09 she does not repeat a DFC in the target sentence in 9 cases. In 5 of these the wh-phrase is monosyllabic.

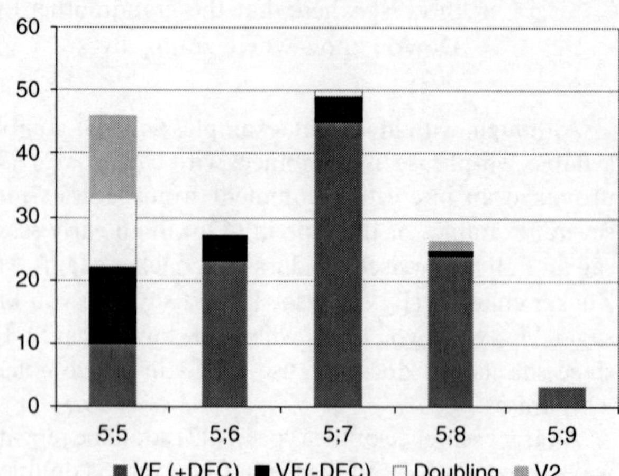

Fig. 2 Wh-complements with a DFC in a sentence-repetition task (Moira: age 5;5–5;9)

In the same elicitation sessions many examples with embedded clauses introduced by a complementizer were used, which are not discussed here, as well as examples with wh-complements without a DFC. When Moira was asked to repeat a target sentence with a wh-complement without a DFC, she often inserted a DFC, as in (45b). This happened in 17 of 20 examples in which the wh-phrase was not monosyllabic and in 1 example with a monosyllabic wh-phrase. Only 'early on', at age 5;05, did Moira not insert *dass* when repeating a target sentence with a non-monosyllabic wh-phrase (3 examples).

(45) a. target sentence:
Ich weiss ned [wiso de Robbi uf t'Nase keit isch].
I know not why the Robbi on the-nose fallen is
'I don't know why Robbi fell on his nose.'
b. Moira's repetition:
Ich weiss ned [wiso dass de Robbi uf t'Nase keit isch].
I know not why that the Robbi on the-nose fallen is

That Moira often inserted *dass* after age 5;05 when she repeated a target sentence that did not contain *dass* can be seen from Fig. 3. In 16 of these examples the wh-phrase was *worum* or *wiso*, both meaning 'why'. Since in these sessions quite a few of the target sentences Moira was asked to repeat contained *worum* or *wiso*, and either a DFC (32 cases) or no DFC (19 cases), there may have been a certain carry-over effect from the former to the latter.[6]

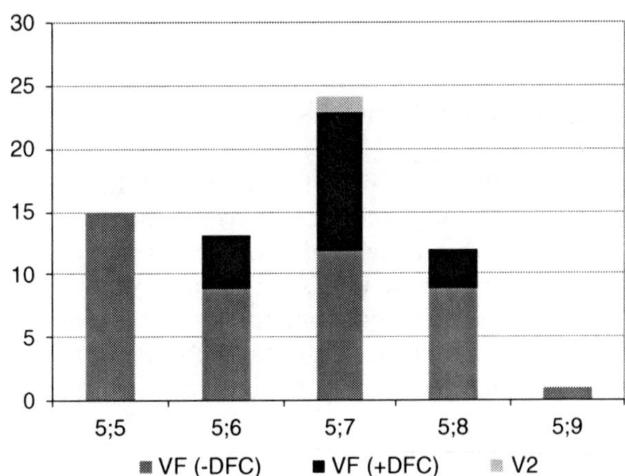

Fig. 3 Wh-complements without a DFC in a sentence-repetition task (Moira: age:5;5–5;9)

---

[6] Only in 5 of the 30 examples with bisyllabic wh-phrases did Moira use *worum* or *wiso* in the natural production data. Three occurred with *dass* and two without *dass*.

The data shown in Figs. 2 and 3 are summarized in Tables 8 and 9. The first column classifies the target sentence according to whether it contained a monosyllabic or polysyllabic wh-phrase. The bisyllabic wh-phrases *worum* and *wiso* are listed separately from other wh-phrases with two or more syllables. The number in parentheses refers to the examples in which Moira used V2 or Verb Doubling instead of the verb-final pattern.

Table 8 Moira's repetition of wh-complements with a DFC in the target sentence

Target wh-phrase	Moira: +DFC	Moira: −DFC
One syllable	3	5
worum/wiso 'why'	24	5 (+3)
Two or more syllables	77	11 (+23)

Table 9 Moira's repetition of wh-complements without a DFC in the target sentence

Target wh-phrase	Moira: +DFC	Moira: −DFC
One syllable	1	43 (+1)
worum/wiso 'why'	16	3
Two or more syllables	1	0

The findings from the sentence-repetition task support the tentative conclusion that for Moira, in contrast to her mother, DFCs are not optional with non-monosyllabic wh-phrases. After age 5;05 she is successful in repeating a wh-complement with a DFC, in particular if the wh-phrase is not monosyllabic, and when repeating a wh-complement without a DFC she generally inserts *dass* if the wh-phrase is not monosyllabic. There may have been a carry-over effect, though.

5 Concluding Remarks

Based on adult data from Lucernese and St. Galler German I have shown that there is dialectal variation concerning the occurrence of DFCs. While in both dialects DFCs are excluded in wh-complements with monosyllabic wh-phrases, in St. Galler German DFCs are obligatory if the wh-phrase is not monosyllabic. There seems to be some optionality in Lucernese with non-monosyllabic wh-phrases. I pointed out certain parallels between the occurrence of DFCs in Swiss German and verb movement in matrix wh-questions in Norwegian dialects. Both phenomena seem to be influenced by the type of wh-phrase. I have not presented an analysis of DFCs, but have argued that an analysis in terms of prosody rather than syntax may be required.

The data of two children acquiring Lucernese were examined to study at what stage they start to use DFCs and in which contexts they use them. These appear around age 5. Based on spontaneous production data and elicitation data I argued that one of the children, Moira, whose mother uses DFCs optionally, may not have converged on optional DFCs. I noted that the mother speaks a mixed dialect and that she also speaks particularly clearly when addressing the child, which may have subtly distorted the data. This may be relevant if prosody plays an important role in the distribution of DFCs. Still, for Moira DFCs seem to be obligatory, even in contexts in which her mother uses them optionally. Moreover, she uses DFCs in certain adverbial adjuncts, in which they either rarely occur (with *bevor* 'before') or do not occur at all (with *bis* 'until') in the adult data. I tentatively conclude that in the face of variation in the distributional pattern of DFCs, Moira is trying to regularize a seemingly irregular pattern. She is also exposed to a certain degree of variation in verb placement in embedded clauses. The fact that both Moira and Eliza initially generalize verb movement to all embedded contexts may further strengthen the conclusion that Moira (and possibly Eliza) are striving for regularization.

Acknowledgments I thank Josef Bayer, Ellen Brandner, Matthias Jilka, Baris Kabak, and Astrid Krähenmann for discussions of this topic and for providing detailed answers to several e-mail questions. I also thank the editors of this volume for helpful comments which allowed me to clarify my argument.

References

Bader, Thomas, and Zvi Penner. 1988. A Government-Binding account of the complementizer system in Bernese Swiss German. *Arbeitspapier* 25, Institut für Sprachwissenschaft, Universität Bern.

Bayer, Josef. 1984. Towards an explanation of certain *that*-t phenomena: The COMP-node in Bavarian. In *Sentential complementation*, eds. Wimde Geest and Yvan Putseys, 23–32. Dordrecht: Foris.

Bayer, Josef. 2004. Decomposing the left periphery: Dialectal and cross-linguistic evidence. In *The Syntax and semantics of the left periphery*, eds. H Horst Lohnstein and Susanne Trissler, 59–95. Berlin: Mouton de Gruyter.

Bayer, Josef, and Ellen Brandner. 2008a. On Wh-head-movement and the doubly-filled-comp filter. In *Proceedings of the 26th West Coast Conference on Formal Linguistics*, eds. Charles B. Chang and Hannah J. Haynie, 87–95. Somerville: Cascadilla Proceedings Project.

Bayer, Josef, and Ellen Brandner. 2008b. Wie oberflächlich ist die syntaktische Variation zwischen Dialekten? Doubly-filled COMP revisited. In *Dialektale Morphologie, dialektale Syntax*, eds. Franz Patocka and Guido Seiler, 9–26. Vienna: Praesens.

Chomsky, Noam. 1986. *Barriers*. Cambridge: MIT Press.

Grimm, Hannelore. 1973. *Strukturanalytische Untersuchung der Kindersprache*. Bern/ Stuttgart: Lawrence Erlbaum.

Haegeman, Liliane. 1992. *Theory and description in generative syntax. A case study in West Flemish*. Cambridge: Cambridge University Press.

Haegeman, Liliane, and Henk van Riemsdijk. 1986. Verb Projection Raising, scope, and the typology of verb movement rules. *Linguistic Inquiry* 17: 417–466.

Henry, Alison. 1995. *Belfast English and Standard English: Dialect variation and parameter setting*. New York and Oxford: Oxford University Press.

Hoekstra, Eric. 1992. *Of* en *dat* nader bekeken. *Die Nieuwe Taalgids* 85: 441–445.

Kabak, Baris, and René Schiering. 2006. The phonology and morphology of function word contractions in German. *Journal of Comparative Germanic Linguistics* 9: 53–99.

Mills, Anne E. 1985. Acquisition of German. In *The crosslinguistic study of language acquisition Vol. 1: The data*, ed. Daniel Isaac Slobin, 141–254. Hillsdale: Erlbaum.

Penner, Zvi. 1996. From empty to doubly-filled complementizers. A case study in the acquisition of subordination in Bernese Swiss German. *Arbeitspapier Nr. 77*, Fachgruppe Sprachwissenschaft der Universität Konstanz.

Penner, Zvi, and Thomas Bader. 1995. Issues in the syntax of subordination: A comparative study of the complementizer system in Germanic, Romance and Semitic languages with special reference to Bernese Swiss German. In *Topics in Swiss German Syntax*, ed. Zvi Penner, 73–290. Bern: Lang.

Pesetsky, David. 1987. Wh-in-situ: movement and unselective binding. In *The representations of (in)definiteness*, eds. Eric Reuland and Alice ter Meulen, 98–129. Cambridge: MIT Press.

Rice, Curt, and Peter Svenonius. 1998. Prosodic V2 in Northern Norwegian. Ms., Tromsø: University of Tromsø.

Rizzi, Luigi. 1997. The fine structure of the left periphery. In *Elements of Grammar: A handbook of generative syntax*, ed. Liliane Haegeman, 281–337. Dordrecht: Kluwer.

Rothweiler, Monika. 1993. *Der Erwerb von Nebensätzen im Deutschen. Eine Pilotstudie.* Tübingen: Niemeyer.

Schönenberger, Manuela. 1995. Constituent order in the VP: Verb Raising and Verb Projection Raising. In *Topics in Swiss German Syntax*, ed. Zvi Penner, 347–411. Bern: Lang.

Schönenberger, Manuela. 2001. *Embedded V-to-C in child grammar: The acquisition of verb placement in Swiss German.* STP. Dordrecht: Kluwer.

Schönenberger, Manuela. 2005. A glimpse of doubly-filled COMPs in Swiss German. In *Organizing grammar. Linguistic studies in honour of Henk van Riemsdijk*, eds. Hans Broekhuis, Norbert Corver, Riny Huybregts, Ursula Kleinhenz and Jan Koster, 572–581. Berlin: Mouton de Gruyter.

Schönenberger, Manuela. 2008. Three acquisition puzzles and the relation between input and output. In *First language acquisition of morphology and syntax. Perspectives across languages and learners*, eds. Pedro Guijarro-Fuentes, Pilar Larranaga and John Clibbens, 87–118. Amsterdam: Benjamins.

Shlonsky, Ur. 1991. Strategies of wh-movement in Palestinian Arabic. Ms., Quebe C: University of Quebec.

Taraldsen, Tarald. 1986. On verb second and the functional content of syntactic categories. In *Verb second phenomena in Germanic languages*, eds. Hubert Haider and Martin Prinzhorn, 7–25. Dordrecht: Foris.

Vangsnes, Øystein. 2005. Microparameters for Norwegian wh-grammars. *Linguistic Variation Yearbook* 5: 187–226.

Westergaard, Marit R. 2003. Word order in wh-questions in a North Norwegian dialect: some evidence from an acquisition study. *Nordic Journal of Linguistics* 261: 81–109.

Westergaard, Marit R. 2005. Optional word order in wh-questions in two Norwegian dialects: A diachronic analysis of synchronic variation. *Nordic Journal of Linguistics* 28(2): 269–296.

Westergaard, Marit R., and Øystein A. Vangsnes. 2005. *Wh*-questions, V2, and the left periphery of three Norwegian dialect types. *Journal of Comparative Germanic Linguistics* 8: 117–158.

The Acquisition of Adjectival Ordering in Italian

Anna Cardinaletti and Giuliana Giusti

Abstract In this chapter, we analyze the syntax of nominal expressions in a corpus of early child speech collected at the University Ca' Foscari of Venice. We focalize on the distribution of quantifiers, determiner-like adjectives, possessive adjectives, and descriptive adjectives. In adult Italian, these elements display a great degree of variation as regards word order. Comparing child production with both the input attested in our corpus and the data found in an electronic corpus of spoken Italian (Lessico di frequenza dell'italiano parlato, LIP, De Mauro et al. 1993), we show that child competence mirrors the adult competence of the spoken register in both syntax and pragmatics and is expectedly deviant from more formal varieties which are usually also taken into account by linguistic literature. From a methodological point of view, we ground our analysis on a well-developed theoretical approach to nominal structure which enables us to make a qualitative analysis in the absence of a large amount of data, as is in fact the case of adjectival modification in child production.

Keywords Adjectives · Nominal expression · . Variable word order · Acquisition · Input

1 Aims and Structure of the Chapter

The acquisition of adjectival ordering in Italian is an empirical question which has not received much attention in previous literature. This lack of attention is certainly not due to lack of interest in the phenomenon of adjectival ordering, which has recently been studied in great detail. Rather, it is probably due to the fact that adjectives are rare in child corpora and often appear in isolation, while the study of their ordering requires that the adjective occurs with other elements such as nouns, determiners, and other adjectives.

A. Cardinaletti (✉)
Università Ca' Foscari di Venezia, Venice, Italy
e-mail: cardin@unive.it

M. Anderssen et al. (eds.), *Variation in the Input*, Studies in Theoretical Psycholinguistics 39, DOI 10.1007/978-90-481-9207-6_4,

Our methodological point here is that, even in the absence of a large amount of data, as is the case of adjectival modification in child production, we should not give up the issue, but rather tackle it from a different perspective. Current theoretical research in the syntax of adjectival ordering allows for hypotheses for acquisition that can be tested against individual utterances by children, which provide what we call qualitative data. We will analyze the early productions of adjectives in our corpus, comparing them with what we know about the adult grammar. Our basic assumption is that, if the child data can be analyzed as being generated by the syntax and pragmatics of adult grammar, there is no reason to do otherwise.

The task is particularly challenging in view of the great variation of possible orders to be found in adult adjectival placement and of the poverty of child data available. We will show that child production mirrors the attested variation in a fully competent way, with an interesting timing in the first appearance of certain orders which mirrors their frequency in the input and in the LIP corpus of spoken Italian (De Mauro et al. 1993). This leads us to conclude that, already in their very earliest production of adjectival modification, children are fully competent in both the syntax and the interpretation of the possible word order variation found in Italian. They master the tripartite architecture of nominal structure and the two very different instances of movement (of the possessive adjective from the NP-internal position to a higher 'subject-like' position and of the noun). They also display discourse sensitivity (e.g. in the case of postnominal possessive adjectives) with respect to the different word orders that can arise in the presence or absence of an application of movement. Children deviate from the input only as far as the lexicon is concerned: some classes of adjectives are not present in the early productions we have analyzed, due to independent reasons.

The chapter is organized as follows. In Section 2, we start with an outline of the most recent analysis of the internal structure of nominal expressions, taking into account determiners and modifiers of the noun, such as quantifiers, determiner-like adjectives, possessive adjectives and descriptive adjectives. In Section 3, we briefly describe the corpora of spontaneous production collected at the University Ca' Foscari Venice, which will provide most of the data. In Section 4, we focus on the analysis of the acquisition data, suggesting that, despite the complexities of Italian nominal syntax, children perfectly master the colloquial variety to which they are exposed.

2 Optionality in the Input and the Complexity of Italian Nominal Structure

An important issue to keep in mind while studying adjectival modification is that modifiers (adverbs as well as adjectives) are optional by definition. They are not frequent in the adult language in any kind of register, and are

Table 1 Occurrences of lexical categories in the LIP corpus

Lexical categories	219,235	100%
Verbs	87,437	39.89
Nouns	77,840	35.49
Adverbs	33,199	15.15
Adjectives	20,759	9.47

particularly rare in the spoken colloquial register. Just to have an idea, in the LIP corpus of spoken Italian, containing 489,178 words and consisting of five different macro-types of spoken genres,[1] adverbs and adjectives are much less frequent than verbs and nouns, and the adjective is the least frequent of the lexical categories, occurring less than 10% in the whole corpus (Table 1).

To give an example of the different frequency of nouns and adjectives, the most common adjective *bello* 'beautiful' occurs less than a third of the times of the most frequent noun *cosa* 'thing' (not including the *wh*-form *che cosa* 'what', lit. 'what thing') (519 vs. 1,747 times). The next most frequent adjective *grande* 'big' occurs 429 times, only a little more than half of the next most frequent noun *anno* 'year', which occurs 798 times. Furthermore, the LIP corpus lists 129 nouns but only 28 adjectives that occur more than a hundred times. This lower frequency with respect to other categories is probably the cause of the slightly delayed acquisition of adjectives. But the delay is by no means as significant as the difference in their occurrence. In the very earliest productions, adjectives already appear as predicates in the one-word stage and as modifiers with nouns or determiners in the two-word stage.

Apart from the optionality of insertion, adjectival syntax also displays a high degree of variation in the distribution of adjectives within the nominal expression. Certain descriptive adjectives such as *simpatica* 'nice' in (1) and possessive adjectives such as *sua* 'his/her' in (2) can appear before or after the noun:

(1) a. una **simpatica** ragazza
a nice girl
b. una ragazza **simpatica**
a girl nice
'a nice girl'

(2) a. una **sua** simpatica amica
a his/her nice friend

[1] The five macro-types of spoken genres are defined as follows (cf. http://languageserver.uni-graz.at/badip/badip/26_typeText.php, April 30th 2008):

Type A. Bidirectional face-to-face free turn-taking communicative exchange, Type B. Bidirectional non-face-to-face free turn-taking communicative exchange, Type C. Bidirectional face-to-face non-free turn-taking communicative exchange, Type D. Unidirectional communicative exchange in the presence of the receiver, Type E. Unidirectional or bidirectional communicative exchange at a distance.

b. una simpatica amica **sua**
a nice friend his/her

c. ?una simpatica sua amica
a nice his/her friend
'a nice friend of his/hers'

In a minimalist framework, word order variability can be derived by different applications of movement. In some cases, it is due to movement of an element across the element under discussion; this is the case of the A – N vs. N – A order in (1), in which the noun is assumed to move to the left of the adjective in (1b) (Cinque 1994). In other cases, it depends on the movement of the element under consideration itself, as is the case for the possessive adjective in (2), which moves from the basic position in (2b) to the prenominal position in (2a) (Cardinaletti 1998). A third case of variation is due to movement triggered by discourse features, which obtains the marked order in (2c) by further moving the adjective *simpatica* across the prenominal position of the possessive. Movement triggered by discourse features is certainly more apparent, and therefore better studied, in the clause than in nominal expressions, but there is evidence that cases such as (2c) are due to discourse features checked in the left peripheral positions of DPs (Giusti 2006). This phenomenon is typical of formal registers which children are not exposed to at the very early stages, as we will observe in the course of the discussion.

A number of questions arise as regards how this variability affects acquisition. We can envisage at least three possible main areas of inquiry.

- What is the effect of such variability on the acquisition of that particular language? Does it re-enforce or delay early production? Does it support the fixation of a single parameter, or is it the result of the interaction of different independent parameters that must be fixed separately?
- In what percentage is variability present in the input? Do adults produce one order more often than others? Do they privilege one order when speaking to children? Can we find a more basic, less marked order and distinguish it from the others due to discourse or pragmatically marked use?
- Do Italian children acquire all possible orders at the same time? And do they use them appropriately in the discourse?

The first issue can be addressed only in a comparative perspective, which is beyond the scope of this chapter. Here, we address the last two issues. Focussing on the acquisition of nominal modifiers, we will show that children's production reflects the frequency in the input, at the same time not excluding marked orders, and displays a target-like competence of the quite complex pattern of variability of adjectival ordering in Italian nominal expressions.

It is important to contrast the variability of certain elements with the fixed position of others. This allows us to compare the process of acquisition of different kinds of elements and to determine the position of the movable elements with respect to the fixed ones. For this reason, we will start our presentation of the nominal structure with quantifiers, determiners, and determiner-like adjectives such as *altro*, which do not display variability. We will assume the tripartite structure of Nominal Expressions in (3) in which each layer (DP, FP, and NP) can be split:

(3) $[_{DP}$ D $[_{FP}$ F $[_{NP}$N]]]

NP realizes the argument structure of the head noun, FP hosts a number of projections in whose specifiers APs are merged according to a universal hierarchy, and DP includes a determiner but may also include other projections headed by discourse features (such as Topic) which may attract movement of elements whose first-merge position is FP-internal or NP-internal.

2.1 Quantifiers and Quantity Adjectives

Quantifiers can be the highest elements in the nominal expression. They can precede the DP and combine with it to obtain a quantifier-variable interpretation. Universal quantifiers occur with a DP headed by a definite determiner, while existential quantifiers and numerals occur with a DP with a null determiner (Cardinaletti and Giusti 2006):

(4) a. $[_{QP}$ **tutti** $[_{DP}$ i suoi amici]]
all the his/her friends
'all his/her friends'
b. $[_{QP}$ **molti** / **tanti** / **pochi** $[_{DP}$ Ø suoi amici]]
many / many / few his/her friends
'many friends of his/hers'
c. $[_{QP}$ **tre** $[_{DP}$ Ø suoi amici]]
three his/her friends
'three friends of his/hers'

A subset of existential quantifiers and numerals can also occur after a definite determiner. In the unmarked order, the quantifier not only follows the determiner but also the possessive adjective; the position preceding the possessive is not excluded, but marked:

(5) a. i suoi **molti** / **tanti** / **pochi** amici
the his/her many / many / few friends

b. ?i **molti / tanti / pochi** suoi amici
the many / many / few his/her friends
'the many friends of his/hers'

(6) a. i suoi **tre** amici
the his/her three friends
b. ?i **tre** suoi amici
the three his/her friends
'his/her three friends'

Cardinaletti and Giusti (2006) take these as instances of a different syntactic category: Quantity Adjectives (QA). Their unmarked position is after the possessive adjective. The order in (5b) and (6b), in which the QAP precedes the possessive adjective, is marked both in the sense of interpretive and prosodic properties and in the sense of frequency. As regards interpretation, it implies an emphasis on the QAP. This emphasis goes with a rising pitch on the emphasized adjective and a dramatic drop of the pitch on the possessive. The unmarked intonation, on the other hand, has a rising pitch, followed by a fall with no abrupt drop. As regards frequency, a search on Google run on Jan 21st 2008 gives 25,800 pages in Italian for *i suoi molti* ('def.art – 3rd.p.poss. – many') as in (5a) and 3,180 for *i molti suoi* ('def.art – many – 3rd.p.poss.') as in (5b). Similarly, the sequence *una sua poca* ('indef.art – 3rd.p.poss. – little') has 6 pages (60 entries), while the sequence *una poca sua* ('indef.art – little – 3rd.p. poss.') has one entry only and this is dated 1856. Notice that *una poca* (with no possessive adjective) displays 792,000 pages in Italian, showing that *poca* as a QAP preceded by the indefinite article *una* is not rare at all, confirming that the higher degree of markedness of *una poca sua* is related to the presence of *poca* at the left of *sua*.

To summarize, Quantifiers in adult Italian can belong to two different categories: Q (a lexical head selecting a full DP) in (7a) or QAP (a high adjective immediately following the prenominal possessive) in (7b). The marked word order in (7c), where the QAP precedes the prenominal possessive, is obtained by raising the quantity adjective to a DP-peripheral position at the left of possessive adjectives (Giusti 2006):

(7) a. [$_{QP}$ Q [$_{DP}$ D]]
b. [$_{DP}$ D [$_{FP2}$ [PossAP] [F2 [$_{FP1}$ [QAP] [F1 [$_{NP}$ N]]]]]]
c. [$_{DP2}$ D2 [$_{DP1}$ [QAP] [D1 [$_{FP2}$ [PossAP] [F2 [$_{FP1}$ [~~QAP~~] [F1 [$_{NP}$ N]]]]]]]]

In our corpus of early productions, we find quantifiers but no quantity adjective in either position. This may be due to two possible reasons. On the one hand, children may need some time to detect the categorial ambiguity of one and the same sub-class of words and may learn the most frequent one first, adjusting the categorial specification later in their lexicon. This hypothesis predicts that the Q-label is the first to be learned and then the QA label is added in the readjustment. On the other hand, the merger of quantity adjectives implies a complex nominal structure which is often favoured by the presence of further specifications (possessive adjectives, relative clauses, demonstratives, etc.). The lack of such complex structures may simply be related to the low MLU of young children's productions.

2.2 Determiner-Like Adjectives

Under this label we include *altro* 'other' and ordinal adjectives (e.g. *primo* 'first'), which contribute referential value to the interpretation of the nominal expression. Parallel to quantity adjectives, determiner-like adjectives are always prenominal, and appear at different sides of the possessive:

(8) a. un'**altra** / l'**altra** sua cara amica
another / the other his/her dear friend
b. *una / *la sua amica **altra**
a / the his/her friend other
c. ?una / ?la sua **altra** cara amica
a / the his/her other dear friend
'another / the other dear friend of his/hers'

(9) a. ?la **prima** sua amica
the first his/her friend
b. *la sua amica **prima**
the his/her friend first
c. la sua **prima** amica
the his/her first friend
'his/her first friend'

The phrase in (8a) displays the unmarked order in which *altro* precedes the possessive adjective. A Google search gives 26,800 pages in Italian for *un'altra sua* ('indef.art – *other* – PossAP') as in (8a) and only 685 for the marked order *una sua altra* ('indef.art – PossAP – *other*') as in (8c). Ordinal adjectives, on the other hand, follow the possessive in the unmarked order as in (9c). A Google search gives 1,090,000 pages for *la sua prima* ('def.art – PossAP – OrdAP') as in (8c) and 1,320 pages for *la prima sua* ('def.art – OrdAP – PossAP') as in (9a).

We conclude that the serialization of these elements is '*altro* – PossAP – OrdAP', as shown in (10a). Marked word orders are again obtained by displacing topic elements to the left-peripheral area, for example raising the possessive adjective in (8c) to the left of *altro*, as in (10b), or the ordinal adjective in (9a) to the left of the possessive, as in (10c) (Giusti 2006):

(10) a. [$_{DP}$ D [$_{FP3}$ [$_{AP}$ *altro*] [F3 [$_{FP2}$ [PossAP] [F2 [$_{FP1}$ [OrdAP] [F1 [$_{NP}$ N]]]]]]]]

b. [$_{DP2}$ D2 [$_{DP1}$ [PossAP] [D1 [$_{FP3}$ [$_{AP}$ *altro*] [F3 [$_{FP2}$ [~~PossAP~~] [F2 [$_{FP1}$ [OrdAP] [F1 [$_{NP}$ N]]]]]]]]]]

c. [$_{DP2}$ D2 [$_{DP1}$ [OrdAP] [D1 [$_{FP2}$ [PossAP] [F2 [$_{FP1}$ [~~OrdAP~~] [F1 [$_{NP}$ N]]]]]]]]

First we must observe that ordinal adjectives are almost absent in our corpus (cf. 4.3) due to the fact that children are not yet able to count. Furthermore, the structure in (10a) is never instantiated in child speech due to the low MLU. Finally, the variation in (10b–c), which is typical of a formal register, is not expected in acquisition data even at a higher MLU, given the fact that children are exposed to and consistently acquire the colloquial register, as will be shown to be the case for descriptive adjectives in Section 4.5.

2.3 Possessive Adjectives

With common nouns, possessive adjectives always co-occur with a determiner. Their unmarked position is before the noun (11a). If focused, possessives can also appear in postnominal position, (11b):

(11) a. la /una/questa **sua** (bella) macchina
the/a /this his/her (nice) car
b. la /una/questa (bella) macchina **sua**
the/a /this (nice) car his/her
'his/her (nice) car', 'a/this (nice) car of his/hers'

The LIP corpus confirms the marked nature of the postnominal position, which occurs only 273 times vs. the 1,660 of prenominal possessive adjectives. In the free turn-taking types, prenominal possessives score 557, while postnominal possessives occur 187 times with common nouns.

Possessive adjectives raise from their first merge position, in which they establish a thematic relation with the noun, to a high functional specifier to the left of ordinal adjectives (Cardinaletti 1998). This position is the counterpart in DPs of the preverbal subject position in the clause. Possessive movement does not take place if the possessive is focalized as in (11b), again parallel to (postverbal) clausal subjects.

In (12a) we observe the first-merge position of the PossAP inside NP. The noun moves out of the NP in Italian and reaches the FP layer, as in (12b). In this way, we get the postnominal position of the possessive adjective (11b), which receives a marked focussed interpretation. In the specifier of this FP a descriptive AP can be merged, as we will see in Section 2.4 below. To obtain the unmarked prenominal position of the possessive adjective in (11a), the PossAP is further moved to the specifier of the upper FP2 across the descriptive AP, as in (12c):

(12) a. [$_{NP}$[PossAP] [N]]→
b. [$_{FP1}$ (AP) [N + F1 [$_{NP}$[PossAP] [~~N~~]]]]→
c. [$_{DP}$ D [$_{FP2}$ [PossAP] F2 [$_{FP1}$ (AP) [N + F1 [$_{NP}$[~~PossAP~~] [~~N~~]]]]]]

The postnominal position of possessive adjectives can arise in another way, namely by N-to-D movement, which takes the noun to the determiner position at the left of the high specifier occupied by the (otherwise prenominal) possessive. In these cases the postnominal position of the possessive adjective is unmarked and the only grammatical option. This is the case in appellatives such as those in (13a), and of certain nouns with quasi-proper-name properties such as *casa* in (13b), and the kinship terms *mamma* and *papà* in (13c) (as argued for by Longobardi 1994). The derivation is given in (13d):

(13) a. piccolo **mio**, amore **mio**, tesoro **mio**
little my, love my, dear my
'my little one, my love, my sweetheart'
b. casa **mia**
house my
'my home'
c. mamma **mia**, papà **mio** (Central Italian)
mom my, daddy my
'my mom, my daddy'
d. [$_{DP}$ D + N [$_{FP1}$ [PossAP] [~~N~~ + F1 [$_{NP}$[~~PossAP~~] [~~N~~]]]]]

Movement of *mamma* and *papà* to D is not found in all varieties of Italian. In Northern Italian, these two kinship terms behave like all the others in (14b) in displaying the possessive in prenominal position in complementary distribution with the article:

(14) a. **mia** mamma, **mio** papà (Northern Italian)
my mom, my daddy
b. **mia** madre, **mio** padre, **mia** sorella, **mia** nonna
my mother, my father, my sister, my grandmother

Notice that both (13c) and (14) are possible only if no descriptive adjective occurs. In this case, the determiner is necessarily present, no N-to-D movement takes place, and the possessive adjective is prenominal:

(15) a. la **mia** cara mamma, il **mio** caro papà
the my dear mummy, the my dear daddy
'my dear mom, my dear dad'

b. la **mia** giovane madre, il **mio** giovane padre
the my young mother, the my young father
'my young mother, my young father'

The facts represented in (11)–(15), which actually just represent part of the complex syntax of possessive adjectives, not only offer a case of quite subtle variability in the position of the possessive with respect to the head noun and to other modifiers, but also display an obvious complexity in the optional vs. obligatory nature of word orders and how these are obtained. It is therefore striking to find that very young children produce both the marked and unmarked patterns (for example, the focused postnominal possessive) in a fully target-like way.

2.4 Descriptive Adjectives

2.4.1 Direct Modification

Following Cinque (1994), we assume that descriptive adjectives are merged in specifiers of functional projections arrayed according to the hierarchical order in (16). The prenominal vs. postnominal position of adjectives is accounted for by N-movement across the adjective. In recent work, Cinque (2005, 2007) proposes to dispense with head movement and replace it with phrasal movement. Under both kinds of analysis, the noun obligatorily crosses over classificatory and nationality adjectives and optionally crosses over the other classes. In the former case, an obligatory postnominal position of the adjective is obtained, (17a,b), in the latter case, both word orders are found, (17c–f):

(16) hierarchy:
det > value > size > shape > colour > nationality > classificatory
$N(P)_{opt}$ $N(P)_{opt}$ $N(P)_{opt}$ $N(P)_{opt}$ $\mathbf{N(P)_{obl}}$ $\mathbf{N(P)_{obl}}$

(17) a. *la materna scuola / la scuola materna
the maternal school / the school maternal
'kindergarten'

b. *l' italiana scuola / la scuola italiana
the Italian school / the school Italian
'the Italian school'

c. le verdi colline della Toscana / le colline verdi della Toscana
the green hills of-the Tuscany / the hills green of-the Tuscany
'the green hills of Tuscany'

d. il tondo ovale del suo viso / l' ovale tondo del suo viso
he round oval of-the his/her face / the oval round of-the his/her face
'the round oval of her face'

e. una grande macchina / una macchina grande
a big car / a car big
'a big car'

f. una bella macchina / una macchina bella
a beautiful car / a car beautiful
'a beautiful car'

As regards the genuine optionality of noun movement climbing up the adjectival hierarchy, it is important to observe that movement across colour, shape and size adjectives displayed in (17c–e) is obligatory in the colloquial register, while the prenominal position has a formal flavour. The only really optional movement in the colloquial register of the input is the one across a value adjective as in (17f). This optionality is perfectly represented in child data, as we argue in Section 4.5 below.

If more than one adjective occurs in the nominal expression, the hierarchy determines the order in which each adjective occurs with respect to the other and with respect to the noun. Phrasal movement instead of head movement accounts for the fact that if two adjectives are found in postnominal position, their order is the mirror image of the hierarchy seen in (16). This is obtained by Cinque (2005) assuming roll-up movement of the constituent containing the NP and the lower adjective across the higher adjective:

(18) det > value > size > NP < classificatory < nationality < colour < shape
la bella grande macchina sportiva italiana rossa aerodinamica
the nice big car sport(ive) Italian red aerodynamic
'the nice big aerodynamic red Italian sport car'

In (18) the NP first moves across the classificatory adjective *sportiva* 'sportive'. The whole functional projection including the moved NP and the classificatory adjective further moves across the nationality adjective *italiana* 'Italian', and so forth. Lack of two postnominal adjectives in the child data can be reduced both to the low MLU and also to the fact that such cases are quite rare in the colloquial register (and in the input).

2.4.2 Indirect Modification

All the examples seen so far are instances of what Cinque (2007) calls direct modification, namely appositive modifiers. The postnominal position, however, can also have the function of a reduced relative clause with restrictive interpretation. This is called indirect modification by Cinque (2007). Indirect modification in Italian is postnominal with no exception. We thus have the following picture. An adjective in prenominal position is non-ambiguous (it can only have the direct modification reading), while an adjective in postnominal position can be either direct or indirect modification:

(19) a. una mia grande amica — prenominal: non-ambiguous
a my big friend
'a close friend of mine' (direct)
b. una mia amica grande — postnominal: ambiguous
a my friend big
(i) 'a close friend of mine' (direct)
(ii) 'a friend of mine who is old(er than me) / who is tall / big' (indirect)

Cinque (2007) proposes that the ambiguity of *grande* in (19b) is to be captured by merger of *grande* in two different positions. In the direct modification interpretation, the position is the one observed in Section 2.4.1 with optional roll-up movement across it, given that direct modification can be prenominal (19a) or postnominal (19bi). In the indirect interpretation modification (19bii), *grande* is merged in a much higher position, as shown in (21a), which has the same basic order of the English (20). In English, no movement takes place and indirect modification precedes direct modification. In Italian, the postnominal position of indirect modification is produced by movement of the whole constituent containing direct modification across indirect modification (21c):

(20)	an	[older	[close	Italian friend]]	
		[indirect	[direct	]]	
(21) a.	una	[grande	[grande	italiana amica]]	→
b.	una	[grande	[grande [amica]	italiana ~~amica~~]]	→
c.	una [grande amica ital.]	[grande	[~~grande [amica] italiana~~	]]	

While certain classes of adjectives can be direct or indirect modification, others can only be of one kind. In particular, stage-level adjectives can only be indirect modification, and for this reason, they can only appear in postnominal position, as in (22):

(22) a. la bottiglia vuota / sporca
the bottle empty /dirty
b. *la vuota / sporca bottiglia
the empty / dirty bottle
'the empty / dirty bottle'

In the child data, indirect modification always appears target-like in post-nominal position.

To conclude, descriptive adjectives even more than other classes of adjectives display a very complex pattern which involves (i) a certain degree of optionality in their position with respect to the noun (as in (16)–(17) above), (ii) ambiguity in the interpretation of one and the same word order (as in (19b)), as well as (iii) quite a high number of different classes, some of which have a fixed position and must be learned with such a specification. We will see that there is no reason to believe that children are not competent in this intricate pattern. If this is the case, the assumption that the classes as well as their structural positions are directly provided by UG seems to us to be not only less costly from a theoretical point of view but also the most plausible account of the empirical data.

3 The Corpora

Our data come primarily from three corpora (Gaia, Sara, and Ernesto) collected by students at the University Ca' Foscari of Venice. The three children and their families live in Venice and are Italian speakers of the Veneto variety (with grandparents coming from other Veneto areas). The three interviewers, who also transcribed the recordings, are native speakers of the Veneto variety of Italian as well.

The Gaia corpus (Gozzi 2004) consists of transcriptions in CHAT format of 14 video-tape recorded sessions of 30 min each, at a distance of roughly 1 month, selected among a number of recordings from age 1;6.29 to 2;6.01. The transcriptions have been made by Roberta Gozzi, mother of the child, who also kept a diary.

The Sara corpus (Ambrosi 2007) consists of 13 video-tape recorded sessions of about 30 min each, from age 1;9.07 to 2;4.19, collected and transcribed by Carlotta Ambrosi.

The Ernesto corpus (Gesmundo 2007) consists of 18 video-tape recorded sessions of about 30 min each, from age 1;8.28 to 3;0.05, collected and transcribed by Daniela Gesmundo.

We also considered the Gregorio corpus available in the CHILDES database (Tonelli) consisting of 8 transcriptions from age 1;7.17 to 2;0.29

Our quantitative data are also based on Zucchet's (2008) analysis of nominal modifiers in Gaia's productions, Ferrari's (2007) analysis of nominal modifiers in Gregorio's productions, and Zampolli's (2007) study of the input in the Sara corpus. Table 2 summarizes the age of the children recorded in the corpus. All the corpora have the property of being representative of the very earliest stage of acquisition:

Table 2 Children's age

Corpus	First recording	Last recording
Gaia	1;6.29	2;6.01
Sara	1;9.07	2;4.19
Ernesto	1;8.28	3;0.05
Gregorio	1;7.17	2;0.29

4 Analysis of the Acquisition Data

The complexity of nominal syntax as depicted in Section 2 above contrasts sharply with the poverty of the input, where adjectives are not abundant at all and, when they appear, they rarely co-occur with other adjectives. How could children learn the hierarchy, the optionality of movement of possessives, the ambiguity in interpretation (corresponding to different structural positions) related to one and the same linear position (the postnominal position of descriptive adjectives) the obligatory postnominal position of stage-level adjectives? If the structure, with the relative height of indirect vs. direct modification and the internal hierarchy of direct modification is given by UG (as proposed by Cinque 1994, 2005, 2007), what is left to be established by the child is how far the noun or a partial nominal constituent moves and whether the possessive stays low or high. As a matter of fact, the input provides plenty of evidence exactly for these properties: (i) postnominal possessives are quite rare and discourse marked, indicating that the possessor moves, (ii) the noun reaches a certain point in the direct modification, and (iii) the nominal constituent formed by direct modification always precedes the indirect modification area.

Under the present approach, it is therefore not surprising to find that children use the entire nominal structure from the very first production containing nominal expressions and master the properties related to word order variation quite early. Like adults, children appear to produce the unmarked orders more abundantly than the marked ones. As regards the first occurrence of the different classes of adjectives, there is no clear evidence that possessive adjectives are produced earlier in one order than they are in the other (see Section 4.4). There is however some hint that prenominal *bello* is produced earlier than postnominal *bello*, while other descriptive adjectives always appear for the first time in postnominal position (see Section 4.5). This may suggest that in cases of genuine optionality, as with *bello*, the most frequent order is produced first, while in the case of different discourse interpretation, as with possessive adjectives, children are perfectly competent in the alternation, and the first occurrence just depends on the context.

4.1 Adjectives with Missing Nouns

In the earliest files, adjectives are often produced in isolation. They can have the function of predicates with a missing copula or modifiers with a missing noun. A remarkable property is that in the great majority of cases, they display the target-like agreement with the noun. We take this to suggest that in the one-word stage, the structure is larger than just the projection of the relevant item. In many cases, adjectives in isolation can be analysed as predicates with copula omission and a null subject (for copula omission, see Caprin and Guasti 2006):

(23) ROB: com'è il gattino?
how is the little-cat MASC.?
'How is the little cat?'
CHI: **totto** [= rotto]! Gaia 1;6.29
broken.MASC.SG
'It is broken.'

(24) MAT: e di che colore sono gli omini?
and of what colour are the little-men.MASC.PL?
'and what colour are the little men?'
CHI: **gialli**. Gaia 2;0.13
yellow.MASC.PL
'They are yellow.'

(25) %com: la mamma esce e torna con l'aranciata che dà a Gregorio.
the mother goes out and comes back with the orange juice (FEM SG) and gives it to Gregorio
CHI: **bona** [= buona]. Gregorio 1;7.17
good.FEM.SG
'It is good.'

(26) SIL: Lo ritiriamo fuori, non c'è problema
[*we*] *take it.MASC.SG out again, no problem*
CHI: **mio**! Ernesto 1;9.22
my.MASC.SG
'It is mine.'

In the case of quantifiers in isolation, it is reasonable to suppose that they are neither predicates nor adjectival modifiers, but Quantifiers with an empty DP (see Section 2.1):

(27) ancora **una** Sara 1;9.07
again one.FEM.SG
'one more'

Table 3 summarizes the figures of the nominal elements we are studying in the presence or absence of a following noun. It shows that these elements are present in a quite substantial quantity, even though they are not as frequent as nouns or verbs in the input. Under the heading 'without the noun', we have included obvious predicative use, with or without a copula, and pronominal use (with a missing noun):

Table 3 Occurrences of nominal elements in the child corpora

		Without a noun	With a noun	Total
Gaia	Quantifiers	39 (62%)	24 (38%)	63
	altro	6 (33%)	12 (67%)	18
	Possessive	2 (15%)	11 (85%)	13
	Descriptive	48 (67%)	24 (33%)	72
Sara	Quantifiers	34 (69%)	15 (31%)	49
	altro	8 (57%)	6 (43%)	14
	Possessive	38 (60%)	25 (40%)	63
	Descriptive	81 (76%)	25 (24%)	106
Ernesto	Quantifiers	27 (93%)	2 (7%)	29
	altro	0 (0%)	4 (100%)	4
	Possessive	28 (93%)	2 (7%)	30
	Descriptive	128 (90%)	15 (10%)	143
Gregorio	Quantifiers	28 (82%)	6 (18%)	34
	altro	4 (67%)	2 (33%)	6
	Possessive	1 (25%)	3 (75%)	4
	Descriptive	46 (75%)	15 (25%)	61

In what follows, we focus our attention on the occurrence of these elements together with a noun.

4.2 Quantifiers

Quantifiers appear quite early together with a nominal expression. With the universal quantifier *tutti*, the determiner can be present or not in child production, (28)–(29). This is not surprising since the determiner is not always produced by young children (Chierchia et al. 1999, Giusti and Gozzi 2006). With existential quantifiers, the determiner is never present (30), as in the adult language[2]:

(28) **tut(t)e** le luci Sara 1;9.07
'all the lights'

[2] It is interesting to observe that of the two synonyms *tanto* and *molto*, only the former appears in our corpus. This mirrors the results found in the LIP corpus, in which *tanto* is more frequent than *molto* (376 vs. 245) in all kinds of spoken genres; the difference becomes more dramatic if the inquiry is restricted to free turn-taking texts, in which *tanto* scores 122 and *molto* only 40. It is therefore not surprising that children use the most frequent form of the colloquial register.

(29) MOT: dove sono gli animaletti?
'where are the animals?'
CHI: **tutti** maetti [= tutti gli animaletti] Gregorio 1;8.07
'all animals' [= all the animals]

(30) a. **tanti** o(r)setti! Gaia 1;11.28
'many teddy-bears'
b. **tanti** [//] **due** o(r)setti +/. Gaia 1;11.28
'many [//] two teddy-bears'

We believe that the presence of the universal quantifier preceding a realized determiner as in (28) shows that, in child grammar, the full extended structure (including Q and its complement DP) is projected. In the hypothesis shared in works on language acquisition and language disorders (Rizzi 1994, Friedmann and Grodzinsky 1997) that only the highest nodes of the utterance structure can be missing or impaired, we take the cases in (29), in which the universal quantifier combines with the noun without a determiner, to also display the whole structure, with a projected DP but a covert determiner. The exact analysis of determiner omission is however not crucial for our discussion of adjectival modifiers, and we will not develop this point any further, but the hypothesis that the whole DP structure is present even if no determiner appears is argued for by Giusti and Gozzi (2006), to which we refer the interested reader.

4.3 Determiner-Like Adjectives

Similar evidence for a rich functional structure inside the DP is provided by the determiner-like adjective *altro*, which is the highest adjective of all, even preceding the prenominal possessive (Section 2.2). In all corpora, *altro* is present from the very earliest files combined with all types of determiners (indefinite or definite article, see (31) and (32), respectively)[3]:

[3] In the Diana corpus of the CHILDES database (Calambrone, see Cipriani et al. 1989), we also find *altro* cooccurring with a demonstrative:

(i) MOT: questa? (%act: Gives the cooker to DIA)
this [*one*]?
CHI: eh quetta no. (%gpx: pointing) Diana 2;0.02
eh this no
'Oh not this one.'
CHI: **quett'atta** **quett'atta** ! (%gpx: pointing)
this other [*one*] *this other* [*one*]
'this other one'

(31) a. **un tanto [= altro]** tato — Gaia 1;11,28
another.MASC.SG boy.MASC.SG
'another child'

b. **nata [= un'altra]** pal(l)ina — Sara 1;9.07
another.FEM.SG little ball.FEM.SG
'another little ball'

c. **tra [= un'altra]** (d)r(ag)ona — Ernesto 1;8.28
another.FEM.SG dragon.FEM.SG
'another dragon'

(32) **l'atta** — Sara 1;10.12
the other.FEM.SG[one]
'the other one'

Assuming as the least costly hypothesis that in child grammar, *altro* is the same element as in the adult grammar, and as a consequence, it is merged in the same structural position, the presence of *altro* in the very early productions suggests that the whole nominal structure is already available to the child.

This assumption is not disconfirmed by the lack of lower nominal modifiers if this can be attributed to independent reasons, as we argue for in this section.

One such case is provided by ordinal adjectives, which follow *altro* and prenominal possessives in the adult grammar (see Section 2.2) and are basically missing in the child data we are examining. We find only two occurrences of ordinal adjectives, each one in a different corpus. In both cases, it is contained in the title of a children's book, and in one case, it is produced as a repetition (33b). However, in both cases, it can be said that the title is not produced as an unanalysed whole since the DP triggers agreement in number with the predicate *sono* 'are' in (33a) and agreement in number and gender with the demonstrative *questa* 'this.FEM.SG' in (33b):

(33) a. ci sono anche <(l)e p(r)ime (r)ime>. — Gaia 2;04.0
there are also the first rhymes
'There are also "the first rhymes".'

b. CAR: uau # <la mia prima banca>
uaugh the my first bank
CHI: <prima banca> questa qua — Sara 2;2.05
first bank this [one] here

Why should ordinal adjectives be almost absent in our corpora? A look at the LIP corpus suggests that this cannot be plausibly related to frequency in the input. In fact, in both the totality of texts and the free turn-taking texts, the number of occurrences of the most frequent ordinal adjective *primo* (518 and 106, respectively) is the same as the number of the most frequent descriptive adjective *bello* 'beautiful' (519 and 102, respectively). A parallel case can be seen for *secondo* 'second' (241 and 75, respectively) and *nuovo* 'new' (275 and 69, respectively).

If in acquisition and language impairment, we do not expect to find pruning of intermediate portions of structure, the fact that ordinal adjectives are missing while structurally higher modifiers such as *altro* and prenominal possessive adjectives (see Sections 2.2 above and 4.4 below) can be present cannot be taken to show that the tree is somehow incomplete in this intermediate position. A reasonable independent motivation for the absence of ordinal adjectives in our corpora is the fact that at this early age, children do not count yet and, as a consequence, they do not have the semantics of ordinal numeral adjectives (but they can learn them as modifiers in fixed expressions and apply concord with the noun correctly, as in (33)).

4.4 Possessive Adjectives

When possessive adjectives are produced with the noun, they appear in prenominal position in the unmarked word order, as in adult Italian. The determiner can be present or absent also with common nouns. Some examples are provided below:

(34) a. (l)a **tua** [= **mia**] tazza # dov'è? — Gaia 2;2.28
the your [= *my*] *cup* # *where is* [*it*]?
'Where is my cup?'

b. **tuo** letto [= il tuo letto] — Sara 1;9.07
your bed [= *the your bed*]

c. du è [= dov'è] la **sua** (a)mica? — Sara 2;0.14
where is the your friend
'Where is your friend?'

d. la **mia** matita — Gregorio 2;0.29
the my pencil
'my pencil'

Again, the null hypothesis is that irrespective of the presence or absence of an article, the status and position of the prenominal possessive in child grammar is the same as in the adult grammar. This implies that it is correctly categorized as an adjective and moved to the high prenominal position.

This is also very clear in the case of postnominal possessives, with which the distribution of the determiner is target-like. The determiner is absent in (35a) because of the presence of the preposition (cf. *a casa* (*tua*) 'at your place'); in this syntactic environment, the possessive adjective can only be postnominal (cf. **in tua bocca* 'in your mouth', **a tua casa* 'at your place').[4] In (35b,c), the possessive is focussed, as it would be in the adult language. Recall that the postnominal position of the possessive implies movement of the noun across it:

(35) a. in bocca **tua** [= mia] Gaia 2;0.28
in mouth your [= *my*]
'in my mouth'
b. aia incastrato il biscotto **mio** Sara 2;2.05
ehi (is) stuck the cookie my
'My cookie got stuck.'
c. il tatore [/] tatore [= registratore] **mio**. Gregorio 2;0.29
the recorder / recorder my
'my recorder'

In Table 4 we report the possessive adjectives present in the corpora we are studying:

Table 4 Possessive adjectives in prenominal and postnominal position

	(det) poss N	(det) N poss
Gaia	10	1
Sara	23	2
Ernesto	2	0
Gregorio	2	1
Total	37	4

Our data replicate Bernardini's (2004: 173) count of the possessives present in the CHILDES Calambrone corpus (Martina, Raffaello, Rosa, and Viola). As is clear from Table 5, most possessives occur in prenominal position with

Table 5 Possessive adjectives in prenominal and postnominal position in the Calambrone corpus

(det) poss N	(det) N poss	(det) poss kin-N	(det) casa/kin-N poss	Total
59	4	–	17	80

[4] Notice that the very sequence *in bocca tua* is idiomatic and can only be interpreted metaphorically, meaning "if said by you". It cannot have the literal interpretation "in your mouth" which is the intended meaning of (35a) and would correspond to *nella tua bocca* in the adult language. It is also highly improbable that the child has been exposed to such an idiom, which occurs only once in the LIP corpus and not even with a possessive adjective. What the child has certainly been exposed to is the determinerless prepositional phrase *in bocca*, which contains a non-overt inalienable possessor typical of Italian. The child's production is non-target only as far as the realization of the possessor is concerned.

common nouns. The postnominal position is widely attested only with *casa* (home) and kinship nouns, as in the target language (see section 2.3).

Notice that the Calambrone corpus was collected in Tuscany, where possessive adjectives are preceded by (determinerless) kinship terms and *casa*. This is not the case in Northern-Italian varieties (see Section 2.3). It is therefore not surprising that these phrases are absent from the Gaia, Sara, and Ernesto corpora, where kinship terms occur with prenominal possessives, with or without the determiner, and always target-like[5]:

(36) a. con la **sua** mamma — Gaia 2;2.28
with the his mother
'with his mother'

b. **mio** papà — Gaia 2;6.01
'my dad'

c. la **mia** mamma — Sara 1;11.27
the my mom
'my mom'

The hypothesis that, from the very beginning, the full nominal structure is present and possessive movement as well as noun movement is available, predicts that the prenominal and postnominal positions are both available to the child. The expectation is that neither order should be produced earlier than the other. This is indeed what we find: Gregorio produces both orders for the first time in the same recording at 2;0.29, Gaia first produces a postnominal possessive at 2;0.28, while Sara first produces a prenominal possessive at 1;9.07. The very small number of postnominal possessives in child speech and the fact that they are appropriate to the context show that children are perfectly aware of their markedness and of their pragmatics.[6]

---

[5] The only example of *mamma mia* 'oh dear!' is an exclamation produced as a repetition:

(i) ANT: mamma mia
CHI: mamma mia # è caduto [%exp: il dentifricio] — Sara 2;3.20
mother my [*it*] *is fallen* [*the toothpaste*]
'Oh my dear, it fell down.'

[6] Antelmi (1997: 90–92) claims that in the Camilla corpus, postnominal possessives come later. She reaches this conclusion excluding from her analysis a number of cases of 'N – Poss' which she interprets as instances of predicative possessives with copula omission.

4.5 Descriptive Adjectives

Inside the nominal expression, children only produce some classes of adjectives. Classificatory, nationality, and shape adjectives are not present in the early stages of children's speech, which is characterized by fewer categories in the hierarchy (15) with respect to adults, presumably due to limited encyclopaedic knowledge.[7] What is interesting is that descriptive adjectives almost always appear in postnominal position. In prenominal position, only two adjectives are found: *bello* is attested 5 times and *grande* once. The data are summarised in Table 6 and exemplified in (37)–(39):

Table 6 Descriptive adjectives in child corpora

		(det) adj N	(det) N adj	Total
Gaia	*grande*	0 (0%)	6 (100%)	6
	other	0 (0%)	18 (100%)	18
Sara	*bello*	3 (50%)	3 (50%)	6
	grande	0 (0%)	1 (100%)	1
	other	0 (0%)	18 (100%)	18
Ernesto	*grande*	1 (20%)	4 (80%)	5
	other	0 (0%)	10 (100%)	10
Gregorio	*bello*	2 (50%)	2 (50%)	4
	other	0 (0%)	11 (100%)	11
Total		6 (7.6%)	73 (92.4%)	79

(37) value

a. questo è gli occhi **belli** Sara 2;2.05
this is the beautiful eyes
'These are beautiful eyes.'

b. e la **bella bella** collalina [=collanina] Sara 1;11.26
and the nice nice necklace
'the very nice necklace'

(38) size

a. un ciuccio **dande** [=grande] Gaia 1;11.28
a pacifier big
'a big pacifier'

[7] One child in our corpora produced one nationality adjective (*italiano*) as a repetition, and one classificatory adjective (*spaziale*) spontaneously:

(i) a. cd italiano Ernesto, 2;5,01
'Italian cd'

b. aer(e)o spaziale Ernesto, 2;4.02
'space aircraft'

b. **g(r)a(n)de** confusione — Ernesto 2;5.01
big confusion
'a big confusion'

(39) colour:
un piatto ## **ve(r)de** — Gaia 1;11.13
a dish green
'a green dish'

Our data replicate Bernardini's (2004: 170) analysis of the CHILDES Calambrone corpus (Martina, Raffaello, Rosa, and Viola): the great majority of adjectives produced by children appear in postnominal position (Table 7):

Table 7 Descriptive adjectives in the Calambrone corpus

(det) adj N	(det) N adj	Total
3	42	45

In Cinque's (2007) terms, postnominal adjectives can either be the low direct modifiers or indirect modifiers, the latter being very high in the structure. As for the former, the data in (37)–(39) suggest that children tend to obligatorily move the NP across all adjectives of the hierarchy in (16) apart from the last two classes, value and size, where NP movement appears to be strongly preferred across size adjectives and freely optional across value adjectives. However, it should be noted that the only instance of prenominal *grande*, which is found in the Ernesto corpus (38b), has a value interpretation. It could therefore be suggested that NP movement is in fact obligatory across size adjectives and optional only across value adjectives, as summarized in (40):

(40) Child-Italian:
det > value > size > (shape) > colour > (nationality > classificatory)
NP_{opt} $\mathbf{NP_{obl}}$ $\mathbf{(NP_{obl})}$ $\mathbf{NP_{obl}}$

This might suggest that child grammar is slightly different from adult grammar in the sense that there is more syntactic movement. This would be unexpected in a minimalist perspective, in that it would mean that children choose the less economical option applying movement more often than adults. Another more plausible explanation is that children's competence reflects the colloquial register which is predominant in the input.

This hypothesis is supported by the study of the input in one of our corpora (Sara corpus) and by the free turn-taking types in the LIP corpus. As shown in Table 8, the input in the Sara corpus contains 83 adjectives inside nominal

Table 8 Adjectives in the input of Sara corpus

	(det) adj N	(det) N adj	Total
Value	9 (45%)	11 (55%)	20
Size	2 (7%)	28 (93%)	30
Colour	0 (0%)	21 (100%)	21
Other	0 (0%)	15 (100%)	15
Total	11 (13%)	72 (87%)	83

expressions, and displays the same tendencies found in child productions: obligatory postnominal position of colour and size adjectives, while value adjectives can be equally prenominal or postnominal.

As a matter of fact, the two only instances of prenominal size adjectives in Sara's input are spurious: one occurrence (41a) has a value interpretation, the other (40b) comes from written Italian:

(41) a. e poi qui c'è una grande confusione
and then here there is a big confusion
'There is a mess here.'
b. (reading a book) sono una piccola mucca curiosa
[*I*] *am a little cow curious*
'I am a little curious cow.'

As for the free turn-taking texts in the LIP corpus, we have searched for two examples of value (*bello* 'beautiful', *brutto* 'ugly'), size (*grande* 'big', *piccolo* 'small') and shape (*tondo* 'round', *ovale* 'oval') adjectives, all colour adjectives, and those adjectives labelled as 'other' in the Sara corpus (including *nuovo* 'new', *personale* 'personal', *strano* 'strange', *fresco* 'fresh', *sporco* 'dirty', etc.). The tendencies observed in Table 8 are confirmed in an interesting way by the results in Table 9: Almost all the instances of *grande* and *piccolo* with value interpretation are prenominal, and, vice versa, almost all instances of real size adjectives occur in postnominal position.

The tendencies shown in Tables 8 and 9 are slightly different as far as the size class is concerned: more prenominal adjectives are found in the LIP corpus than in the input to Sara. In both cases, however, there is a clear tendency to locate

Table 9 A and B types of spoken genres (free turn-taking) in the LIP corpus

	(det) adj N	(det) N adj	Total
Value (*bello*, *brutto*)	74 (76%)	24 (24%)	98
Value (*grande*, *piccolo*)	58 (95%)	3 (5%)	61
Size (*grande*, *piccolo*)	7 (17%)	35 (83%)	42
Shape (*tondo*, *ovale*)	0 (0%)	3 (100%)	3
Colour	0 (0%)	52 (100%)	52
Other	30 (28%)	78 (72%)	108
Total	169 (46%)	195 (54%)	364

size, (shape), and colour adjectives in postnominal position, which means, in Cinque's terms, that NP-movement is obligatory across these classes too. This result is not in line with what we observed in (16) above, where NP-movement is obligatory across the lower classes of classificatory and nationality adjectives only. This difference can be made sense of by hypothesizing that (i) Cinque's (2007) proposal regards all registers of Italian, (ii) the prenominal positioning of size, shape and colour adjectives is typical of the high or written registers of Italian, and (iii) adult spoken grammar can be partially influenced by these more formal registers, as is apparent in Table 9.[8]

To conclude, children are exposed to a variety of Italian where NP-movement must reach the left of size adjectives and they are perfectly competent in this variety. They reproduce the most frequent order in their first utterance of individual classes, as is shown by the fact that *bello* is produced prenominally earlier than postnominally in those child corpora that contain it (Sara and Gregorio, see (37) and (42) respectively):

(42) a. **belli** piedini Gregorio 1;9.10
nice little-feet
'nice little feet'
b. Pegaso **bello** Gregorio 1;9.24
Pegasus nice
'nice Pegasus'

4.6 Stage-Level Adjectives

Let's now consider the other possible interpretation of postnominal adjectives, i.e., indirect modification. Notice that individual-level indirect modification can be detected in the presence of two postnominal adjectives if the order is not reversed with respect to what we have seen in (16) (if the order is opposite, Cinque's theory predicts that it is direct modification whose order has been inverted by roll-up, see (18)). In (43), indirect modification *rossa* 'red' is merged higher than direct modification *grande* 'big'. After movement across indirect modification, the order of postnominal adjectives is the same as in (16):

(43) la [$_{\text{ind. mod}}$ rossa [$_{\text{dir. mod}}$ grande [macchina]]]→
the red big car
la [$_{\text{ind mod}}$ rossa [$_{\text{dir mod}}$ [macchina] [grande ~~macchina~~]]]→
la [[$_{\text{dir mod}}$macchina grande][$_{\text{ind mod}}$ rossa [~~macchina grande~~]]]

---

[8] The prenominal position of certain classes of adjectives in high and written registers can be related to the fact that in Old Italian, more prenominal adjectives were possible than in Modern Italian (cf. Giusti 2010).

At the early stages that we are studying, two postnominal adjectives are never found.[9] In order to check the acquisition of indirect modification and the subsequent movement of the whole direct modification constituent across it, we can only analyse stage-level adjectives, which are considered by Cinque as being inserted exclusively in the indirect modification area. Once again, it is in principle impossible to establish whether children acquire this portion of structure through the input or whether the complex structure is given by UG and the only process to be learned through acquisition is the relevant movement. What is interesting to notice is that (i) stage-level adjectives are never produced prenominally, suggesting that, as soon as they are produced, the constituent movement of direct modification has been acquired, and (ii) stage-level adjectives are produced slightly later than individual-level adjectives.

Some examples of stage-level adjectives present in our corpora are provided below[10]:

(44) a. i bibi **vuoti** — Gaia 2;2.28
the bottles empty
'the empty bottles'

b. (l)a tetta(r)ella **(s)po(r)ca**! — Gaia 2;2.28
the pacifier dirty
'the dirty pacifier'

c. gli occhi **chiusi** — Sara 2;3.0
the eyes closed
'the closed eyes'

d. luce **accesa** — Gregorio 1;9.10
light turned-on

[9] Two postnominal adjectives are indeed very rare also in adult speech. We have found none in the input to Sara.

[10] In isolation, stage-level adjectives are present from the very first files:

(i) a. totto [= rotto] — Gaia 1;6.29
broken

b. uadda [= guarda] focca [= sporca] — Sara 1;9.7
look! dirty
'Look, it is dirty.'

The same is true of English (Blackwell 2000, 2005). This shows that the observed delay is not due to a delayed lexical acquisition of the class of stage-level adjectives, as is the case with other classes of adjectives (quantity, Section 2.1, ordinal, Section 4.3, classificatory, nationality, shape, Section 4.5).

It is interesting that no stage-level adjective is present in the Ernesto corpus, which does not contain many adjectives in general, suggesting that the child has not yet reached the relevant stage.

In Cinque's analysis, indirect modification is merged higher than direct modification (20) and (22). One hypothesis for the observed delay in the acquisition of stage-level adjectives could be that the highest portion of the FP in (3) containing indirect modification is expanded slightly later. This does not contradict the general approach taken here that assumes the presence of the entire DP structure, given the presence of higher functional structure at the very earliest stages witnessed by the production of elements such as *altro* (see Section 4.3) and prenominal possessives (see Section 4.4). Since indirect modification must be analysed as (reduced) relative clauses (Cinque 2007), the observed delay can be related to the apparent absence of (reduced) relative clauses and other subordinate clauses in the early stage we have analysed. As soon as children produce indirect modification, this is done in a target-like way: no such adjectives are ever found in prenominal position. This implies that they master the movement of the large constituent including direct modification across indirect modification. Notice that indirect modification clearly appears much earlier than any kind of subordinate clauses including relative clauses, probably due to its reduced nature.

Our observations are in line with what is independently observed by Blackwell (2000, 2005) for English. In her study of the acquisition of English adjectives, based on Dixon's (1982) and Frawley's (1992) semantic typology, Blackwell observed that adjectives that denote 'unstable properties' (e.g., *dirty*, *clean*, *wet*, *dry*, *hot*, *cold*; *happy*, *sad*, *sick*) appear in prenominal position later than adjectives denoting 'more stable properties' (e.g., *round*, *straight*, *pretty*). The two classes clearly correspond to stage-level and individual-level adjectives, respectively. We can therefore reformulate Blackwell's results by saying that in English, the two prenominal positions in (20a) above are acquired at different times, first direct and then indirect modification.

In conclusion, there is a parallel delay in the acquisition of indirect modification in Italian and English, the parallel delay being independent of the roll-up movement that takes place in Italian. This can be related to the fact that indirect modification and relative clauses are in fact an expansion of the intermediate FP layer.

5 Concluding Remarks

In this chapter, we have studied the distribution of adjectives in early spontaneous productions by Italian children. Given the unavailability of a large amount of data (due to independent factors: i.e., optionality of insertion and a low frequency of adjectives w.r.t. other lexical categories), we have undertaken a qualitative analysis based on well-established theoretical assumptions on the internal structure of nominal expressions.

We have shown that Italian children master the complexities of adjectival placement in a target-like fashion:

(i) adjectives like *altro*, which have a unique prenominal position, are used in the correct way;
(ii) possessive adjectives, whose prenominal or postnominal position depends on discourse features, are also used in a target-like fashion;
(iii) descriptive adjectives, which display the largest degree of variability, are used following the tendencies characterizing the colloquial register;
(iv) indirect modification, which has a unique postnominal position, is used in the correct way as soon as it appears (slightly later than direct modification).

Learning the colloquial register first, children do not produce orders that are only found in the formal register, such as topicalized adjectives. The only difference between child and adult grammar that we have detected concerns the lexicon, namely some classes of adjectives are not yet produced by children at the stage we have analysed. We have argued that this is not related to their syntactic competence, but is due to independent reasons: problems with categorial ambiguity with quantity adjectives, incomplete cognitive development with ordinal adjectives, limited encyclopaedic knowledge with descriptive adjectives.

Acknowledgments This paper has been presented at the XXX GLOW Workshop on Language Acquisition *Optionality in the Input: Children's Acquisition of Variable Word Order*, held in Tromsø on April 11, 2007, at the University of Trondheim on April 16, 2007, at the University of Geneva on April 30, 2007, and at the Seconda giornata di Linguistica applicata *Acquisizione del linguaggio e disturbi linguistici dell'età evolutiva*, held at the University Ca' Foscari of Venice on June 1, 2007. We thank the audiences for comments and criticism. In particular we thank Adriana Belletti, Petra Bernardini, Mila Dimitrova-Vulchanova, Maria Teresa Guasti, Gabriella Hermon, and the editors of this volume for very helpful comments.

References

Ambrosi, Carlotta. 2007. *Some aspects of the cognitive and linguistic development of a two-year-old child. Tesi di laurea*. Venice: University Ca' Foscari of Venice.

Antelmi, Donella. 1997. *La prima grammatica dell'italiano*. Bologna: Il Mulino.

Bernardini, Petra. 2004. *L'italiano come prima e seconda (madre) lingua. Indagine longitudinale sullo sviluppo del DP*. Etudes romanes de Lund 71. Lund: Lunds Universitet.

Blackwell, Aleka 2000. On the acquisition of the syntax of English adjectives. In *CLS36: The Panels. The Proceedings from the Panels of the Chicago Linguistic Society's Thirty-Sixth Meeting, vol. 36–2*, eds. Arika Okrent and John P. Boyle, 361–375. Chicago: Chicago Linguistic Society, University of Chicago.

Blackwell, Aleka 2005. Acquiring the English adjective lexicon: relationships with input properties and adjectival semantic typology. *Journal of Child Language* 32: 535–562.

Caprin, Claudia, and Maria Teresa Guasti. 2006. A cross-sectional study on the use of "be" in early Italian. In *The acquisition of syntax in Romance languages*, eds. Vincent Torrens and Linda Escobar, 117–133. Amsterdam: Benjamins.

Cardinaletti, Anna. 1998. On the deficient/strong opposition in possessive systems. In *Possessors, predicates, and movement in the determiner phrase*, eds. Artemis Alexiadou and Christopher Wilder, 17–53. Amsterdam/Philadelphia: Benjamins.

Cardinaletti, Anna, and Giuliana Giusti. 2006. The syntax of quantified phrases and quantitative clitics. In *The blackwell companion to syntax*, vol. V, eds. Martin Everaert and Henk van Riemsdijk, 23–93. Oxford: Blackwell Publishers Ltd.

Chierchia, Gennaro, Maria Teresa Guasti, and Andrea Gualmini. 1999. Nouns and articles in child grammar and the syntax/semantics map. Paper presented at GALA, Postdam.

Cinque, Guglielmo. 1994. On the evidence for partial N movement in the Romance DP. In *Paths towards universal grammar. Studies in honour of Richard S. Kayne*, eds. Guglielmo Cinque et al., 85–110. Washington: Georgetown University Press.

Cinque, Guglielmo. 2005. Deriving Greenberg's Universal 20 and its exceptions. *Linguistic Inquiry* 36: 315–332.

Cinque, Guglielmo. 2007. The syntax of adjectives. A comparative study. Ms., Venice: University Ca' Foscari of Venice.

Cipriani, Paola, Pietro Pfanner, Anna M. Chilosi, Lorena Cittadoni, Alessandro Ciuti, Anna Maccari, Lucia Pfanner, Paola Poli, Stefania Sarno, Piero Bottari, Giuseppe Cappelli, C. Colombo and E. Veneziano. 1989. *Protocolli diagnostici e terapeutici nello sviluppo e nella patologia del linguaggio* (1/84 Italian Ministry of Health), Stella Maris Foundation.

De Mauro, Tullio, Federico Mancini, and Massimo Vedovelli. 1993. *Lessico di frequenza dell'italiano parlato*. Milano: Etas Libri.

Dixon, Robert M.W. 1982. *Where have all the adjectives gone?* The Hague: Mouton.

Ferrari, Chiara. 2007. *Noun phrases and functional categories in early child production. Tesi di laurea*. Venice: University Ca' Foscari of Venice.

Frawley, William. 1992. *Linguistic semantics*. Hillsdale: Erlbaum.

Friedmann, Naama, and Yosef Grodzinsky. 1997. Tense and agreement in agrammatic production: Pruning the syntactic tree. *Brain and Language* 56: 397–425.

Gesmundo, Daniela. 2007. *Some aspects of the linguistic development of an Italian child. Tesi di laurea*. Venice: University Ca' Foscari of Venice.

Giusti, Giuliana. 2006. Parallels in clausal and nominal periphery. In *Phases of interpretation*, ed. Mara Frascarelli, 163–184. Berlin: Mouton.

Giusti, Giuliana. 2010. Il sintagma aggettivale. In *Grammatica dell'italiano antico*, eds. Giampaolo Salvi and Lorenzo Renzi, 593–616. Bologna: il Mulino.

Giusti, Giuliana, and Roberta Gozzi. 2006. The acquisition of determiners: Evidence for the full competence hypothesis. In *Language acquisition and development: Proceedings of GALA 2005*, eds. Adriana Belletti et al., 232–237. Newcastle: Cambridge Scholars Press.

Gozzi, Roberta. 2004. *The acquisition of determiners. A longitudinal study on an Italian child. Tesi di Laurea*. Venice: University Ca' Foscari of Venice.

Longobardi, Giuseppe. 1994. Reference and proper names: a theory of N-movement in syntax and logical form. *Linguistic Inquiry* 25: 609–665.

Rizzi, Luigi. 1994. Some notes on linguistic theory and language development: The case of root infinitives. *Language Acquisition* 3: 371–393.

Zampolli, Serena. 2007. *Adjectives and Winnie Pooh: On the input for first language acquisition. Tesi di laurea*. Venice: University Ca' Foscari of Venice.

Zucchet, Silvia. 2008. *L'acquisizione del sintagma nominale in una bambina italiana. Tesi di laurea*. Venice: University Ca' Foscari of Venice.

Input Factors in Early Verb Acquisition: Do Word Frequency and Word Order Variability of Verbs Matter?

Anja Kieburg and Petra Schulz

Abstract While simplex verbs show word order variability in main clauses and subordinated clauses in standard German, the verb particle of morphologically complex particle verbs is syntactically less variable: It generally occurs in sentence final position. Acquisition data reveal that telic verb particles appear in German-speaking children's speech around 14 months of age, even earlier than the first simplex verbs. Using a longitudinal design, we examine whether children's early preference for telic verb particles can be explained by word frequency and/or word order variability in the ambient language. The analysed data comprises 5,001 utterances from three mothers recorded in eight 1-h home sessions when the children's ages were 14, 16, 18, and 20 months. While simple input frequency does not influence children's early verb acquisition, it is shown that the factor 'word order variability', i.e. less syntactic variation in the input, favours children's early acquisition. Thus, it is concluded that children seem to adhere to learning mechanisms that make use of the parental input in a specific way, by taking into account the structural properties of the target language.

Keywords Early verb acquisition · Endstate-orientation · Telic verb particles · Simplex verbs · Word frequency · Word order variability · Parental input

1 Introduction

Verbs differ from nouns in a number of aspects that are of relevance not only for linguistic theory but also for language acquisition. Unlike nouns, verbs do not express reference to objects, but express relationships between objects via predication. Verbs often designate events that are transient, such as *open,* and hence less readily extracted as perceptual units than objects, which are typically

P. Schulz (✉)
Johann Wolfgang Goethe-University Frankfurt, D-60323 Frankfurt am Main, Germany
e-mail: P.Schulz@em.uni-frankfurt.de

M. Anderssen et al. (eds.), *Variation in the Input*, Studies in Theoretical Psycholinguistics 39, DOI 10.1007/978-90-481-9207-6_5,

non-transient. Thus, the event designated by verbs such as *open* is more difficult to grasp than the object referred to with nouns such as *door*. What is more, often the event designated by a verb is complex. The verb *open*, for example, designates an event, where a component passes through a transition from a process of being opened to an endstate of being open. In addition, the relationship between verbs and the event type they designate is often ambiguous. An event like ‘move a broom across the floor causing leaves to change their location on the floor’ could be expressed as *sweep* or *clean*. Only the latter verb, however, expresses the endstate of being clean. These facts among others should make verb learning difficult.

Despite the difficult acquisition task the child is faced with, German-speaking children use verbs already in their second year of life. Typically they log into the verb lexicon with verb particles like *auf* ‘open’ that can be semantically classified as telic, and some time later start producing non-telic verb particles, simplex verbs, and particle verbs (Mills 1985, Behrens 1998, Schulz et al. 2001, Schulz et al. 2002, Penner et al. 2003, Schulz 2005). Moreover, telic verb particles are the most frequent verb expressions in the speech of 1-year-olds (Schulz 2003, 2005). This finding has been accounted for by drawing on language-internal properties of the target language (cf. Schulz et al. 2001, 2002, Penner et al. 2003).

In this chapter, extending previous work (Kieburg 2005, Kieburg and Schulz 2008), we will investigate whether and how different input factors such as word frequency as well as word order variability have a bearing on the early verb acquisition of German-speaking children. In line with continuity assumptions of language acquisition (e.g., Pinker 1984) and contrary to the view that children’s earliest linguistic productions do not show evidence of abstract syntactic categories (e.g., Tomasello 2000), we assume that at least by age one children possess a knowledge of lexical categories such as ‘verb’. Many studies on early syntax acquisition (e.g., Tracy 1991, Weissenborn 1994) have shown that children obey the structural constraints for verb positions from early on. This finding seems difficult to account for, if language learning is based on purely surface properties of the ambient target language. Furthermore, given that the learner is equipped with the ability to assign words in the input to their lexical category, e.g., by making use of prosodic and morphological cues including finiteness or tense markers (Golinkoff et al. 2001), the question arises of how the frequency patterns and the specific structural properties within this word class contribute to the child’s acquisition path. More specifically, in this study we will address the following questions: (1) Does the frequency with which particle verbs, simplex verbs, and verb particles appear in the parental input influence the order of verb acquisition? (2) Does the fact that particle verbs, simplex verbs, and verb particles differ with regard to their word order variability shape the child’s acquisition path? Furthermore, we will explore how the two factors are connected.

In order to address these questions a longitudinal study was conducted, in which the parental input to three children between the ages of 14 and 20 months was analyzed with respect to the verbs used. Following previous research into frequency, word frequency was calculated using three different measures: types, tokens, type token ratio (TTR). The second factor 'word order variability' has traditionally been addressed focusing on the saliency of certain positions such as the edge of an utterance (e.g., Tardif et al. 1997), without taking into account the underlying structure of an utterance. Under the view that children have knowledge not only of categories but also of the structural positions able to host verbal elements, it can be asked whether differences regarding this structural word order variability can account for the acquisition patterns observed in children. Therefore, word order variability was calculated based on (a) the possible surface positions a verb appeared in, ignoring the underlying sentence structure (henceforth called surface perspective) and (b) the two syntactic positions hosting verbal elements in German: V2 and Verbend (henceforth called structural perspective).

For the first factor word frequency the results reveal that simple word frequency, i.e. measured via token or type frequency does not play a causal role in children's early verb acquisition. With regard to the more complex frequency measure TTR we found partial evidence that word frequency may influence the order of verb acquisition. Concerning the second factor word order variability, the results for the structural as well as the surface perspective reveal that less syntactic variability favours the early acquisition of verb particles in German speaking children.

The paper is organized as follows. Section 2 sketches the classification of verb categories in German according to their morpho-syntactic properties. Section 3 deals with semantic properties of verb categories in German. Section 4 gives an overview of verb acquisition, focusing on the acquisition of verb particles and simplex verbs in German-speaking children. Section 5 summarizes the various factors that have been proposed in the literature to play a role in the acquisition of the early lexicon. Section 6 presents our study on word frequency and word order variability of verb categories in the input. The results of this study are discussed in Section 7. Section 8 concludes with implications of these findings for further research.

2 Morpho-Syntactic Properties of Verb Categories in German

West Germanic languages differentiate between simplex verbs such as *spielen* 'to play' (1) and complex predicates, which consist of a verb root and an affix as shown in (2) and (3). Complex predicates can be further distinguished according to the type of affix they host. In particle verbs such as *aufmachen* 'to open', the affixal particle can be separated from the verb root in verb second structures such as (2b), but not when some other finite verbal element, such as a modal verb, occupies the verb second position as in (2a). In prefix verbs such as *enthüllen* 'to uncover', the prefix cannot be separated from the verb root, as illustrated in (3a) and (3b) (cf. also Behrens 1998).

(1) Er will mit dem Ball *spielen*.
he wants with the ball *play*
'He wants to play with the ball'

(2) a. Er will die Flasche *aufmachen*
he wants the bottle *open.make*
'He wants to open the bottle'

b. Sie *macht* die Flasche *auf*.
she *makes* the bottle open
'She opens the bottle'

(3) a. Er will das Geheimnis *enthüllen*.
he wants the secret *un.cover*
'He wants to uncover the secret'

b. Sie *enthüllt* das Geheimnis.
she *un.covers* the secret
'She uncovers the secret'

Note that the separated verb particle may appear without the verb root in informal requests (4a) or questions (4b). Importantly, the meaning is equivalent to the particle verb structures in (4a') and (4b').

(4) a. Tür *auf!*
door open
'Open the door'

a.' *Mach* die Tür auf!
make the door open
'Open the door'

b. Alle *weg?*
all *gone*
'Is everybody gone?'

b.' *Sind* alle *weg?*
are all gone
'Is everybody gone?'

Verbs in German are assumed to be base generated in verb final position (cf. Koster 1975). German is a XVO language that shows verb second (V2) word order in finite main clauses (5a). In subordinate clauses, the finite verb remains in verbend (VE) position, as shown in (5b).

(5) a. Peter *kauft* den Apfel.
Peter *buys* the apple

b. Anna weiß, dass Peter den Apfel *kauft*.
Anna knows that Peter the apple *buys*
'Anna knows that Peter is buying the apple.'

It is well known that the structural position of the verb and its surface position with regard to the other elements of the sentence do not necessarily correspond. For example, V2 may coincide with the sentence final position (6a), and VE with a prefinal sentence position (6b).

(6) a. Peter *schläft*.
Peter *sleeps*
b. Peter hat den Apfel *reingelegt* in die Tasche.
Peter has the apple *in-put* in the bag
'Peter put the apple in the bag.'

Generally speaking, while V2 and VE are the two structural options for verbal elements, according to the surface perspective in German there are three positions the verb can appear in: at the beginning, in the middle, and at the end of a sentence (henceforth sentence initial, sentence medial, and sentence final). As this will become important for the two analyses of word order variability carried out in Section 6, the differences between surface and structural perspective will be illustrated in the following in more detail. For ease of comparison with the surface perspective, the structural perspective will employ the topological field model (e.g., Höhle 1986), which remains open with regard to the specific functional projections postulated for V2 and VE structures in German (cf. Table 1).

Table 1 A simplified topological field model of German

		Sentence bracket		
Prefield	Left sentence bracket	Middle field	Right sentence bracket	Postfield
(6a) Peter	schläft	–	–	–
(6b) Peter	hat	den Apfel	reingelegt	in die Tasche
(5b)	dass	Peter den Apfel	kauft	–

Regarding the morphologically complex particle verbs, in main clauses the finite verb root occurs in the left sentence bracket, while the verb particle occurs in the right sentence bracket as seen in (7a). From the surface perspective, in (7a) the verb root occurs in sentence medial and the verb particle in sentence final position. In subordinated clauses such as (7b), the finite particle verb, which forms one complex word, occupies the right sentence bracket, which in this example coincides with the sentence final position.

(7) a. Peter *isst* den Apfel *auf*.
Peter *eats* the apple *up*
b. Anna weiß, dass Peter den Apfel *aufisst*.
Anna knows that Peter the apple *up.eats*
'Anna knows that Peter eats the apple up.'

Importantly, the right sentence bracket hosts the verb particle of a particle verb, either separated from the verb root as in (7a) or affixed to the verb root as in (7b). Note that verb particles that appear without a verb root as in (4a) and (4b) above are also located in the right sentence bracket. Taking a surface perspective, the verb particle may thus appear in sentence final position as in (7a). Whether the position of the verb particle in (7b) is sentence final as well, is unclear. In order to classify *auf* as being 'at the end of the sentence', the particle verb has to be treated as one element.

In extraposition structures such as (8) the difference between the structural and the surface perspective is evident as well. In colloquial German, the *post-field* may host extraposed constituents such as prepositional phrases (see Haider 1995 for constraints on extraposition), preceded by the verb particle, which occupies the right sentence bracket, just as in (7a). From a surface perspective however, unlike the verb particle in (7a), the verb particle in (8) appears in sentence medial position.

(8) Du *machst* das *rein* in die Kiste.
you *make* this *into* into the box
'You put this into the box.'

Non-separated particle verbs occupy the right sentence bracket as illustrated with a simple subordinate clause in (7b) and with a modal or an auxiliary added as shown in (9). From a surface perspective, the picture looks more diverse. While in (7b) the particle verb appears in sentence final position, in (9) it appears in sentence medial position.

(9) a. Anna weiß, dass er die Flasche *aufmachen* möchte.
Anna knows that he the bottle *open.make* wants
'Anna knows that he wants to open the bottle.'
b. Anna weiß, dass er die Flasche *aufgemacht* hat.
Anna knows that he the bottle *open.made* has
'Anna knows that he has opened the bottle.'

Aside from the left and right sentence bracket as the typical positions hosting the verbal elements, the *prefield* may host the particle verb or the verb particle when they are topicalized, as demonstrated in (10a–b). Note that these topicalized structures are marked (see also Lüdeling 2001: 53) and occur less frequently. From a surface perspective, both the particle verb (10a) and the verb particle (10b) appear in sentence initial position.

(10) a. ?*Zugemacht* hat er die Tür.
close.made has he the door
'He has closed the door.'
b. ?*Zu macht* er die Tür!
close makes he the door
'He closes the door.'

In short, the verb particle of a complex predicate is located in the right sentence bracket or – in specific contexts – in the *prefield*. From a surface perspective, the verb particle may appear in sentence final, and – more marked – in medial, or initial position.

Turning to simplex verbs, let us first look at their position in main clauses. Finite simplex verbs are located in the left sentence bracket, as illustrated in (5a), repeated here as (11), corresponding to a sentence medial position.

(11) Peter *kauft* den Apfel.
Peter *buys* the apple

Nonfinite simplex verbs occur in the right sentence bracket as can be seen in (12a–b); the left sentence bracket is occupied by the modal or the auxiliary carrying the finiteness features. (12b) illustrates that in colloquial German the simplex verb may be followed by an extraposed constituent (Haider 1995: 9); the prepositional phrase occurs in the *postfield*. From a surface perspective, the simplex verb appears in sentence final position in (12a) and in sentence medial position (12b).

(12) a. Er will/ hat mit ihr *sprechen/gesprochen.*
he wants to/has with her *talk/ talked*
'He wants to talk/has talked to her.'
b. Er hat *gesprochen* mit ihr.
he has *talked* with her
'He talked to her.'

Moreover, simplex verbs may occur in sentence initial position, as shown in both examples (13) and (14). However, the structural position of the verb differs.

In requests (13a) and yes/no questions (13b), the simplex verb occupies the left sentence bracket, and the *prefield* is unfilled. In answers to wh-questions such as (13c), in colloquial German the subject may be omitted, resulting in the same structure as for (13a–b): the *prefield* is empty, and the simplex verb is hosted by the left sentence bracket. In contrast, in (14) the topicalized non-finite simplex verb is hosted by the *prefield,* and the finite auxiliary occupies the left sentence bracket.

(13) a. *Gieß* die Blumen!
water the flowers
b. *Gießt* du die Blumen?
water you the flowers
'Are you watering the flowers?'
c. Question: Wo ist Jan gerade?
'Where is Jan at the moment?'
Answer: *Liegt* im Bett.
lying in bed
'He is lying in the bed.'

(14) Question: Was hat Jan mit den Blumen gemacht?
'What has Jan done with the flowers?'
Answer: *Gegossen* hat er sie.
watered has he them
'He watered them.'

In subordinated verb final clauses, simplex verbs occupy the right sentence bracket, as shown in (5b), repeated here as (15).

(15) Anna weiß, dass Peter den Apfel *kauft.*
Anna knows that Peter the apple *buys*
'Anna knows that Peter is buying the apple.'

In the example above, the right sentence bracket coincides with the sentence final position. If, however, the embedded predicate also contains an auxiliary or a modal as in (16), the simplex verb appears in sentence medial position. Hence, although the simplex verb occurs in the right sentence bracket followed by no other constituent occupying the *postfield,* this does not necessarily mean that the simplex verb concurrently occurs in sentence final position.

(16) Anna weiß, dass er einen Apfel *kaufen* möchte/*gekauft* hat.
Anna knows that he an apple *buy* wants/*bought* has
'Anna knows that he wants to buy/has bought an apple.'

Furthermore, in subordinated clauses the *postfield* may be filled by an extraposed constituent as shown in (17) below, following the simplex verb in the right sentence bracket. Thus, from a surface perspective, both in (16) and in (17) the simplex verb appears in sentence medial position.

(17) Ich möchte nicht, dass er Ball *spielt* in dem Zimmer.
I want not that he ball *plays* in the room
'I don't want, that he is playing ball in the room.'

In short, the simple verb may be located in the left and in the right sentence bracket and – in specific contexts – in the *prefield*. From a surface perspective, the simplex verb may appear in sentence initial, medial, or final position.

Summarizing, German simplex verbs show more word order variability regarding their sentence position than verb particles of morphologically complex particle verbs, both from a structural and from a surface perspective. Verb particles generally occupy the right sentence bracket, while simplex verbs may occupy the right and the left sentence bracket. Verb particles generally occur sentence finally, while simplex verbs may occur in sentence initial, medial, and final position. Following a surface perspective, Tardif et al. (1997) argued that the sentence final position is salient. However, this view disregards the underlying syntactic positions that the child may be aware of. In addition to the morpho-syntactic differences, verbs also differ semantically. These semantic properties are described in the next section.

3 Semantic Properties of Verb Categories in German

Verbs designate events including states such as *being poor* and actions like *walking around, sweeping*, or *opening*. Verbs differ in terms of the temporal make-up of the event they designate (cf. Comrie 1976). While some events have a terminal endpoint built into them leading to a natural culmination point, some events are without such a terminal endpoint allowing the event to continue indefinitely or stop at any moment in time. Verbs designating events with terminal endpoints are referred to as telic verbs, and verbs designating events without such an endpoint are called non-telic. Following Pustejovsky's (1995) model of event typology, events can be distinguished according to their complexity. Verbs like *walk* designate a single event, while verbs like *open* and *sweep* designate a complex event, i.e. a transition from a process to a state. Telic verbs like *open* designate a complex event, called endstate-oriented transition, with the endstate subevent being more prominent than the process subevent. In contrast, non-telic verbs like *sweep* designate a complex event, called process-oriented transition, where the process subevent is more prominent than the endstate subevent. In telic verbs, the endstate is entailed by the verb meaning (18a), and the endstate cannot be cancelled (18b).

(18) a. She opened the bottle. entails 'the bottle is open'
b. She opened the bottle, *but it is still closed.

Non-telic transitional verbs like *sweep* designate events with an endstate often implicated (19a), but not entailed (19b) (cf. Jeschull 2007, Schulz and Ose 2008, for an analysis in terms of pragmatic vs. semantic telicity).

(19) a. She swept the floor, and the floor was clean.
b. She swept the floor, but the floor wasn't clean.

Finally, verbs like *laugh* or *walk around* designate events without a terminal endpoint. For the purposes of this study, verbs like *sweep, laugh*, and *walk around* will be called non-telic.

Telicity is determined by the lexical semantics of the verb and/or by the event-semantic properties of other elements in the sentence (cf. Krifka 1989). The event type of simplex verbs like *find* or *open* or *laugh*, for example, is determined by their lexical semantics. In the case of particle verbs, the verb particles may contribute to the event marking of the complex verb hosting the particle. Assuming for the purposes of classification that the verb root is formed by a light verb like *machen* 'make', several types of verb particles can be distinguished regarding their telicity properties. Some particles mark the prominent endstate of a transition (e.g., *auf* 'open', *aus* 'out'), while others are ambiguous, marking the process or the endstate of a transition (e.g., *rauf* 'up', *runter* 'down'). Furthermore, some particles are atelic, as they exclusively mark the process (e.g., *rum* 'around'). In the present study, the first group of verb particles is referred to as telic and the second group as non-telic, including both ambiguous and atelic particles.

Before we look at the input properties of the syntactic and semantic categories described in this section and in Section 2, an overview of the early acquisition of simplex verbs and verb particles will be given in the next section.

4 Verb Particles and Simplex Verbs in Child Language

German-speaking children start using verb expressions already in their second year of life (e.g., Mills 1985, Behrens 1998, Kauschke 2000, Schulz 2003, 2005). Comparing children's production of simplex and complex verbs, Behrens (1998) found that simplex verbs are generally the first verbs to appear, but that both simplex and particle verbs are used frequently already before age 2, while prefix verbs are used only rarely.

Isolated verb particles play an important role for early verb acquisition as they often assume the function of a full verb (cf. Mills 1985). This is illustrated in (20) (from Penner et al. 2003: 298):

(20) Adult: Was soll ich denn damit machen?
'what should I do with that'
Child: AUF!
open
'open it'

In one word utterances such as in (20) the verb particle is assumed to be located in the right sentence bracket. Clear evidence for this structural position is provided by two-word utterances containing verb particles or simplex verbs as (21a–b) below (from Tracy 1991: 166f.):

(21) a. Child tries to take adult's shoe off:
shoe *on ... off*
'put the shoe on – eh off'
b. Brezel *essen.*
Pretzel *eat*
'I want to eat Pretzels'

Studies of children's early verb lexicon based on data from spontaneous speech corpora and from the parent report RELATIONAL WORD INVENTORY (RWI, cf. Schulz, 2002, unpublished manuscript) showed that isolated verb particles are first used between the ages of 14 and 18 months (Penner et al. 2003, Schulz 2003, 2005). The results of these studies indicate that most children log into the verb lexicon with isolated verb particles only, and that few children start out simultaneously with simple verbs and isolated verb particles. In line with previous findings, Schulz (2003) found that the verb particles are used in the function of a full verb. Particle verbs occur some time later, around 18 months of age (Penner et al. 2003).

Examining the frequency of verb particles, particle verbs, and simplex verbs in the early verb lexicon of German-speaking children between the ages of 14–18 months, Schulz (2005) found that 66% of the children's spontaneous early verb expressions were typically isolated verb particles such as *auf* 'open' or *ab* 'off', compared to only 7% simplex verbs, and 2% particle verbs. Notably, a quarter of the verb expressions were other non-adultlike complex verbs formed by the light verb *machen* 'make' and a child expression such as *heia*, meaning *going to sleep*, or *ei*, meaning *caress*. Presumably, these verbs function as precursors to other complex predicate types. Thus, verb particles make up nearly two thirds of children's early verb lexicon, while simplex verbs and particle verbs play a minor role in the early stages of child verb acquisition.

With regard to the semantic classification of the verb particles used, telic verb particles such as *auf* 'open', *aus* 'out', and *ab* 'off' were used more frequently than ambiguous verb particles like *hoch* 'up'. Atelic particles did not occur at all.

Comparing the event type of verb particles used first by the child according to the RWI, Schulz (2005) found that 90% of the children log into the verb lexicon with telic particles.

To account for these acquisition findings, Schulz and colleagues (see Schulz et al. 2001, 2002, Penner et al. 2003) suggested a learning strategy of endstate-orientation that guides children's early verb learning. The strategy of endstate-orientation works as follows. When logging into the verb lexicon, children first focus on the event structure of the verb rather than on other properties such as its syntactic arguments. More specifically, the language learner focuses on event types with an unambiguous event structure. Because of their prominent endstate, endstate-oriented transitions possess an unambiguous event structure and are therefore preferred by the children. As mentioned above, endstate-oriented transitions are expressed by telic verbs. Within the class of telic verbs, telic particle verbs like *aufmachen* 'to open' or *zumachen* 'to close' express the complex event more transparently than morphologically simple verbs like *öffnen* 'to open' and are therefore among the first telic verbs to be used. Telic particle verbs are composed of a (light) verb encoding the process component like *machen* 'make' and a verb particle encoding the telicity like *auf* 'open'. When acquiring their first verb expressions, children produce first the prominent subevent of the particle verb, i.e. *auf* 'open' or *zu* 'closed', before producing the full particle verb.

Note that the strategy of endstate-orientation described above is based on linguistic properties of the German verb system that are assumed to guide children's early verb learning. In other words, these specific features of the target language are prominent for the child from a linguistic perspective. The strategy of endstate-orientation is therefore closely connected to the so-called 'language-driven processes' (Behrend 1995), which are learning algorithms that are based on the child's knowledge of the architecture of the verb lexicon. This knowledge primarily concerns the internal organization of specific modules such as argument structure and event structure as well as their interaction with syntactic, morphological, and semantic features. In this learning process, aspects of the learning environment such as frequency of a certain structure in the input to the child play a minor role in explaining the order of verb acquisition.

According to Behrend's classification of verb learning mechanisms, in addition to language-driven processes, two other types of learning processes can be distinguished: child-driven processes and environment-driven processes. According to Behrend, child-driven processes are pre-existing perceptual, cognitive, or linguistic strategies or constraints that the child brings to the learning context like the *manner bias* (cf. Gentner 1978). The notion of environment-driven learning processes emphasizes the role of the environment of the language learner and includes factors such as frequency, timing, or variability as well as real world characteristics of verb usage in the input to which the child is exposed (cf. Behrend 1995). In the present study we explore the possible role of environment-driven learning processes in accounting for children's early verb acquisition. We will argue that not all of the factors characterized as environment-driven can in fact be subsumed under what is traditionally referred to as input-driven (cf. Tomasello 2003). The following section introduces various input factors that have been identified in the literature as influencing the early acquisition of the lexicon.

5 Input Factors in Previous Research on Lexical Acquisition

Mainly the noun-verb-difference across different languages has been studied from an input perspective, while little research has been done to examine the role of the input in the early verb acquisition by German-speaking children. Several properties of the input have been argued to influence the child's acquisition of the lexicon: word frequency, overall amount of input, saliency of the sentence position, morphological transparency, and variability of the linguistic environment. Common to these accounts is the notion that '... the process of acquiring a lexicon is clearly a process of learning from experience, and the relevant experience must be conversational interaction, because that is the context in which exposure to language occurs' (Hoff and Naigles 2002: 418).

Among these input factors, the role of word frequency has received the most attention and has been investigated in a variety of learning contexts. Brown (1958) was among the first to consider word frequency as an explanation for the order of acquisition of noun classes, more precisely for the fact that basic level nouns like *bird* are produced earlier than subordinate nouns like *sparrow*. Brown assumes that highly frequent words in the input, i.e. basic level nouns, correlate with the children's cognitive requisites and are therefore acquired earlier than other nouns. Word frequency has also played a key role in the controversy regarding the question of why nouns seem to be acquired before verbs. Goldfield (1993), for example, argued that a high noun type frequency in the parental input causes the early noun bias in English-speaking children. Additionally, cross-linguistic studies (e.g., Tardif et al. 1997, Choi 2000) found that language specific differences in the initial production of nouns and verbs are due to word frequency in the input. With regard to the category of verbs, Naigles and Hoff-Ginsberg (1998) observed a positive correlation between the frequency of verb categories in the input and the children's verb production 10 weeks later. While most of these studies examined either type or token frequency, Sandhofer et al. (2000) analyzed the proportion of both types and tokens in parental input to explain the early noun bias in English-speaking children and the early verb bias in Chinese-speaking children. They found that a high number of tokens combined with a low number of types favoured verb acquisition, while a high number of types combined with a low number of tokens favoured noun acquisition. This proportion of number of types and number of tokens corresponds to the type-token ratio (abbreviated as TTR), calculated by dividing the number of types by the number of tokens (e.g., Richards and Malvern 1996). Thus, a high TTR for nouns in the input explains English-speaking children's early noun production, and a low TTR for verbs favours Chinese-speaking children's early verb production.

Concerning the factor 'overall amount of input', Pearson et al. (1997) found that the size of the lexicons of Spanish-English bilingual 1- and 2-year-olds depended on the amount of input that the children were exposed to in each language. Furthermore, it has been reported for English-speaking children that the rate of lexical growth correlates with the overall amount of language input (Huttenlocher et al. 1991).

With regard to the input factor 'saliency of the sentence position', Tardif et al. (1997), among others, claimed that words that appear at the edge of an utterance, i.e. sentence initial or sentence final, are more accessible to children and are therefore acquired earlier than words in medial sentence positions. When Tardif et al. compared the spontaneous speech of English- and Chinese-speaking mothers they found that nouns were used significantly more often than verbs in sentence final position by English-speaking mothers, while Chinese-speaking mothers used significantly more verbs than nouns in final position. According to the authors, these data can account for the finding mentioned above that English-speaking children have more nouns than verbs in their productive lexicon, while Chinese-speaking children produce more verbs than nouns.

In addition, the early noun bias of English-speaking children has been explained by the input factor 'morphological transparency' (Gentner 1982, Tardif et al. 1997). According to Gentner (1982), words that always appear in more or less the same morphological form, are morphological transparent and hence easier to acquire than morphologically more variable words. Unlike verbs, nouns in English are claimed to be morphologically transparent and are therefore assumed to be learned earlier.

In sum, the results from previous studies highlight several input factors that could play a role for the acquisition order and for the composition of the child's early lexicon. Importantly, investigation of factors such as frequency of nouns or verbs presupposes that the child has knowledge of the respective categories, while the underlying structure of the utterances may be ignored by the child. Even the input factor 'saliency of the sentence position' only pays attention to what we referred to as the surface perspective (cf. Section 2). Looking at word order variability from a structural perspective has not been the focus of this line of research. Note that this mode of analysis goes beyond the notion of classical environment-driven language mechanisms, as it combines characteristics such as saliency with structural properties of the target language that adult speakers provide in the input.

Therefore, in the present study, we will explore the influence of two major input factors, 'word frequency' and 'word order variability', on German-speaking children's early verb lexicon. Word frequency will be examined using three different measures: types, tokens, and TTR. Word order variability will be examined using two measures: surface and structural sentential positions, as detailed in Section 2. More specifically, the following two hypotheses can be formulated:

Frequency Hypothesis: Frequent verbal elements in the parental input, to be defined via token, types, or via TTR, influence the composition of the verb lexicon and the order of acquisition of verb categories in German-speaking children.

Word Order Variability Hypothesis: Verbal elements that show less variation in the input, to be defined either from a surface or a structural perspective, are favoured in the acquisition of verb categories in German speaking children.

Assuming that the child is equipped with knowledge of categories such as 'verb' and that by age 1 the child is aware of the two possible structural positions for verbal elements, we expect that rather than frequency restricted syntactic variation plays a role for early acquisition.

6 The Study

This study is based on the analysis of the parental input of three German-speaking children in their second year of life. The data stems from the large longitudinal German Language Development (GLAD) study in Berlin, which investigates children's language acquisition and precursors of language impairment between birth and age four (cf. acknowledgment).

6.1 Data Sample

The sample included three caregiver-child dyads chosen from the spontaneous speech corpus of the GLAD study. The children (two girls, one boy) and their families spoke German as their only language. All the families belonged to the lower middle class and lived in Berlin. Data collection involved observations of spontaneous interactions between the child and other interaction partners present in the children's homes, such as for example mother, father, grandparents, siblings, and the research assistant. All utterances made by these conversation partners in the child's presence were considered as input to the child. As the mother was the primary caregiver in all three families, the mothers contributed overall 72% of the utterances in the children's ambient language. For reasons of readability, in the following, the term 'parental input' is used to refer to all utterances in the child's presence. Bimonthly video recordings were made for each child, starting at the age of 12 months and ending at the age of 30 months. Each session lasted approximately 60 min and was recorded by a research assistant with a portable video camera. The sessions typically involved free play with toys as well as everyday situations like getting dressed or meal and snack times. Since the primary aim of the GLAD study was to collect language data from the children, the child's interaction partners were not aware that their utterances would be of interest. For the present study, we analyzed the parental utterances across 8 speech samples: four samples of one mother-girl dyad at the child's age of 14, 16, 18 and 20 months and two samples each of the other two mother-child dyads at the age of 14 and 20 months (see Table 2). This selection was based on two factors: The spontaneous speech of the participating children had previously been analyzed, and the age range was chosen so that the children started producing verb particles and verbs.

Table 2 Spontaneous speech samples studied

Child	Number of analyzed samples	Age (months)	Transcript code
Anne	4	14, 16, 18, 20	A14, A16, A18, A20
Maria	2	14, 20	M14, M20
Tim	2	14, 20	T14, T20

6.2 Data Analysis

For each session, first all adult utterances containing a verb (i.e. full verb, modal verb, auxiliary, or copula), a verb particle, or a preposition[1] were transcribed. Additionally, all remaining utterances were counted to compute the overall number of utterances in that recording. The computation of the number of adult utterances was based on the following assumption: A unit for analysis roughly corresponds to a main clause or to a conversational turn. Maximally, it consisted of a sentence with one full verb such as *mach die Tür zu* 'close the door', or of a phrase like *auf dem Tisch*; minimally it consisted of a single word like *zu* 'closed' or *Tasse* 'cup'. Thus, complex sentences were counted separately. For reasons of readability in the following the term 'utterance' is used throughout.

To facilitate multiple analyses, the utterances were divided into several subcategories. There were two main categories: WITH FULL VERB OR VERB PARTICLE and WITHOUT FULL VERB AND WITHOUT VERB PARTICLE. Furthermore, utterances with a full verb or verb particle were subdivided into more specific categories: SIMPLEX VERBS (e.g., *schlafen* 'to sleep'), PARTICLES WITHOUT VERB ROOT

[1] In German, some lexemes such as *auf* 'open' are ambiguous wrt. their lexical class; they could be a preposition as well as a verb particle. To control for misclassifications, in our analysis we also analysed all occurrences of prepositions. Confirming Behrens' (1998) results, we did not find any structural ambiguity between utterances containing a verb particle and utterances containing a preposition. The most frequently produced verb particles did only partly match the most frequent prepositions *mit* 'with', *auf* 'on', and *in* 'in', of which only *mit* and *auf* exist both as verb particles and as prepositions in German. For further details see Kieburg (2005).

(e.g., *auf* 'open'), PARTICLE VERBS (e.g., *aufmachen* 'to open'), and OTHER COMPLEX VERBS (e.g., *kaputtmachen*, broken.make, 'to break'). The category of particle verbs was subdivided into PARTICLE VERBS SEPARATE (e.g., *machen auf,* make open, 'to open') and PARTICLE VERBS NON-SEPARATE (e.g., *aufmachen*, open.make, 'to open'). Finally, there were two meta-categories, combining relevant basic categories. The meta-category ALL SEPARATELY PRODUCED VERB PARTICLES contained all the verb particles of the categories PARTICLE VERBS SEPARATE and PARTICLES WITHOUT VERB ROOT. The meta-category ALL VERB PARTICLES OR PARTICLE VERBS contained all verb particles, regardless of whether they were produced separately or non-separately.

6.2.1 Calculating Word Frequency

For each category, the number of tokens as well as the number of types was computed. The token analysis is purely quantitative, while the type analysis gives information on how many different simplex verbs, verb particles, and particle verbs the mothers use (Choi 2000). Thus, the type analysis can also indicate the degree of lexical diversity in parental speech. Note that all inflected forms of a specific verb were counted as belonging to the same type. Due to the fact that some complex verbs, i.e. particle verbs, are morphologically separated in certain sentence structures (cf. Section 2), this means that a particle verb such as *aufmachen* (open.make, 'to open') was counted as belonging to the same type as all inflected variants, including *macht auf* (make open, 'to open') and *aufgemacht* (open.made, 'opened').[2]

Three matrixes were used to measure word frequency. First, we determined the total token frequency for each verb category across all sessions by dividing the number of tokens per category by the number of all utterances. Second, following Sandhofer et al. (2000), we determined the relative token frequency per session for each verb category by dividing the number of tokens of one category by the sum of all tokens of simplex verbs, complex verbs, and verb particles. The relative type frequency was determined in a parallel fashion. Third, we determined the type-token ratios per session for each category by dividing the number of types by the number of tokens of one category.

[2] Note that for the verb particle and particle verb subcategories, the type analysis is more complex than the token analysis. We could not simply add the number of types of two basic categories to arrive at the type number of the superordinate category: The separately counted verb types in the basic categories PARTICLE VERBS SEPARATE (e.g., *macht auf,* make open, 'open') and PARTICLE VERB NON-SEPARATE (e.g., *aufmachen*, open.make, 'open') were only one verb type in the category ALL PARTICLE VERBS (e.g., *auf+machen*, open + make). Instead we had to determine the number of types separately for each category. Furthermore, in the categories ALL SEPARATELY PRODUCED VERB PARTICLES the verb particles alone determined the particle type. Hence, a particle type in this category (e.g., *auf* 'open' or 'up') may label different events, as the verb root in the complex verb may differ (*aufmachen* 'open', *aufessen* 'eat up').

6.2.2 Calculating Word Order Variability

For the four basic categories SIMPLEX VERBS, PARTICLE VERBS NON-SEPARATE, SEPARATE VERB PARTICLE IN PARTICLE VERBS, and VERB PARTICLES WITHOUT VERB ROOT we counted the occurrences of the verb or the verb particle, respectively across the eight spontaneous speech samples of the three mothers. We distinguished (a), following the surface perspective, between the three positions 'sentence initial', 'sentence final', and 'sentence medial', and (b) following the structural perspective, between V2 and VE (and *prefield*). In Table 3 examples from the spontaneous speech corpus are given for the four verbal categories and the classification regarding the surface sentence position.

Table 3 Examples of verb occurrences in the spontaneous speech samples from a surface perspective

Surface sentence position	SIMPLEX VERBS	PARTICLE VERBS NON-SEPARATE	SEPARATE VERB PARTICLE IN PARTICLE VERBS	VERB PARTICLES WITHOUT VERB ROOT
Initial	*hol* den ball (A14) 'fetch the ball'	*aufessen* die mama[a] (M14) 'the mum eats up'	n.a.	*rein* da (M14) 'in there'
Medial	wir *nehmen* den schuh (A16) 'we take the shoe'	soll ich die Tür *aufmachen* für dich (A14) 'shall I open the door for you'	*mach* mal fein wieder *rauf* da (T14) 'put on there'	soll das *rauf* auf dein brötchen (A18) 'shall this onto your bread roll'
	was sie *sagen* könnte (M20) 'what she could say'			
	und er is *gekrabbelt* zu unserem Standtelefon (T14) 'and he crawled to our telephone'			
Final	milch kannst du *trinken* (A18) 'you can drink milk'	jetzt nicht die tür *zumachen* (A14) 'don't close the door now'	*mach* mal *rein* (M14) 'put in'	wieder *ab* (M20) 'off again'
				weg (M20) 'away'
	wenn du hier *spielst* (A16) 'if you play here'			

[a] Note that this ungrammatical structure – a particle verb in sentence initial position – is the only one attested in this corpus.

In Table 4 examples from the spontaneous speech corpus are given for the structural categories left and right sentence bracket as well as for the *prefield* which is highly marked.

Table 4 Examples of verb occurrences in the spontaneous speech samples from a structural perspective

Structural sentence position	SIMPLEX VERBS	PARTICLE VERBS NON-SEPARATE	SEPARATE VERB PARTICLE IN PARTICLE VERBS	VERB PARTICLES WITHOUT VERB ROOT
Prefield	*gegessen* hat er sie schon (T20) 'he did eat it, however'	*aufessen* die mama (M14) 'the mum eats up'	n.a.	*rein* da (M14) 'in there'
Left sentence bracket	*hol* den ball (A14) 'fetch the ball'	n.a.	n.a	n.a
	wir *nehmen* den schuh (A16) 'we take the shoe'			
Right sentence bracket	was sie *sagen* könnte (M20) 'what she could say'	soll ich die Tür *aufmachen* für dich (A14) 'shall I open the door for you'	*mach* mal fein wieder *rauf* da (T14) 'put on there'	soll das *rauf* auf dein brötchen (A18) 'shall this onto your bread roll'
	milch kannst du *trinken* (A18) 'you can drink milk'	jetzt nicht die tür *zumachen* (A14) 'don't close the door now'	*mach* mal *rein* (M14) 'put in'	wieder *ab* (M20) 'off again'
	wenn du hier *spielst* (A16) 'if you play here'			*weg* (M20) 'away'

With regard to the morphologically complex predicates, we focused on the position of the verb particle as this verbal element rather than the verb root is produced first by the children. Therefore, for the category PARTICLE VERBS NON-SEPARATE a final position means that the whole complex verb is situated in the final position with the verb root following the verb particle. In contrast, for the SEPARATE PARTICLES in PARTICLE VERBS the classification as final corresponds to the verb particle only. In addition, single word utterances consisting of a verb particle, a particle verb, or a simplex verb were classified as 'sentence final' as well.

6.3 Predictions

Recall that there are two empirical facts about children's early verb acquisition in German that have to be accounted for. First, German-speaking children log into the verb lexicon using verb particles rather than simplex verbs or particle verbs. Second, the first verb particles used by children learning German belong to the class of telic verb particles (see Section 4). Following the hypothesis proposed for the input factor 'word frequency', the following two predictions can be derived. Note that for the semantic analysis necessary for testing P2, we examined the 10 verb particles and particle verbs used most frequently by the mothers and classified them as telic or non-telic, applying the semantic tests employed by Dowty (1979).

Prediction 1 (P1): The frequency of particle verbs and verb particles in the parental input should be higher than the frequency of simplex verbs, where frequency is measured via types, tokens, or the type-token-ration.

Prediction 2 (P2): There should be more telic than non-telic verb particles or particle verbs in the parental input.

Regarding the input factor 'word order variability', recall that in standard German simplex verbs are syntactically more variable than verb particles that predominantly appear in the same position (see Section 2). If parents use verb particles and simplex verbs in their speech to 1-year-olds in the same way as suggested by this characterization, the following prediction can be derived:

Prediction 3 (P3): In the parental input verb particles and particle verbs occur in fewer different positions than simplex verbs, where position can be analysed from a surface or a structural perspective.

6.4 Results

The analysis of the parental input was based on 5,001 utterances across the eight spontaneous speech samples. Section 6.4.1 contains the results regarding the effect of word frequency, and Section 6.4.2 presents the results regarding the input factor word order variability.

6.4.1 Results for Word Frequency

As demonstrated in Fig. 1, 62% of the utterances contained a full verb or a verb particle. The total token frequencies reveal that 39% of the utterances contained a simplex verb and only 19% a particle verb. Verb particles without a verb root accounted for 3% of the utterances. Other complex verbs like *kaputtmachen* (broken.make, 'to break') were only found in 1% of the utterances and were not taken into account in the subsequent analyses.

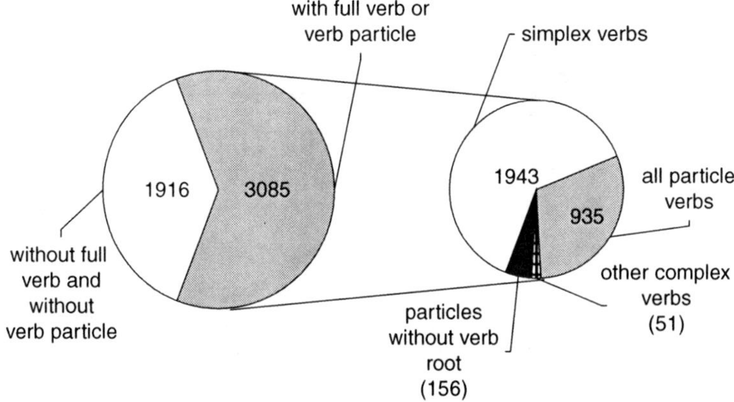

Fig. 1 Total token frequencies in parental utterances, $n = 5{,}001$ utterances (8 samples)

We also examined whether there were any differences in the parental verb category use depending on the children's age. The relative token frequencies per age (i.e. at 14, 16, 18 and 20 months) revealed no changes depending on the child's age. For all child ages, we found that the children's mothers produced nearly twice as many simplex verb tokens as particle verb tokens and very few verb particles. The relative type frequencies revealed that the degree of lexical diversity remained stable with regard to age. Therefore, in the subsequent analyses the factor 'child age' was not taken into account.

Verb Particles/Particle Verbs Versus Simplex Verbs

Prediction 1 (P1) states that the word frequency of verb particles and particle verbs in the parental input is higher than the word frequency of simplex verbs. In order to test (P1), we compared the frequencies of verbs and verb particles in the spontaneous speech of the three mothers. First, we examined whether individual differences exist with regard to the mothers' verb category use. As can be seen in Fig. 2, the mothers' input showed a very similar profile in each sample. Simplex verbs were used twice as often as particle verbs; verb particles without the verb root were used in about 5% of the utterances. Therefore, all input data were subsequently analyzed together.

Relative token frequencies: The relative token frequencies of the basic categories (see Table 5) and meta-categories (see Table 6) show a distribution that is similar to the total token frequencies reported in Fig. 1. The children were exposed to nearly twice as many simplex verbs as verb particles or particle verbs. The Friedman test indicated a highly significant effect of verb category ($\chi_r^2 = 22.200$, $p < 0.001$). A pair-wise comparison, using the Wilcoxon test, confirmed that the relative token frequency of simplex verbs in the input was significantly higher than the relative token frequency of verb particles or particle verbs ($Z = -2.521$, $p < 0.05$). In other words, among all utterances

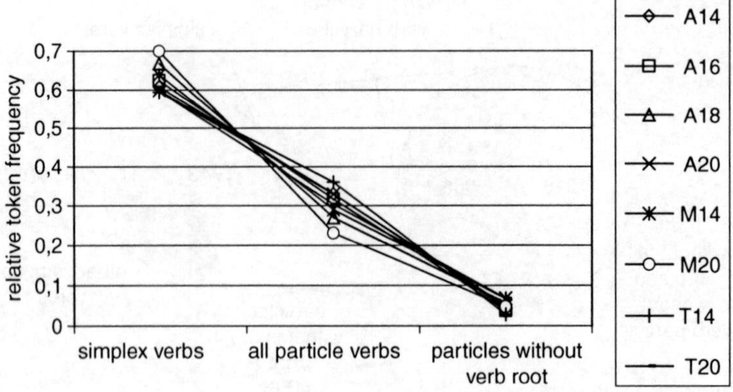

Fig. 2 Relative token frequency in parental input per transcript, $n = 8$ samples

with a full verb or a verb particle there were significantly more simplex verbs than verb particles or particle verbs.

Relative type frequencies: As shown in Tables 5 and 6, the mothers used nearly the same number of simplex verb types as separate or non-separate verb particle and particle verb types. The Friedman test showed a highly significant effect of verb category ($\chi_r^2 = 22.200$, $p < 0.001$). A pair wise

Table 5 Basic verb categories: Relative token frequency, relative type frequency, and TTR in parental input by means (standard deviation), $n = 8$ samples

Basic category	Tokens M (S.D.)	Types M (S.D.)	TTR M (S.D.)
SIMPLEX VERBS	0.63 (0.04)	0.47 (0.03)	0.34 (0.04)
PARTICLE VERBS NON-SEPARATE	0.14 (0.02)	0.23 (0.03)	0.75 (0.11)
PARTICLE VERBS SEPARATE	0.16 (0.03)	0.21 (0.03)	0.60 (0.08)
VERB PARTICLES WITHOUT VERB ROOT	0.05 (0.01)	0.06 (0.02)	0.50 (0.07)
OTHER COMPLEX VERBS	0.02 (0.01)	0.03 (0.01)	0.66 (0.19)

Table 6 Selected Meta-categories: Relative token frequency, relative type frequency, and TTR in parental input by means (standard deviation), $n = 8$ samples

Meta-category	Tokens M (S.D.)	Types M (S.D.)	TTR M (S.D.)
PARTICLE VERBS (PARTICLE VERBS NON-SEPERATE + PARTICLE VERBS SEPERATE)	0.30 (0.04)	0.39 (0.03)	0.57 (0.05)
ALL SEPARATELY PRODUCED VERB PARTICLES (PARTICLE VERBS SEPERATE + VERB PARTICLES WITHOUT VERB ROOT)	0.21 (0.04)	0.13 (0.01)	0.28 (0.05)
ALL VERB PARTICLES OR PARTICLE VERBS (PARTICLE VERBS NON-SEPERATE + PARTICLE VERBS SEPERATE + VERB PARTICLES WITHOUT VERB ROOT)	0.35 (0.04)	0.44 (0.03)	0.56 (0.05)

comparison using the Wilcoxon test indicated no significant difference in the relative type frequencies of simplex verbs and of verb particles or particle verbs ($Z = 2.521$, $p = 0.167$). However, when comparing the category ALL PARTICLE VERBS with the category SIMPLEX VERBS, the statistical analysis revealed that mothers produced more simplex verb types than verb particle types ($Z = -2.521$, $p < 0.05$).

Type-token ratios: The type-token ratios of each category were determined in order to examine whether an individual verb particle or particle verb occurs more often in the mothers' spontaneous speech than an individual simplex verb. Recall that the lower the TTR, the more often an individual word type is repeated in a specific data sample. The Friedman test revealed a highly significant effect of verb category ($\chi_r^2 = 22.950$, $p < 0.001$). A pair wise comparison using the Wilcoxon test indicated that the mothers of the three typically developing children repeated an individual simplex verb significantly more often than an individual verb particle or particle verb ($Z = 2.521$, $p < 0.05$). The mean TTR of simplex verbs was 0.34 (see Table 5), compared to a TTR of 0.56 for verb particles and particle verbs (see Table 6). However, when comparing the TTR of the category ALL SEPARATELY PRODUCED VERB PARTICLES with the TTR of SIMPLEX VERBS, a different result was achieved. The mothers produced an individual verb particle (TTR = 0.28) significantly more often than an individual simplex verb, $Z = -2.521$, $p < 0.05$. Recall that in the category ALL SEPARATELY PRODUCED VERB PARTICLES, a particle type was counted independently from the verb root, e.g., the particle *auf* 'open' could belong to *machen auf* 'to open' as well as to *essen auf* 'to eat up'. Thus, the number in this category does not refer to actual particle verbs, but to specific verb particles.

Telic Versus Atelic Verb Particles/Particle Verbs

Prediction 2 (P2) states that there are more telic than non-telic verb particles or particle verbs in the input. Using the tests for determining telicity in Dowty (1979), we determined the semantic type of the 10 most frequently uttered verb particles or particle verbs in the mothers' spontaneous speech. As illustrated in Fig. 3, telic verb types occurred more often than non-telic verb types in each category.

The particle verb structures that the mothers produced most often were *herkommen* (here.come, 'to come here') and *kommen her* (come here, 'to come here'). The most frequently used verb particle without a verb root was *weg* 'off'. In sum, the particle verbs and the verb particles the children most often heard in the input were telic.

6.4.2 Word Order Variability

Following the Word Order Variability Hypothesis, prediction 3 (P3) stated that in the parental input verb particles and particle verbs should occur in fewer

Fig. 3 Total token frequency of the 10 most frequent verb particle and particle verb types in parental input, $n = 5{,}001$ utterances (8 samples)

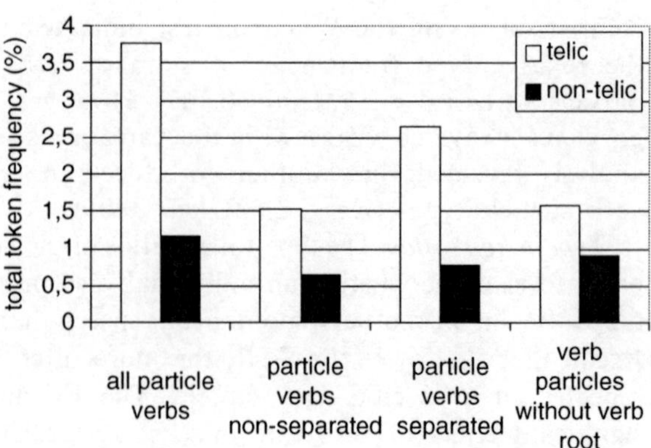

different positions than simplex verbs. To examine the variation both from the surface and from the structural perspective, we counted the number of occurrences of simplex verb, particle verb and verb particle tokens across the eight spontaneous speech samples in two ways. Table 7 shows the raw numbers and the percentile distribution in each of the verb categories across the three surface sentence positions initial, medial, and final.

Table 7 Number of occurrences (n) and percentile distribution (%) of simplex verb, particle verb and verb particle tokens in different surface sentence positions across the 8 samples

Sentence position	SIMPLEX VERBS n (%)	PARTICLE VERBS NON-SEPARATE n (%)	VERB PARTICLES IN PARTICLE VERBS SEPARATE n (%)	VERB PARTICLES WITHOUT VERB ROOT n (%)
Initial	390 (20%)	1 (0.002%)	0	5 (3%)
Medial	646 (33%)	72 (17%)	39 (8%)	10 (6%)
Final	907 (47%)	362 (83%)	460 (92%)	141 (90%)
Total	1,943 (100%)	435 (100%)	499 (100%)	156 (100%)

From a surface perspective the data shows that of the 1,943 occurrences of simplex verb tokens in the parental input simplex verbs were mostly produced in sentence final position (47%). They were also frequently used in medial (33%) and sentence initial position (20%). The main share of the 435 non-separated particle verb tokens occurred in sentence final position (83%). Seventeen percent were produced in medial sentence positions. There was one occurrence in sentence initial position (*aufmachen die mama* (M14) see also Table 3), a sentence structure which is ungrammatical in Standard German. Of the 499 separately produced particle verb tokens there were no verb particles produced in sentence initial position.

The main share of these particles was produced in sentence final position (92%), while 8% were used in sentence medial position. Particles without a verb root were also mostly produced in sentence final position (90%); only 6% of the 156 particle tokens were produced in sentence medial position and 3% in sentence initial position.

Let us turn to the structural perspective. Table 8 shows the raw numbers and the percentile distribution in each of the verb categories across the possible structural positions.

Table 8 Number of occurrences (*n*) and percentile distribution (%) of simplex verb, particle verb and verb particle tokens in different structural sentence positions across the 8 samples

Structural sentence position	SIMPLEX VERBS *n* (%)	PARTICLE VERBS NON-SEPARATE *n* (%)	VERB PARTICLES IN PARTICLE VERBS SEPARATE *n* (%)	VERB PARTICLES WITHOUT VERB ROOT *n* (%)
Prefield	2 (0.001%)	1 (0.002%)	0	2 (1%)
Left sentence bracket	1,078 (55%)	0	0	0
Right sentence bracket	863 (44%)	434 (99%)	499 (100%)	154 (99%)
Total	1,943 (100%)	435 (100%)	499 (100%)	156 (100%)

As can be seen in Table 8, simplex verbs frequently appear in the left sentence bracket (55%) as well as in the right sentence bracket (44%). In contrast, as the structural position of the verb particle in particle verbs is grammatically restricted they almost always appear in the right sentence bracket in the categories particle verbs non-separate (99%), verb particles in particle verbs (100%) and verb particles without a verb root. Less than 1% of the simplex verbs were produced in the *prefield* which also contains only the ungrammatical non-separate particle verb occurrence (see above) and 1% of the verb particles without a verb root.

Unlike simplex verbs verb particles can appear in three different morpho-syntactic environments (i.e. in non-separated particle verbs, separated particle verbs, and as verb particles without verb root). Thus, in order to compare the word order variability of simplex verbs and verb particles in a different way, in a second analysis all occurrences of verb particles were combined. Figure 4 illustrates the variability of occurrences of simplex verbs across the different surface positions compared to the occurrences of verb particles.

The graph in Fig. 4 shows that in the parental input simplex verbs are used in more different surface sentence positions than are verb particles. Although both simplex verbs and verb particles occur most often in sentence final position, simplex verbs are also frequently used in sentence medial position and to a considerable amount in sentence initial position. Figure 5 illustrates the

Fig. 4 Variability of occurrences of simplex verbs and verb particles across different surface sentence positions

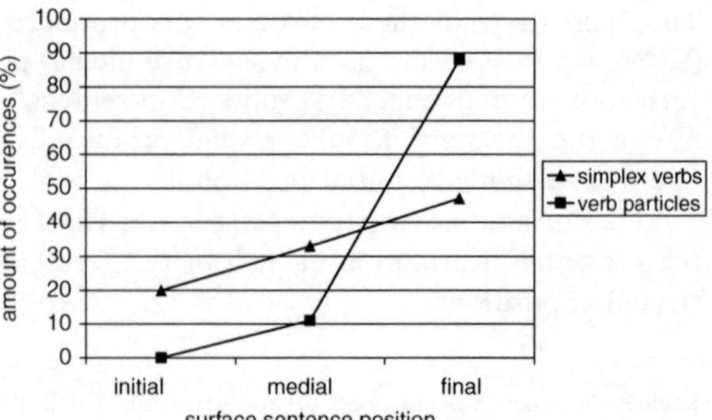

variability of occurrences of simplex verbs across the different structural positions compared to the occurrences of verb particles (i.e. of non-separated particle verbs, separated particle verbs, and particles without verb root).

As can be seen from Fig. 5, in concordance with the structural restrictions described in Section 2, almost all verb particles are attested to occur in the right sentence bracket (and only one in the *prefield*), while simplex verbs are attested in the left and the right sentence bracket, with a light predominance of the left sentence bracket. In sum, in the parental input studied here verb particles show limited word order variability, while simplex verbs show a greater diversity of sentence positions. This difference is more prominent in the structural than the surface analysis.

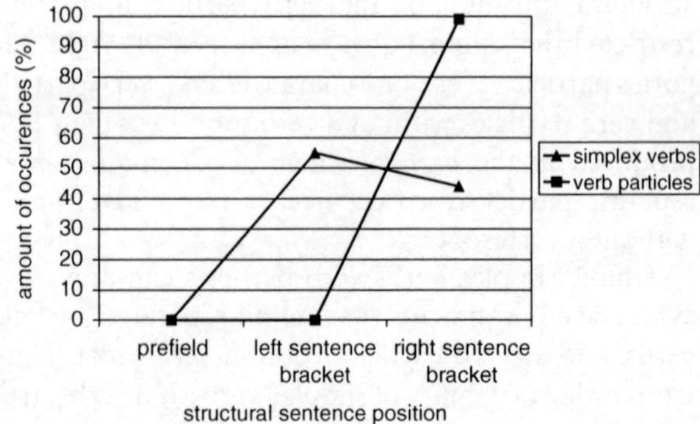

Fig. 5 Variability of occurrences of simplex verbs and verb particles across different structural sentence positions

7 Discussion

This study was designed to test the research questions of whether word frequency and word order variability of verb expressions in the input matter in the early acquisition of simplex verbs and verb particles by German-speaking children. The input factors 'word frequency' and 'word order variability' will be discussed in turn.

In order to test prediction 1 (P1) derived from the Frequency Hypothesis, word frequency was calculated in three different ways: token, types, and type-token ratio. First, let us consider the results from the token analysis. Contrary to prediction, the token frequency of verb particles and particle verbs in the parental input was lower than the token frequency of simplex verbs. In fact, the mothers produced significantly more simplex verb tokens than verb particle or particle verb tokens, while in children's speech verb particles generally occur before simplex verbs and are used more frequently than simplex verbs. Thus, word frequency measured via token cannot explain the early verb acquisition in German-speaking infants. Naigles and Hoff-Ginsberg (1998) hypothesized that the more frequently a verb occurs in the parental speech, the more likely a child is to produce it several weeks later. Our design did not allow for a direct test of this hypothesis. However, since mothers' verb use was constant across the child's age (cf. Fig. 2), we can infer that this hypothesis is not confirmed for the verb acquisition order in German.

Next, let us turn to the type frequency in the parental speech. According to the Frequency Hypothesis, the type frequency of verb particles and particle verbs in the parental input should be higher than the type frequency of simplex verbs. However, the results from a type frequency analysis are not compatible with prediction 1 either. Although the children listened to a similar amount of verb particle, particle verb, and simplex verb types, they produced verb particles earlier and more frequently than simplex verbs. This result stands in contrast to the finding reported in Section 5 that a high number of noun types relative to a low number of verb types gives rise to the early noun bias in English-speaking children. Therefore, it can be argued that type frequency is not a causal factor in early verb acquisition.[3]

Third, let us examine the results for the type-token ration. Sandhofer et al. (2000) argued that a low TTR, corresponding to many repetitions of one type of verb, favours verb acquisition. Consequently, it was predicted that the TTR for verb particles and particle verbs is lower than the TTR for simplex verbs. Contrary to this prediction, the TTR for simplex verbs was significantly lower than the TTR for verb particles and particle verbs. In other words, the mothers of the three typically developing children repeated an individual simplex verb significantly more often than an individual verb particle or particle verb. However, when comparing the TTR of the category ALL SEPARATELY PRODUCED VERB PARTICLES with the TTR of SIMPLEX VERBS, it was found that the mothers produced a specific verb particle significantly more often than a specific simplex verb. The latter result seems to provide partial support for the Frequency Hypothesis. However, note that this finding directly follows from the German

[3] Note, moreover, that type analyses have also been criticized on principled grounds. Richards and Malvern (1996), for example, pointed out that the number of types varies depending on the size of the language corpus.

verb particle inventory. In German, a limited number of verb particles can be combined with different verb roots to form a wide range of different particle verbs. In other words, the number of simplex verbs itself is much higher than the number of verb particles. It is therefore not surprising that mothers used few verb particles in combination with various verb roots repeatedly and more often than specific simplex verbs. Nevertheless, the frequent repetition of specific verb particle types in the input could favour their early acquisition in 1-year-old children and hence provide evidence that input factors influence the acquisition of different verb categories. Note, however, that the verb particles used by the mothers most frequently (i.e. *her* 'here', *hin* 'there', *rein* 'in', *weg* 'off') differed from those initially produced by their children (i.e. *auf* 'open', *ab* 'off', *aus* 'off', *an* 'on', *zu* 'closed'). Thus, the language learner, while being sensitive to categories such as 'verb particle', must clearly employ additional strategies in building her productive verb lexicon. In previous work we suggested the language driven mechanism of endstate-orientation (cf. Section 4).

In sum, with regard to the three methods of input analysis carried out in the present study, neither the type nor the token analysis nor the calculation of the TTR satisfyingly explained the order of acquisition of verb particles, particle verbs, and simplex verbs in children's speech and the composition of the early verb lexicon.

Now let us turn to the semantic analysis. As children initially prefer telic over atelic particles, following the Frequency Hypothesis it was predicted (P2) that there should be more telic than non-telic verb particles and particle verbs in the input. This prediction was born out. However, it should be taken into account that we classified only the 10 most frequent verb particles and particle verbs in the input. A further note of caution concerns the specific telic verb particles used by mothers and children. As mentioned above, the mothers used other telic verb particles than those initially preferred by the children. Thus, in line with the argumentation above regarding the TTR, it remains to be explained why the children produced other verb particles than the ones they most frequently heard in the input.

Let us now turn to the input factor 'word order variability'. According to the Variable Word Order Hypothesis it was predicted that verb particles show less syntactic variation than simplex verbs in the parental input (P3) and are therefore favoured in language acquisition. Two methods of analysis were used: calculating surface and structural sentence positions. From a surface perspective we determined the verb occurrences in sentence initial, medial, and final position. The results show that verb particles appeared in nearly 90% of the cases in sentence final position. They almost never appeared in sentence initial and rarely in sentence medial position. In contrast, simplex verbs were frequently used in sentence final, medial, and initial position. Thus, the three mothers under investigation used verb particles much more invariable than simplex verbs across the different surface sentence positions confirming prediction 3. The prominence of verb particles in children's early verb lexicon also supports the assumption that the sentence final position – that verb particles most often appear in – is salient (e.g. Tardif et al. 1997). Note, however, as detailed in Section 2 that the notion of sentence positions such as 'final' is by far uncontroversial. First, the classification of verb particles according to their sentence position did not take into account the presence of a verb root. Therefore, the label 'sentence final' included verb particles that are affixed to the verb root as well as separated verb particles and verb particles without verb root. Sentence final particle verbs such as *aufmacht* 'opens' or *aufisst* 'eats up' may well be perceived differently by a child than a verb particle in sentence final position such as *auf* 'up'. Second, even if the child is able to identify sentence final verb particle structures such as *aufisst* 'eats up' and *isst ... auf* 'eats ... up' as morpho-syntactic variants of the same verb, she still has to realize that the same particle can be affixed to many different verb roots giving rise to a range of verbs including *aufisst* 'eats up', *aufmacht* 'opens', *aufsteht* 'gets up', *aufhört* 'stops', and *auftaucht* 'appears'. Third, the notion 'sentence final', disregards the internal syntactic structure of a sentence, as for example characterized by the topological field model.

In our structural analysis we determined the verb occurrences according to the topological field model, i.e. the left sentence bracket, the right sentence bracket (and the *prefield*). We found that verb particles appeared to 99% in the right sentence bracket and to less than 1% in the *prefield*. In concordance with the structural restrictions described in Section 2 they never appeared in the left sentence bracket. Hence, the difference in the syntactic variability between simplex verbs and verb particles is even more prominent than in the surface analysis. Verb particles show less syntactic variation than simplex verbs in the parental input. These results confirm the Variable Word Order Hypothesis.

Taken together, our results confirm that pure frequency measures of the input provided by the three mothers under investigation cannot sufficiently explain the acquisition order of the different verb categories observed in their 1- to-2-year-old children. The invariant word order of verb particles, on the other hand, was shown to favour their early acquisition.

8 Summary and Conclusion

This study addressed the question of whether input factors such as word frequency and word order variability matter in the early verb acquisition in German-speaking children. Based on the Frequency Hypothesis, it was predicted that the word frequency of verb particles and particle verbs in the parental input is higher than the word frequency of simplex verbs (P1) and that there are more telic than non-telic verb particles or particle verbs in the input (P2). Based on the Word Order Variability Hypothesis, it was predicted that verb particles and particle verbs occur in fewer different positions than simplex verbs.

Regarding word frequency in the input, prediction 2, but not prediction 1 was confirmed. The results of our study revealed that the order of verb acquisition and the composition of the verb lexicon in 1- to 2-year-olds is independent of simple word frequency, i.e. total token, relative token and type frequency, in parental input. With regard to the type-token ratio, we found partial evidence for the Input Hypothesis as an individual verb particle was repeated more often in the input than an individual simplex verb. However, since children initially produced different verb particle types than the ones occurring in the input, this result provides no support for a causal role of word frequency in verb learning. Similarly, even though mothers used more telic than non-telic verb particles or particle verbs in the input, the specific items used did not match the verb particles initially preferred by the children. Children, while being predominantly exposed to simplex verbs, log into the verb lexicon with telic particles like *auf* 'open' and *ab* 'off', a strategy that is compatible with the endstate-orientation (cf. Section 4).

Concerning word order variability in the input the advantage of an invariant word order for verb particles was confirmed. This difference was stronger for the structural than for the surface analysis. Note that this finding is in line with the constraints for verb and particle occurrences in standard German supplied by the target language. Thus, while simplex verbs frequently occur in V2 and VE structures, verb particles predominantly occur in the right sentence bracket and are hence syntactically more invariant. Note that this learning mechanism goes beyond the environment-driven processes as classified by Behrend (1995) and shows more parallels with what Behrend calls language-driven learning mechanisms.

In sum, our findings provide first evidence that input, calculated via simple frequency measures does not play a major role in the acquisition of verb order and the composition of the verb lexicon in 1- to 2-year-olds learning German, while restricted variability can account for children's early preference of verb particles. More specifically, the little syntactic variation in the input attested for verb particles that predominantly occur in the right sentence bracket seems to favour the early production of verb particles in children's spontaneous speech. Importantly, the structural position does not necessarily coincide with the sentence final position that has been assumed to be more salient than sentence medial positions. Therefore, it was argued that even though word order variability has been regarded as an input factor, once structural characteristics of the target language are taken into account, word order variability can be seen as a language-driven mechanism. In this respect, the results of this study provide a new account of the composition and acquisition of children's early verb lexicon that can be regarded as an alternative to the language-driven account of early verb acquisition, the strategy of endstate-orientation (Schulz et al. 2001, 2002, Penner et al. 2003) suggested in our previous studies. Recall that according to this learning strategy, German-speaking children initially focus on the verb's event-semantic structure and follow an endstate-orientation in acquiring the verbs' meanings. When learning languages that provide verb particles children start with telic particles rather than with full verbs, since telic particles encode the event-semantic type 'Endstate' most transparently. They specifically favour telic particles of particle verbs with a light verb as the verb root as it does not contribute to the meaning of the complex verb. Note that only the latter account can explain why children start out with particles such as *auf* 'open', *ab* 'off', *aus* 'off', *an* 'on' and *zu* 'closed', and not with particles like *her* 'here', *hin* 'there', *rein* 'in' and *weg* 'gone'. The corresponding particle verbs are primarily *herkommen* 'come here', *hingehen* 'go there', *reingehen* 'go into' and *weggehen* 'go away' and do not encode the endstate as transparently as *aufmachen* 'open', *abmachen* 'untake', *ausmachen* 'put out', *anmachen* 'put on' and *zumachen* 'close'. Future research with a wider range of parental data is needed to see whether this observation can be generalized.

Acknowledgments This chapter is based on the first author's diploma thesis and is part of the project 'Language production and language comprehension' within the research group German Language Development (GLAD), supported by the German Research Foundation (DFG, FOR 381) and the Max Planck Institute for Human Cognitive and Brain Sciences Leipzig. Portions of this work were presented at the conference on 'Emergence of linguistic abilities' (ELA) 2005, the GLOW (2007) Acquisition Workshop 'Optionality in the input', and at the University of Frankfurt. We are very grateful for the comments and suggestions from the audiences at these presentations. Furthermore, we like to thank Anne Ballhorn, Anja Kersten, Anja Müller, Katalin Sebestyen und Ramona Wenzel for their help in collecting the spontaneous speech data and Sybille Reif for help with the analysis of the child data.

References

Behrend, Douglas A. 1995. Processes involved in the initial mapping of verb meanings. In *Beyond names for things*, eds. Michael Tomasello and William E. Merriman, 251–273. Hillsdale: Lawrence Erlbaum.

Behrens, Heike. 1998. How difficult are complex verbs? Evidence from German, Dutch and English. *Linguistics* 36: 679–712.

Brown, Roger. 1958. How shall a thing be called? *Psychological Review* 65: 14–21.

Choi, Soonja. 2000. Caregiver input in English and Korean: use of nouns and verbs in book-reading and toy-play contexts. *Journal of Child Language* 27: 69–96.

Comrie, Bernard. 1976. *Aspect*. Cambridge: Cambridge University Press.

Dowty, David R. 1979. *Word meaning and Montague grammar*. Dordrecht: Reidel.

Gentner, Dedre. 1978. On relational meaning: The acquisition of verb meaning. *Child Development* 49: 988–998.

Gentner, Dedre. 1982. Why nouns are learned before verbs: Linguistic relativity versus natural partitioning. In *Language development, Vol. 2 Language, thought, and culture*, ed. Stan A. Kuczaj, 301–339. Hillsdale: Lawrence Erlbaum.

Goldfield, Beverly. A. 1993. Noun bias in maternal speech to one-year-olds. *Journal of Child Language* 20: 85–99.

Golinkoff, Roberta M., Kathy Hirsh-Pasek, and Melissa A. Schweisguth. 2001. In *Approaches to bootstrapping: phonological, lexical, syntactic and neuropsychological aspects of early language acquisition*, vol. 1, eds. Jürgen Weissenborn and Barbara Höhle, 167–294. Amsterdam: John Benjamins Publishing.

Haider, Hubert. 1995. *Studies on phrase structure and economy*. Stuttgart: Universität Stuttgart, Institut für Linguistik.

Höhle, Tilman N. 1986. Der Begriff 'Mittelfeld', Anmerkungen über die Theorie der topologischen Felder. In *Akten des VII. Kongresses der Internationalen Vereinigung für germanische Sprach- und Literaturwissenschaft. Göttingen 1985*, eds. Walter Weiss, Herbert E. Wiegand, and Marga Reis, 329–340. Tübingen: Max Niemeyer.

Hoff, Erika, and Letitia R. Naigles. 2002. How children use input to acquire a lexicon. *Child Development* 73: 418–433.

Huttenlocher, Janellen, Wendy Haight, Anthony Bryk, Michael Seltzer, and Thomas Lyons. 1991. Early vocabulary growth: Relation to language, input and gender. *Developmental Psychology* 27: 236–248.

Jeschull, Liane. 2007. The pragmatics of telicity and what children make of it. In *Proceedings of the 2nd Conference on Generative Approaches to Language Acquisition North America*, eds. Alyona Belikova, Luisa Meroni and Mari Umeda, 180–187. Somerville: Cascadilla Proceedings Project.

Kauschke, Christina. 2000. *Der Erwerb des frühkindlichen Lexikons: Eine empirische Studie zur Entwicklung des Wortschatzes im Deutschen*. Tübingen: Gunter Narr.

Kieburg, Anja. 2005. *Die Rolle des sprachlichen Inputs beim Erwerb von Verbpartikeln und Simplexverben im zweiten Lebensjahr: Eine Analyse der Wortfrequenz*. Unpublished Diploma Thesis, University of Potsdam.

Kieburg, Anja, and Schulz, Petra. 2008. The role of parental input in early verb acquisition: Evidence from child German. In *Emergence of linguistic abilities: From gestures to grammar*, eds. Sophie Kern, Frédérique Gayraud and Egidio Marsico, 237–260. Cambridge: Cambridge Scholars Publishing.

Koster, Jan. 1975. Dutch as an SOV Language. *Linguistic Analysis* 1: 111–136.

Krifka, Manfred. 1989. Nominal reference, temporal constitution, and quantification in event semantics. In *Semantics and contextual expression*, eds. Renate Bartsch, Johan F. A. K. van Benthem and Peter van Emde Boas, 75–115. Dordrecht: Foris.

Lüdeling, Anke. 2001. *On particle verbs and similar constructions in German*. Stanford: CSLI Publications.

Mills, Ann E. 1985. The acquisition of German. In *The cross-linguistic study of language acquisition. Vol. I: The data*, ed. Dan I. Slobin, 141–254. Hillsdale: Erlbaum.

Pearson, Barbara. Z., Maria. C. Fernandez, Vanessa L. Lewedag, and D. Kimbrough Oller. 1997. The relation of input factors to lexical learning by bilingual learning infants. *Applied Psycholinguistics* 18: 41–58.

Naigles, Letitia R., and Erika Hoff-Ginsberg. 1998. Why are some verbs learned before other verbs? Effects of input frequency and structure on children's early verb use. *Journal of Child Language* 25: 95–120.

Penner, Zvi, Petra Schulz, and Karin Wymann. 2003. Learning the meaning of verbs: What distinguishes language-impaired from normally developing children? *Linguistics* 41: 289–319.

Pinker, Steven 1984. *Language learnability and language development*. Cambridge: Harvard University Press.

Pustejovsky, James. 1995. *The generative lexikon*. Cambridge: MIT Press.

Richards, Brian J., and David D. Malvern. 1996. Swedish verb morphology in language impaired children: Interpreting the type-token ratios. *Logopedics, Phoniatrics, Vocology* 21: 109–111.

Sandhofer, Cathrine M., Linda B. Smith, and Jun Luo. 2000. Counting nouns and verbs in the input: Differential frequencies, different kinds of learning? *Journal of Child Language* 27: 561–585.

Schulz, Petra. 2003. *Frühes Verblernen als Prädikator für Wortschatz- und Grammatikentwicklung*. Paper presented at the Research Colloquium of the SFB 538, "Mehrsprachigkeit" at the University of Hamburg, Hamburg.

Schulz, Petra. 2005. *Are children's first event expressions telic? Evidence from child German.* Paper presented at the X. Conference of the International Association for the Study of Child Language (IASCL), Berlin.

Schulz, Petra, and Ose, Julia. 2008. *Semantics and pragmatics in the acquisition of telicity.* Paper presented at the 29th Annual Conference of the Deutsche Gesellschaft für Sprachwissenschaft DGfS, Bamberg.

Schulz, Petra, Zvi Penner, and Karin Wymann. 2002. Comprehension of resultative verbs in normally developing and language impaired German children. In *Investigations in clinical phonetics and linguistics*, eds. Fay Windsor, M. Louise Kelly and Nigel Hewlett, 115–129. Mahwah: Lawrence Erlbaum.

Schulz, Petra, Karin Wymann, and Zvi Penner. 2001. The early acquisition of verb meaning in German by normally developing and language impaired children. *Brain and Language* 77: 407–418.

Tardif, Twila, Marilyn Shatz, and Letitia Naigles. 1997. Caregiver speech and children's use of nouns versus verbs: A comparison of English, Italian and Mandarin. *Journal of Child Language* 24: 535–566.

Tomasello, Michael 2000. Do young children have adult syntactic competence? *Cognition* 74, 209–253.

Tomasello, Michael 2003. *Constructing a language: A usage-based theory of language acquisition.* Cambridge: Harvard University Press.

Tracy, Rosemarie. 1991. *Sprachliche Strukturentwicklung.* Tübingen: Narr.

Weissenborn, Jürgen. 1994. Constraining the child's grammar: Local wellformedness in the development of verb movement in German and French. In *Syntactic theory and language acquisition: Crosslinguistic perspectives. Vol. 1: Phrase structure*, eds. Barbara Lust, Margarita Suner and John Whitman, 273–287. Hillsdale: Lawrence Erlbaum.

Word Order in the Development of Dative Constructions: A Comparison of Cantonese and English

Chloe C. Gu

Abstract This chapter investigates the development of word order of dative constructions in English and Cantonese speaking children. Corpus data from English monolingual and Cantonese-English bilingual children show that the children who are late in producing English prepositional datives also use the preposition *to* with fewer meanings and structures. It is argued that the ambiguity of English *to* influences the development of English prepositional datives. In contrast, Cantonese does not have ambiguity in its dative marker, and Cantonese monolingual children acquire serial verb datives (similar to English prepositional datives) before double object datives, exhibiting a pattern that is the opposite of English children's. Also, it is shown that the order of emergence of different Cantonese dative constructions has a great impact on the acquisition of a language-specific inverted double object dative structure in Cantonese monolingual and bilingual children. Optionality per se does not slow down the development of a particular dative structure. Word order development in dative constructions is mainly affected by input ambiguity, and non-transparency in derivation also makes the Cantonese inverted double object datives difficult to acquire.

Keywords Dative constructions · Word order · Input ambiguity · Acquisition

1 Introduction

Dative constructions are one of the areas where word order variation and optionality are frequently observed both within language and cross-linguistically. The direct object and the indirect object in a dative construction can be presented in different orders and structures. In English, there are two argument realization patterns for dative verbs. The double object dative (DOD) (1a) puts the goal DP ('Mary') before the theme DP ('a book'), and the prepositional

C.C. Gu (✉)
University of Massachusetts Amherst, Amherst, MA, USA
e-mail: cgu@linguist.umass.edu

M. Anderssen et al. (eds.), *Variation in the Input*, Studies in Theoretical Psycholinguistics 39, DOI 10.1007/978-90-481-9207-6_6,

dative (PD) (1b) puts the goal in a PP ('to Mary'), and the PP has to follow the theme DP in their linear order:

(1)	a.	John gave Mary a book.	(DOD)
	b.	John gave a book to Mary.	(PD)

(1a) and (1b) are syntactically different, as the direct object and the indirect object are positioned in different order/type of phrases. However, they are very close in meaning. In fact, English dative verbs that do not have Latinate origin can all participate in dative alternation, and both double object datives and prepositional datives are legitimate forms for such verbs. Thus, English-speaking children are confronted with two options based on the input of dative constructions.

For children acquiring other languages, the case can be quite different. For example, in Cantonese, there are dative constructions which look similar to English double object datives and prepositional datives, but there is also a third inverted double object dative construction (IDOD) which puts the theme and the goal in the reversed order of a double object dative (2).

(2)	Ngo5	bei2	zo2	jat1	zi1	bat1	keoi5	(IDOD)
	I	give	PERF	one	CL	pen	3sg	
	'I gave a pen to him/her.'							

Plus, in Cantonese, each dative verb can only appear in one type of dative constructions. For example, for *bei2* ('give'), the inverted double object dative is the only legitimate form. Thus, children acquiring Cantonese are confronted with variation in word order and non-optionality in the corresponding form in the acquisition of dative constructions.

The case becomes more complicated if a child is acquiring Cantonese and English simultaneously. In the bilingual first language acquisition literature, it is frequently observed that the development of certain constructions in one language is influenced by corresponding constructions in the other language (Paradis and Genesee 1996, Müller 1998, Yip and Matthews 2000, 2007, Müller and Hulk 2001, among others). It is very likely that Cantonese-English bilinguals will demonstrate some cross-linguistic influence in the acquisition of dative constructions.

In this chapter, I would like to examine the development of dative constructions in three groups of children: English monolinguals, Cantonese-English bilinguals and Cantonese monolinguals. The three groups together offer a more comprehensive perspective on the issue of word order in acquisition, optionality in the input, and developmental gap between syntactically related constructions. There are three basic questions to ask: (1) In what order do dative constructions emerge in each language for each group of children? (2) What delays the emergence of certain constructions? (3) Do the same factors hold for both monolinguals and bilinguals? By answering these questions, I would like to show that children regard both double object datives and prepositional datives as legitimate options for dative verbs in natural languages, and the developmental lag and non-target usages emerge based on language-particular reasons.

The basic acquisition pattern of the English dative construction in monolingual children can be found in previous studies such as Snyder and Stromswold (1997) and Viau (2006). I do not intend to study more children to enrich the data; rather, I use their results to analyze the delay of prepositional datives. For Cantonese-English bilinguals and Cantonese monolingual children, I investigate spontaneous corpus data of five bilingual children from age 1;3 to 3;6, and eight monolingual Cantonese children from age 1;7 to 3;8.

The results show that bilingual children exhibit a similar pattern in the development of English datives, but there is a much wider gap between their early double object datives and prepositional datives. It is found that bilingual children who have better mastery of different prepositional *to*s make faster progress in the acquisition of *to*-datives, and the same pattern is observed in monolingual children as well. This suggests that the ambiguity in *to* (and also *for*) influences children's development of prepositional datives.

Such ambiguity does not exist in Cantonese, and Cantonese monolingual children in general acquire serial verb datives (which is parallel to English prepositional datives) before they start to produce double object datives. Both monolingual and bilingual children produce more non-target *bei2*-double object datives than target inverted double object datives, but the monolinguals unlearn the non-target structures faster, and they are more likely to have linked the surface inverted order to the underlying serial verb dative structure.

The paper is organized as follows. Section 2 discusses the (il)legitimate word order options in English and Cantonese dative constructions. Section 3 summarizes previous work on the acquisition of English and Cantonese dative constructions. Section 4 presents the methodology and results of each group of children. Section 5 discusses various factors that affect the late development of dative constructions in each language. Section 6 summarizes this study.

2 Dative Constructions in English and Cantonese

As noted in Section 1, dative constructions in English and Cantonese share many similarities. Both languages have double object datives, and English prepositional datives are parallel to Cantonese serial verb dative constructions.

An example of Cantonese double object dative construction is given in (3). Only 'teach' class dative verbs can appear in this construction (Tang 1998).[1]

---

[1] Such verbs include *ceng2gaau3* 'to inquire', *gaau3* 'to teach', *haau2* 'to test', *kau4* 'to request', and *man6* 'to ask'.

(3) Ngo5 gaau3 keoi5 Gwong2dung1waa2 (**DOD**)
I teach 3sg Cantonese
'I teach him/her Cantonese.' (Tang 1998)

In Cantonese serial verb dative constructions (SVD), the goal (indirect object) is introduced by a dative marker *bei2*, which means 'give' when used as a main verb.[2] The word order in serial verb dative constructions and English prepositional datives is the same.

(4) Siu2ming4 gei3 zo2 jat1 fung1 seon3 bei2 ngo5 (**SVD**)
Siuming send PERF one CL letter give I
'Siuming sent a letter to me.' (Tang 1998)

Note that the preposition in English prepositional datives can either be *to* or *for*, depending on the thematic roles of the indirect objects. *To* is used if the indirect object is non-benefactive, and *for* is used if the indirect object is benefactive (5b). However, the *to/for* distinction is not reflected overtly in Cantonese, as the dative marker in serial verb datives is always *bei2*.

(5) a. John baked Mary a cake.
b. John baked a cake for Mary.

Most dative verbs in Cantonese are used in the serial verb dative form. According to Tang (1998), such verbs can be sub-categorized into 'send', 'fry' (verbs of creation), and 'pluck' (verbs of obtaining) types of verbs.[3] However, there is no dative alternation in Cantonese, and one class of verbs only appears in one type of constructions.

---

[2] As there is no conclusive evidence to show that *bei2* in (4) is a preposition, the construction cannot be called as prepositional datives.

[3] The 'pluck' verbs are separated from 'fry' verbs as verbs of obtaining in Cantonese (as well as in Mandarin Chinese) can be used in a construction which has the same surface form as double object datives, but different semantics and syntax. This construction is similar to the possessive datives in Hebrew and other languages (Landau 1999).

(i) Ngo5 zaak6 zo2 keoi5 sap6jat1 zi1 mui4gwai6 faa1.
I pluck PERF 3sg eleven CL rose
'I plucked his/her eleven roses.'
(not 'I pluck eleven roses for him/her.')

Cantonese has a third dative construction – the inverted double object dative. In Modern Cantonese, this construction is restricted to the verb *bei2* ('give'). It is observed that the inverted order is most natural, but if the theme becomes very heavy or is the focus of the sentence, the double object dative and serial verb dative form may also be judged as acceptable (Matthews and Yip 1994, Tang 1998).

(6) a. Ngo5 bei2 zo2 jat1 zi1 bat1 keoi5 **(IDOD)**
I give PERF one CL pen 3sg
'I gave a pen to him/her.'

b. ?? Ngo5 bei2 zo2 keoi5 jat1 zi1 bat1 **(DOD)**
I give PERF 3sg one CL pen
'I gave him/her a pen.'

c. ?? Ngo5 bei2 zo2 jat1 zi1 bat1 bei2 keoi5 **(SVD)**
I give PERF one CL pen give 3sg
'I gave a pen to him/her.' (Tang 1998)

The inverted double object datives can be analyzed as a derived form of the serial verb dative, with the dative marker *bei2* deleted due to avoidance of repetition of the same phonological element (the haplology effect) (Tang 1998, Yip and Matthews 2007). The major evidence to support (7) comes the fact that the serial verb dative becomes acceptable when the theme becomes heavier (8).

(7) SVD: *bei2* – Theme – *bei2* – Goal
IDOD: *bei2* – Theme – Ø – Goal (adapted from Tang 1998)

(8) Ngo5 bei2 zo2 [jat1 bun2 hou2 jau5jung6 ge3 syu1]$_{\text{THEME}}$
I give PERF one CL very useful GE book
bei2 [keoi5]$_{\text{GOAL}}$
give 3sg
'I gave a very useful book to him/her.'

Heavy NP shift may explain why double object datives with the verb *bei2* can be acceptable, but it does not predict that the serial verb dative form will also be available when the theme gets heavy.[4] The haplology effect offers a better

---

[4] An example of such double object dative is given below:

(i) Ngo5 bei2 zo2 [keoi5]$_{\text{GOAL}}$ [jat1 bun2 hou2 jau5jung6 ge3 syu1]$_{\text{THEME}}$
I give PERF 3sg one CL very useful GE book
'I gave him/her a very useful book.' (Chan, 2003)

Table 1 Dative verbs classes and dative constructions in Cantonese

Constructions	*bei2* ('give')	*Send, fry, pluck* verbs	*Teach* verbs
DOD	Heavy theme	No	OK
SVD	Heavy theme	OK	No
IDOD	OK	No	No

Adapted from Tang (1998: 40, Table 9) and Chan (2003: 11, Table 1.2)

solution, as the repetition of *bei2* is less undesirable when more materials are added between the main verb *bei2* and the dative marker *bei2*. In this case, the deleted dative marker *bei2* has a reason to surface from the underlying form.

Table 1 summarizes the one-to-one correspondence between verb class and type of dative constructions in Cantonese.

There are several different approaches to the syntax of double object datives and prepositional datives. Larson (1988) argues that double object datives and prepositional datives are derived from the same underlying form. Harley (2002) focuses on the semantic differences between double object datives and prepositional datives and proposes that different primitives (P_{HAVE} and P_{LOC}) are involved in these constructions.[5] Pylkkänen (2002) offers a low applicative account to double object datives and remains open on the structure of prepositional datives. The discussion on the syntactic properties of double object datives and prepositional datives reveals the complexity in dative constructions, but for children, there is another level of difficulty in the acquisition. In the input, *to* and *for* are ambiguous in many ways in English. Both can be infinitival, and the prepositional *to* and *for* each have several different meanings.

For instance, the preposition *to* is dative in (9a) and (9c), and directional in (9b) and (9d). Only dative *to* entails a possessive relationship between the arguments, which is a prerequisite for dative alternation – as the double object dative indicates a transfer of possession (Harley 2002, Pylkkänen 2002, among others). The directional *to* has no such meaning, and cannot participate in dative alternation (compare (9d) and (10d)).

(9) a. The bag belongs to Mary. (dative *to*)
b. John went to London yesterday. (directional *to*)
c. Mary gave the bag to John. (dative *to*)
d. John sent the package to London. (directional *to*)

[5] According to Harley (2002), P_{HAVE}, a silent preposition accounting for the possessive relationship between the goal and the theme, is involved in double object datives, and P_{LOC}, which indicates the location of the theme, is involved in prepositional datives. In addition to Harley, several other researchers also argue for similar decomposition approaches to dative constructions (Beck and Johnson 2004, Pesetsky 1995, Richards 2001, and others).

(10) a. John sent the package to Mary. (dative *to*)
b. John sent Mary the package. (DOD)
c. John sent the package to London. (directional *to*)
d. *John sent London the package.

Levinson (2005) argues that the dative *to* and the directional *to* are different syntactic elements. The directional *to* corresponds to *where* in *wh*-interrogatives (11b), and can undergo British English *do* ellipsis (11c). The dative *to*, according to Levinson (2005), corresponds to *to who/what* in *wh*-interrogatives (12b), and cannot undergo *do* ellipsis (12c).

(11) a. John sent the letter to London.
b. Where did John send the letter?
c. John didn't send the letter to London, but he will do to Sydney.
(Levinson 2005)

(12) a. John sent the letter to Mary.
b. Who did John send the letter to?
c. ?*John didn't send the letter to Mary, but he will do to Jane.
(Levinson 2005)

In contrast, such ambiguity does not exist in Cantonese, as the distinction between dative *to* and directional *to* is lexically marked in serial verb dative constructions. The dative marker *bei2* corresponds to dative *to* in English prepositional datives (13), and *heoi3*, which means 'go' when used as a verb, corresponds to directional *to* (14).

(13)	a.	Ngo5	gei3	zo2	go3	baau1gwo2	**bei2**	maa1mi4
		I	send	PERF	CL	package	give	mother
		'I sent a package to my mother.'						
	b.	*Ngo5	gei3	zo2	go3	baau1gwo2	**heoi3**	maa1mi4
		I	send	PERF	CL	package	go	mother
		'I sent a package to my mother.'						

(14)	a.	Ngo5	gei3	zo2	go3	baau1gwo2	**heoi3**	Leon4deon1
		I	send	PERF	CL	package	go	London
		'I sent a package to London.'						
	b.	*Ngo5	gei3	zo2	go3	baau1gwo2	**bei2**	Leon4deon1
		I	send	PERF	CL	package	give	London
		'I sent a package to London.'						

The preposition *for* in English is also ambiguous. It is a dative maker, but also has other readings (e.g. deputy 'on behalf of'). An English sentence like (15) can be interpreted in two different ways (16), depending on the reading of *for*. Only the sentence with dative *for* (16a) resembles the double object dative counterpart (16c).

(15) I baked a cake for my mother.

(16) a. I baked a cake for my mother (as a birthday present). (dative *for*)

b. I baked a cake for my mother (since she is very busy right now). (*on behalf of*)

c. I baked my mother a cake.

This ambiguity does not exist in Cantonese, either, as two different types of serial verb constructions are involved to differentiate the intended possessor vs. event benefactor readings. (17a) is the serial verb dative construction that corresponds to dative *for*, and (17b) is a different serial verb construction in which the benefactive argument *maa1mi4* 'mother' is linked by another verb *bong1* 'help' to the baking event.

(17) a. Ngo5 guk6 zo2 go3 daan6gou1 **bei2** maa4mi4
I bake ASP CL cake give mother
'I baked my mother a cake.'

b. Ngo5 **bong1** maa4mi4 guk6 zo2 go3 daan6gou1
I help mother bake ASP CL cake
'I helped my mother to bake a cake.'
(i.e. 'I helped with the baking but the cake was not to my mother.')

Thus, though Cantonese differs from English in its inverted double object datives and lack of dative alternation, it does not involve as much input ambiguity as English does in prepositional datives. In the next section, I will review several previous studies on the acquisition of dative constructions, and discuss the research questions of this study.

3 Previous Research on the Acquisition of Dative Constructions

One basic question in the study of word order acquisition of dative constructions is the developmental patterns of different dative constructions in different languages/groups of children. We would like to know if there exists a universal pattern, and if children hold a general preference/bias against certain order of the theme and the goal. And if there exists no universal explanation for the delay of a dative construction, we expect that language-specific reasons can account for each individual pattern.

Snyder and Stromswold (1997), using age of first use as a measure, study the order of acquisition and the correlation of double object datives and *to*-datives in 12 English monolingual children. They find that the acquisition of the two dative constructions is highly correlated with each other, and children acquire double object datives significantly earlier than *to*-datives. The mean age of acquisition of double object datives is 2;2.5, while the mean age of acquisition of *to*-datives is 2;6.9. There is an average gap of 4.4 months between the acquisition of double object datives and *to*-datives.

Snyder and Stromswold (1997) suggest that the developmental lag between double object datives and *to*-datives is connected to the lag between V-NP-Particle constructions and V-Particle-NP constructions. They argue against the possibility that input frequency or children's MLU delays the acquisition of *to*-datives. Instead, they hypothesize that two different parameters are involved in the acquisition of double object datives and prepositional datives. The first parameter alone determines the acquisition of double object datives (and causative/perceptual constructions, *put*-locatives, V-NP-Particle constructions – as the acquisition of these constructions is all highly correlated with each other), while the second parameter, when combined with first one, determines the acquisition of *to*-datives and V-Particle-NP constructions.

Viau (2006), adopting a decomposition approach to dative constructions, reexamines the developmental lag between the two dative constructions and argues that the late acquisition of prepositional datives can be attributed to the late development of the primitive GO, which is related to the use of directional *to*. His argument is based on the assumption that complex predicates can be decomposed into different primitive heads, and constructions that are headed by more than one primitive will emerge only when each primitive is acquired individually. In his system, double object datives are composed of the primitives CAUSE and HAVE, and prepositional datives CAUSE and GO (Table 2).

Viau (2006) analyzes the utterances of 22 monolingual English children from the CHILDES corpus (MacWhinney 2000). He shows that there is a strong

Table 2 The syntactic-semantic primitives in Viau (2006) and their instantiations

Primitive	Instantiation	Examples
CAUSE	Double object dative	[x CAUSE [z HAVE y]]
	Prepositional dative	[x CAUSE [y GO z]]
	Causative verbs e.g. *open, close, break, grow*	[x CAUSE [y BECOME XP_{state}]]
HAVE	Double object dative	[x CAUSE [z HAVE y]]
	get	[BECOME [x HAVE y]]
	have	[BE [x HAVE y]]
	want	*want* [x HAVE y]
GO	Prepositional dative	[x CAUSE [y GO z]]
	Directional *to*, e.g. *to the store*	[x GO $XP_{location}$]

correlation between the ages of acquisition of CAUSE/HAVE and those of double object datives, and between the ages of acquisition of GO and those of prepositional datives, but predicates containing the primitive GO are acquired at a later time compared with CAUSE and HAVE. According to Viau, the late development of preposition datives (which involves both CAUSE and GO) can be attributed to the late acquisition of GO.

However, why is the primitive GO, representing the goal of an action, difficult to acquire? Viau (2006) notices that GO is difficult only in the linguistic sense, as perceptual studies of non-linguistic motion events demonstrate that infants, as early as 12-month-old, can interpret events as goal-related (Lakusta 2005, Wagner and Carey 2005). However, one possibility, raised by Viau (2006), is that English does not distinguish directional *to* clearly from dative *to*, and this ambiguity may cause confusion in children's mapping between different types of goals to their surface structures, and hence delay the acquisition of GO.

One of the goals in this study is to assess this hypothesis. If it is the ambiguity in *to* that makes prepositional datives difficult to acquire, children who are late in acquiring prepositional datives should also show little evidence of distinguishing dative *to* from directional *to*.[6] This prediction is expected to hold for both monolingual and bilingual children. Though Cantonese makes a lexical distinction between dative *to* and directional *to*, it cannot be applied directly to English, as no such lexical items are available.

For Cantonese monolingual children, there may not exist a developmental gap between double object datives and serial verb datives. Though target double object datives in Cantonese are restricted to 'teach' class verbs and such verbs may not be part of children's early vocabulary, previous research reports that both monolingual and bilingual children use the verb *bei2* ('give') in the non-target double object order (like English *give*-double object datives) at an early age (Chan 2003). However, it is not clear what the ages of acquisition of serial verb datives are. This study is going to compare the emergence of non-target *bei2*-double object datives with serial verb datives. As Cantonese does not have an ambiguous dative marker in serial verb dative constructions, the serial verb datives construction may not be more difficult to produce than double object datives.

4 Methodology and Findings

This chapter investigates longitudinal data of three groups of children. For English monolinguals, 9 out of 12 children are selected from the study of Snyder and Stromswold (1997) (Table 3). Three children are excluded because of

[6] In Snyder and Stromswold (1997), it is observed that some children exhibit a huge gap between double object dative and prepositional datives, while others acquire them at the same time or with a short gap.

Table 3 Background information of monolingual English-speaking children

Child	Gender	Corpus	Age range	Total child lines
Adam	M	Brown	2;3–5;2	21,070
Eve	F	Brown	1;6–2;3	9,282
Mark	M	MacWhinney	1;5–6;0	13,889
Naomi	F	Sachs	1;2–4;9	7,593
Nathaniel	M	Snow	2;6–3;9	10,591
Nina	F	Suppes	2;0–3;3	22,535
Peter	M	Bloom 1970	1;10–3;2	26,764
Sarah	F	Brown	2;3–5;1	26,067
Shem	M	Clark	2;3–3;2	15,077

infrequent recordings during an age period when first double object datives are expected to emerge.[7]

For Cantonese-English bilingual children, I use data from the Hong Kong Bilingual Child Language Corpus (Yip and Matthews 2007). This corpus contains data of six children who are exposed to both Cantonese and English naturally after birth. For each child, one of the parents is a native English speaker, and the other a native Cantonese speaker. The children are recorded weekly or biweekly in an age period between 1;03 and 4;06. Previous work from Snyder and Stromswold (1997) and Viau (2006) show that 1;06–3;06 constitutes the best age range for studies of early double object datives and prepositional datives. One child in the corpus is excluded from this study, because her transcribed recordings are available only after 3;01.

Among the 5 bilingual children, 4 are dominant in Cantonese, and 1 is dominant in English.[8] 3 children (Timmy, Sophie and Alicia) are siblings in the same family. Information on age range, gender, dominant language and numbers of sessions in each language is summarized in Table 4.

For Cantonese monolingual children, I use data of 8 children recorded in the Hong Kong Cantonese Child Language Corpus (Lee et al. 1996). All these children were born to Cantonese-speaking parents and speak Cantonese as the first and only language. Each child is recorded on a biweekly basis. Information on age range, gender, and number of sessions is summarized in Table 5.

---

[7] Recordings of Allison are infrequent after 1;10, and recordings of April are infrequent from 1;10 to 2;09. Recordings of Ross have a huge gap between 1;06.09 and 2;06.17, and Ross has already produced a double object dative at 1;06.09.

[8] Language dominance here is determined by comparing children's MLUw in both languages. Though it is an independent research question whether MLU values of different languages are fully comparable, Yip and Matthews (2005) show that MLU differential (the difference between MLU scores in each language) is a reliable measure of language dominance for children in the Hong Kong bilingual child language corpus, and children's MLU differentials match patterns of transfer effects and language preference.

Table 4 Background information of bilingual children

Child	Gender	Dominant language	Age range	Cantonese sessions	English sessions
Alicia	F	Cantonese	1;03.10–3;00.24	40	40
Charlotte	F	English	1;08;28–3;00.03	19	19
Llywelyn	M	Cantonese	2;00.12–3;04.17	17	17
Sophie	F	Cantonese	1;06.00–3;00.09	40	40
Timmy	M	Cantonese	1;05.20–3;06.25	34	38

Table 5 Background information of monolingual Cantonese-speaking children

Child	Gender	Age range	No. of sessions
CCC	M	1;10.08–2;10.27	22
CGK	F	1;11.01–2;09.09	19
CKT	M	1;05.22–2;07.22	25
HHC	M	2;04.08–3;04.14	16
LLY	F	2;08.10–3;08.09	20
LTF	F	2;02.10–3;02.18	16
MHZ	M	1;07.00–2;08.06	26
WBH	F	2;03.23–3;04.08	16

This chapter chooses age of first non-imitative use as a measure of emergence.[9] Following Snyder and Stromswold (1997) and Viau (2006), I consider the age of emergence to be the age of acquisition of a construction, if a child produces no non-target structures after their first use of such constructions. For English monolingual children, the two are the same – as children do not produce non-target dative constructions (Snyder and Stromswold 1997). However, as Chan (2003) reports that children acquiring Cantonese dative constructions are prone to error with the inverted double object datives, a Cantonese dative construction will not be considered as being fully acquired until its accuracy rate reaches and remains more than 90% after a certain age.[10]

In the current study, when ages of emergence differ from ages of acquisition, I take ages of emergence to be the measurement of children's grammatical development. By acquisition we expect children to have very low error rates in certain constructions for a continuous period of time, while by emergence we only expect children to have some basic syntactic structures of those

[9] To qualify as a non-imitative utterance, children must produce an utterance which is not identical to the preceding adult utterance (i.e. children's utterance must contain at least one different element – which indicates that they have processed the preceding adult utterance and produced their own version afterwards). However, when children produce a very similar sentence after several such adult utterances, it would be regarded as imitative.

[10] It is arbitrary to set the accuracy rate at higher than 90%, but it is found that when children produce non-target structures alongside with target structures, their accuracy rate is around 50%. After that period, children suddenly stop producing non-target structures and their accuracy rates rise to nearly 100%.

constructions, with or without making a choice between target and non-target structures. Chan (2003) reports that non-target *bei2*-double object datives and target *bei2*-inverted double object datives coexist in children's grammar for years. As children's use of non-target *bei2*-double object datives reflects a non-target grammar they have internalized at that point, the emergence of such non-target structures offers valuable information on children's development of dative constructions.

The procedures to identify English dative constructions are as follows. The CLAN program was used to extract children's utterances that contained any potential dativizable verbs – these verbs are summarized in a list in Snyder and Stromswold (1997).[11] The results were hand-checked to make sure they were not imitations of a preceding adult utterance. For prepositional datives, the CLAN program were used to extract all children's utterances containing *to* and *for*, and these sentences were checked by hand for possible prepositional datives, including ungrammatical ones. To be counted as a prepositional dative, the utterance must have two objects and an overt preposition *to* or *for*. If there is no overt preposition, the utterance will be counted as a double object dative.

The procedures to identify Cantonese dative constructions are similar to the procedures for English ones. The CLAN program was used to extract all children's utterances containing the verb *bei2*, and the results were checked by hand to select possible non-target double object datives ([*bei2*-Goal-Theme]) and target inverted double object datives ([*bei2*-Theme-Goal]). For serial verb constructions and double object datives, the CLAN program was used to extract all children's utterances that contain potential dativizable verbs identified by Tang (1998).[12] The results are hand-checked to make sure they are full dative constructions.

[11] These verbs included: address, admit, afford, allocate, allocating, allow, ask, assign, bake, baking, bought, bring, broadcast, brought, build, building, built, buy, buying, commend, communicate, communicating, concede, conceding, convey, demonstrate, demonstrating, denied, denies, deny, describe, describing, devote, devoting, dictate, dictating, did, dig, do, does, doing, done, dug, explain, gave, get, give, giving, got, gotten, grant, guarantee, impart, lend, lent, made, make, making, mention, order, ordering, orders, preach, prescribe, prescribing, promise, promising, radio, read, refer, refuse, refusing, relate, relating, relay, reserve, reserving, restore, restoring, reveal, sell, send, sent, serve, serving, show, sold, submit, take, taking, taught, teach, telegraph, tell, told, took, transmit, unveil, volunteer, whisper, wire, wiring, write, writing, and wrote.

[12] These verbs include: sung3 'to give (a present)', zoeng2 'to award', bun1 'to move', daai3 'to bring', dai6 'to hand to', deng3 'to pelt', gaau1 'to deliver', gaap3 'to lift food with chopsticks', gei3 'to send', lau4 'to reserve', ling1 'to carry with hand/to take', lo2 'to bring', maai6 'to sell', paai3 'to deliver', tek3 'to kick', wui6 'to remit', caau2 'to fry', jing2 'to photocopy', pai1 'to cut', sai2 'to wash', tong3 'to iron', waak6 'to draw', zam1 'to pour', zik1 'to knit', zing2 'to make', zak3 'to compose', zyu2 'to cook', coeng2 'to snatch', gaan2 'to choose', maai5 'to buy', lo2 'to get', tau1 'to steal', zaak6 'to pluck', ceng2gaau3 'to inquire', gaau3 'to teach', haau2 'to test', kau4 'to request', and man6 'to ask'.

4.1 The Late Acquisition of English Prepositional Datives

I will first present data on the acquisition of English dative constructions in bilingual children, and compare children (both bilingual and monolingual) who are late in prepositional datives with those that acquire both double object datives and prepositional dative at the same time.

English double object datives emerge before prepositional datives in all five bilingual children. Llywelyn does not produce any target-like prepositional datives before the recording ends. No target *to*-datives are attested in Alicia's transcripts, and no target *for*-datives are attested in Sophie's transcripts. The ages of emergence of double object datives range from 1;5.2 to 2;2.9, and the ages of emergence of prepositional datives range from 2;4.9 to >3;4.6.[13] The mean age of acquisition of double object datives is 2;0.1. The mean age of acquisition of prepositional datives is >2;9.8.[14] The average gap between first double object datives and first prepositional datives is more than 9.7 months. Compared with the 3.3 months gap in monolingual English-speaking children (Viau 2006), Cantonese-English bilingual children exhibit a much wider temporal gap between their first double object datives and prepositional datives.

Viau (2006) reports that monolingual children produce directional *to* before prepositional datives. Bilingual children's age of emergence of directional *to* is also examined to figure out whether prepositional datives in bilingual children are acquired at a relatively later time. The ages of emergence of directional *to* in bilingual children range from 2;1.3 to 2;5.5, and the mean age of emergence is 2;3.1. Children's ages of emergence of double object datives, prepositional datives, and directional *to* are provided in Table 6.

There is an average temporal gap of more than 6.7 months between the emergence of directional *to* and prepositional datives in bilingual children, but the gap in monolingual English-speaking children is only 0.9 months

Table 6 Emergence of double object datives, prepositional datives and directional *to* in bilingual children

Child	Double object datives	Prepositional datives	Directional to
Timmy	2;2.9	2;4.9	2;1.3
Sophie	2;1.7	2;9.8	2;5.5
Alicia	1;5.2	2;11.2	2;1.5
Llywelyn	2;2.1	>3;4.6	2;5.3
Charlotte	2;0.8	2;6.5	2;1.7
Mean	2;0.1	>2;9.8	2;3.1

[13] '>3;4.6' means later than 3;4.6. The exact age of acquisition is not known because the child never produces any target construction before the recording ends.

[14] Note that the mean age for prepositional datives is calculated from the age of emergence of *to*-datives and *for*-datives (whichever comes first).

Table 7 Comparison of average temporal gaps of DOD/PD/directional to between bilingual and monolingual children

	DOD – PD	Directional *to* – PD	DOD – directional *to*
Bilingual	>9.7	>6.7	3.0
Monolingual	3.3	0.9	2.4

(Viau 2006). However, the average gap between the emergence of double object datives and directional *to* in bilingual children is 3.0 months, which is very close to the 2.4 months gap in monolingual children (Viau 2006) (Table 7).

The mean ages of emergence of double object datives and directional *to* in bilingual children and monolingual children are similar, but the mean age of emergence of prepositional datives in bilingual children is much greater than that of monolingual children.[15] This, combined with the fact that bilingual children have wider gaps between the emergence of double object datives and prepositional datives, shows that bilingual children are further delayed in the acquisition of prepositional datives.

Among the five bilingual children, Timmy has the smallest gap (2.0 months) between first double object datives and first prepositional datives. The gaps in other bilingual children range from 5.7 months to >14.5 months. Note that Charlotte, an English-dominant child, does not progress as fast as Timmy (a Cantonese-dominant child) does in the development of prepositional datives. This deviates from the general language development pattern in Cantonese-English bilingual children, in which language dominance greatly influences children's mastery of a language (Yip and Matthews 2000).

Examination of Timmy's production of *to* shows that he produces triadic directional *to* (18) at a remarkably early age of 2;04.14, which is even before his first *to*-dative (2;04.28).

(18) I take him to the hospital. (Timmy 2;04.14)

In contrast, among other bilingual children, only Charlotte produces such triadic directional *to* (19) at 3;03.03, which is 5.3 months after her first *to*-datives.

(19) Daddy can't do take her to the park. (Charlotte 3;03.03)

No other bilingual children produce triadic directional *to* in their recordings. Children's utterances with the verb 'take' are also examined, and it is found that

[15] The mean age of acquisition of double object datives in monolingual children is 2;2.5, the mean age of acquisition of prepositional datives is 2;4.9, and the mean age of acquisition of directional *to* is 2;4.0 (Viau 2006).

all 5 bilingual children are able to use the verb 'take' in Verb-Particle constructions before their recordings end. This shows that it is not the difficulty in learning individual verbs that delays production of triadic directional *to* in these children.

Among the five bilingual children, the three children (Sophie, Alicia and Llywelyn) who exhibit a huge gap between double object datives and prepositional datives fail to produce both triadic dative *to* and triadic directional *to* in a short period of time. This suggests that the ability to separate triadic dative *to* from triadic directional *to* is related to the ability to make fast progress from double object datives to prepositional datives.

The same pattern is also observed in English monolingual children. Snyder and Stromswold (1997) provide children's ages of acquisition of double object datives and *to*-datives in their paper, and I also check these children's first *for*-datives.[16] The information is summarized in Table 8.[17,18]

Table 8 The acquisition of English dative constructions

Child	Double object datives	*to*-datives	*for*-datives
Adam	2;3.1	2;11.9	2;11.0
Mark	2;7.2	3;4.2	3;4.5
Eve	1;7.9	2;0.0	1;11.3
Naomi	2;0.9	2;5.1	2;3.6
Nathaniel	2;5.6	2;7.0	Unclear
Nina	2;0.0	2;1.5	2;1.7
Peter	2;0.2	2;0.2	2;4.5
Sarah	2;10.7	3;2.8	3;0.6
Shem	2;2.8	2;4.8	2;5.1
Mean	2;2.9	2;6.8	2;6.8

[16] Children use *for*-datives frequently after their first such usages, and only one child makes one mistake in producing a *for*-dative in the [V-PP-DP] order:

(i) write for me a Patsy. (Peter 2;05.22)

Peter produces a total of 17 *for*-datives during the age period 2;04.15–3;01;20, and only one token is in the non-target order. It is very likely that this case is a performance error. More information on children's early *for*-datives can be found in Gu (2007).

[17] Nathaniel's age of acquisition of *for*-datives is unclear. Although he does not produce any *for*-datives in his corpus, the recordings become infrequent after 3;0.6 with intervals of more than 1 month. There may be missing *for*-datives between 3;0.6 and 3;9.1.

[18] Monolingual children's ages of acquisition of double object datives and *to*-datives are based on data reported by Snyder and Stromswold (1997). The mean ages of acquisition are slightly different from their mean ages because I do not include Allison, April and Ross in this study.

It is found that children (Adam and Mark) who are late in producing *to*-datives are also late in *for*-datives. Adam and Mark demonstrate a gap of about 8–9 months between their first double object datives and first *to*-datives, as well as first double object datives and first *for*-datives. Except Adam and Mark, no child exhibits a gap that is far bigger than the mean gap of monolingual children. Compared with other children, Adam and Mark are relatively slow in the development of prepositional datives (Table 9).

Table 9 Developmental gaps between DOD and *to*-datives/*for*-datives

Child	DOD - *to*-datives	DOD - *for*-datives
Adam	8.8	7.9
Mark	9.0	9.3
Eve	4.1	3.4
Naomi	4.2	2.7
Nathaniel	1.4	Unclear
Nina	1.5	1.7
Peter	0	4.3
Sarah	4.1	1.9
Shem	2.0	2.3
Mean	3.9	4.2

However, Adam and Mark do not have problems with the primitive GO. A search of children's early uses of prepositional *to* shows that Adam produces his first directional *to* at age 2;3.0, which is concurrent with his first double object dative (2;3.1), and Mark produces his first directional *to* at 2;6.2, which is earlier than his first double object dative (2;7.2).[19] However, Adam produces his first *to*-dative at 2;11.9, and Mark produces his first *to*-dative at 3;4.2.

According to Viau (2006), use of dyadic directional *to* indicates knowledge of the primitive GO, and the late acquisition of prepositional datives is a result of late development of GO. Thus, we would expect Adam and Mark to be slow in both prepositional datives and directional *to*, but instead, they are not behind other children in terms of the acquisition of directional *to*.[20] Contrary to what Viau (2006) has proposed, emergence of dyadic directional *to* (indicating knowledge of the primitive GO) fails to predict the emergence of *to*-datives in Adam and Mark.

A further investigation on children's various uses of prepositional *to* shows that Adam and Mark are late in producing triadic directional *to*.[21] Both of them demonstrate a gap between first triadic dative *to* and first triadic directional *to*

[19] Such directional *tos* are dyadic – the sentence only has two arguments (e.g. (9b)).

[20] The mean age of acquisition of directional *to* is 2;4.2 (Snyder and Stromswold 1997), and the mean gap between first double object datives and first directional *to* is 1.7 months.

[21] Triadic directional *to* is a directional *to* in a sentence that has three arguments (e.g. (9d)). Triadic dative *to* is a dative *to* in a sentence that has three arguments (e.g. (9c)).

Table 10 Developmental gaps between triadic directional *to* and triadic dative *to*

Child	Triadic directional *to*	Triadic dative *to*	Gap between triadic directional *to* and triadic dative *to*
Adam	3;4.6	2;11.9	4.7 *
Mark	3;10.6	3;4.2	6.4 *
Eve	2;1.9	2;0.0	1.9
Naomi	2;5.0	2;5.1	0.1
Nathaniel	2;5.6	2;7.0	1.4
Nina	Unclear	2;1.5	Unclear
Peter	2;1.6	2;0.2	1.4
Sarah	3;4.9	3;2.8	2.1
Shem	2;5.5	2;4.8	0.7
Mean	2;9.1	2;6.8	2.3

* Children who exhibit a gap that far exceeds the average gap.

that exceeds the mean gap in monolingual children. Information on children's first triadic directional *to*, triadic dative *to*, and the gap between the two *to*s is summarized in Table 10.[22]

Children who produce triadic directional *to* late do not have problems using verbs like *take* or *throw* in complex constructions from early on. Adam starts to use *take* in verb-particle constructions from 2;03.04, and Mark starts to use *throw* in verb-particle construction from 2;6.14. It is unlikely that the acquisition of the verb delays children's production of triadic directional *to*.

Putting information in Tables 8, 9 and 10 together, it is found that among the 9 monolingual children, only Adam and Mark exhibit a gap that far exceeds the average gap between first double object datives and first prepositional datives. Also, Adam and Mark have an above-average gap between triadic directional *to* and triadic dative *to*.[23] This pattern, like the pattern observed in bilingual children, suggests that the ability to produce both triadic directional *to* and triadic dative *to* in a short period of time greatly influences children's progress from double object datives to prepositional datives.

4.2 Development of Cantonese Dative Constructions

It is found that most monolingual Cantonese-speaking children acquire serial verb dative constructions before they produce their first non-target *bei2*-double

[22] There is a gap in Nina's recordings between 2;5.28 and 2;9.13. Nina produces a triadic directional *to* at 2;5.28, but the sentence is marked as being produced in soft voice. Her next triadic directional *to* is produced at 2;9.21. However, there may be missing triadic directional *to* during that age period.

[23] However, Nina also seems to exhibit such an above-average gap, though she acquires *to*-datives soon after double object datives. Right now there is no clear explanation for Nina's delay in producing of triadic directional *to*.

object datives ([bei2-Goal-Theme]) and first target inverted double object datives ([*bei2*-Theme-Goal]), while bilingual children start to use non-target *bei2*-double object datives at an earlier stage.

All the 8 monolingual children produce serial verb dative constructions in their recordings. Only 1 child (HHC) has problems with word order in serial verb dative constructions.[24] There are 4 children who produce target inverted double object datives before their recordings end. Also, 4 children produce non-target *bei2*-double object datives in the recording periods. Except HHC, all the other 7 children acquire serial verb dative constructions before or at the same time with their first non-target *bei2*-double object datives and target inverted double object datives. Target double object datives with 'teach' class of verbs come in relatively late. Only 2 children produce such constructions at age 3;02.18 and 3;03.15. Each child's ages of first use of serial verb datives, non-target *bei2*-double object datives and target inverted double object datives are summarized in Table 11.[25]

Table 11 Monolingual children's ages of emergence of Cantonese dative constructions

Child	[V-Theme-*bei2*-Goal]	Non-target [*bei2*-Goal-Theme]	Target [*bei2*-Theme-Goal]
CCC	2;9.8	n.a.	>2;10.9
CGK	2;2.7	2;3.4	2;3.4
CKT	2;6.6	n.a.	2;7.1
HHC	2;11.3	2;10.4	>3;4.5
LLY	2;11.3	2;11.3	3;1.4
LTF	2;4.0	2;4.0	2;4.9
MHZ	2;3.3	n.a.	>2;6.6
WBH	2;11.9	n.a.	>3;1.0
Mean	2;7.6		>2;9.5

The mean age of acquisition of serial verb datives is 2;7.6, while the mean age of first inverted double object datives is >2;9.5.[26] There are 5 monolingual children who produce at least one of the target inverted double object datives or non-target *bei2*-double object datives, and 4 of them produce non-target double object datives before or at the same time with target inverted double object datives. The order of emergence of these three constructions in monolingual children is summarized in Table 12.

[24] These non-target serial verb dative constructions are in the [V-*bei2*-Goal-Theme] order.

[25] Children who do not produce non-target *bei2*-double object datives in their recording periods are listed as 'not attested (n.a)'. However, these children's recordings end relatively early (1–2 months after their first serial verb datives), so it is very likely for them to use non-target *bei2*-double object datives after the recordings end.

[26] The mean age of first non-target *bei2*-double object datives is not calculated, as it is uncertain whether children who do not produce this non-target construction in the corpus will produce it afterwards.

Table 12 Monolingual children's order of emergence of Cantonese dative constructions

Child	Order of emergence	
CCC	Serial verb dative	No [*bei2*-G-T], no [*bei2*-T-G]
CGK	Serial verb dative < [*bei2*-T-G] = [*bei2*-G-T]	
CKT	Serial verb dative < [*bei2*-T-G]	No [*bei2*-G-T]
HHC	[*bei2*-G-T] < serial verb dative	No [*bei2*-T-G]
LLY	Serial verb dative < [*bei2*-G-T] < [*bei2*-T-G]	
LTF	Serial verb dative = [*bei2*-G-T] < [*bei2*-T-G]	
MHZ	Serial verb dative	No [*bei2*-G-T], no [*bei2*-T-G]
WBH	Serial verb dative	No [*bei2*-G-T], no [*bei2*-T-G]

There is 1 bilingual child (Charlotte) who does not produce any full dative constructions in her corpus. Among the other 4 children, only 3 produce serial verb datives in the recording periods, and Sophie has problems with word order in her serial verb datives.[27] There are 4 bilingual children who produce non-target *bei2*-double object datives in the recordings, while 3 bilingual children produce target inverted double objects before their recordings end. Only 1 child produces target double object datives with 'teach' class verbs in her corpus at age 3;00.10. Each bilingual child's ages of first use of serial verb datives, non-target *bei2*-double object datives and target inverted double object datives are summarized in Table 13.

Table 13 Bilingual children's ages of emergence of Cantonese dative constructions

Child	Serial verb datives	*bei2*-Goal-Theme	*bei2*-Theme-Goal
Timmy	2;8.6	2;7.5	2;4.9
Sophie	2;5.5	2;3.8	2;8.7
Alicia	1;11.2	2;3.5	>3;0.8
Llywelyn	>3;4.6	2;9.2	2;10.1
Charlotte	>3;0.1	n.a	>3;0.1
Mean	>2;7.5		>2;9.1

Contrary to the developmental pattern observed in monolingual children, there is no consistent pattern in bilingual children. Alicia produces serial verb datives before the non-target *bei2*-doubel object datives, but Sophie, Timmy and Llywelyn produce their first non-target *bei2*-double object datives before their first serial verb dative constructions. The order of emergence of these three constructions in bilingual children is summarized in Table 14.

Bilingual children also demonstrate a strong preference for the non-target *bei2*-double object datives. The average accuracy rate of inverted double object

[27] Similar to HHC, Sophie produces serial verb datives in the [V-*bei2*-Goal-Theme] order.

Table 14 Bilingual children's order of emergence of Cantonese dative constructions

Child	Order of emergence	
Timmy	[*bei2*-T-G] < [*bei2*-G-T] < serial verb dative	
Sophie	[*bei2*-G-T] < serial verb dative < [*bei2*-T-G]	
Alicia	Serial verb dative < [*bei2*-G-T],	No [*bei2*-T-G]
Llywelyn	[*bei2*-G-T] < [*bei2*-T-G],	No serial verb dative

datives in bilingual children is 20%. Alicia has the lowest accuracy rate (0%), and Timmy has the highest accuracy rate (41.2%). Table 15 presents each bilingual child's number of tokens of target inverted double object datives and non-target *bei2*-double object datives and their accuracy rates.

Table 15 Accuracy rates of inverted double object datives in bilingual children

	Alicia	Llywelyn	Sophie	Timmy	Average
Tokens of target [bei2-T-G]	0	1	2	7	10
Tokens of non-target [bei2-G-T]	9	4	17	10	40
Accuracy rate	0%	20%	10.5%	41.2%	20%

Alicia only produces non-target *bei2*-double object datives in her corpus. Llywelyn and Sophie do produce target inverted double object datives once or twice, but their target constructions only appear in one transcript while their non-target *bei2*-double object datives appear several times before and after the target inverted double object datives. Timmy has the highest accuracy rate, and he produces target constructions 10 times in 5 different sessions throughout his corpus.

It is observed that when both target and non-target constructions appear in the same transcript of a bilingual child, the non-target constructions always outnumber (or appear as often as) the target ones. Timmy's accuracy rate of inverted double object datives reaches 100% only in the last recording at 3;06.25.

Monolingual children, on the other hand, demonstrate higher accuracy rates and more frequent uses of target inverted double object datives throughout their recordings. The average accuracy rate is 50%. One child (CKT) solely uses the target construction in the corpus.[28] Three children (CGK, LLY and LTF) produce both target and non-target constructions, and among them, LTF has the highest accuracy rate (63.6%), while CGK has the lowest accuracy rate (40%). HHC only produces non-target *bei2*-double object datives. CCC, MHZ and WBH do not produce any target or non-target inverted *bei2*-double object datives in their recordings. Each monolingual child's number of tokens of target

[28] Note that CKT overall only produces two target inverted double object datives in one transcript. It is possible that later he will also use the non-target [*bei2*-Goal-Theme] form.

Table 16 Accuracy rates of inverted double object datives in monolingual children

	CGK	CKT	HHC	LLY	LTF	Average
Tokens of target [*bei2*-T-G]	6	2	0	4	7	19
Tokens of non-target [*bei2*-G-T]	9	0	2	4	4	19
Accuracy rate	40%	100%	0%	50%	63.6%	50%

inverted double object datives and non-target *bei2*-double object datives and their accuracy rates are summarized in Table 16.

Except for HHC, every monolingual child demonstrates a higher accuracy rate in the inverted double object datives than most bilingual children. The highest accuracy rate in monolingual children is 100%, while the lowest accuracy rate in monolingual children (CGK: 40%) is close to the highest rate in bilingual children (Timmy: 41.2%), and much higher than rates of Alicia (0%), Llywelyn (20%) and Sophie (10.5%).

In addition to higher accuracy rates, monolingual children also use the target constructions more frequently than bilingual children. The number of target inverted double object datives generally exceeds (or equals to) the number of non-target double object datives in the second half of the recordings of monolingual LLY and LTF. LLY stops using the non-target double object form at age 3;0, and LTF's last non-target [*bei2*-Goal-Theme] construction appears at age 2;9.[29]

5 Discussion

It is observed that 2 out of 9 monolingual English-speaking children and 3 out of 5 Cantonese-English bilingual children are relatively delayed in English prepositional datives, and they also fail to produce both triadic dative *to* and triadic directional *to* within a short period of time. However, these children, contrary to what the decomposition approach predicts, do not have problems with the primitive GO, and their first prepositional datives emerge months after their first dyadic directional *to*. If the decomposition approach alone explains the late emergence of prepositional datives, why should Adam, Mark and the 3 bilingual children, who produce directional *to* from early on, wait another 8 (or more) months to produce their first prepositional datives?

One possibility is that after acquiring each primitive, children need some additional time to combine the primitives together. However, according to Viau (2006), there is no statistical difference between children's ages of acquisition of

[29] However, it cannot be concluded firmly that LLY and LTF have acquired the inverted double object datives at the end of their recordings, because later development may not be captured in the corpus.

primitives CAUSE and HAVE and double object datives, which means that children almost need no additional time to combine CAUSE and HAVE together to produce their first double object datives. Thus, it seems unjustifiable to assume that children take longer time to combine CAUSE and GO, if these primitives equip children with all the necessary syntactic representation of the prepositional datives.

Another possibility, as proposed earlier in Section 3, is that the ambiguity in *to* (and also *for*) makes English prepositional datives difficult to acquire. One sign of not being able to distinguish dative *to* from directional *to* is limited usage of different meanings of *to* for a period of time. This is confirmed on both monolingual and bilingual children, as those who are late in prepositional datives only produce one type of triadic *to* for several months, while other children who make faster progress from double object datives to prepositional datives have a shorter gap between first triadic dative *to* and first triadic directional *to*.

Note that children's knowledge of dyadic directional *to* and dyadic dative *to* may not be helpful in distinguishing triadic dative *to* and triadic directional *to*, because dyadic dative *to* is lexically selected by verbs (e.g. *happen*, *belong*, etc.) that do not take dyadic directional *to* and location as arguments. Thus, no true ambiguity exists between the two dyadic *to*s as the ambiguity between triadic dative *to* and triadic directional *to*, which are taken by the same ditransitive verb.

However, it is still unclear how children acquire the syntactic and semantic differences between triadic dative *to* and triadic directional *to*. Levinson (2005) argues that dative *to* corresponds to *who*/*what* in *wh*-interrogatives, while directional *to* corresponds to *where*. Therefore, one possibility is that the corresponding *wh*-interrogatives help children to capture the difference between triadic dative *to* and triadic directional *to*.

An analysis of adult input in CHILDES reveals that this kind of crucial evidence, for many children, is very rare. The adults' utterances containing both 'who/what' and 'give/send/take' and both 'where' and 'send/take' were extracted from the 9 monolingual English-speaking children's corpora, and the results are summarized in Table 17. Correspondence of triadic dative *to* with the verb *give* is found in the investigators' utterances of Peter and Shem, and the mother's utterances in Nina's transcripts. Correspondence of triadic directional *to* with the verb *send* and/or *take* is found in mother's utterances of Adam, Nina, Sarah and Shem. However, no parents use both *to who* and *where* with the same verb, suggesting that the crucial evidence to disambiguate triadic dative and directional *to* is not vastly available to children in the input.

Thus, it seems that children need to rely on other means to acquire the distinction between the two types of *to*. The syntax and semantics of double object datives may lend support to children, as the alternation between double object datives and prepositional datives is only available to triadic dative *to*, and triadic dative *to*, which suggests a possessive relationship between the goal and the theme, should be semantically related to double object datives. The ordering relation between the acquisition of double object datives and prepositional

Table 17 *Wh*-correspondence of triadic *to* in adult's speech

Child	Dative *to–who/what*	Directional *to–where*	Both[a]
Adam	No	1 (from mother)	No
Eve	No	No	No
Mark	No	No	No
Naomi	1 (from mother)	No	No
Nathaniel	No	No	No
Nina	7 (from mother)	27 (from mother)	No
Peter	1 (from investigator)	No	No
Sarah	No	1 (from mother)	No
Shem	1 (from investigator)	3 (from investigator)	No

[a] *Both* here means both *wh*-correspondences (*where* and *to whom/what*) are produced for the same verb.

datives also shows that acquiring double object dative is possibly a necessary step in acquiring prepositional datives.

However, it is less likely that the late acquisition of prepositional datives and [V-Particle-NP] constructions are both influenced by one parameter. Adam, who has a gap of 8.8 months between his first double object and prepositional datives, only takes 0.5 months to produce [V-Particle-NP] constructions after his first [V-NP-Particle] construction. Different factors may be involved in the delay of each construction, and the proposal of a second parameter does not explain the different developmental patterns observed in these children.

Though most English dative verbs participate in dative alternation and the input can demonstrate true optionality, the two dative constructions do not emerge at the same time for some children. The acquisition of prepositional datives requires extra knowledge of the ambiguities in *to* and *for*. Also, the fact that monolingual Cantonese-speaking children produce serial verb datives before non-target *bei2*-double object datives shows that the double-object-dative-first pattern is specific to English speaking children.

However, *bei2*-double object datives are ungrammatical in Cantonese, and there is a possibility that children may produce such double object datives earlier if such constructions were legitimate choices in that language. In fact, Cantonese-English bilingual children do produce non-target *bei2*-double object datives earlier than monolingual children do, but the bilinguals are more likely to do so due to the influence from their English grammar.

Cantonese inverted double object datives are expected to be difficult to acquire, as the acquisition process involves a discovery of an underlying serial verb structure which is very different from its surface form (see (7)). To acquire the inverted double object datives, children need to link this construction to serial verb datives, and discover the *bei2*-deletion rule to derive the surface [*bei2*-Theme-Goal] order. The most relevant evidence for a *bei2*-deletion analysis is adult serial verb dative [*bei2*-Theme-*bei2*-Goal] input. However, Chan (2003) looks at child-directed speech in CANCORP (Lee et al. 1996) and finds that only 1.65% of all dative constructions that contain a main verb *bei2* are in this form.

Though the input does not provide much direct evidence for the derivation of inverted double object datives, acquisition of the serial verb datives is nonetheless a necessary step in the discovery of the underlying [*bei2*-Theme-*bei2*-Goal] structure. If children do not produce any serial verb dative before their first inverted double object datives, it is questionable whether the underlying structure is in place for the inverted double object datives, and it follows that children may not apply the *bei2*-deletion rule but use other analyses to form the surface [*bei2*-Theme-Goal] sequence.

Analysis of the order of emergence of serial verb datives and inverted double object datives in Section 4.2 shows that it is very unlikely that the bilingual children have formed a syntactic connection between serial verb datives and inverted double object datives. The early inverted double object datives of these children are produced before their serial verb datives, and children who have produced serial verb datives do not produce any target inverted double object datives in their recordings. Monolingual children, on the other hand, acquire serial verb dative constructions before they produce their first inverted double object datives. It is more likely for them to build a syntactic connection between the two constructions. In terms of quantity and frequency, bilingual children generally produce more non-target *bei2*-double object datives than monolingual children do. Some monolingual children stop producing non-target double object datives in the second half of their recordings, while bilingual children continue to use the non-target structure throughout their corpus.

As we can see from the different developmental patterns in bilingual and monolingual children, it is crucial to form the correct analysis for the inverted double object dative at the beginning of acquisition, otherwise the non-target [*bei2*-Goal-Theme] structures will emerge at a relatively earlier developmental stage, and delay the acquisition of inverted *bei2*-double object datives.

It seems that the syntactic connection between the surface inverted order and the underlying serial verb dative structure is also a key factor in unlearning the non-target *bei2*-double object datives. In fact, there is a learnability problem, as children are mainly exposed to target constructions, which include the inverted [*bei2*-Theme-Goal] constructions, topicalized [Theme-*bei2*-Goal] constructions, null-object [*bei2*-Goal]/[bei2-Theme] constructions, and sometimes serial verb [*bei2*-Theme-*bei2*-Goal] constructions. No positive input can inform children that *bei2*-double object datives are non-target-like.

Children also do not follow the Subset Principle but start to produce both target inverted double object datives and non-target double object datives from the beginning. There is no straightforward mechanism to remove the non-target double object order from their grammar.

The null-object [*bei2*-Goal] constructions are also potentially misleading to children. Chan (2003) reports that among all adult input containing a main verb *bei2*, 48.46% consists of [*bei2*-Goal] constructions while only 5.05% consists of [*bei2*-Theme] constructions. Since [*bei2*-Goal] is highly frequent while [*bei2*-Theme] is restricted to a small range of themes, Chan (2003) suggests that children treat [*bei2*-Goal] as an entrenched unit with the theme tagged on at the end.

However, it is observed that children use both [*bei2*-Theme-Goal] and [*bei2*-Goal-Theme] orders at the same time. The [*bei2*-Goal] is not a fixed sequence for both bilingual and monolingual children, and the prolonged coexistence period of the two constructions shows that children have formed their own analyses for each structure. The null-object [*bei2*-Goal] utterances may be a trigger for non-target double object datives, but children definitely hold more knowledge than putting *bei2* and the goal in a strict order. The learnability problem is still unsolved, and the ambiguity in null-object [*bei2*-Goal] constructions seems to be more difficult for children to resolve than the ambiguity in *to*, as most monolingual and bilingual children have not fully acquired the inverted double object datives at the end of their recordings.

The findings of this study, when put together, show that various syntactic and semantics factors affect the development of dative constructions in different languages. Though optionality in word order is observed in the adult English grammar, children do not always start by producing double object datives and prepositional datives at the same time. No evidence shows that an avoidance strategy is adopted in the development of dative constructions (for a comprehensive discussion on the avoidance strategy and optionality in word order, see 'The Acquisition of Apparent Optionality: The Word Order in Subject- and Object-Shift Constructions in Norwegian' by Anderssen et al. (this volume)). In fact, many monolingual English-speaking children acquire double object datives and prepositional datives at the same time, and the children who spend longer time on prepositional datives also have difficulty with certain usages of *to*. Compared with double object datives, English prepositional datives involve input ambiguities in the syntax and semantics of dative/directional *to* and various usages of *for*, and children are sensitive to this property of English prepositions and dative constructions.

The large proportion of non-target double object datives in Cantonese-speaking children (both monolingual and bilingual) suggest that children naturally utilize a grammar that allows double object structure for dative verbs, even though no such input may be provided. Also, the serial verb dative constructions, which are parallel to English prepositional datives, are acquired early in Cantonese monolingual children. These facts together suggest that children can accept optionality in the case of dative constructions, and the universal grammar may already provide them with both word order options. Input ambiguities may interfere in the development of a particular dative construction, but children seem to accept both double object datives and prepositional datives as legitimate structures for a dative verb.

6 Conclusion

This study investigates the development of dative constructions in English monolingual, Cantonese-English bilingual and Cantonese monolingual children. With regard to the acquisition of English dative constructions, it is found that monolingual and bilingual children who are relatively slow in acquiring prepositional datives also fail to produce triadic dative *to* and triadic directional *to* within a short period of time. The distinction between triadic dative *to* and triadic directional *to* is crucial to the acquisition of prepositional datives, as the two types of *to* can be selected by the same verb, and yet they have different meanings and take different types of arguments. It is also shown that it is not the primitive GO that delays the acquisition of prepositional datives.

The double-object-datives-first pattern is language-specific to English. Cantonese does not have input ambiguity with its dative marker, and Cantonese dative constructions are acquired in a different order. Cantonese monolingual children produce serial verb datives first, and this developmental pattern helps them to acquire the inverted double object datives. Cantonese-English bilingual children, due to influence from their English grammar, use non-target *bei2*-double object datives at an earlier stage, and show no evidence that they have linked the inverted double object datives to the syntactically related serial verb dative constructions.

Acknowledgments The author would like to thank Yang Gu, Richard Larson, Thomas Lee, Yafei Li, Gladys Tang, Joshua Viau, Virginia Yip, audiences at BUCLD31 and ISB6, GLOWXXX acquisition workshop organizers, and the editors and reviewers of this volume for their helpful comments and discussion. This research is supported by a postgraduate studentship by the Chinese University of Hong Kong.

References

Beck, Sigrid, and Kyle Johnson. 2004. Double objects again. *Linguistic Inquiry* 35: 97–123.

Chan, Wing-Shan. 2003. *The development of bei2 dative constructions in early child cantonese*. Unpublished M.Phil. Thesis. The Chinese University of Hong Kong.

Gu, Chenjie. 2007. *The acquisition of dative constructions in cantonese-English bilingual children*. Unpublished M.Phil. Thesis. The Chinese University of Hong Kong.

Harley, Heidi. 2002. Possession and the double object construction. In *The yearbook of linguistic variation 2*, eds. Pierre Pica and Johan Rooryck, 31–70. Amsterdam: John Benjamins.

Lakusta, Laura. 2005. *Source and goal asymmetry in non-linguistic motion event representations*. Doctoral dissertation, Johns Hopkins University.

Landau, Idan. 1999. Possessor raising and the structure of VP. *Lingua* 107: 1–37.

Larson, Richard K. 1988. On the double object construction. *Linguistic Inquiry* 19: 335–391.

Lee, Thomas Han-Tak, Colleen Wong, and Samuel Leung. 1996. The Hong Kong Cantonese Child Language Corpus (CANCORP). Accessed 31 March 2006.

Levinson, Lisa. 2005. 'To' in two places and the dative alternation. *Penn Working Papers in Linguistics* 11: 136–147.

MacWhinney, Brian. 2000. *The CHILDES project: Tools for analyzing talk. Third edition.* Mahwah: Lawrence Erlbaum Associates.

Matthews, Stephen, and Virginia Yip. 1994. *Cantonese: A comprehensive grammar*. London: Routledge.

Müller, Natascha. 1998. Transfer in bilingual first language acquisition. *Bilingualism: Language and Cognition* 1: 151–171.

Müller, Natascha, and Aafke, Hulk. 2001. Crosslinguistic influence in bilingual language acquisition: Italian and French as recipient languages. *Bilingualism: Language and Cognition* 4:1, 1–21.

Paradis, Johanne, and Fred Genesee. 1996. Syntactic acquisition in bilingual children: autonomous or interdependent? *Studies in Second Language Acquisition* 18: 1–25.

Pesetsky, David. 1995. *Zero syntax: Experiencers and cascades*. Cambridge: MIT Press.

Pylkkänen, Liina. 2002. *Introducing arguments*. Doctoral dissertations, MIT.

Richards, Norvin. 2001. An idiomatic argument for lexical decomposition. *Linguistic Inquiry* 32: 183–192.

Snyder, William, and Karin Stromswold. 1997. The structure and acquisition of English dative constructions. *Linguistic Inquiry* 28: 281–317.

Tang, Sze-Wing. 1998. On the 'inverted' double object construction. In *Studies in Cantonese linguistics*, ed. Stephen Matthews, 35–52. Hong Kong: Linguistic society of Hong Kong.

Viau, Joshua. 2006. Give = CAUSE + HAVE/GO: Evidence for early semantic decomposition of dative verbs in English Child Corpora. In *Proceedings of the 30th annual Boston University Conference on Language Development*, eds. David Bamman, Tatiana Magnitskaia and Colleen Zaller, 665–676. Somerville: Cascadilla Press.

Wagner, Laura, and Susan Carey. 2005. 12-month-old infants represent probable endings of motion events. *Infancy* 7: 73–83.

Yip, Virginia, and Stephen Matthews. 2000. Syntactic transfer in a Cantonese-English bilingual child. *Bilingualism: Language and cognition* 3: 193–208.

Yip, Virginia, and Stephen Matthews. 2005. Dual input and learnability: null objects in Cantonese-English bilingual children. In *Proceedings of the 4th International Symposium on Bilingualism*, eds. James Cohen, Kara T. McAlister, Kellie Rolstad and Jeff MacSwan, 2421–2431. Somerville: Cascadilla Press.

Yip, Virginia, and Stephen Matthews. 2007. *The bilingual child: Early development and language contact*. Cambridge: Cambridge University Press.

Using Early ASL Word Order to Shed Light on Word Order Variability in Sign Language

Deborah Chen Pichler

Abstract This study examines the early multi-sign utterances of four deaf children between the ages of 20 and 30 months acquiring American Sign Language (ASL) as their first language from deaf, signing parents. Results show that during this early stage, children are very inconsistent in their adherence to canonical VO word order, producing a high proportion of utterances with noncanonical OV order. Although such a pattern could indicate failure to set the Head Parameter, this chapter argues the contrary: that these children have not only set the Head Parameter, they have already begun to employ word order variation licensed by specific types of ASL verbal morphology. In addition to this early development of morpho-syntactically motivated OV, one of the children in this study also produces what appears to be early topicalisation structures, exhibiting a developing awareness that noncanonical OV word order has pragmatic as well a syntactic sources in ASL.

Keywords Sign language · Acquisition · Word order · Topicalisation · Variability

1 Introduction

This study examines the production of four deaf American children acquiring American Sign Language (ASL) as their first language. ASL has traditionally been categorized as a flexible word order language with canonical SVO order. In particular, verb-final constructions have been reported by many researchers (Fischer and Janis, 1992, Matsuoka 1997, Chen Pichler 2001), although details of their syntactic distribution and relative frequency are still fairly unclear. In certain cases, VO order appears to alternate freely with OV order, leading some to argue that syntactic labels such as subject and object are ill-suited to ASL,

D.C. Pichler (✉)
Gallaudet University, Washington, DC, USA
e-mail: deborah.chen.pichler@gallaudet.edu

M. Anderssen et al. (eds.), *Variation in the Input*, Studies in Theoretical Psycholinguistics 39, DOI 10.1007/978-90-481-9207-6_7,

because sign languages in general are pragmatically rather than syntactically organized (Friedman 1977, Deuchar 1983, Bouchard and Dubuisson 1995, Bouchard 1996).

While an accurate account of ASL grammar must clearly incorporate the significant influence of pragmatic factors (e.g. figure/ground distinctions, newness/shared information, etc.) on ASL structure, this fact does not preclude the possibility that sign languages also employ identifiable subjects, objects and verbs, and that these traditional syntactic notions are useful for explaining some of the word order variability in ASL. This study turns to language development data to throw light on the issue of ASL word order, investigating the response of children acquiring ASL to the word order variability in their input. Our main question is whether young learners themselves produce variable word order, and if they do, whether this variation follows any sort of pattern. The data discussed in this chapter suggest that young signers vary word order for both syntactic and pragmatic reasons, but that these two categories follow distinct acquisition timetables. These results support the view that a syntactic approach to ASL word order phenomena is valid, even though this area of the grammar is also subject to significant pragmatic influence.

This chapter will begin with a brief summary of relevant word order patterns in adult ASL (Section 2), followed by a review of previous acquisition studies on early ASL word order in Section 3. As we will see, these previous studies present contradictory characterizations of early ASL word order, motivating the present study, described in detail in Section 4. In Section 5, I will discuss data from one child in the study, ABY, that may represent a very early stage in object topicalisation. Finally, Section 6 consists of a summary and conclusion.

2 Word Order Variability in Adult ASL

Fischer (1975) first classified ASL as a canonically SVO language, based on the observation that 'reversible' noun-verb-noun sequences (i.e. sequences in which either noun could function as a semantically appropriate agent or patient) as in (1) were consistently interpreted by native signers as SVO.

(1) CHILD NOTICE MAN
'The child noticed the man'
#'The man noticed the child'

Fischer noted that despite being the canonical word order of ASL, SVO is not the only order available. Adult signers make frequent use of other orders, such that preverbal objects and postverbal subjects are both common. In our discussion of noncanonical word order, this chapter will focus only on preverbal objects (the reader is referred to Chen Pichler (2001) for a summary of word order patterns featuring postverbal subjects and the early appearance of these patterns in children's signing).

2.1 OV Due to Topicalisation

Often described as a topic-comment language, ASL makes frequent use of topics to express contrastive focus, establish a new discourse topic or introduce new information (Aarons 1994). A variety of sentential elements may appear as topics, including noun phrases (both subject and object), verb phrases, adjectives, and adverbs. Topics appear in sentence-initial position and are accompanied by a grammatical nonmanual marker. Although the exact description of the topic nonmanual is a matter of debate, researchers generally agree that the major components are brow raise and (often) head tilt. In addition, topics are held or lengthened, giving the impression of a pause between the topic and remaining elements of the sentence. Fischer (1975) first described this particular constellation of nonmanual features, illustrated in Fig. 1, as 'intonational breaks.' She observed that they occurred in sentences where the word order departed from the canonical SVO pattern in ASL. This intonational break has since come to be known as the *ASL topic(alisation) nonmanual marker*, one of multiple nonmanual markers with grammatical status in ASL (and other sign languages). Current characterization of the ASL topic nonmanual includes obligatory brow raise on the topicalised constituent only (notated in examples by a scope line over the topic labeled *top*), followed by a hold or pause (notated with a comma) between the topicalised constituent and the remainder of the

Fig. 1 SISTER signed with the ASL topic nonmanual marker

sentence (Humphries and Padden 1992). An example of a topicalised object is shown in (2a).[1] Crucially, the topicalisation nonmanual marker in (2a) is obligatory, such that the same sentence signed without the nonmanual (consisting of both raised brows and pause) is ungrammatical (2b).

      ‾‾‾‾‾top
(2a) SISTER, (PRO-1) MEET FINISH.
     'His/her sister, I've met.'
(2b) *SISTER (PRO-1) MEET FINISH.

Even more specific description of the topicalisation nonmanual was proposed by Aarons (1994) (see also Neidle et al. 2000), whose detailed analysis distinguishes between three classes of topics in ASL, depending on their relation to the canonical object position following the verb. Type 1, represented by (3a), is the only true moved topic, forming an argument chain with the object trace in canonical postverbal position. Aarons claims that moved topics "can be contrastive focus," often introducing new information within a limited set. Type 2 topics are base-generated topics, and may co-occur with an independent NP in canonical object position. The topic NP in this case is not a true argument of the verb, although it is not uncommon for it to be in a class-member relation with the object, as in (3b). Alternatively, type 2 topics may be coreferential with a pronominal argument, as shown in (3c). According to Aarons, base-generated topics serve to change discourse topic or introduce new information. Finally, type 3 topics are also base-generated, but are always coreferential with an argument in canonical position in the sentence, as illustrated in (3d). Aarons claims that these can only be used when the referents are already known to the interlocutor and serve to introduce a major change in discourse topic.

     top
(3a) MARY$_i$, JOHN LIKE t$_i$
     '*Mary*, John likes.'
     top
(3b) VEGETABLE, JOHN LIKE CORN
     'As for vegetables, John likes corn.'
     top
(3c) MARY$_i$, JOHN LIKE HER$_i$
     'As for Mary, John likes her.'

[1] Because ASL allows null subjects, sentences such as (2a) may surface with OV word order, as long as PRO-1 is understood in the discourse.

$\overline{\text{top}}$

(3d) MARY$_i$, JOHN LIKE HER$_i$
'You know Mary? John likes her.'

Aarons claims that in addition to differing in structure, distribution and function, the three topic types are marked by distinct nonmanual markers. According to her analysis, topic 1 is marked by brow raise, widened eyes, and the head tilting slightly back and to side, then moving down and forward. Topic 2 is marked by very wide eyes and a large movement of the head back and to the side, then down and forward. Topic 3 has the most distinct nonmanual marking of the three topic types: raised brow, widened eyes with fixed gaze, open mouth and raised upper lip and the head forward and slight, rapid head nods.

A consistent and exact characterization of the topic nonmanual is elusive in the literature, due to the fact that so much variation seems to exist across and even within signers. Aarons' approach is attractive in that it makes highly specific claims about the form exhibited by each type of nonmanual marker. To illustrate the differences between topic markers, Aarons (1994) and Neidle et al. (2000) provide still photos of each nonmanual marker as produced by a native signer, and video clips are available on the American Sign Language Linguistic Research Project site hosted by Boston University at http://www.bu.edu/asllrp/book/ch4.html. However, the nonmanual expressions displayed in these examples strike me as very deliberate and somewhat affected. The nonmanual distinctions described by Aarons, especially between type 1 and type 2, are difficult to detect in natural, running signing, and they are unlikely to be observed in the production of small children. Furthermore, young children's utterances tend to be short and frequently contain null arguments, such that distinguishing between topic types based on structural grounds (e.g. whether or not there is a resumptive pronoun) may prove implausible. For these reasons, there have been no acquisition studies yet, to my knowledge, testing Aarons' proposed classification of topic types. However, if it turns out that different topic types *can* be distinguished in early ASL, Aarons' classification could help us determine whether some topic types are acquired earlier than others.

2.2 OV Due to Reordering Morphology

In addition to noncanonical OV order accompanied by 'intonational breaks,' early ASL researchers also noted variation accompanied by certain kinds of 'modification' of the verb (Fischer and Gough 1974, Fischer 1975, Kegl 1976, Liddell 1980). Today 'modification' is understood to mean inflection, not only for person and number (i.e. 'classic' verb agreement), but for other features as well, such as aspect, location and instrument (Fischer and Janis 1990, Matsuoka 1997, Braze 2004, Chen Pichler 2001). In example (4), the verb EAT is marked for continuative aspect (an *aspectual verb*), resulting in a reduplicated form that is phonologically heavier than the citation form of EAT. Example (5), in contrast, features a verb inflected for location (a *spatial verb*). This form is not phonologically heavier than its uninflected counterpart, yet it occurs in noncanonical OV order. Likewise, example (6) involves a *handling verb*, in which the hand configuration suggests the grasping of a specific object (in this case, the instrument, although the hand configuration of other handling verbs reflect the shape of the theme). While spatial and aspectual verbs appear to require verb-final word order, many handling verbs are judged to be equally grammatical in both OV and VO word orders. Crucially, the preverbal objects in (4)–(6) are not topicalised, because they are not marked with the obligatory topicalisation nonmanual marker described earlier.

(4) MEAT $\text{EAT}_{\text{[aspect:continuative]}}$
'(I) just ate and ate meat'

(5) MONEY $\text{PUT}_{\text{[location:can]}}$
'(He) put the money in the can'

(6) BALL $\text{HIT}_{\text{[handling:bat]}}$
'(He) hit the ball (with a bat)'

Considering their effect on word order, I will collectively refer to the aspectual, spatial and handling morphemes as *reordering morphology*. Following previous proposals for aspectual verbs in ASL (Fischer and Janis 1990, Matsuoka 1997, Braze 2004, inter alia), I will assume that these morphemes license OV order because the verb is required to raise to a right-branching functional projection such as Aspect Phrase, leaving the object in a preverbal position.[2] If the same mechanism underlies the derivations of aspectual, spatial and handling OV, then these constructions could also be expected to form a natural class with respect to acquisition.

3 Early Word Order in Sign Language: Previous Reports

As we have just seen in the previous section, adult ASL allows variation in word order, including several options for noncanonical preverbal objects. Faced with variable word order in their input, children could conceivably react in several different ways. They might ignore the variability, insisting on a single order in their own output. Alternatively, they might note the variability but overlook the syntactic nuances distinguishing one order from another; in this case, we could expect the children to vary word order randomly. Finally, if ASL word order is exclusively determined by pragmatic factors, children's order variation might reflect these.

[2] In all of the proposals cited here, the raising verb leaves behind a copy of itself that need not be deleted, giving rise to the so-called *verb sandwich construction*, (S)VO$\text{V}_{\text{[inflection]}}$.

In this section, I will first summarize two previous studies on ASL word order in child ASL, Hoffmeister (1978, unpublished manuscript) and Schick (2002). These two studies come to very different conclusions regarding the degree of word order variability in their data, prompting my own study in this area, Chen Pichler (2001), which I will discuss in Section 4. I will also summarise previous research on the development of topicalisation in ASL, focusing mainly on the noted absence of the obligatory topic nonmanual in child signing. This will become relevant to later discussion in Section 5.

3.1 Hoffmeister (1978)

The first study of child ASL word order, Hoffmeister (1978, unpublished manuscript), was based on the spontaneous production of three deaf children of deaf, signing parents: Alice and Anne (twin sisters), and Thomas. Filming of the twins began when they were 24 months old, and continued until Alice was 3;0 years and Anne 4;6 years. Thomas was filmed from 3;7 until 5;7. Their collective data was arbitrarily divided into four stages of development, based loosely on age and MLU. Videotapes were transcribed by deaf adults and all multi-sign utterances containing a verb were classified according to word order, focusing on subjects, verbs, objects and locatives.

At stage I, both Anne and Alice produced many noncanonical OV sequences, accounting for 42 and 40% of all their utterances containing both a verb and overt object. In subsequent stages, the percentage of OV utterances fell for Anne and Alice (data for Thomas began only at Stage II), but rose again in stage IV for Alice and Thomas (see Table 1).

Hoffmeister (1978, unpublished manuscript) did not provide a list of the actual utterances produced by the children, but noted that OV utterances tended to occur with verbs that 'allow modulation' (most likely referring to agreement for person and number, but possibly also location) although most of

Table 1 Percentage of noncanonical OV in Hoffmeister (1978, unpublished manuscript) data

Child, stage	Total utterances with verb and object	Percentage of utterances with OV order
Anne, stage I	26	42
Anne, stage II	34	38
Alice, stage I	15	40
Alice, stage II	57	12
Alice, stage III	100	12
Alice, stage IV	259	14
Thomas, stage II	134	19
Thomas, stage III	75	13
Thomas, stage IV	171	20

the forms actually produced by the children in the early stages were uninflected. Once children began inflecting verb forms, Hoffmeister reports that they still favored canonical VO order over noncanonical OV. He interpreted this finding, in addition to the higher frequency of VO compared to OV overall, as evidence that deaf children show a strong preference for canonical VO order in ASL. Newport and Meier (1984) subsequently commented that such a preference was unexpected, given the high degree of word order variability permitted in adult ASL, presumably the input deaf children receive. However, Hoffmeister's interpretation of his data was consistent with other reports at that time of children initially resorting to a 'fixed word order strategy' when faced with word order variation in their input.

3.2 Schick (2002)

The second study to investigate early ASL word order, Schick (2002), draws from a large set of spontaneous data from 12 deaf children of deaf parents, each filmed for 5 h, within 2 weeks of their second birthday. Like Hoffmeister, Schick (2002) coded all multi-sign combinations that contained a verb, and reported very little verbal morphology at that stage. However, whereas Hoffmeister highlighted the canonical qualities of his subjects' ASL, Schick (2002) reports that her data is characterized by high variability in word order. Of the total multi-sign utterances including a verb and overt theme argument,[3] 57–68% (mean, 56%) appear in canonical order. While these percentages are comparable to those reported by Hoffmeister (1978, unpublished manuscript) for stage I, they are much higher than the percentages in subsequent stages, leading Schick to conclude that there is no evidence for a canonical word order strategy in her data.

Next, Schick investigates whether her data are consistent with the Verb Island Hypothesis proposed by Tomasello (1992), in which children assign grammatical properties to verbs on an individual basis, rather than generalizing across the entire class of verbs. If this is so, she predicts there should be positional preferences for individual verbs, giving the overall appearance of mixed word order. She selected the three children with the highest MLW (mean length of utterance in words) score for closer examination and found only weak positional preferences. For example, one subject used noncanonical theme-verb order almost exclusively for the verbs LOOK-FOR and PUT-IN, but canonical verb-theme order for the verbs EAT, SEE and DRINK. The same child produced WANT and LIKE in canonical and noncanonical orders with roughly equal frequency. Thus Schick concludes that the evidence for children using word order patterns on a verb-to-verb basis is weak at best.

In her discussion, Schick (2002) summarizes her findings thus: 'The data provide little evidence that children use a word order strategy to communicate

---

[3] Schick (2002) refers to themes and agents rather than subjects and objects, to avoid claiming that such syntactic notions are acquired by children at this age.

grammatical role for common semantic functions in early multi-word utterances in ASL' (2002: 154). She offers two pragmatic alternatives as possible sources of the word order variation she observes in her data. First, she considers the possibility that deaf children, through frequent exposure to topicalised structures in their input, are aware that objects are not limited to post-verbal position. They therefore produce fronted, preverbal objects in their own production. However, these preverbal objects are not properly marked as topics because children at this age are 'simply not aware of the nonmanual markers needed to indicate a dislocation' (2002: 156). She cites supporting reports by Reilly et al. (1990) that the topic nonmanual is acquired late in ASL (see the next subsection).

Second, Schick (2002) suggests that children may conclude from the word order variation of their input that order is not used in ASL to signal grammatical function, but rather discourse status such as new vs. given information. She notes that studies of another languages with highly variable word order, Turkish, have reported that children manipulate order in pragmatically appropriate ways by the tender age of 2;0 (Aksu-Koç and Slobin 1985).

Although Schick (2002) does not ultimately settle on a single explanation for her data, she does conclude that whatever motivation young children have in varying word order is better characterized as pragmatic than as syntactic. This is in opposition to the staunchly syntactic analysis advanced by Hoffmeister, who concluded that his young subjects depended so strongly on word order to encode grammatical role, that they even extended this strategy in contexts where it became redundant.

3.3 Reilly et al. (1991)

The most comprehensive study to date on the acquisition of ASL grammatical nonmanuals has been conducted by July Reilly and colleagues (Reilly et al. 1990, 1991, inter alia). Nonmanuals are notoriously challenging to study, and their execution by child signers tends to be even more varied and ephemeral than in adult signing. Nevertheless, Reilly and her colleagues succeed in establishing rough timelines for the development of various ASL nonmanuals and identify two important generalizations relevant to our discussion. First, when faced with multiple grammatical forms all marked with the same nonmanual feature, children apply the principle of Unifunctionality (Slobin 1985) and seek distinct ways of marking each grammatical form. Thus, once brow raise is coopted as the marker for yes-no questions around 1;9, it is temporarily unavailable as a marker for topics or conditional; the child must then find alternate ways of marking these latter structures. Here Reilly et al. (1991) point out a second generalization: young deaf children consider the hands as their primary linguistic articulators, reserving the face (nonmanuals) for affective, paralinguistic information. Thus, when both a manual and nonmanual marker exist for a particular structure, children will opt for the manual marker first. Reilly et al. (1991) illustrate with the case of ASL conditionals, which are obligatorily marked with brow raise on the *if*-clause, and optionally (and redundantly) marked with a lexical (manual) sign such as #IF, SUPPOSE or JUDGE.

(7a) MILK SPILL, MOTHER ANGRY (MILK SPILL marked "cond")
'If the milk gets spilled, Mom'll get angry.'

(7b) SUPPOSE MILK SPILL, MOTHER ANGRY (SUPPOSE MILK SPILL marked "cond")
'If the milk gets spilled, Mom'll get angry.' (Reilly et al. 1990:16)

While a lexical/manual marker is available for ASL conditional structures, no such marker is available for topicalisation structures. The latter are identifiable solely by the presence of the topic nonmanual marker and, in the case of object topics, a departure from canonical word order. Interestingly, Reilly et al. report that their subjects produced sentences like (8), featuring a preposed object at the front of the sentence.

(8) BANANA MOTHER EAT
'Banana, Mommy (is) eat(ing) it.' (Reilly et al. 1990:15)

Although the sentence-initial position occupied by BANANA suggests that it is a topic, Reilly et al. refrain from labeling it as such, due to the absence of raised brows. As a conservative measure, they do not consider word order alone sufficient evidence that the children are producing topic structures. In their words, only explicit marking with the topic nonmanual marker constitutes 'inescapable evidence of the child's competence.' Again, this view is consistent with the prevailing assumption that brow raise is the most salient and critical component of the ASL topic nonmanual.

On the other hand, Reilly et al. concede that examples like (8) give a strong impression that 'the child is beginning to develop a notion called "topic,"' presumably because of the noncanonical position of the object, but possibly also because of the pragmatic status of the fronted object. As we will discuss in Section 5, some deaf children in their second year seem to have awareness of the pragmatic effects of fronting, even though they lack the adult form of the topic nonmanual marker at this age.

4 Early Word Order in Sign Language

In light of the contradictory conclusions reached by Hoffmeister (1978, unpublished manuscript) and Schick (2002), I set out to analyze a new set of spontaneous ASL data from four deaf children of deaf parents, observed longitudinally on a weekly or biweekly basis from the age of roughly 20–30 months (Chen Pichler 2001, 2008). All multi-sign utterances containing a verb and overt object[4] were coded as either canonical VO or noncanonical OV. Noncanonical utterances were initially analyzed only for evidence of reordering morphology on the verb (syntactically-motivated OV).

Results, shown in Table 2, indicate that all four children were highly variable in their word order with respect to verbs and objects in the data sample. They produced canonical VO order with nearly the same frequency as noncanonical OV order (mean percentage of canonical VO utterances, 46%). Examples (9a–b) exhibit canonical order, while examples (10a–d) feature noncanonical preverbal objects with an aspectual verb, a spatial verb, a handling verb where the hand configuration corresponds to the instrument, and a handling verb where the hand configuration corresponds to the theme, respectively.[5]

Table 2 Percentage of canonical VO in Chen Pichler (2001, 2008) data

Child	Total utterances with verb and object	Utterances with VO order (%)
NED	25	52
SAL	44	32
JIL	50	50
ABY	76	50

(9a) PRO-1 WANT CAT [ABY, 29.5 mo.]
'I want the cat.'

(9b) DRINK WATER [JIL, 23.5 mo.]
'(I want to) drink some water.'

(10a) CAT LOOK-FOR$_{\text{[aspect:continuative]}}$ [JIL, 26.0 mo.]
'I'm looking and looking for the cat.'

(10b) YELLOW THROW$_{\text{[location:corner]}}$ [SAL, 20.75 mo.]
'(I) threw the yellow (ball) there (in the corner)'

(10c) IX(picture of man) BOAT ROW$_{\text{[handling:small cylinder]}}$ [NED, 27.5 mo.]
'He's rowing a boat.'

(10d) IX(cup) PUT-DOWN$_{\text{[handling:med cylinder]}}$ IX(living room) [ABY, 24.5 mo.]
'Put it (the cup) down over there (in the living room).'

Not only were children variable in their overall production of canonical and noncanonical word orders, but this variation persisted through the entire period

---

[4] Index points (IX) clearly directed towards the object (i.e. object pronouns) were counted as overt objects. As far as I can tell, this practice is consistent with that employed by both Hoffmeister (1978) and Schick (2002).

[5] It should be noted that many of these OV examples could be categorized as involving *depiction* (Liddell 2003, Dudis 2004). Although I do not have the means to analyze the effects of depiction on word order here, it is a line of investigation worth pursuing as cognitive linguistic models of sign language develop and extend into the field of acquisition.

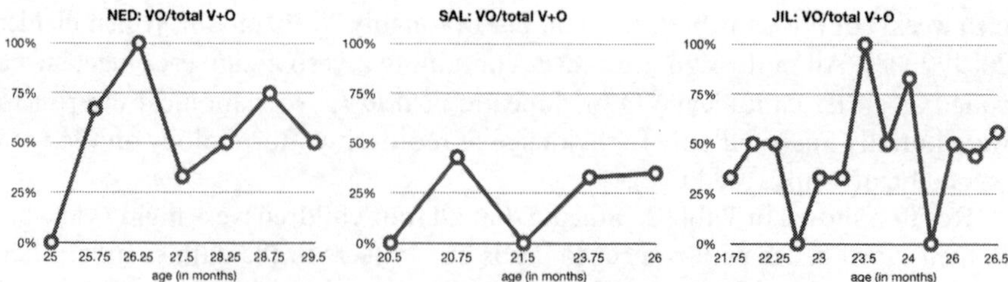

Fig. 2 Production of canonical VO order for NED, SAL and JIL

of study, as shown by the graphs in Fig. 2 (graphs for ABY will be analyzed separately in Section 5). From a parameter-setting viewpoint, one might be led to the conclusion that these children have yet to set the Head Parameter and are assigning random word order to verbs and objects.

However, once we take into account noncanonical OV utterances *with reordering morphology* as grammatical strings, the graphs show a different picture. Figure 3 shows the percentage of *grammatical* or adult-like utterances containing a verb and an object.

Now we see that NED reaches ceiling for grammatical V + O combinations around 28 months, while SAL does so just before 22 months. JIL reaches ceiling from about 24 to 26 months, although she then dips again in her final two sessions.[6] In contrast to the first set of graphs, this second set of graphs indicates that the vast majority of verb + object utterances at this age are grammatical, leading to a very different conclusion from before: these children have set the Head Parameter correctly (resulting in correct VO utterances) *and* have already learned to modify this order when the verb is marked with certain types of morphology (resulting in correct OV utterances). If this interpretation of the data is accurate, it would support the view that ASL makes grammatical use of word order, contra the claims of Bouchard (1996) and others. It is also worth noting that such an analysis might apply to at least some of the Schick (2002) data as well. Although she has published only very limited examples from her

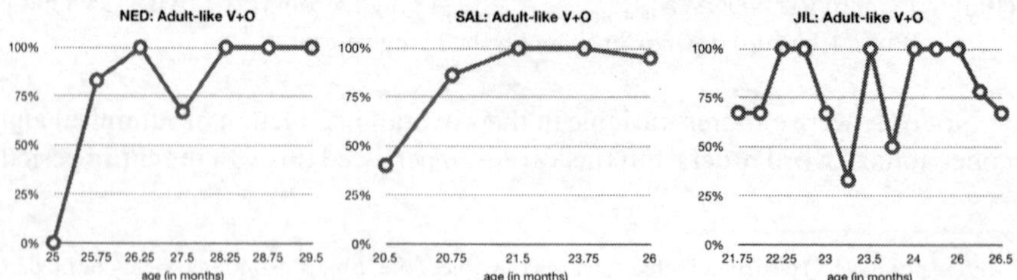

Fig. 3 Production of canonical VO or noncanonical OV with reordering morphology

[6] Unfortunately, I currently have no good explanation for this dip, but the reader is referred to Chen Pichler (2001) for further details and discussion.

data, recall that she reports theme-verb order for the verbs LOOK-FOR and PUT-IN. Both of these verbs are very likely to be verbs with reordering morphology (aspectual and spatial, respectively), and as such would be expected to appear with preverbal objects.

Although the account presented here has been very promising so far, it must be tested with additional data, both from more children and from sessions beyond those analyzed in Chen Pichler (2001, 2008). It will be important to examine word order in the input these children receive from adults in their environment. As noted by Newport and Meier (1985), Schick (2002) and others, ASL input is commonly assumed to involve considerable variation in word order. However, some studies focused on ASL input report that deaf mothers actually use *more* canonical SVO order with their deaf children than they would in adult-to-adult signing (Spencer and Harris 2006). If this is generally true, then the variation in early word order observed by Schick (2002) and Chen Pichler (2001, 2008) would be rather mysterious, and warrant serious reconsideration.

As a final point, children in the Chen Pichler (2001, 2008) study begin producing noncanonical OV order with all three verb types at approximately the same age, between 20 and 30 months. Operating on the assumption that structures sharing a common etiology can be expected to be acquired at the same point in development, these results suggest that aspectual, instrumental and locational morphology may form some sort of natural class in ASL, triggering noncanonical order, or (in the case of handling verbs) at least making it a possible option. In claiming a syntactic source for early word order variation, my results are similar in spirit to those of Hoffmeister (1978, unpublished manuscript). However, this does not preclude the possibility that deaf children are also sensitive to pragmatic effects of word order, the conclusion proposed by Schick. I will pursue this option in more detail in the next section.

5 Word Order Variation Due to Topicalisation: A Closer Look

Although an analysis based on the effects of reordering morphology can account for most of the noncanonical OV constructions in the Chen Pichler (2001, 2008) data, it does not account for all of them. Most notably, the majority of ABY's noncanonical OV constructions do not involve reordering morphology and are therefore not amenable to the analysis advanced in Section 4. In this section, I will pursue the possibility that a portion of ABY's unexplained OV constructions are early topics, marked with a more general form of the topic nonmanual employed by adult ASL signers.

5.1 A Closer Look at the Adult Topicalisation Nonmanual

While researchers noted from early on that the ASL topic nonmanual marker may involve more than just raised brows, this feature has come to be regarded as the most salient and obligatory component of the marker. Traditionally, discussions of the topic nonmanual have made little or no mention of the role played by other nonmanual features. However, a very different approach has been proposed by Nespor and Sandler (1999) and Rosenstein (2001) in their analyses of topics in Israeli Sign Language (ISL). While they report that brow raise is associated with topics in ISL, the true topic marker is not limited to that or any other single nonmanual feature, but rather, involves combinations of features such as widened eyes, raised brows, head nods, eye blinks and holds. However, all topic-bearing sentences share a striking feature: following the topic, the configuration of the nonmanual features up to that point changes all at once.

For example, in Fig. 4 the brows, eyes, mouth, etc. assume one position during the signing of the topic CAKE, then a new position for the remaining elements of the sentence. In addition, there is a hold on CAKE (indicated by the = symbol) and an eye blink (X) immediately following it.

Fig. 4 Prosodic analysis of CAKE I EAT-UP DEPLETE (Nespor and Sandler 1999)

	CAKE		I EAT-UP DEPLETE	
brows	up___			
eyes	squint_	X		X
mouth	O --> o		lip sputter	
head	forward		tilt______________	
mouthing	'cake'			
hold			=	

The simultaneous change in nonmanual features described above results in a general prosodic break separating the topic sign from the rest of the sentence. Nespor and Sandler (1999) claim that it is this break, rather than raised brows specifically, that constitutes the true topic nonmanual marker for ISL. Such an analysis is worth considering for ASL also, despite the long-held assumption that brow raise is an obligatory component of the topicalisation marker. It also has great potential to enlighten our understanding of the development of topicalisation in child signing. Recall from Section 3 that neither Schick (2002) nor Reilly et al. (1990) pursue an analysis of topicalisation before age 3;0 due to the absence of consistent brow raise prior to that age. In the next section, I will argue that one of my child subjects, ABY, does in fact produce topics, but marks them with a general, ISL-style nonmanual marker that does not necessarily involve brow raise.

5.2 *Prosodic Analysis of OV Structures in ABY Data*

As mentioned in Section 4, ABY's verb + object production does not pattern like that of the other children in the Chen Pichler (2001, 2008) study. Unlike the

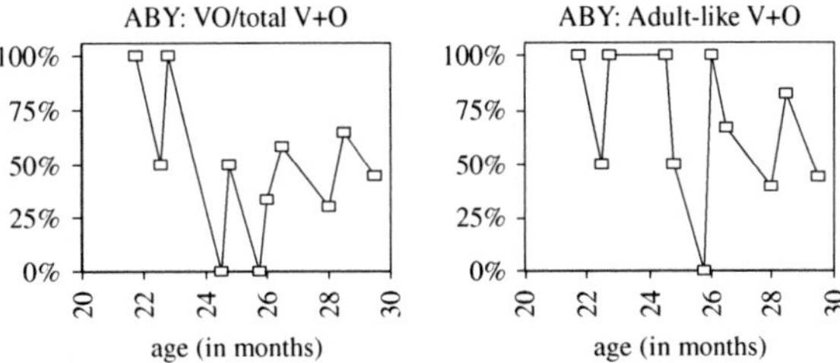

Fig. 5 ABY graphs for canonical VO (*left*) and grammatical verb + object (*right*)

other children, ABY makes very little use of reordering morphology, with the result that there is little difference between her graphs for canonical VO structures and grammatical verb + object structures, as shown in Fig. 5.

A sample of ABY's unexplained OV structures is given in (11)–(13). In these examples, the line marked *br* indicates the scope of brow raise; the equal sign (=) indicates a hold, as in the Nespor and Sandler (1999) analysis cited earlier.

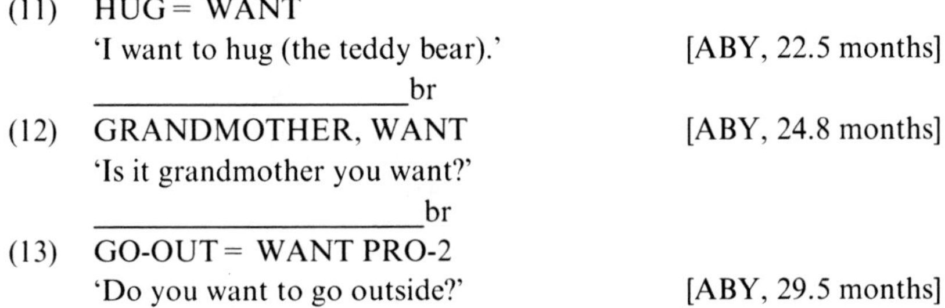

(11) HUG= WANT
'I want to hug (the teddy bear).' [ABY, 22.5 months]

____________________br
(12) GRANDMOTHER, WANT [ABY, 24.8 months]
'Is it grandmother you want?'

____________________br
(13) GO-OUT= WANT PRO-2
'Do you want to go outside?' [ABY, 29.5 months]

As the examples show, ABY fronts both noun phrase objects (GRANDMOTHER) and clausal objects (albeit very simple clauses consisting only of a verb: HUG and GO-OUT). Most, although not all, of her unexplained OV sentences are characterized by the verb WANT (17/25 sentences) and the tendency to be yes/no questions (13/25 sentences). The connection between WANT and OV order is yet unclear, so I will not discuss it here (although see Chen Pichler 2001 for more details). I will focus instead on the nonmanual aspect of ABY's unexplained OV sentences.

The line marked *br* in examples (12) and (13) indicates that the brow raise is sustained for the entire sentence, extending over the object in initial position. While it is possible that the segment of the raised brows over the fronted object is the topic nonmanual marker, it is important to recognize that these sentences are yes/no questions, which also happen to be marked with brow raise in ASL. Reilly et al. (1991) report that this nonmanual is acquired exceptionally early, and ABY uses it correctly during the entire period under investigation. In adult signing, topics occupy a position outside the scope of question nonmanuals (Liddell 1980). Thus, a yes-no question with topicalisation should technically be marked with two separate instances of brow raise, one over the topic and another over the matrix question. However, these two adjacent nonmanuals are perceived as a single, continuous brow raise in fluid adult signing, and this is also the case in ABY's OV yes-no questions here. We must thus turn to other means of identifying topics.

Aside from brow raise, there is another, more subtle nonmanual feature that characterizes ABY's OV constructions. In 14/25 cases, there is some sort of prosodic break, of the type described by Nespor and Sandler (1999) for adult ISL, between the initial object and the remainder of the sentence. Typically, ABY's prosodic breaks are very simple, characterized by repetition or holding of the topic sign, followed by a change in head position or slight nodding of the head for the remainder of the sentence. Two examples are presented in Fig. 6.

Fig. 6 Examples of prosodic analysis for two of ABY's problematic OV utterances

	GRANDMOTHER	WANT
brows	up________________	________________
eyes	wide______________	________________
mouth	/aa/______________	________________
hold	=	=

	GO-OUT	WANT	PRO-2
brows	(up__________	__________	__________)
head	low__________	__________	__________
nod		slight______	__________
hold	=		

Whereas brow raise is largely limited to OV yes/no-questions, this simple prosodic break occurs in both questions and declaratives. ABY produces two OV declaratives with a prosodic break, including the earlier example (11). Although rare in my data sample, these sentences present the clearest evidence for topics, since they avoid the complicating factor of yes/no brow raise.

The prosodic breaks produced by ABY in this data set are admittedly very simple, sometimes consisting of little more than a hold, as in example (12). I propose that these examples represent the very earliest stages of development of the topic nonmanual, at a point when ABY has understood the general pragmatic effect of fronting the object to topic position, as well as the requirement that she mark the topic nonmanually. What she has yet to learn is that in her target sign language, a general prosodic break is not sufficient (although it is sufficient in other natural sign languages), but must include brow raise as one of its components.

Of course, as mentioned earlier, the long-standing assumption that all ASL topics are obligatorily marked by brow raise may not be accurate, and deserves renewed scrutiny. As early as 1980, Liddell demonstrated that the duration of signs in topic (sentence-initial) position is significantly longer than in any other position in the sentence. Interestingly, Liddell (1980) includes a description of the ASL topic nonmanual that does not specifically mention brow raise,[7] but defines it in terms that are strikingly similar to those used by Nespor and Sandler (1999) for ISL: 'a sharp change between the facial expression and the head position ... which marks topics and the facial expression and head position which are used during the rest of the sentence' (Liddell 1980: 80). Future work on adult ASL will determine whether brow raise is indeed an obligatory component of the ASL topic marker, but in the meantime, it is perhaps wiser to characterise this marker as a prosodic break, rather than focusing on any single nonmanual feature. If this is so, then it should be no surprise if children initially conceive of the topic marker precisely in this way, only incorporating language-specific features (such as brow raise) later in development.

5.3 A Word on the Pragmatic Context of ABY OV Constructions

Earlier in Section 2.1, I summarized the analysis of ASL topic types presented by Aarons (1994). The categorisation she proposes is based on syntactic, pragmatic and nonmanual distinctions she observes in her adult data, but they have yet to be tested in the field of acquisition. If Aarons is accurate in her proposal for multiple classes of topics in ASL, we might expect that some class(es) might be acquired before others. Unfortunately, the minimalistic nature of the nonmanual markers that I observed in ABY's data severely limit their usefulness in testing the Aarons (1994) categorisation. Certainly ABY does not produce the very specific changes in head position described by Aarons for topic types 1 and 2, and her use of brow raise and widened eyes is inconsistent. Topic type 3 is generally easier to identify in adult signing, thanks to nonmanual features unique to this topic type, such as rapid head nods or nose crinkle, but these features do not occur in my current sample of ABY's signing.[8] Structurally speaking, ABY's data are also too simple at this stage to determine which topic type(s) she has acquired.

The only conclusions we might be able to draw from the present, limited data come from pragmatic context. In roughly half of the 14 OV constructions with a prosodic break that I considered here, the fronted object could qualify as new information within a limited set, consistent with the Aarons' definition of type 1 topics. For instance, the question in example (12) above occurs in a context where ABY is asking the litter of newborn kittens in her home (with whom she converses often and fondly) who they want to be with them. She produces a

[7] However, elsewhere in Liddell (1980), he does specify brow raise as a component of the ASL topic nonmanual.

[8] ABY does produce rapid head nods, as in example (13), but these nods occur on signs that come *after* the prosodic break.

string of utterances in which she suggests various family members, first her grandmother (who had recently visited), then her father:

(14) *ABY: GRANDMOTHER WANT
%eng: is it grandma you want?
*ABY: GRANDMOTHER WANT
%eng: is it grandmother you want?
*ABY: DAD WANT
%eng: is it dad you want?
*ABY: DAD WORK
%eng: dad is working/at work

Similarly, the excerpt in (15) shows that example (13) above is uttered within the context of offering two choices: going outside or staying inside (DCP is the adult whom ABY is addressing):

(15) *ABY: GO-OUT WANT PRO-2
%eng: do you want to go outside?
*DCP: GO-OUT
%eng: go out?
*ABY: STAY
%eng: or stay (inside)?
...
*ABY: STAY WANT
%eng: do you want to stay (inside)?

These very preliminary observations suggest that ABY's earliest topic production includes Aarons' type 1 topics, a finding that would be compatible with recent studies on the development of information packaging in ASL and Brazilian Sign Language. Lillo-Martin and de Quadros (2005) examine the position and discourse status (e.g. new vs. given) of NPs in the naturalistic signing of their two Brazilian and two American deaf subjects (one of which is ABY) to determine the relative time course of acquisition for informational focus, contrastive focus and emphatic focus. They report that the earliest type of focus used consistently by all four subjects is information focus, which they equate with Aarons' (1994) type 1 topic. Thus there is at least preliminary evidence that in addition to their grasp of the syntactic sources for word order variation, discussed in Section 4, young signers are also aware of the pragmatic consequences of word order emphasized by Friedman (1977), Bouchard (1996) and others. However, whereas order variation for syntactic purposes appears well in place by 20–30 months, variation for pragmatic purposes seems to develop later, with only one of my four subjects exhibiting what appears to be an early form of topicalisation. Alternatively, it may be that children differ in their initial analysis for word order variation, some beginning with a syntactic approach while others begin with a pragmatic approach. Clearly, further information is needed from these and other signing children to before we can determine which of these two alternatives is correct.

6 Summary and Conclusion

The study of ASL word order development, although it begun more than 30 years ago, is still in its early stages. Previous reports offer opposing conclusions on the role of word order in the earliest multi-sign combinations of deaf signing children: whereas Hoffmeister (1978, unpublished manuscript) reports that deaf children exhibit a strong dependence on a canonical word order scheme to express grammatical role, Schick (2002) finds no evidence for a word order scheme, concluding that deaf children vary word order for pragmatic reasons.

Chen Pichler (2001, 2008) considers the possibility that word order variation in early signing has both syntactic and pragmatic motivation. First, I presented evidence that the four deaf children in my study produced OV word order with verbs inflected with aspectual, spatial and handling morphology, all associated with preverbal objects in adult ASL. Because these three types of morphology have a similar effect on word order and appear together within the 10-month period under study, I proposed that they form a natural class, which I refer to as *reordering morphology*. Once reordering morphology is taken into account, word order for verb + object combinations by NED, JIL and SAL look target-like by the end of the observation period.

However, reordering morphology account for only a few of the OV utterances produced by the fourth child in this study, ABY. Detailed prosodic analysis revealed that more than half of ABY's OV sequences feature a very simple prosodic break between the preverbal object and the verb. This prosodic break is not considered target-like unless it involves brow raise, commonly assumed to be an obligatory component of the ASL topic nonmanual marker. Despite this fact, I argued that a prosodic break following the topic has been noted before in the ASL literature and is perhaps a more accurate characterization of the ASL topic maker than one that specifies any particular nonmanual feature such as brow raise. I concluded that ABY is producing topics that are correctly fronted and are marked by a simple prosodic break, following a mistaken initial assumption that any change in prosody is sufficient to mark ASL topics, as is the case in Israeli Sign Language (Nespor and Sandler 1999). The topic nonmanual will become adult-like once ABY recognizes that ASL accords special status to brow raise (if this is indeed true), and that this particular nonmanual feature is an obligatory component in marking topics.

Note that the attribution of topicalisation structures to ABY at 25 months is nearly a year earlier than the age at which Reilly et al. (1990) reported such structures occurring in their data. Both Reilly et al. (1990) and others have noted preposed objects in their child data in the past, but refrained from labeling them as topic structures due to children's unreliable control of brow raise over the topicalised element. Although the simple prosodic break employed by ABY is not completely target-like in many instances, it occurs in pragmatic contexts appropriate for topicalisation, supporting the claim that she is developing pragmatically-motivated strategies for word order variation. These structures were not attested in the production of the other three children during the 20–30 month age period under investigation, although presumably they will appear later. Investigation of subsequent video sessions for these three children is currently underway to determine if this prediction is accurate.

In conclusion, the patterns observed in this study indicate that young children exposed to variable word order in ASL also vary word order in their own production. This variation is not random, but is attributable to specific factors, both syntactic and pragmatic. These results support an approach to ASL word order that incorporates both syntactic and pragmatic features, rather than simply one or the other.

Acknowledgments This work was supported by NIH grant #NIDCD DC-00183 to Diane Lillo-Martin. Many thanks to her, and to our Deaf families and consultants, who make the study of their language possible! Thanks also to the many research assistants at the University of Connecticut and Gallaudet University for their invaluable help in filming and transcription. All errors in the present work are entirely my own.

References

Aarons, Debra. 1994. *Aspects of the syntax of American Sign Language*. Ph.D. dissertation, Boston University.

Aksu-Koç, Ayhan, and Dan Slobin. 1985. The acquisition of Turkish. In *The crosslinguistic study of language acquisition*, ed. Dan Isaac Slobin, 839–878. Mahwah: Lawrence Erlbaum Associates.

Bouchard, Denis. 1996. Sign languages and language universals: The status of order and position in grammar. *Sign Language Studies* 91: 101–160.

Bouchard, Denis, and Colette Dubuisson. 1995. Grammar, order & position of wh-signs in Quebec Sign Language. *Sign Language Studies* 87: 99–139.

Braze, David. 2004. Aspectual inflection, verb raising, and object fronting in American Sign Language. *Lingua* 114: 29–58.

Chen Pichler, Deborah. 2001. *Word order variation and acquisition in American Sign Language*. Ph.D. dissertation, University of Connecticut.

Chen Pichler, Deborah. 2008. Views on early word order in early ASL: Then and now. In *Signs of the time: Selected Papers from TISLR 8*, ed. Josep Quer, 293–318. Hamburg: Signum Press.

Deuchar, Margaret. 1983. Is BSL an SVO language? In *Language in sign: International perspectives on sign Language*, eds. Jim Kyle and Bencie Woll, 69–76. London: Croom Helm.

Dudis, Paul. 2004. *Depiction of events in ASL: Conceptual integration of temporal components*. Ph.D. dissertation, University of California- Berkeley.

Fischer, Susan. 1975. Influences on word-order change in American Sign Language. In *Word order and word order change*, ed. Charles Li, 3–25. Austin: University of Texas Press.

Fischer, Susan, and Bonnie Gough. 1974. Verbs in ASL. *Sign Language Studies* 18: 17–48.

Fischer, Susan, and Wynne Janis. 1990. Verb sandwiches in American Sign Language. In *Proceedings of the fourth international symposium on sign language research*, ed. S. Prillwitz and T. Vollhaber, 75–85. Hamburg: Signum Verlag.

Fischer, Susan, and Wynne Janis. 1992. License to derive: Resolving conflicts between syntax and morphology in ASL. Ms.

Friedman, Lynn. 1977. Formational properties of American Sign Language. In *On the other hand*, ed. Lynn Friedman, 13–56. New York: Academic Press.

Humphries, Tom, and Carol Padden. 1992. *Learning American Sign Language*. Englewood Cliffs: Prentice Hall.

Kegl, Judy. 1976. *Relational grammar and American Sign Language*. Unpublished manuscript, MIT.

Liddell, Scott. 1980. *American Sign Language Syntax*. The Hague: Mouton de Gruyter.

Liddell, Scott. 2003. *Grammar, gesture and meaning in American Sign Language*. Cambridge: Cambridge University Press.

Lillo-Martin, Diane, and Ronice Muller de Quadros. 2005. The Acquisition of focus constructions in American Sign Language and Lingua de Sinais Brasileira. In *BUCLD 29: Proceedings of the 29th Annual Boston University Conference on Language Development*, eds. Alejna Brugos, Manuella Clark-Cotton and Seungwan Ha, 365–375. Somerville: Cascadilla Press.

Matsuoka, Kazumi. 1997. Verb raising in American Sign Language. *Lingua* 103: 127–149.

Neidle, Carol, Judy Kegl, Dawn MacLaughlin, Benjamin Bahan, and Robert G. Lee. 2000. *The syntax of American Sign Language*. Cambridge, MA: MIT Press.

Nespor, Marina, and Wendy Sandler. 1999. Prosody in Israeli Sign Language. *Language and Speech* 42: 143–176.

Newport, Elissa, and Richard Meier. 1984. The acquisition of American Sign Language. In: *The crosslinguistic study of language acquisition, volume 1: the data*, eds. Dan I. Slobin, 881–938. Hillsdale, NJ: Erlbaum.

Newport, Elissa, and Richard Meier. 1985. The acquisition of American Sign Language. In *The crosslinguistic study of language acquisition*, ed. Dan Isaac Slobin, 881–938. Mahwah: Lawrence Erlbaum Associates.

Reilly, Judy, Marina McIntire, and Ursula Bellugi. 1990. Conditionals in American Sign Language: Grammaticized facial expressions. *Applied Psycholinguistics* 11: 369–392.

Reilly, Judy, Marina McIntire, and Ursula Bellugi. 1991. Baby face: A new perspective on universals in language acquisition. *In Theoretical issues in sign language research*, vol. 2, eds. Patricia Siple and Susan Fischer, 9–23. Chicago: University of Chicago Press.

Rosenstein, Ofra. 2001. *Israeli Sign Language: A topic prominent language*. MA thesis, University of Haifa.

Schick, Brenda. 2002. The development of word order in deaf toddlers learning ASL. In *An international perspective on the acquisition of sign languages*, eds. Bencie Woll and Gary Morgan, 143–158. Amsterdam: John Benjamins Publishing.

Slobin, Dan I. 1985. Crosslinguistic evidence for the language-making capacity. In *The crosslinguistic study of language acquisition*, Vol. 2, ed. Dan Isaac Slobin, 1157–1249. Mahwah: Lawrence Erlbaum Associates.

Spencer, Patricia, and Margaret Harris. 2006. Patterns and effects of language input to deaf infants and toddlers from deaf and hearing mothers. In *Advances in the sign language development of Deaf children*, eds. Brenda Schick, Marc Marschark, and Patricia Spencer, 71–101. New York, NY: Oxford University Press.

Tomasello, Michael. 1992. *First verbs*. Cambridge: Cambridge University Press.

Variable Word Order in Child Greek

Konstantia Kapetangianni

Abstract This chapter investigates the acquisition of subject-verb word order in Greek. Based on naturalistic production data from three monolingual Greek-speaking children (ages 1;9–2;9), it is shown that overt DP subjects and variable word order (SV, VS and OV(S)) are attested in child Greek at the earliest stages of linguistic production (before age 2;0). Furthermore, based on a detailed investigation of the grammatical properties of early word order, evidence is presented for early setting of the Null Subject parameter and for early knowledge of the syntactic, semantic and pragmatic principles that govern subject-verb word order in the adult grammar.

Keywords Greek · Null-subject parameter · Information structure · Input · Left periphery

1 Introduction

Within the generative grammar tradition and specifically the Principles and Parameters (P&P) approach (Chomsky 1981), knowledge of a particular language is developed from: (i) principles of Universal Grammar (UG), which are genetically inherited as part of our biological endowment, and (ii) the choices that UG makes available (i.e. parameters), which are based on the stimuli that an individual receives from a specific linguistic environment. According to this approach, the process of grammar construction in first language acquisition can be described as in Fig. 1.

Within the theory of Universal Grammar, the task of the learner is to discover and set the particular values of parameters of the target grammar, based on the Primary Linguistic Data (PLD i.e. the input). Thus, the input that an individual receives – influencing the genetic endowment via parameter setting – affects the grammar that will be acquired. This chapter investigates

K. Kapetangianni (✉)
University of Michigan, Ann Arbor, MI, USA
e-mail: kapetang@umich.edu

M. Anderssen et al. (eds.), *Variation in the Input*, Studies in Theoretical Psycholinguistics 39, DOI 10.1007/978-90-481-9207-6_8,

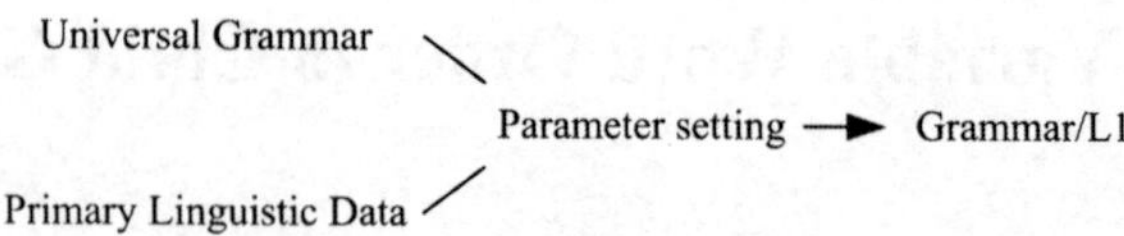

Fig. 1 Process of grammar development within the principles and parameters framework

the acquisition of word order in Greek and examines how children exposed to null subject language data analyze the optionality regarding the phonological realization of subjects and the variability of the structural positions in which overt subjects surface.

I specifically address the following three questions with respect to the development of word order: (i) How early do children exposed to Greek acquire the Null Subject parameter? (ii) How early do children acquire the grammatical principles that determine pre- and postverbal subjects in adult Greek? (iii) When do child data provide evidence that children have the grammatical and pragmatics/discourse knowledge that governs Subject-Verb order in the adult Greek grammar? In order to answer these questions, I examine word order in early child Greek. Based on naturalistic production data from three monolingual Greek children, I present evidence for (i) early setting of the Null Subject parameter, (ii) emergence of variable Subject-Verb order by age 2;0 and (iii) early knowledge of the syntactic, semantic and pragmatic constraints that govern Subject-Verb order in the adult grammar.

The paper is organized as follows: In Section 2, I discuss cross-linguistic empirical facts regarding the development of word order. In Section 3, I discuss the grammatical properties of the 'subject' in adult Greek. In Section 4, I review previous work on the development of null subject languages and provide the background for the present study. In Section 5, I present the data regarding the development of Subject-Verb order in child Greek and show that variable word order is attested before age 2;0. In Section 6, I provide a detailed analysis of the properties of early word order and argue that the child language production data presented here provide evidence for early knowledge of the grammatical mechanisms that govern word order in the adult Greek grammar. Finally, in Section 7, I provide the conclusions.

2 Acquisition of Word Order Across I-Languages

Two central issues in the field of language acquisition have been: (i) how early in children's development are the correct values of parameters set and (ii) when do children come to know the formal properties that characterize their language? Several studies of early child language have provided evidence for Very Early Parameter Setting (as formalized by Wexler 1998). Specifically, it has been shown that parameters that govern the word order properties of adult grammars are set correctly in the earliest observed stages of syntactic development, as soon as learners start producing two-word utterances. It has been demonstrated, for instance, that the verb movement parameter which regulates V-to-I movement in adult grammars is set early by young French children (see Pierce 1992), a parameter that distinguishes the grammar of French from the grammar of English in that overt movement of finite verbs to the Inflectional Head takes place in the former but not in the latter (Pollock 1989). Similarly, children exposed to English distinguish between lexical verbs and auxiliaries and they appear to know that lexical verbs do not move to I (Harris and Wexler 1996).

In fact, according to Bloom (1970) and Brown (1973), word order is among the first grammatical properties to be acquired by children exposed to English. This is evidenced by early setting of the head direction parameter, which governs the order of head and complements distinguishing head-initial grammars (e.g. English) from head-final grammars (e.g. Japanese). Finally, there is evidence for early setting of the V2 parameter, showing that children exposed to German place finite verbs in second position, whereas they place non-finite verbs in final position (Poeppel and Wexler 1993). All these findings suggest that learners, by being exposed to PLD, discover the correct value of the word order parameters that characterize the target grammar from the onset of syntactic (i.e. two-word) production.

Turning now to the acquisition of word order in null subject languages, we observe that the PLD that a learner is exposed to exhibit a great deal of variability (and optionality). Learners of null subject grammars (e.g. Spanish, Italian, Greek) hear sentences both with and without overt subjects in the input. Furthermore, when subjects are phonologically realized, they may surface in different structural positions (VS, SV, VSO, SVO, etc).

In sum, children exposed to null subject languages receive highly variable input compared to children exposed to non-null subject languages. This empirical fact raises then the following related questions: (i) How does the variation in the input affect the course of word order development in null subject languages? (ii) Do children exposed to such variable word order input experience any difficulties or delays in determining the correct values of parameters? (iii) Do we observe early setting of the relevant parameter (i.e. the Null subject parameter) similar to what is attested in the acquisition of languages with fixed word order? (iv) Do early grammars exhibit variability relative to word order phenomena and, if they do, is this variability consistent with the adult grammar? This study seeks to provide answers to these questions by investigating the development of Subject-Verb order in the grammar of Greek, which, as we will see in the following section, exhibits a great deal of variation.

3 Adult Greek: Optionality and Variation of Subject-Verb Surface Order

In this section, I discuss basic properties of adult Greek and the theoretical assumptions that have been advanced regarding the properties of word order, specifically the syntactic and semantic properties of what has been traditionally referred to as the 'subject' of the clause.

Adult Greek is a null subject language with rich verbal agreement morphology. Inflection on the verb form marks aspect, voice, tense, person, and number, as illustrated in the example below:

(1) O skilos kinigise ti gata (SVO)
the dog.NOM chase.3SG.PAST.ACT.PERF the cat.ACC
'The dog chased the cat'

Greek is also a language with overt verb movement to I (e.g. Rivero 1994, Philippaki-Warburton 1989, Tsimpli 1990). Furthermore, Greek exhibits a great deal of variation in word order. Observe, for example, that the constituents of a typical finite main clause like (1), namely subject, verb, and object, can surface in different positions, as shown in (1), (2), and (3), or the subject may be omitted entirely as in (4):

(2) Kinigise o skilos ti gata (VSO)
chase.3SG.PAST.ACT.PERF the dog.NOM the cat.ACC
'The dog chased the cat'

(3) Ti gata kinigise o skilos (OVS)
The cat.ACC chase.3SG.PAST.ACT.PERF the dog.NOM
'The dog chased the cat'

(4) Kinigise ti gata (VO)
chase.3SG.PAST.ACT.PERF the cat.ACC
'He/she/it chased the cat'

In the examples above, the syntactic function of the noun phrases is indicated by morphological case and hence they do not have to surface in a fixed position in the clause in order to specify their function.[1] Notice also that all major word orders are allowed (including OSV, VOS, and SOV), but among those SV(O) (1) and VS(O) (2) orders are the predominant ones, with VS(O) being the least marked order (Philippaki-Warburton 1985).

As can be seen, DP subjects in Greek can surface pre- and postverbally or can be omitted. Despite the variation and optionality observed on the surface, word order (including Subject-Verb order) is heavily constrained by syntactic, semantic and pragmatic principles. First, notice that postverbal subjects occur with all eventive predicates, transitive and intransitive predicates, as illustrated in examples (5), (6), and (7):

---

[1] Nouns in Greek are inflected for gender, number, and case, while pronouns are marked for person, gender, number, and case.

Transitive (example 2, repeated here as 5)

(5) Kinigise o skilos ti gata
chase.3SG.PAST.ACT.PERF the dog.NOM the cat.ACC
'The dog chased the cat'

Unergative

(6) Pezun ta pedia
play.3PL.PRES[2] the children.PL.NOM
'The children are playing'

Unaccusative

(7) Efige i maria
leave.3SG.PAST the Mary.NOM
'Mary left'

In terms of its structural position, it is assumed that the DP subject in VS(O) orders (including unaccusatives, unergatives and passives) occupies its thematic position; it has not moved outside of the VP (Alexiadou and Anagnostopoulou 1998 among others). In terms of interpretation, the predominant view in the literature is that in Greek, postverbal subjects differ from preverbal subjects relative to information structure: A postverbal DP subject conveys 'new' information whereas a DP subject in preverbal position is associated with a topic reading; it is a constituent which is part of the background context and thus it presents 'old' (known) information. For illustration, consider the examples in (8).

(8) a. i maria mu estile ena grama.
the Mary.NOM me.CL send.3SG.PAST a letter.ACC
'Mary sent me a letter'
to grama irthe simera
the letter.NOM arrive.3SG.PAST today
'The letter arrived today'

b. ?? i maria mu estile ena grama.
the Mary.NOM me.CL send.3SG.PAST a letter.ACC
'Mary sent me a letter
irthe **to grama** simera
arrive.3SG.PAST the letter.ACC today
'The letter arrived today'
(from Alexiadou & Anagnostopoulou 2000)

[2] For ease of exposition, I will indicate in the gloss of the examples only person, number and tense marking on the verb forms.

Example (8) shows that a DP conveying 'old' information (the DP *the letter* is part of the background information, i.e. it has been introduced in the discourse) cannot occupy a postverbal position as in (8b). It is associated with a Topic reading and occurs preverbally as in (8a).

Furthermore, as shown in example (9), a DP subject in preverbal position can be associated with a Focus interpretation.[3] In this case, the DP receives a [+contrastive, +exhaustive] interpretation (what Kiss 1998 terms 'identificational' focus).

(9) Q: Pios perase tis eksetasis?
who.NOM pass.3SG.PAST the exam.PL.ACC
'Who passed the exams?'
A: O YANIS perase tis eksetasis
the John.NOM pass.3SG.PAST the exams.PL.ACC
'John passed the exam'

Following Tsimpli (1990, 1995), focusing in Greek involves overt movement of a Focus operator to the relevant peripheral functional projection, FocusP. I will adopt this analysis and assume that, in example (9), the focused argument o YANIS 'John' has moved to the Specifier of FocusP (Rizzi 1997).

Regarding the structural position of preverbal subjects that are not focused constituents, it has been argued that the DP subject and the Inflectional Head (where the verb moves to) are not in a Spec, Head relation in Greek (Philippaki-Warburton 1985, Alexiadou and Anagnostopoulou 1998, Spyropoulos and Philippaki-Warburton 2001). The evidence that supports this view comes from a number of distributional facts. When a DP subject surfaces in a (matrix or embedded) subjunctive clause introduced with the subjunctive marker *na*, the DP must surface either postverbally or in a position to the left of the [marker *na* + verb] complex as shown in (10) and (11). In other words, the subjunctive marker *na* and the verb must be contiguous; hence a DP subject cannot intervene between the two.

(10) O yanis **na** (*o yanis) **figi** (o yanis)
the John.NOM SUBJ the John.NOM leave.3SG the John.NOM
'May John not leave'

[3] Notice that a focused DP subject can also appear in situ, as the following example illustrates:

a. Perase tis eksetasis O YANIS
pass.3SG.PAST the exams the John.NOM
'John passed the exam'

(11) I maria elpizi o yanis
the Mary.NOM hope.3SG.PRES the John.NOM

na (*o yanis) **figi** (o yanis)
SUBJ the John.NOM leave.3SG the John.NOM
'Mary hopes John will leave'

The same restriction is also observed in negative clauses. The DP subject cannot intervene between the negation marker *den* and the verb, nor the negation marker *den* and the future marker *tha*: it must either be realized in a postverbal position or to the left of the negation marker, as example (12) indicates:

(12) (O yanis) **den** (*o yanis) **tha** (*o yanis) **figi** (o yanis)
the John.NOM **NEG** **FUT** the John.NOM **leave.3SG** the John.NOM
'John will not leave'

It is standardly proposed that the negation and the mood particle (i.e. *den* and *na*) head the functional projections of NegP and MoodP respectively, each located above IP, as illustrated in the schemas in (13) and (14).[4] A DP subject may not occupy the position generally associated with the EPP, namely the Specifier position of IP (Chomsky 1995), because it will interrupt the sequence of particles (i.e. *na* and *tha*) and the verb, which form a single phonological unit in Greek (Spyropoulos and Philippaki-Warburton 2001).

(13) [$_{CP}$ [0] [$_{MOODP}$ Subj [NA] [$_{NEGP}$ Neg [min] [$_{IP}$... (Subjunctive)

(14) [$_{CP}$ [oti/pu[5]] [$_{MOODP}$ Ind [0] [$_{NEGP}$ Neg [den] [$_{FUIP}$ [tha] [$_{IP}$... (Indicative)
(Philippaki-Warburton 1998: 169)

It is also worth observing that in both matrix and embedded subjunctive clauses a DP subject realized with neutral intonation can surface only in a postverbal position (Philippaki-Warburton 1982, 1985). When a DP subject surfaces preverbally it always carries focalized stress or is realized with an intonational gap. This restriction, however, does not hold in indicative matrix and embedded clauses realized with neutral intonation, where preverbal and postverbal DP subjects are both equally felicitous.

---

[4] A different analysis of the particle *na* is advanced by Agouraki (1991), who treats it as a complementizer. This is not crucial for the discussion here, since also under this account *na* will be located above IP, in the CP domain.

[5] *Oti* and *pu* are treated as complementizers introducing indicative complements.

Such facts have led researchers to hypothesize that in Greek the basic structural position of the Subject is the postverbal position, i.e. Spec,vP/VP. Preverbal subjects are analyzed as Clitic Left-dislocated constituents, occupying an A′ position in the left periphery of the clause, either Spec,TopicP or Spec, FocusP (Philippaki-Warburton 1985, Alexiadou and Anagnostopoulou 1998, Spyropoulos and Philippaki-Warburton 2001).[6]

However, the analysis of preverbal subjects as topics in Greek has been challenged recently by Roussou and Tsimpli (2006) and Spyropoulos and Revithiadou (2009), who provide evidence that DP subjects in SV(O) order do not always receive a Topic interpretation. More precisely, Spyropoulos and Revithiadou convincingly show that similar to postverbal subjects, preverbal subjects are felicitous answers to questions that require all new information, as the example in (15) illustrates:[7]

(15) Q: Ti egine?/ Ti nea?
what.ACC happen.3SG.PAST / what.PL.NOM new.PL.NOM?
'What happened? /What's up?'
A1: O yanis filise ti maria
the John.NOM kiss.3SG.PAST the Mary.ACC
'John kissed Mary'
A2: Filise o yanis ti maria
kiss.3SG.PAST the John.NOM the mary.ACC
'John kissed Mary'
(from Spyropoulos & Revithiadou 2009)

Given these considerations, the hypothesis that will be defended here is that preverbal subjects in Greek are of at least two types syntactically (see also Kapetangianni 2010).[8] That is, they may be associated with a Topic interpretation and be Clitic Left-Dislocated elements, and thus realized in the CP domain, specifically in Spec, TopicP, or they may involve a non-topic reading and thus be TP-internal elements, realized in the position associated with the EPP, i.e. Spec, TP, as shown in Fig. 2.

To summarize this section, we have seen that adult Greek exhibits a great deal of variability in word order. The different word order options attested in

[6] There are also relevant interpretational and binding facts that, given space limitations, will not be discussed here. See Alexiadou and Anagnostopoulou (1998) for details.

[7] There is further evidence that supports the analysis of preverbal subjects as non-topics that I will not review here. The interested readers are referred to Roussou & Tsimpli (2006) and Spyropoulos & Revithiadou (2007) for more details.

[8] See also Pires (2009) for arguments that preverbal subjects in Brazilian Portuguese exhibit similar 'mixed' properties, i.e. preverbal subjects may be realized as left-dislocated elements (as topics) or as arguments internal to the clause, in Spec, IP, depending on the structural properties of different clauses.

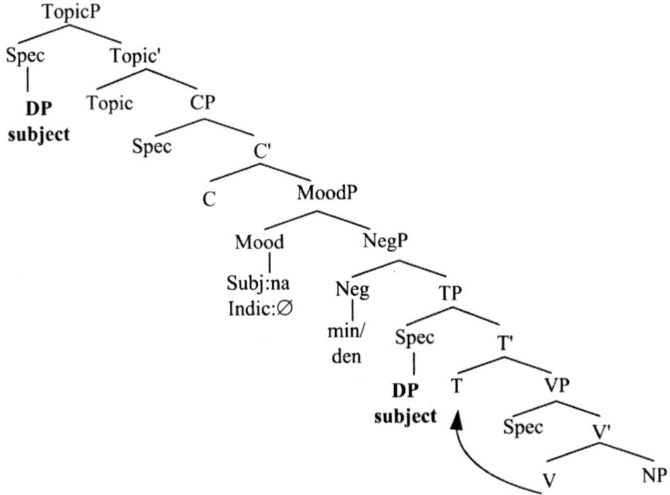

Fig. 2 Basic clause structure of Greek[9]

the adult grammar, summarized in Table 1, are heavily constrained by different (syntactic and semantic) principles, and thus there is a strict correspondence between syntactic position and semantic interpretation.

Table 1 Properties of overt DP-subjects in Greek

DP- Subject	Preverbal	Preverbal	Preverbal	Postverbal
Interpretation	Old information/ Topic	Contrastive/ Focus	New information	New information
Structural Position	Spec, TopicP	Spec, FocusP	Spec, TP	Spec, vP

This means that the learner has to acquire both the syntactic and the semantic-pragmatic/discourse knowledge, i.e. the correspondences expressed in Table 1, in order to achieve competence regarding word order in the adult grammar of Greek. During the process of language acquisition, the learner's task then is to figure out the different mechanisms that govern the different word order 'options' in the adult grammar. But how does the learner deal with the variability in the PLD? Do learners' early productions exhibit variability with respect to word order phenomena? If they do, is early variable word order governed by the same grammatical principles that constrain word order in the adult grammar? Before examining children's production data, I review some previous work on the acquisition of null subject languages relevant to the phenomena discussed here in the following section.

---

[9] See Roussou (2000) for a more finely structured CP domain including TopicP and FocusP.

4 Previous Studies

In a previous study of Child Spanish and Catalan, Grinstead (2004) observed that there is a stage in the linguistic development of children exposed to null subject languages during which no overt subjects are attested. More precisely, Grinstead noticed that in contrast to children exposed to overt subject languages, such as English, who produce overt subjects well before the age of 2, overt subjects do not appear until around the age of two in Child Spanish and Catalan. Grinstead has argued that this crosslinguistic variation in child grammars results from independent differences between the adult target grammars, specifically the setting of a parameterized UG principle of subject-licensing. According to Grinstead, the parameter that is responsible for this difference is what he calls the *Pronominal Argument Subject Parameter*, which he formulates as follows: 'Overt subject licensing may permit subjects either in the Specifier of IP or in its head'(p. 50). This parameter divides languages into two types: languages which realize overt subjects in the Specifier of IP, such as English and French, and languages which realize overt subjects pronominally on the verb, i.e. subject agreement, such as Spanish and Catalan. Given this parametric option and following Ordónez's (1997) proposal that preverbal overt subjects in Spanish are not IP-internal elements but rather occupy a left peripheral topic position, Grinstead (2004) accounts for the absence of overt subjects in child Spanish and Catalan as follows:[10]

> ... these languages do not have overt subjects, where *overt subject* is defined as the element that occurs in [Spec, IP]. Rather, the overt nominal elements that are used in a subject-like way in these languages are located in the left periphery in Rizzi's (2000) topic-focus field, which is not active in the beginning. (p. 56)

According to this account, Spanish and Catalan children set the *Pronominal Argument Subject Parameter* to the adult value very early and thus, their grammar is adult-like in that it does not express overt subjects in Spec, IP. However, according to Grinstead, what the children lack at an early stage (before they are 2 years old), is the adult competence to syntactically generate the left periphery of the clause, namely the Topic/Focus projections, and express overt subjects in this domain. This inability is explained as an interface delay between the grammar and the discourse-pragmatics domain. The evidence that he provides to support this claim is that focus, topicalization and wh-questions, which all involve movement of constituents to left peripheral positions, do not appear before the age of two but emerge at the same time

[10] Providing evidence from ellipsis, negative quantifier extraction and quantifier scope, Ordónez (1997) has argued that preverbal overt subjects are not located in Spec,IP (contra Belletti 1990, Rizzi 1990, Cardinaletti 1996), but that they are A′ elements, located outside of IP, at the left periphery of the clause.

as do overt subjects in child Spanish and Catalan (for details and data see Grinstead (2004)).

There is, however, empirical evidence that children exposed to Spanish and Catalan PLD do not appear to display the interface delay Grinstead postulates: Specifically, the 'no-overt subject' stage was not confirmed by Aguado-Orea and Pine (2002) for the two Spanish children in CHILDES, Juan (Linaza corpus) and Maria (López-Ornat corpus), and by Bel (2003) for the three Spanish children (López-Ornat, Vila and Linaza corpus in CHILDES) as well as the three Catalan-speaking children she studied (Serra-Solé corpus).

Given that the data from Spanish and Catalan are controversial and do not unequivocally support Grinstead's theory, in previous work (Kapetangianni 2007a) I investigated the development of aspects of Greek syntax that interface with pragmatic knowledge, namely A′ subjects, focused, topicalized constituents and wh-movement, in order to examine whether the predictions that Grinstead's theory makes for Spanish can be confirmed in another null subject language.[11] The working hypothesis of that earlier work was as follows: Grinstead specifically argued that the interface delay is, 'a more general phenomenon ..., which implicates areas of cognition and their relationships with linguistic cognition' (p. 69), such as spatial cognition or numerical competence and linguistic competence. If this claim is on the right track, then we expect that the interface delay will uniformly affect other child grammars as well.

After analyzing production data from three Greek-acquiring children and comparing the results with the child Spanish and Catalan data presented by Grinstead, Kapetangianni (2007a) showed that the 'no-overt subject' stage is not attested in Early Greek. Preverbal DP subjects are found even at the earliest stages of syntactic development, before age 2;0, from the onset of two-word production. In addition, focus, topicalization and wh-movement are also attested at the same stage, and thus peripheral positions, TopicP and FocusP, appear to be available in Early Greek (see also Tsimpli 2005). Based on this evidence, I argued that the lack of overt subjects observed by Grinstead at early stages of development is not universal. In this chapter, I provide evidence for early setting of the Null Subject parameter in Child Greek and also for early knowledge of the grammatical (i.e. syntactic) and discourse (pragmatic) principles/constraints that govern the Subject-Verb order attested in the adult grammar of Greek.

---

[11] Adult Greek and Spanish share a number of grammatical properties which allows comparison with the early production data. First, Greek, like Spanish, is a null subject language with rich morphological agreement. Second, preverbal subjects in Greek are considered to be A′ elements, located in the left periphery (as discussed in Section 3). Thus, assuming that adult grammars of Greek and Spanish are similar in this respect, we expected to find similar developmental patterns in Early Greek.

5 Data and Results

5.1 Data and Method

The present study is based on the analysis of naturalistic production data samples of three monolingual Greek children. The data are drawn from the Stephany Corpus of the CHILDES database (MacWhinney and Snow 1985, Stephany 1997). The children's age and MLUs are provided in Table 2.

Table 2 Greek children, Ages and MLUs

Child	Age	MLU
Spiros	1;9	1.6–1.7
Yanna	1;11–2;9	1.4–2.8
Mairi	1;9–2;9	1.9–3.1

To measure the co-occurrence of subjects and verbs, all child utterances were extracted from the files, using the CLAN Combo program developed for the CHILDES project (MacWhinney 1995). Verbs were counted and coded for person, number and tense. A manual search was performed for instances of null and overt subjects. Overt subjects were coded for type (postverbal-preverbal, lexical-pronoun).

5.2 Results

Recall from the introduction that the central questions addressed here are: (i) How early do Greek children acquire the Null Subject parameter? (ii) How early do Greek children acquire the grammatical properties that determine pre- and postverbal subjects? Let us consider first the evidence regarding the knowledge of the Null Subject parameter. Table 3 presents the early production of null and overt DP subjects in child Greek.

Table 3 Distribution of null and overt DP subjects with verbs

Child	Age	Null subjects (%)	Overt subjects (%)	Total utter/s
Spiros	1;9	78	22	135
Yanna	1;11	94	6	161
	2;5	91	9	243
	2;9	83	17	252
Mairi	1;9	89	11	411
	2;3	74	26	147
	2;9	72	28	397

The data in Table 3 show that from the earliest stages of syntactic production, null and overt DP subjects are evidenced in each child's grammar. The data also show that in early production, null subjects outnumber overt DP subjects. Yanna and Mairi's data show that null subjects constitute the vast majority at the earliest stages, but gradually decrease in favor of overt subjects after age 2;0. Nevertheless, the prevalence of null subjects is also attested at later stages. This observation is not surprising given that the omission of a DP subject is the most 'frequent option' in adult Greek: an overt pronominal or lexical DP subject is realized to indicate emphasis or contrast (Holton et al. 1997). An issue that arises is whether early overt DP subjects are used emphatically or contrastively. Consider the following example from Mairi (at 1;9):

(16) MOT: pinai to alogaki.
be.hungry.3SG.PRES the horsie.NOM
'The horsie is hungry'
MOT: dos tu na fai!
give.2.SG.IMP he.GEN.CL SUBJ eat.3SG
'Give him to eat'
MOT: ti thelis?
what want.2SG.PRES
'What do you want?'
CHI: (n)a to taiso **ego**
SUBJ it.CL feed.1SG I
'I will feed it'

In this example, Mairi is presumably using an overt subject, the first person pronoun 'I', for emphasis, i.e. to emphasize that 'she is the one who will feed the horse'. Consider also another example from Spiros (at 1;9). In (17), the child is apparently using an overt DP subject, his own name 'Spiros', to indicate contrast: 'It is Spiros who will sweep the closet'. These examples indicate that early overt subjects show the same properties that characterize overt subjects in the adult grammar: they are at least in some cases arguably realized to mark either emphasis or contrast.

(17) MOT: ti dulapa tha skupisi
the closet.ACC FUT sweep.3SG
'She will sweep the closet'
MOT: jati den tin epline i mama.
because not it.CL clean.3SG.PAST the mom.NOM
'Because mom didn't clean it'
CHI: a (s)kupisi **o spiros**.
FUT sweep.3SG the Spiros.NOM
'Spiros will sweep'

Let us now examine children's production of null subjects. The following are examples of null subjects found in the data.

(18) MOT: ti n afto, aɣapi mu ? (Spiros 1;9)
what be.3SG.PRES this love my
'What is this, my love?'
CHI: o likos
the wolf.NOM
'The wolf'
ULL:[12] Den ine o likos.
neg be.3SG.PRES the wolf.NOM
'This is not the wolf'
ULL: elafi ine afto.
deer be.3SG.PRES this
'This is a deer'
MOT: afto ine elafi, aɣapi mu.
this be.3SG.PRES deer love my
'This is a deer, my love'
CHI: (s)toma **exi.**
mouth **have.3SG.PRES**
'It has a mouth'

(19) ULL: pinai? (Mairi, 1;9)
be.hungry.3SG.PRES
'Is he hungry?'
ULL: ti teli?
what want.3SG.PRES
'What does he want?'
ULL: ti fajito teli ?
what food want.3SG.PRES
'What food does he want?'
MOT: ti teli na fai o piθikos?
what want.3SG.PRES SUBJ eat.3SG the monkey.NOM
'What does the monkey want to eat?'
CHI: **sei** piguni
want.3SG.PRES fork
'(He) wants a fork'

[12] Ull is the abbreviation of the investigator's name Ulla (Ursula Stephany).

In (18) and (19), we observe that children use null subjects appropriately, in felicitous pragmatic contexts, i.e. in contexts where the reference of a null subject can be established through an antecedent. The referent of the null subjects in the examples above, i.e. 'the wolf' in (18), 'the monkey' in (19), has already been introduced in the previous discourse, and is part of the knowledge shared with interlocutors. Thus, children appear to know the pragmatic conditions that license null subjects in the adult grammar. As a first proposal then, we see that Greek child language provides evidence for early knowledge of the Null Subject parameter as the children realize both null and overt subjects from the earliest stages in their development, in accordance with the PLD they are exposed to (see also Bel (2003) for Child Spanish and Catalan).

Notice also that the high production of null subjects in the early stages, which decreases with age, as shown in Table 3, is consistent with the adult production. Null subjects also outnumber overt subjects in the adult grammar: the proportion of overt subjects produced by Mairi's mother (found in the same corpus, when mother is addressing Mairi) ranges from 22 to 30%. Thus, we observe a similar production by children and adults regarding null and overt subjects. It could thus be argued that children produce a high number of null subjects in response to frequencies in the input and not due to lack of grammatical knowledge. If it were the case that in the very early stages of acquisition, children do not have knowledge of the grammatical constraints on the realization of subjects and overextend the use of null subjects, we would expect to observe a high proportion of null subjects or rather a low occurrence or absence of overt subjects in the early stages of the acquisition of null subject languages.

The developmental data from different studies on Child Greek, Spanish and Catalan show that not all children start with a high production of null subjects. More precisely, Tsimpli (2005) reports that one of the Greek-acquiring girls she studied, Alexia, started with a high production of overt subjects (79%) in the first recording at age 1;11, whereas the other girl, Elli, started with a high production of null subjects (77%) at age 1;9. Similarly, in Bel's (2003) study of Child Spanish and Catalan, Maria (Spanish, age 1;7) produced a small number of null subjects in the first recording (26.1%) whereas Julia (Catalan, age 1;11) produced a high number of null subjects (92.8%), similar to the Greek children of the present study. The combined results of these studies show that there is individual variation regarding the early production of null subjects across languages. The rate of null subjects reported here in Early and Adult Greek seems to indicate that the frequencies of null vs. overt subjects in the PLD may influence children's production, and that children's 'preference' for null subjects in the early stages of development occurs in response to the input.

We now turn to the distribution of overt DP subjects in order to address our second question, i.e. when do children acquire the grammatical principles that determine the realization of subjects in pre- or post-verbal positions. The results are given in Table 4.

As indicated, both pre- and postverbal DP subjects (i.e. SV and VS orders) are attested in all children's early production during the three stages. A high

Table 4 Pre- and post-verbal DP subjects

Child	Age	Preverbal (%)	Postverbal (%)	Total # overt subjects
Spiros	1;9	19	81	31
Yanna	1;11	70	30	10
	2;5	44	56	23
	2;9	45	55	42
Mairi	1;9	17	83	46
	2;3	46	54	39
	2;9	40	41	110[a]

[a] The remaining 21 subjects are wh-phrases.

number of postverbal subjects are observed in Spiros' and Mairi's data during the first period. Yanna's data show a different pattern: during the first period, we find a relatively large number of preverbal subjects, whereas in the following two stages, preverbal subjects are realized in roughly half of the child's utterances. The same can be seen in Mairi's data. Examples of children's overt subjects (pre- and post-verbal ones) are given in (20)–(25):

(20) **to** **pe(d)aki** ta bi (s)tin t(r)ipa (Spiros, 1;9)
the child FUT enter.3SG to.the hole
'The child will go into the hole'

(21) na to anik(s) **i** **ula** (Spiros, 1;9)
SUBJ it.CL open.3SG the Ulla
'Ulla will open it'

(22) **i** **dada** ine koko mu (Yanna, 1;11)
the purse.NOM be.3SG.PRES mine
'The purse is mine'

(23) mesa ine **to** **treno** (Yanna, 1;11)
inside be.3SG.PRES the train
'The train is inside'

(24) to pi(re) **i** **mama**, to da(x)tiliði (Mairi, 1;9)
it.cl get.3SG.PAST the mom.NOM the ring.ACC
'Mom got the ring'

(25) **i** **meri** na to vali (Mairi, 1;9)
the Mary.NOM SUBJ it.CL put.3SG
'Mary will put it'

As the data indicate, pre- and post-verbal subjects emerge at roughly the same age in all children's grammar (see also Tsimpli 2005). When compared to the adult language, children's early production of SV and VS orders does not deviate significantly from the adult production data. Mairi's mother's production of post-verbal subjects (VS order) amounts to 74% (Stephany 1997), which is approximately similar to Spiros' and Mairi's production during the first developmental period. Yanna's production, however, appears to be different, in that she is showing a preference for preverbal subjects at the earliest stage. In order to understand why Yanna's data show such a distinct pattern, a closer examination of her early production is needed. Examples (26)–(30) illustrate some of the preverbal subjects produced by Yanna during the first period.

(26) **i** **jana** pije (s)ton kipo
the Yanna.NOM go.3SG.PAST to.the garden
'Yanna went to the garden'

(27) **tuto** **o** **kilo** ehi mimi
this the dog have.3SG.PRES wound
'This dog has a wound'

(28) **afto** beni mesa
this go.3SG.PRES inside
'This goes inside'

(29) **tuto** **o** **kilo** meto ekane
this the dog vomit do.3SG.PAST
'This dog vomitted'

(30) **tuto** papai
this walk.3SG.PRES
'This one walks'

In all of these examples, Yanna's preverbal subjects are apparently associated with a contrastive or emphatic reading, evidenced by the use of the child's name or the use of the demonstrative element 'tuto' with a DP subject or the demonstrative pronoun 'afto', and thus they have to be realized in the structural position associated with Focus/Contrast. This is the preverbal position, specifically the peripheral position Spec,FocusP. Thus, it is not the case that Yanna's production is different from that of the other two children, but that the semantic information that her early subjects convey require the realization of the subject in a preverbal position, in accordance with the adult grammar.

Finally, notice that the findings presented here constitute empirical evidence against the predictions of Grinstead's theory regarding the development of word order in null subject languages. Specifically, the data from Greek challenge the hypothesis that there is an initial stage in the development of null subject languages during which no overt preverbal subjects are realized. Second, the data do not confirm the prediction that postverbal subjects, by virtue of being VP-internal elements, emerge earlier than preverbal subjects, which are, by hypothesis, topics. If it were the case that the peripheral position that hosts preverbal subjects, i.e. TopicP, was not available at an early stage, as suggested by Grinstead, preverbal subjects would have emerged later than postverbal ones. However, this is not borne out by the data from Greek. Interestingly, the 'simultaneous' emergence of overt preverbal and postverbal subjects observed in Greek is also attested in Spanish and Catalan. In both Grinstead's (1998) and Bel's (2001, 2003) reported data, preverbal and postverbal subjects emerge *at the same time and age*, a fact that fails to support the hypothesis that the peripheral position that hosts these subjects is not available in Early Spanish and Catalan.

6 Grammatical Properties of Early Word Order

6.1 Properties of SV(O) and VS(O) Orders

Thus far, we have seen that the variability of subject-verb order attested in the adult grammar is also evidenced in early child grammar. In this section, I discuss the grammatical properties of early word order and show that children have early knowledge of the syntactic, semantic and pragmatic constraints that govern the adult word order.

The first piece of evidence comes from the distribution of overt DP subjects relative to other constituents in the clause. As can be seen in the following example from Mairi (at 1;9), early preverbal DP subjects precede the mood marker *na*

(31) CHI: puzo ze to valome?
where cl.NEUT.SG put.1PL.PRES
'Where will we put it?'
ULL: ne.
yes
'Yes'
CHI: kala.
good
'Ok'
CHI: **i meri na to vali.**
the Mary.NOM subj cl.NEUT.SG.ACC put.3SG
'Mary will put it'
ULL: ti les?
what say.2SG.PRES
'What are you saying?
CHI **i meri na to vali.**
the Mary.NOM subj cl.NEUT.SG.ACC put.3SG
'Mary will put it'
CHI: (e)ki kato.
there down
'Over there'

In Section 3, we saw that *na* is the head of a MoodP situated above IP, and that no element (except negation and clitics) can intervene in the structure [*na* + V]. It appears then that in example (31), the preverbal lexical subject *i meri* 'Mary' does not occupy Spec, TP but a position higher than the mood marker, more specifically a position in the left periphery, as illustrated in Fig. 3.

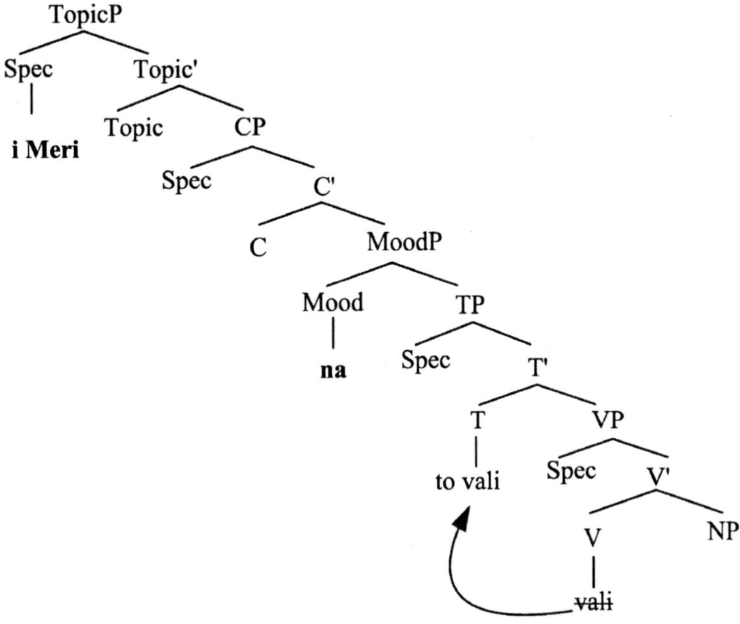

Fig. 3 Clause structure illustrating the preverbal subject position in child grammar

Further evidence comes from Spiros' and Yanna's data. In examples (32) and (33), preverbal subjects occur before the future marker *tha* (*ta* in child language), as well as the negation marker in (34).

(32) **to pe(d)aki ta** bi (s)tin t(r)ipa (Spiros, 1;9)
the child.DIM FUT enter.3SG to-the hole
'The little child will go into the hole'

(33) ke **ego tha** (r)θo sto spiti (Yanna, 2;9)
and I FUT come.1SG at.the home
'I'll come home too'

(34) **i mama** tora **den** klei. (Yanna, 2;9)
the mom.NOM now NEG cry.3SG.PRES
'Mommy does not cry now'

Given that preverbal subjects in (31)–(34) precede modality markers (i.e. *na* and *tha*, situated in the head of MoodP above TP) as well as the negation marker situated in the head of NegP also above TP, they cannot occupy the Specifier of TP, but must occupy a peripheral position, external to TP.

Furthermore, it should be noted that no instances of incorrect subject placement are found in the children's production in clauses that contain mood particles or the negation marker (during both the early and later stages of development). Overt DP subjects are correctly realized either in a postverbal position (see example (21) above) or in a position to the left of the [particles + verb] complex. These facts suggest that the structural positions that host overt subjects in the adult grammar can be projected in the early child grammar of Greek from the onset of syntactic development.

In addition to distribution, there is also evidence that early word order is constrained by the same semantic and pragmatic principles that regulate word order in the adult grammar. Consider the following excerpt from Mairi's data: In (35), a postverbal subject is used to convey new information (i.e. the DP 'bogeyman' has not been introduced in the previous discourse, it is considered 'new' information and surfaces in a postverbal position).

(35) k(l)ista ta xe(r)ja!
closed.CL.PL the hands.ACC
'Close your hands!
tha(r)thi **(o)** **babulas** tha se fai
FUT come.3SG (the) bogeyman.NOM FUT you.CL.ACC eat.3SG
'Bogeyman will come and get you' (Mairi, 1;10 – from Stephany 1997)

In contrast, early preverbal subjects appear to have a Topic interpretation. Consider example (36) from Mairi. When the DP 'the monkey' is first introduced in the discourse, it is realized in postverbal position. Once it is part of the 'known' information, the DP surfaces in a preverbal position.

(36) n ehi **pisiko** kapelo.
not have.3SG.PRES monkey.ACC hat.ACC
'The monkey does not have a hat.
na to vali kani nani
SUBJ it.CL put.3SG make.3SG beddy-bye
'Let me make him go beddy-bye'
o **pisiko** kani nani
the monkey make.3SG.PRES beddy-bye
'The monkey goes beddy-bye' (Mairi 1;10, from Stephany 1997)

The same pragmatic constraint on subject position is also attested in Yanna's data. In example (37), we observe a postverbal DP subject (i.e. *aera* 'air') in a context of new information, followed by a sentence where the DP subject is used as a topic and occurs in a preverbal position:

(37) ehi halasi i pota mas
have.3SG broken.PART the door.NOM ours
'Our door is broken'
beni **aera** ke ti aniji
enter.3SG.PRES air and it.CL.ACC open.3SG.PRES
'Air comes in and opens it'
aera beni. tin aniji
air enter.3SG.PRES it.CL.ACC open.3SG.PRES
'Air comes in. It opens it' (Yanna 2;10, from Stephany 1997)

It should also be noted that not all preverbal subjects found in the children's data occupy peripheral positions in the CP domain. Early preverbal subjects are also realized in the Specifier of TP (recall that, in Section 3, it was argued that preverbal subjects in adult Greek are either A-bar constituents or TP-internal elements). Consider the following examples:

(38) ULL: Dose mu
give.2SG.IMP me
'Give me (the purse)
CHI: i **dada** ine kokomu
the purse.NOM be.3SG.PRES mine
'The purse is mine'
ULL: aliθja?
really
'Really?'
CHI: ne.
yes
'Yes' (Yanna, 1;11)

(39) CHI: Pu pai a(f)to ?
where go.3SG.PRES this
'Where does this go?'
CHI: i **mama** to pi(re) a(f)to.
the mom it.CL get.3SG.PAST this
'Mom got this one' (Mairi 1;9)

Notice that the DP subjects in (38) and (39) are not associated with a Topic reading (like other preverbal subjects that we have seen in this section): they all present new information (similarly to postverbal subjects) – i.e. they introduce new referents into the discourse ('the purse' and 'mom'). As can be seen, these DPs surface in a preverbal position; given that these DPs are not interpreted as Topics, they cannot occupy the peripheral Topic position. They must occupy a position in the TP domain which I take to be the Specifier of TP. Table 5 presents in more detail the instances of children's preverbal subjects and their properties relative to information structure. We focus here only on preverbal subjects since much of the variability attested in the adult grammar concerns the semantic interpretation of subjects realized in preverbal structural positions.

Table 5 Properties of children's preverbal subjects[a]

Child	Age	Topic #	Contrastive/ emphatic: focus #	New information #	Total preverbal DP-subjects #
Spiros	1;9	1	4	1	6
Yanna	1;11	1	6	–	7
	2;5	2	7	1	10
	2;9	–	13	6	19
Mairi	1;9	–	7	1	8
	2;3	1	15	2	18
	2;9	1	31	7	39

[a] For the analysis of the properties of children's preverbal subjects, the following criteria were used: (a) a preverbal DP subject was labeled as Topic when that DP was already introduced in the previous discourse and was part of the context; (b) a preverbal DP subject was taken as expressing new information when that DP was the first occurrence in the discourse. Finally, due to lack of prosodic information in the transcripts, the criterion used to determine whether preverbal DP subjects were expressing contrast, i.e. were focused constituents, was their distribution with respect to modal particles (e.g. the mood particle *na*), tense markers (e.g. the future marker *tha*), wh-phrases (e.g. *pu* 'where'), the negation marker *den*, as well as discourse gaps/pauses marked on the transcripts.

On the basis of this evidence, it is reasonable to conclude that children have early grammatical knowledge of the mechanisms that determine the subject verb order in the adult grammar and that the variability of word order observed in their early production is not arbitrary but constrained by syntactic, semantic and pragmatic principles.

6.2 Further Evidence (OV(S))

In addition to SV and VS orders, the more marked OV(S) order is also attested in children's early production.[13] In the adult grammar, instances of OV(S) order are analyzed as involving focus movement of the DP object into the Specifier of

[13] See Stephany (1997) and Tsimpli (2005) for the emergence and development of other constituent orders (e.g. VOS, SOV) in Child Greek.

FocusP, in the left periphery of the clause (Tsimpli 1998, Kiss 1998). Kiss (1998) has distinguished two types of focus: *identificational* focus and *informational* focus. This distinction is based on both semantic and syntactic properties. Semantically, identification focus 'represents the value of the variable bound by an abstract operator expressing exhaustive identification' and syntactically 'the constituent called identificational focus itself acts as an operator, moving into the scope position in the Specifier of a functional projection (called FocusP), and binding the variable' (Kiss 1998: 245). In contrast, informational focus marks the non-presupposed nature of the information it carries and does not involve movement (i.e. it can appear in any position in the sentence and is marked by pitch accents).

In Greek, the distinction between these two types of focus can be illustrated in the following pair of examples, where in (40) the focused argument (STON PETRO) involves an identificational focus and has moved to the Specifier of the left peripheral projection FocusP, whereas in (41) the focused argument (STON PETRO) remains in situ and constitutes an informational focus.

(40) [$_{FP}$ STON PETRO [$_{IP}$ dhanisan to vivlio]
to.the Peter lend.3PL.PAST the book.ACC
'It was to Peter that they lent the book'

(41) [$_{IP}$ Dhanisan [$_{VP}$ to vivlio STON PETRO]
lend.3PL.PAST the book.ACC to.the Peter
'They lent the book to Peter'

In previous work (Kapetangianni 2007a, b), I have shown that movement of constituents to peripheral positions, including movement to the Specifier of FocusP, is evidenced in early Greek. Instances of OV(S) order are found in the earliest data of the Greek children, at the same stage where we find instances of SV and VS. The children's data in examples (42)–(44) display the use of focus structures with DP objects displaced from their thematic position inside VP and surfacing in preverbal position (see also Tsimpli (2005) for additional evidence regarding early emergence of OV order in Child Greek).

(42) **vi(v)lio** exi (Spiros, 1;9)
book.ACC have.3SG.PRES
'Book, I have'

(43) **tuto** exo ego, na (Janna, 1;11)
this.one have.1SG.PRES I DEM
'This one, I have, look'

(44) **agalitsa** sa se parume (Mairi, 1;9)
hug FUT you.CL take.1PL
'We'll give you a hug'

To sum up this section, it was shown that early Greek exhibits similar word order variability of Subject and Verb as well as of Object-Verb-(Subject) in accordance with the adult grammar. That is, variable word order in early Greek is not arbitrary but is constrained by the same syntactic, semantic and pragmatic principles that constrain word order in adult Greek. Based on these findings, it can be concluded that children appear to have both syntactic competence and pragmatic/discourse knowledge from the earliest stages of their syntactic development. Similar conclusions regarding the early acquisition of pragmatic principles have been formulated by a number of researchers who investigate the development of word order in other child grammars. For instance, De Cat (2003) has shown that French-acquiring children have the pragmatic competence that governs the structural realization of topics early on. Similarly, Westergaard (2003, 2008) has concluded that the pragmatic principles that regulate word order in wh-questions in a North Norwegian dialect are acquired at early stages of development, evidenced by children's competence in distinguishing between given and new subjects in terms of information structure. Furthermore, Russian-acquiring children appear to be sensitive to information structure principles governing the distribution of null elements in Russian, as demonstrated by Gordishevsky and Avrutin (2004). The present study adds to previous findings and further supports the claims that pragmatic principles of this sort are acquired early.[14]

The findings reported here also provide evidence for an early grammar with a fully structured CP and operable movement operations to peripheral positions (contra the no functional structure hypothesis formulated by Radford 1990). Furthermore, the findings go against the proposed immature interface delay between grammar and discourse as formulated by Grinstead (2004), given that children appear to have both syntactic and pragmatic knowledge from the earliest stages examined.

7 Conclusions

This chapter has addressed three related but separate questions: (i) How early do Greek children acquire the Null Subject parameter? (ii) How early do children acquire the grammatical properties that determine pre- and postverbal subjects? and (iii) When do child data provide evidence that children have the

[14] An anonymous reviewer raises the question of what children do when the pragmatic principles are not yet acquired. The empirical data presented here come from the first recordings available in the CHILDES database for child Greek and correspond to the earliest stages of children's syntactic production (ages 1;9 and 1;11). There are no available recordings for ages earlier than 1;9, which would be needed in order to further investigate this interesting issue. As we have seen, there is ample evidence even in the first recordings that suggests that pragmatic principles are already part of children's early grammar before the age of 2.

grammatical and pragmatics/discourse knowledge that governs Subject-Verb order in the adult Greek grammar?

By analyzing the properties of word order in child Greek, it was demonstrated that learners of Greek realize early that the language they are exposed to is a null subject language at an early age. Thus they set the correct value for the Null Subject parameter before age 2;0 and alternate between null and overt subjects in the earliest observed stages of development when they start producing two-word utterances. This finding provides further support for the hypothesis of Very Early Parameter Setting in language development cross-linguistically.

In addition, it was shown that the word order variability attested in the adult grammar is also evidenced in early child grammar. It was shown specifically that SV and VS, including OV(S) orders, are found in the earliest data and exhibit the syntactic and semantic properties of adult word order. Based on the distribution and interpretation of early overt subjects, it was argued that children have the syntactic, semantic and pragmatic knowledge that governs word order in the adult grammar from early on.

Finally, the findings of the present study indicate that, despite the apparent variability in the input, learners succeed very early in their development in acquiring the different mechanisms that govern word order in the adult grammar. This is similar to what is attested in the acquisition of grammars that do not exhibit a high level of word order variability (e.g. English).

Acknowledgments For important, helpful suggestions and discussion of the analyses and the data, I would like to thank my advisors Profs. Samuel Epstein, Acrisio Pires and Marilyn Shatz. Thanks also to the audience of the GLOW XXX workshop on Language Acquisition 'Optionality in the Input: Children's Acquisition of Variable Word Order' for their comments. I would like also to thank the organizers of the workshop Merete Anderssen, Kristine Bentzen and Marit Westergaard for taking the time to prepare this volume and for providing their valuable feedback on this paper. All remaining errors are mine.

References

Agouraki, Georgia. 1991. A modern Greek complementizer and its significance for universal grammar. *UCL Working Papers in Linguistics* 3: 1–24.

Aguado-Orea, Javier, and Julian M. Pine. 2002. There is no evidence for a 'no overt subject' stage in early child Spanish: A note on Grinstead (2000). *Journal of Child Language* 29: 865–874.

Alexiadou, Artemis, and Elena Anagnostopoulou. 1998. Parametrizing AGR: Word order, V-movement and EPP-checking. *Natural Language and Linguistic Theory* 16: 491–539.

Alexiadou, Artemis, and Elena Anagnostopoulou. 2000. Greek syntax: A principles and parameters perspective. *Journal of Greek Linguistics* 1: 171–222.

Bel, Aurora. 2003. The syntax of subjects in the acquisition of Spanish and Catalan. *Probus* 15: 1–26.

Bel, Aurora. 2001. The projection of aspect: A key in the acquisition of finiteness? In *Research on child language acquisition. Proceedings of the 8th Conference of the International Association for the Study of Child Language*, 1300–1316. Somerville/Massachusetts: Cascadilla Press.

Belletti, Adriana. 1990. *Generalized verb movement*. Turin: Rosenberg and Sellier.

Bloom, Lois. 1970. *Language development: Form and function in emerging grammars*. Cambridge: MIT Press.

Brown, Roger. 1973. *A first language*. Cambridge: Harvard University Press.

Cardinaletti, Anna. 1996. Subjects and clause structure. *University of Venice Working Papers in Linguistics* 6: 55–95.

Chomsky, Noam. 1981. Principles and parameters in syntactic theory. In *Explanation in linguistics. The logical problem of language acquisition*, eds. Norbert Hornstein and David Lightfoot, 32–75. London and New York: Longman.

Chomsky, Noam. 1995. *The minimalist program*. Cambridge: MIT Press.

De Cat, Cécile. 2003. Syntactic manifestations of very early pragmatic competence. In *Proceedings of the 27th Annual Boston University Conference on Language Development*, eds. Barbara Beachley, Amanda Brown and Frances Conlin, 209–219. Somerville: Cascadilla Press.

Gordishevsky, Galina, and Sergey Avrutin 2004. Optional omissions in an optionally null subject language. In *Proceedings of GALA 2003*, vol. 1, eds. Jacqueline van Kampen and Sergio Baauw, 187–198. LOT Occasional series 3, Utrecht: University of Utrecht.

Grinstead, John. 2004. Subjects and interface delay in child Spanish and Catalan. *Language* 80: 40–72.

Grinstead, John. 1998. Subjects, sentential negation and imperatives in child Spanish and Catalan. Ph.D. dissertation, University of California, Los Angeles.

Harris, Tony, and Kenneth Wexler. 1996. The optional infinitive stage in child English: Evidence from negation. In *Generative perspectives on language acquisition*, ed. Harald Clahsen. Amsterdam: John Benjamins.

Holton, David, Peter Mackridge, and Irene Philippaki-Warburton. 1997. *Greek: A comprehensive grammar of the modern language*. London: Routledge.

Kapetangianni, Konstantia. 2007a. Is there a syntax-pragmatics interface delay in early child grammars? Evidence from Greek. In *Proceedings of the 30th Annual Penn Linguistics Colloquium, Penn Working Papers in Linguistics* 13.1, eds. Tatjana Scheffler, Joshua Tauberer, Aviad Eilam, and Laia Mayol, 99–112. Penn Working Papers in Linguistics.

Kapetangianni, Konstantia. 2007b. The development of peripheral positions in early child grammars. In *Proceedings of the 31st Boston University Conference on Language Development* 2, eds. Heather Caunt-Nulton, Samantha Kulatilake and I-hao Woo, 358–369. Somerville: Cascadilla Press.

Kapetangianni, Konstantia. 2010. The Minimalist Syntax of Control in Greek. Ph.D. dissertation, University of Michigan.

Kiss, Katalin. 1998. Identificational focus versus informational focus. *Language* 74: 245–273.

MacWhinney, Brian. 1995. *The CHILDES project: Tools for analyzing talk*. Hillsdale: Lawrence Erlbaum Associates.

MacWhinney, Brian, and Catherine Snow. 1985. The Child Language Data Exchange System. *Journal of Child Language* 12: 271–295.

Ordonez, Francisco. 1997. Word order and clause structure in Spanish and other Romance languages. New York: CUNY dissertation.

Philippaki-Warburton, Irene. 1982. Προβλήματα σχετικά με τη σειρά των όρων στιζ ελληνικέζ προτάσειζ. *Γλωσσολογία* 1: 99–107.

Philippaki-Warburton, Irene. 1985. Word order in Modern Greek. *Transactions of the Philological Society*, 114–143.

Philippaki-Warburton, Irene. 1989. Subjects in English and Greek. *Proceedings of the 3rd Symposium on the description and/or comparison of English and Greek*. Thessaloniki: Aristotle University, School of English.

Philippaki-Warburton, Irene. 1998. Functional categories and Modern Greek syntax. *The Linguistic Review* 15: 159–186.

Pierce, Amy. 1992. *Language acquisition and syntactic theory: A comparative analysis of French and English child grammar*. Dordrecht: Kluwer.

Pires, Acrisio. 2009. The subject, it is here! The varying structural positions of preverbal subjects, DELTA (Documentation of Studies in Theoretical and Applied Linguistics) 23, 113–146.

Poeppel, David, and Kenneth Wexler. 1993. The full competence hypothesis of clause structure in early German. *Language* 69: 365–424.

Pollock, Jean-Yves. 1989. Verb movement, universal Grammar, and the structure of IP. *Linguistic Inquiry* 20: 365–424.

Radford, Andrew. 1990. *Syntactic theory and the acquisition of English Syntax*. Oxford: Blackwell.

Rivero, Maria Luisa. 1994. Clause structure and V-movement in the languages of the Balkans. *Natural Language and Linguistic Theory* 12: 63–120.

Rizzi, Luigi. 2000. *Comparative syntax and language acquisition*. London: Routledge.

Rizzi, Luigi. 1997. The fine structure of the left periphery. In *Elements of grammar: Handbook in generative syntax*, ed. Liliane Haegeman, 281–337. Dordrecht: Kluwer.

Rizzi, Luigi. 1990. *Relativized minimality*. Cambridge: MIT Press.

Roussou, Anna. 2000. On the left periphery: Modal particles and complementizers. *Journal of Greek Linguistics* 1: 65–94.

Roussou, Anna, and Ianthi Maria Tsimpli. 2006. On Greek VSO again. *Journal of Linguistics* 42: 317–354.

Spyropoulos, Vassilios, and Irene Philippaki-Warburton. 2001. 'Subject' and EPP in Greek. *Journal of Greek Linguistics* 2: 149–186.

Spyropoulos, Vassilios, and Anthi Revithiadou. 2009. Subject chains in Greek and PF processing. *MIT Working Papers in Linguistics* 57, 293–309, *Proceedings of the 2007 Workshop in Greek Syntax and Semantics at MIT*.

Stephany, Ursula. 1997. The acquisition of Greek. In *The crosslinguistic study of language acquisition* 4, ed. Dan Isaac Slobin, 183–333. New Jersey: Lawrence Erlbaum Associates.

Tsimpli, Ianthi Maria. 1990. The clause structure and word-order in Modern Greek. *UCL Working Papers in Linguistics* 2: 226–255.

Tsimpli, Ianthi Maria. 1995. Focusing in modern Greek. In *Discourse configurational languages*, ed. Katalin Kiss. Oxford: Oxford University Press.

Tsimpli, Ianthi Maria. 1998. Individual and functional reading for focus, Wh- and negative operators evidence from Greek. In *Themes in Greek Linguistics II*, eds. Brian D. Joseph, Geoffrey C. Horrocks and Irene Philippaki-Warburton, 197–227. Amsterdam and Philadelphia, PA: John Benjamins.

Tsimpli, Ianthi Maria. 2005. Peripheral positions in early Greek. In *Advances in Greek generative syntax*, eds. Melita Stavrou and Arhonto Terzi, 178–216. Linguistics Today 76. Amsterdam: John Benjamins.

Westergaard, Marit. 2003. Word order in wh-questions in a North Norwegian dialect: Some evidence from an acquisition study. *Nordic Journal of Linguistics* 26: 81–109.

Westergaard, Marit. 2008. Verb movement and subject placement in the acquisition of word order: Pragmatics or structural economy? In *First language acquisition of morphology and syntax: Perspectives across languages and learners*, eds. Pedro Guijarro-Fuentes, Pilar Larranaga and John Clibbens. Language Acquisition and Language Disorders 45, Amsterdam: John Benjamins.

Wexler, Kenneth. 1998. Very early parameter setting and the unique checking constraint: A new explanation of the optional infinitive stage. *Lingua* 106: 23–79.

Optional Scrambling Is Not Random: Evidence from English-Ukrainian Acquisition

Roksolana Mykhaylyk and Heejeong Ko

Abstract In this chapter, we investigate the role of specificity in the acquisition of a 'free-word-order', article-less language – Ukrainian. Particularly, we are interested in the acquisition of direct object scrambling as a means to encode the feature [+specific] on the scrambled direct object DP. An elicited production study is used to show that bilingual English-Ukrainian children have the knowledge of specificity in their grammar, and they are able to match it with appropriate syntactic movement in Ukrainian. We argue that the high rate of optionality in child scrambling can be better accounted for with syntax-semantics notions, contrary to discourse-pragmatic approaches to the phenomenon. We show that children do not overuse scrambled constructions with non-specific objects, and argue that the optionality of scrambling in children's utterances is unlikely to be due to a pragmatic deficit.

Keywords Acquisition · Object scrambling · Optionality · Specificity · Ukrainian

1 Introduction

A variety of types of word order permutations have been unified under the descriptive term of scrambling. Previous research has provided evidence for an interaction between scrambling and the semantic feature 'specificity'.[1] The specificity effect in scrambling has been extensively studied for Germanic languages (see Thrainsson 2001 for an overview) and also for Slavic languages such as Russian (Avrutin and Brun 2001, Dyakonova 2004) and Serbo-Croatian (Ilić and Deen 2004).

R. Mykhaylyk (✉)
Stony Brook University, Stony Brook, NY, USA
e-mail: rmykhayl@ic.sunysb.edu

[1] A precise definition of specificity will be provided in Section 3. Roughly, we use the term 'specific' to mean that the speaker presupposes the existence of an individual.

M. Anderssen et al. (eds.), *Variation in the Input*, Studies in Theoretical Psycholinguistics 39, DOI 10.1007/978-90-481-9207-6_9,

The acquisition of scrambling in first language acquisition (L1A) and second language acquisition (L2A) has been widely investigated in recent studies (see Otsu 1994 for Japanese; Clahsen and Muysken 1986, Penner et al. 2000, Hopp 2005 for German; Josefsson 1996 for Swedish; Westergaard 2008 for Norwegian; Powers 2000 for English inter alia). In a number of acquisition studies, it has also been shown that a scrambled object in L1 and L2 learners' speech is usually interpreted as specific (Schaeffer 2000a, b, Unsworth 2005).

In this chapter, we focus on three main studies on the acquisition of the interaction between scrambling and specificity.

Schaeffer's (2000b) approach can be best defined as discourse-pragmatic. Schaeffer argues that scrambling in Dutch is triggered by a discourse-related feature – specificity.[2] She further proposed that young children lack the pragmatic concept of non-shared knowledge, so they are not able to correctly mark specificity on the direct object DP, and thus the specificity feature is underspecified in their grammar. Therefore, scrambling does not occur consistently in child speech due to lack of pragmatic knowledge.

Avrutin and Brun (2001) proposed a discourse-syntactic approach to the acquisition of scrambling. They based their research on the assumption that word order interacts with specificity and definiteness, especially in Russian. It was shown that Russian children (age 1;7–2;3) place most arguments in the correct positions, which suggests that they have the knowledge of specificity/definiteness from a very early age. Errors, if they exist, are due to children's egocentric assumption that the elements they refer to are known to the speaker and the hearer.[3]

Unsworth (2004, 2005) showed some inadequacies of the pragmatic analysis and put forward a syntactic-semantic approach to the acquisition of object scrambling. She suggested that errors in the acquisition of scrambling are not likely to be due to the lack of pragmatic knowledge, since even adult learners show the same problems with scrambling as child learners (e.g., in L2 Dutch). In her view, errors in scrambling (especially in production) are linked to an unstable mapping between a semantic feature and syntactic movement.

There are many issues left open, however: how specificity interacts with scrambling in child grammars of other languages, which theoretical account concerning the acquisition of scrambling can be supported by cross-linguistic data, and how bilingual children acquire scrambling especially if their L1 lacks scrambling, to list a few. In the current chapter, we provide experimental

---

[2] In Section 2, we discuss what 'specificity' means under Schaeffer (2000b) with concrete Dutch examples.

[3] As a reviewer suggests, both Schaeffer (2000b) and Avrutin and Brun (2001) associate children's errors in scrambling with a discourse related factor (i.e. lack of the distinction between the speaker's and hearer's knowledge). The two studies, however, diverge in some crucial respects. In Section 2, we provide more detailed reviews on the differences between the two approaches.

evidence for an interaction between specificity and scrambling in Ukrainian and propose a syntactic-semantic analysis of optionality in scrambling.

The base structure of Ukrainian is SVO, and it has object scrambling across the verb.[4] Similarly to Dutch, Ukrainian allows object scrambling only when the object is specific: (1) is acceptable with specific reading of the object, but (2) is unacceptable because the context forces non-specific reading of the object.

(1) Elmo **jabluko**$_i$ jist' t_i - vono take smačne.
Elmo apple$_{[+\text{specific}]}$ eats it such delicious
'Elmo is eating a specific apple - it is such a delicious apple.'

(2) #Elmo **jabluko**$_i$ jist' t_i bo vin holodnyj.
Elmo apple$_{[+\text{specific}]}$ eats because he hungry
'Elmo is eating a specific apple because he is hungry.'

Unlike other languages, e.g., Dutch, in-situ objects in Ukrainian can be specific or non-specific, as in (3) and (4). Adults, however, strongly prefer a non-specific reading for in-situ objects.

(3) Elmo jist' **jabluko** bo vin holodnyj.
Elmo eats apple$_{[\text{-specific}]}$ because he hungry
'Elmo is eating some apple because he is hungry.'

(4) Elmo jist' **jabluko** jake jomu dav Bert.
Elmo eats apple$_{[+\text{specific}]}$ which him gave Bert
'Elmo is eating a specific apple, which Bert gave to him.

The pragmatic approach to the acquisition of scrambling in Ukrainian predicts that young children will produce sentences with a scrambled object even in non-specific contexts, as in (2) (cf. Avrutin and Brun 2001). On this analysis, children might misinterpret hearer knowledge, and thus mark a [−specific] object as specific/definite according to their own beliefs, which in turn will trigger more scrambling of non-specific objects (see also Westergaard (2008), Anderssen et al. ('The Acquisition of Apparent Optionality. Word Order in Subject and Object Shift Construction in Norwegian', this volume) for the same argument regarding subject and object shift in Norwegian). In this chapter we will show that such an approach fails to account for the optional child scrambling in Ukrainian.

We argue that bilingual children acquiring Ukrainian have access to the specificity feature in UG and to the UG-defined 'scrambling rule' (regardless of their L1), assuming Full Access to UG in child L2 (Schwartz 2003). However,

[4] We adopt Shevelov's (1993) view that unmarked word order in Ukrainian is Subject-Verb-Object. We abbreviate the unmarked order as SVO hereafter.

we propose that children and adults may show different scrambling patterns in certain contexts because children, unlike adults, might have difficulties in correlating syntactic and semantic components of the grammar (see also White (2003) for adult L2). Specifically, we hypothesize that Ukrainian adult speakers resolve the semantic ambiguity of the SVO structure by syntactic movement, but that children may scramble at a lower rate than adults due to an unstable mapping between a syntactic feature (EPP) and a semantic feature (specificity).

The current approach to optional direct object scrambling will be shown to be supported by our experimental study, an elicited production task based on Schaeffer (2000b) with 41 English-Ukrainian bilingual children. The results of the study reveal that there is no significant overuse of object scrambling in non-specific contexts, contrary to what is predicted under the pragmatic approach. They further indicate that children have the specificity value in their grammar, but employ syntactic movement only optionally.

The paper is organized as follows. First, previous experimental research on scrambling acquisition is surveyed in Section 2. Next, the theoretical background of the syntactic mechanism of scrambling in adult Ukrainian is presented in Section 3. The hypothesis and predictions for child acquisition of object scrambling in Ukrainian are defined in Section 4. Section 5 provides a detailed description of the experimental study, and in Section 6 the results are summarized. The paper concludes with a discussion of the findings and their implications for language acquisition theory.

2 Reviews of Previous Studies

A number of studies on the acquisition of object scrambling have been conducted on languages with scrambling, such as Dutch and Russian. They report optionality of scrambling in different age groups of L1 and L2 learners, attributing this phenomenon either to a pragmatic deficit (e.g., Schaeffer 2000b, Avrutin and Brun 2001) or to a syntactic-semantic mismapping (Unsworth 2004, 2005). Although the authors account for the optionality of the process in different terms, their findings document several convergent patterns in the acquisition of scrambling that can be tested cross-linguistically.

2.1 Schaeffer (2000a, b): The Discourse-Pragmatic Approach

Schaeffer (2000a, b) assumes that object scrambling is driven by the feature [+specific]; [+specific] objects undergo scrambling, but [–specific] objects do not. Specificity (or 'referentiality' in Schaeffer's 2000b terms) was defined as follows:

(5) A nominal expression is understood to be referential if it has a 'fixed referent' in the (model of the) world, meaning that it can be identified by the speaker and/or by one of the people whose propositional attitudes are being reported (Schaeffer 2000b:24).

Importantly, Schaeffer argues that the specificity feature is *underspecified* in early child grammar. She predicts that at an early stage of acquisition, children may lack the concept of specificity and thus cannot associate it with scrambling. Consequently, children at this stage may scramble only optionally even in the contexts where scrambling is obligatory.

This hypothesis was tested with an experimental study which consisted of an elicited production task and a truth value judgment task. The subjects (49 Dutch children age 2;4–6;10 and 23 adults) were shown short puppet shows with direct objects incorporated into a definite specific, indefinite specific, or indefinite non-specific context. These contexts were designed to elicit a certain type of production from the language learners. The target sentence may be accompanied with or without scrambling (across adverbs or negation), as exemplified in (6).[5]

(6) a. Dat Marieke **een (bepaald/zeker) boek** gisteren gekocht heeft.
that Marieke a certain book yesterday bought has
'That Marieke bought a certain book yesterday.'
b. Dat Marieke gisteren **een (of ander) boek** gekocht heeft.
that Marieke yesterday a/one or other book bought has
'That Marieke bought some book or other yesterday.'

Schaeffer observes two developmental stages in the acquisition of scrambling: At Stage 1, 2-year-old children scramble highly optionally, and at Stage 2, 3-year-old and older children behave more adult-like: they scramble specific objects at a high rate (over negation). This is illustrated by Table 1.

Schaeffer claims that the optionality of object scrambling at the early stage of acquisition results from the optional marking of specificity, which in turn depends on the acquisition of 'the Concept of Non-Shared Knowledge' – speaker and hearer knowledge are always independent. Under this view, young children lack a specific pragmatic principle which leads to the lack of a distinction between discourse-related (mentioned in the discourse, e.g., *the tree*) and non-discourse-related (part of the long-term shared knowledge, e.g., *the sun*) object DPs. The object, then, is not constantly marked with a relevant feature, and the syntactic process of scrambling does not always take place in child Dutch.

[5] A similar experiment was also conducted with 35 Italian children (2;1–5;11) in order to show that the object scrambling across negation and adverbs in Dutch and object cliticization in Italian are similar syntactic processes (Schaeffer 2000b).

Table 1 Placement of definite and indefinite direct objects with respect to negation

	Definite		Indefinite	
Age	Pre-neg. (%)	Post-neg. (%)	Pre-neg. (%)	Post-neg. (%)
2	30	70	33	67
3	72	28	56	44
4	82	18	57	43
5	76	24	59	41
6	83	17	57	43
Adults	96	4	66	34

However, this analysis was developed mostly for definite DPs (including proper names and pronouns) and specific indefinite DPs that must precede the adverb and negation. Since the results from indefinite specific and indefinite non-specific were collapsed together (see Table 1), it is unclear whether children optionally scramble only in specific (or referential in Schaeffer's term) contexts or in any contexts across-the-board. We will return to this issue in Section 4.

2.2 *Avrutin and Brun (2001): The Discourse-Syntactic Approach*

Avrutin and Brun (2001) (and later Brun 2005) challenged Schaeffer's (2000a, b) claim about underspecification of specificity in child grammar. In their study, the terms 'specificity' and 'non-specificity' are used in 'an intuitive pre-theoretical sense' and are defined along the lines of Yokoyama's (1986) description of different states of interlocutors' knowledge in discourse.[6]

(7) Specific expression denotes an individual already mentioned in the conversation and, therefore, familiar ('old') with respect to a given discourse (Avrutin and Brun 2001:70).

The observation of Russian facts, which constitute the basis of the study, may be summarized as follows: independently of the grammatical function (subject or object), preverbal elements are interpreted as specific and postverbal as non-specific.

(8) a. **Mal'čik** činit igrušku.
(the)boy.NOM is-fixing (a/some)toy.ACC
'The boy is fixing a toy.'

[6] In fact, Avrutin and Brun's definition of specificity corresponds to definiteness, and in the follow up study, Brun (2005), the term 'definiteness' was used.

b. **Igrušku** <u>činit</u> mal'čik.
(the)toy.ACC is-fixing (a/some)boy.NOM
'A boy is fixing the toy.'

The authors pose a specific research question: to what extent are young children aware of this dependency between word order and specificity and use it in their speech. If it is true that children lack knowledge of specificity, Russian children should misinterpret preverbal and post-verbal arguments. Nonetheless, naturalistic data from four Russian children (1;7–2;3) show that most of the arguments are placed correctly (90% of specific subjects and 89.4% of specific objects occurred preverbally) (Table 2).

Table 2 Distribution of subjects and objects in child speech (Avrutin and Brun 2001: 73)

Interpretation	Preverbal subject (%)	Postverbal subject (%)	Preverbal object (%)	Postverbal object (%)
Specific	90.0	10.0	89.4	10.6
Non-specific	**32.2**	67.8	**9.7**	90.3

Interestingly, only 9.7% of non-specific objects were scrambled over the verb. Therefore, Avrutin and Brun concluded that Russian children (unlike the Dutch children from Schaeffer's study) show knowledge of specificity from a very early age. However, the high rate of preverbal non-specific subjects (32.2%) weakened the argument, so the authors suggested that this is due to pragmatic factors: 'that is, to the child's erroneous presupposition that the referred individual is known to the listener and hence specific' (Avrutin and Brun 2001: 79). It has remained unclear, however, why the object behaves in a different way from the subject in scrambling.

To sum up, Avrutin and Brun show that children know and make use of the mapping between object scrambling and specificity at an early age. This mapping can thus be considered a part of an innate (or very early acquired) knowledge of the *syntax-discourse interface* rules. Furthermore, Avrutin and Brun suggested that the optionality of scrambling is related not to the featural underspecification (cf. Schaeffer 2000b), but to the optionality of the syntactic representation of the discourse referent. 'While in adult language the discourse referents are introduced by syntactic means, children may (optionally at some stage) rely on discourse presupposition as the source of introducing discourse entities' (Avrutin and Brun 2001: 79).

2.3 Unsworth (2005): The Syntactic-Semantic Approach

Unsworth (2005) compared child L1, child L2 and adult L2 acquisition of scrambling in Dutch. The main goal of her research was to examine whether

English-speaking adult and child L2 learners go through the same developmental sequences in their acquisition of object scrambling in Dutch as L1 Dutch children. Unsworth employed both production and comprehension tasks in the experiment. The production task focuses on object scrambling over negation (based on Schaeffer's 2000b experiment). In the comprehension task, scrambling across the frequency adverbial *twee keer* 'twice' and negation was examined (based on Krämer's 2000 experiment).

Unsworth assumes that scrambling is movement to some VP-external position that has interpretive semantic effects. She notes that scrambled indefinite objects have been variously labeled as 'specific' (in the sense of Enç 1991), 'referential' (Fodor and Sag 1982), or 'presuppositional' (Diesing 1992). To avoid any confusion, she uses the cover-term 'specific', although, strictly-speaking, the reading which was tested in the relevant experimental conditions is partitive or 'strong', in de Hoop's (1992) terms.

The goal of Unsworth's experimental production study was to determine whether learners know the interpretive constraints on scrambling. For instance, scrambling over negation is obligatory for specific direct objects, as in (9b), but it is not allowed for non-specific direct objects, as in (9a).

(9) a. Brigit heeft <u>geen</u> (niet + een) **roos** geplukt.
Brigit has no (not + a) rose picked
'Brigit didn't pick a(ny) rose.'
b. Brigit heeft **een roos** <u>niet</u> geplukt.
Brigit has a rose not picked
'Brigit didn't pick a (certain) rose.'

Based on the elicited production task conducted with three different learner groups (13 L1 children, 25 L2 children, and 23 L2 adults), Unsworth analyzed the developmental stages of acquisition scrambling of (Table 3 and 4).

Table 3 L1 child and L1 adult (target) object scrambling (Unsworth 2005: 226)

Age	Definite (%)	Specific indefinite (%)	Non-specific indefinite (%)
5	71.7	61.3	**15.2**
Adults	98.5	92.9	**0**

The results showed that adult Dutch L2 learners' initial stage corresponds to their L1 (English SVO) word order, but the next stages are similar for L1 and child and adult L2 learners. It was concluded, then, that since both adults and children pass through the same optional scrambling stage (see the shaded row in Table 4, for example), they make use of the same mechanisms in language acquisition.

Table 4 L2 child and L2 adult object scrambling per condition (Unsworth 2005: 243, 244)

	Definite		Specific indefinite		Non-specific indefinite	
Proficiency in Dutch	Children	Adults	Children	Adults	Children	Adults
Low	22.1%	19.3%	23.3%	14.3%	23.3%	20.0%
Mid	80.0%	88.9%	71.7%	58.3%	30.0%	13.3%
High	88.1%	87.5%	91.7%	85.7%	16.7%	0%

Overall, the results of Unsworth's study demonstrate that L2 children and adults are able to overcome the poverty-of-the-stimulus in the infrequent input for scrambling and make a connection between the semantic notion of specificity and syntactic movement. The existence of an optional scrambling stage in the L2 data was claimed to be inconsistent with Schaeffer's (2000b) approach discussed above. The adult L2 subjects tested were old enough to know pragmatic principles, and yet, they scrambled optionally.

These findings imply that syntactic-semantic factors might play a more important role in Dutch scrambling acquisition than knowledge of a certain pragmatic concept. However, more research on languages other than Dutch is needed in order to evaluate the validity of the syntax-semantic approach to scrambling and specificity in general. The current study aims to contribute to this by presenting evidence from the acquisition of object scrambling in Ukrainian.

2.4 *Summary of the Literature Overview*

To summarize, previous research on free-word-order languages has provided evidence for the interaction between specificity and scrambling. In particular, it was shown that the direct object that was moved out of the VP is usually interpreted as specific in L1 and L2 learners' production. One of the most disputable questions has been whether the specificity feature is available in child grammar. Noticing that young children fail to scramble in obligatory contexts, Schaeffer argued for underspecification of specificity in child Dutch. On the other hand, studies conducted on Russian and Serbo-Croatian show that even the youngest children are aware of the correlation between specificity (definiteness, more precisely speaking) and word order, which suggests that the underspecification of specificity is not universal. Interestingly, all studies mentioned above reported optionality of scrambling in different age groups, attributing this phenomenon either to a pragmatic deficit (Schaeffer 2000a, b, Avrutin and Brun 2001, Ilić and Deen 2004) or to a syntactic-semantic mismapping (Unsworth 2004, 2005). The current study aims to resolve these conflicting accounts by presenting evidence from acquisition of direct object scrambling in Ukrainian.

3 Direct Object Scrambling in Adult Ukrainian Grammar

3.1 Theoretical Background

Three main concepts need to be defined in order to set the theoretical framework for the research: specificity, definiteness and object scrambling.

We assume that definiteness and specificity are different semantic notions related to the speaker's and hearer's knowledge in the following way:

(10) If a Determiner Phrase (DP) of the form [D NP] is ...
  a. [+definite], then the speaker assumes that the hearer shares the speaker's presupposition of the existence of a unique individual in the set denoted by the NP (based on Heim 1991)
  b. [+specific], then the speaker presupposes the existence of an individual in the set denoted by the NP regardless of the hearer's knowledge (based on Enç 1991; cf. Diesing 1992 for presuppositionality; Ko et al. 2007 for partitivity).[7]

Ukrainian lacks articles and there is no lexical item that directly marks a DP as definite. Demonstratives can be used to refer to a referential definite in some contexts. As shown in (11), demonstratives such as *cej, cja, ce, ci* 'this' and *toj, ta, te, ti* 'that' strongly imply shared knowledge between the speaker and hearer about a particular individual.

(11)	Čy	ty	bačyla	<u>tu</u>	<u>ihrašku</u>,	jaka	meni	spodobalasja?
	Q-Part	you	saw	that	toy.ACC	that	I.DAT	liked

'Have you seen that/the toy that I liked?'

Note, however, that Ukrainian demonstratives are only optional (unlike English articles), and they do not have the same semantics as the English definite article *the*. Hence, in Ukrainian, no demonstrative is used to mark definiteness even when the uniqueness presupposition is satisfied for the object 'author'.

---

[7] A cautionary note on the term specific is required here. Enç (1991) suggests that there are two sub-types of specificity: specificity encoded by *partitive* DPs, which are related to a previously mentioned set, and specificity encoded by elements such as *a certain* in English, which involve *speaker intent to refer* (see also Fodor and Sag 1982, Ionin 2003, Ionin et al. 2004, among others). In this paper, we are mainly interested in the former notion of specificity – which is often termed as partitive (Ko et al. 2004, 2007) and 'presuppositional' (Diesing 1992). Although we also present examples relevant to the latter notion of *specificity as speaker intent to refer* here for concreteness (e.g., (13), (14)), our experiment is mainly designed to test the effects of specificity in the sense of 'presuppositionality', as given in (10b). We acknowledge, however, that we call these two sub-types of DPs as *specific* only for convenience. These two notions are known to be independent semantic features at work in L2 acquisition (Ko et al. 2004, 2007). We wish to investigate how this fine-grained distinction of specificity interacts with L2- Ukrainian scrambling in our future research.

(12) ja xoču zustrity avtora cijeji kartyny, ale ja ne znaju xto vin.
I want meet author.ACC this painting but I not know who he
'I want to meet the author of this painting, but I do not know who it is.'

Indefiniteness can be used based on the speaker's knowledge only, as in (13) (specific reading), or it can be related neither to the speaker nor to the hearer, as in (14) (non-specific reading). In Ukrainian, the cardinal numeral 'one' in its various gender and number forms *odyn, odna, odne, odni* can have a specific meaning of 'a certain', and thus it often serves as a specificity marker (cf. (11) for the use of demonstratives in [+definite, +specific] contexts):

(13) Cej recept meni dala odna žinka, jaku ty ne znaješ.
this recipe.ACC I.DAT gave one woman that you not know
'I got this recipe from a woman who you do not know.'

Non-specific interpretation is usually associated with the commonly used indefinite determiner *jakyjs', jakas', jakes',* and *jakis'* ('some/any') or other indefinite pronouns *byd'-jakyj, dejakyj, jakyj-nebud'* with the reinforced indefinite meaning 'whichever'. Cummins (1998) describes different nuances of similar pronouns in Czech and classifies them as marking different degrees of indefiniteness.[8]

(14) Cej recept napysala jakas' žinka, jaku ja ne znaju.
this recipe.ACC wrote some woman that I not know
'This recipe was written by a woman who I do not know.'

In some contexts, word order can also encode definiteness and specificity in Ukrainian. As discussed briefly in the introduction, object scrambling into preverbal position is allowed only when the object is specific (see (1) and (2)). In-situ objects can be specific (e.g., definite DP, specific indefinite DP) or non-specific (i.e. non-specific indefinite DP) (see (3) and (4)).[9]

Another concept to be defined is *object scrambling*.[10] Without delving into different definitions of scrambling offered in the literature, we simply assume its

[8] In Ukrainian, too, they differ slightly in the degree of indefiniteness.

[9] It has also been argued for Russian that all preverbal elements are interpreted as specific while postverbal elements are interpreted as non-specific (Avrutin and Brun 2001: 71) (Note that 'specific' in Avrutin and Brun 2001 actually refers to 'definite': see note 6). Crucially, however, Ukrainian direct objects can be either specific or non-specific in postverbal position.

[10] Given that this paper deals with the reordering of sentential constituents, namely direct objects, *within* clause boundaries, the term *object shift* could be used to refer to the process under the analysis. However, *object shift* is usually reserved for Scandinavian languages and has not been applied to Ukrainian. The term *object shift* has been used to refer to a process restricted by the position of the main verb (Holmberg 1999), whereas in Ukrainian, there is no such restriction concerning verb raising and object scrambling. Since it is not our intention to find a consensus in the terminological disputes, in this paper we use a neutral term for Ukrainian object movement – *direct object scrambling*.

pre-theoretical meaning, that is, a change in word order from the base order. Since the constituent that is the focus of the current research is the direct object, its movement leftward will be described in terms of scrambling. Therefore, object scrambling is defined as the movement of a direct object from its base position within the VP to a higher pre-verbal landing site. The choice of the landing site, the mechanism of the movement, and the change in object interpretation associated with scrambling in Ukrainian will be discussed in detail in the following section.

3.2 The Syntactic-Semantic Mechanism of Object Scrambling

In Ukrainian, the direct object can take different positions in the sentence, but since the base structure of the language is SVO, all other orders of constituents are considered derived. In the current chapter we are concerned mostly with an SOV structure that exhibits direct object scrambling to a position higher than the verb, but lower than the subject, as in (16):

(15) Taras čytaje **knyžku.**
Taras.NOM reads book.ACC

(16) Taras **knyžku** $_i$ čytaje t_i
Taras.NOM book.ACC reads
'Taras is reading a/the book.'

3.2.1 Landing Sites

To locate the landing site of a scrambled object, it is necessary to find elements that can index the moved position of the object. Adverbs and negation figure prominently as such landmarks (Thrainsson 2001). In this chapter, we also employ them to detect the landing site of the scrambled object.

As has been shown in Cinque (1999), different types of adverbs can occur in different positions in the clause. In Ukrainian, too, both high (sentential) and low (manner) adverbs precede the main verb in the typical transitive structure S-Adv-V-O, but there are important structural differences between them. In particular, vP-ellipsis tests show that the high adverb *napevno* 'certainly' cannot be elided and, thus, it is situated outside of vP:

(17) Taras *napevno* ne bude čytaty knyžku, a Ivan napevno bude.
Taras certainly not will read book.ACC but Ivan certainly will
'Taras is certainly not going to read a book, but Ivan certainly will [read a book].'

(18) #Taras <u>napevno</u> ne bude čytaty knyžku, a Ivan bude.
Taras certainly not will read book.ACC but Ivan will
'Taras is certainly not going to read a book, but Ivan certainly will [read a book].'

In contrast, deletion of the low adverb *švydko* 'quickly' in vP-ellipsis contexts does not make the sentence unacceptable, which suggests that it is a vP-internal element:

(19) Taras bude <u>švydko</u> čytaty knyžku, a Ivan ne bude.
Taras will quickly read book.ACC but Ivan not will
'Taras will read a book quickly, but Ivan will not [read a book quickly].'

Assuming that the low adverb is situated in a vP domain (see also Adger 2003), its position in scrambled structures such as (20) indicates that the landing site of the scrambled object is (at least) as high as the edge of *v*P.

(20) Taras knyžku$_i$ <u>švydko</u> čytaje t_i
Taras book.ACC quickly reads
'Taras is reading the book quickly.'

The scrambled specific object must precede the negation in Ukrainian. When the object precedes the negation, the sentence gets a sentential negation reading over the object, as shown in (21). If the object follows the negation, a constituent negation reading is obtained instead, as illustrated in (22).

(21) Taras knyžku $_i$ ne čytaje t_i
Taras book.ACC not reads
'Taras is not reading the/a certain book.'

(22) Taras ne knyžku $_i$ čytaje t_i (a žurnal)
Taras not book.ACC reads
'Taras is reading not a book, (but a journal).'

Following Pollock (1989: 397), we assume that negation is the head of NegP, and that NegP can be left-adjoined to *v*P in some languages (see Schaeffer 2000b and Thrainsson 2001 for Germanic and Scandinavian). This assumption is in line with previous proposals for Slavic languages which argue that the sentential negation marker is pronounced on the finite verb, but checks its [NEG] feature in the head of NegP (Brown 1999). Similar proposals have also been suggested for Czech, in which quantifiers are able to precede the negative marker, but remain under the scope of the negation (Zeijlstra 2004). Ukrainian exhibits a similar phenomenon with the negative pronoun 'nothing':

(23) Taras ničoho$_i$ ne čytaje t$_i$
Taras nothing.GEN not read
'Taras reads nothing/Taras does not read anything.'

Post-verbal objects take scope under negation, as in (22):

(24) Taras ne čytaje žodnoji knyžky
Taras not reads any book.GEN
'Taras is not reading any book.'

We argue that in Ukrainian, as in other Slavic languages (Zeijlstra 2004), the negative marker is base-generated within *v*P and the negative feature moves out of *v*P to create a sentential scope of negation. Consequently, if a direct object moves to a pre-verbal position via scrambling (i.e., *v*P adjunction), the linear order of the sentence becomes Subject > Direct Object > Neg + Verb, as shown in the tree (25). We thus assume that the negation can be treated on a par with the low adverb as a marker of the structural border of *v*P in Ukrainian.

(25)
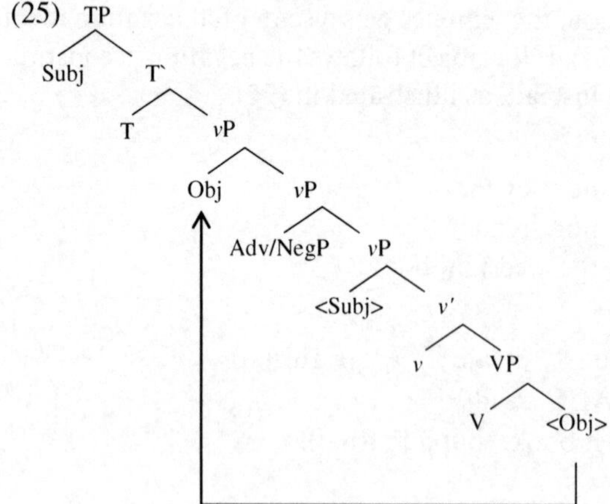

Thus, the change from the basic SVO structure to SO(Adv/Neg)V involves the direct object moving to the left edge of the vP, which is clearly detectable if the sentence contains NegP or low adverbs. The details of the movement will be discussed in Section 4.2.2, but it is clear that in both cases the shifted direct object precedes these elements.

3.2.2 Semantic Interpretation of the Direct Object

We argue that scrambling under analysis is used to mark a change in the semantic interpretation of the direct object. This approach is based on Dutch/Ukrainian parallels. In Dutch, a direct object scrambled over a high adverb (and/or negation) always receives a specific interpretation for the speaker, as shown in the example (26) from (Schaeffer 2000b).[11] Corresponding Ukrainian examples with a high adverb are given in (27), where (27) is parallel to Dutch in that it is understood as 'Maria bought a certain, specific book yesterday', although there is no determiner in (27), compared to (26).[12]

(26) a. Dat Marieke gisteren een (of ander) boek gekocht heeft.
that Marieke yesterday a/one or other book bought has
'That Marieke bought some book or other yesterday'
b. Dat Marieke een (bepaald/zeker) boek gisteren gekocht heeft.
that Marieke a certain book yesterday bought has
'That Marieke bought a certain book yesterday'

(27) a. Marija včora kupyla knyžky.
Maria yesterday bought book.ACC
'Maria bought a book yesterday.'
b. Marija knyžku včora kupyla.
Maria book.ACC yesterday bought
'Maria bought a certain book yesterday.'

Furthermore, personal pronouns that are considered to be inherently specific (see also Koopman 1998) must raise both in Dutch (28) and in Ukrainian (29)[13]:

[11] Schaeffer mentions that indefinite objects with the indefinite article *een* 'a' are slightly awkward in pre-high-adverb position, and the sentence sounds better if the determiner *één* 'one' is used. Unsworth (2005), however, notes that there is a clear interpretational difference between scrambled and non-scrambled word orders in both cases.

[12] High adverbs can appear in different positions in Ukrainian, but only the post-subject and pre-verbal position of the object as in (27b) is indicative of object scrambling. In the following discussion and in the experimental design, we use mostly low adverbs because they appear more consistently in a pre-verbal position.

[13] The analysis of pronominal movement in Ukrainian is a separate topic that will not be discussed in this paper. These examples (as well as the pronominal condition in the experiment) are used as additional evidence of object scrambling, but the nature of pronominal movement is more complex than the movement of DP and needs a more careful investigation.

(28) dat Marieke haar niet gezien heeft.
that Marieke her not seen has
'that Marieke didn't see her'

(29) Marija jiji ne bačyla.
Maria her not seen
'Maria didn't see her.'

Object scrambling in Ukrainian may alter the semantic interpretation of the sentence. In particular, *cja* 'this' and *jakas'* 'some/any' can be used to test the possible changes in the meaning of scrambled sentences. In the basic structure (30), either of these determiners is acceptable and the sentence can have the following readings: (a) there is *a certain book* that will be read by Taras *or* (b) there will be some event of reading *of any book*.

(30) a. Taras bude švydko čytaty [cju] knyžku.
Taras be.FUT quickly read.IN this book
'Taras is going to read the/this book quickly.'
b. Taras bude švydko čytaty [jakus'] knyžku.
Taras be.FUT quickly read.INF any book
'Taras is going to read a book quickly.'

After object scrambling, however, the sentences become unacceptable with *jakas'* 'some/any', as shown in (31a) and (31b). This indicates that only a specific interpretation is possible with the scrambled object.

(31) a. Taras bude [#jakus'] knyžku$_i$ švydko čytaty t_i.
Taras be-FUT any book.ACC quickly read$_{INF}$
'Taras is going to read a book quickly.'
b. Taras [#jakus'] knyžku$_i$ bude švydko čytaty t_i
Taras any book be.FUT quickly read$_{INF}$
'Taras is going to read a book quickly.'

3.2.3 The Syntactic-Semantic Account

With the theoretical background presented above, we now turn to the mechanism of direct object scrambling in Ukrainian. In this chapter, we adopt the *Phase Theory* proposed by Chomsky (2001) to implement scrambling. Specifically, we argue that scrambling is triggered by a probe-goal Search (Chomsky 2001, Ko 2005). The direct object, as a *goal*, is selected by the *probe v*, and the object may undergo overt movement to *v*P-edge position after Agree.

To be more concrete, we argue that the probe and goal has a [SPEC] feature, which marks the specificity value. The goal has an interpretable [SPEC] feature [*i*SPEC], and the head *v* contains an uninterpretable [SPEC] feature [*u*SPEC], which must undergo agreement with [*i*SPEC].[14] When the [SPEC] features of the object and *v* match with each other, they undergo syntactic Agree.

After Agree between *v* and D, the object undergoes movement due to the presence of EPP on *v*. Following Pesetsky and Torrego (2001), we propose that EPP is a sub-feature of [*u*SPEC]. The goal moves to the specifier position of the head *v* when the EPP with [*u*SPEC] on *v* triggers movement. On this view, movement of the object is a consequence of Agree between *v* and D, and optionality of movement comes from optional insertion of EPP with [*u*SPEC].

The tree diagram in (32) illustrates this process: Agree between the probe-goal is established between *v* and D for [SPEC] feature; the association between [*u*SPEC] and EPP triggers movement of the DP *book* to the *v*P edge that is marked by the adverbial *quickly*. Note that this proposal is in harmony with Chomsky's view that movement to edge positions (e.g., *v*P-edges, CP-edges) yields discourse-related effects such as focus and specificity. (In (32), the subject undergoes additional movement from Spec*v*P to SpecTP due to the EPP-requirement of T.)

(32)

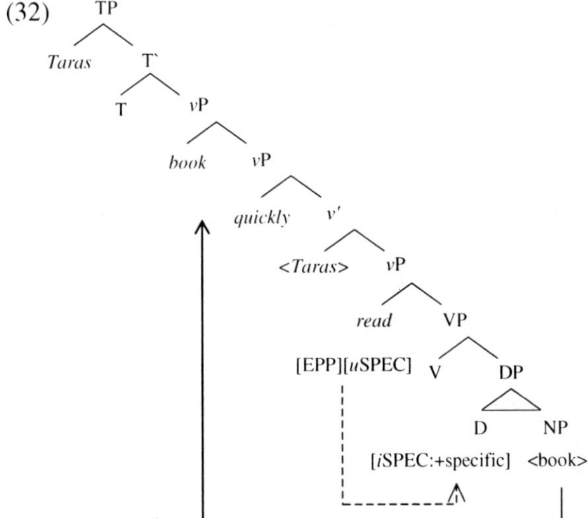

[14] Placement of the specificity feature in *v* is justified by the fact that specificity can be realized by verbal morphology in some languages. For instance, in Swahili, specificity is marked by an object agreement affix (OA) on the verb (Deen 2006):

(i) Juma a- li- **mw-** on-a m- tu.
Juma SA.3sg- past- **OA.3sg-** see-IND I- person
'Juma saw the person/ *a person.'

For completeness of the overall structure, we also note that the direct object marked as [+specific] can undergo further movement to a position higher than the *v*P-edge. As shown in (33), when the *v*P is elided, the scrambled object *journal* remains intact. This indicates that the scrambled object can be situated outside of *v*P.

(33) Taras knyžku$_i$ švydko čytaje t_i, a Ivan žurnal ni.
Taras book.ACC quickly reads but Ivan journal not
'Taras is reading the book quickly, but Ivan is not [reading quickly] the journal.'

In Ukrainian, the auxiliary verb (e.g., *bude* 'will') may occur with a non-finite main verb, as in (34). In such cases, the object may scramble to the left of the low adverb, as in (35), or it may scramble further to the left of the auxiliary and negation, as in (36).[15]

(34) *Basic Structure with auxiliary*
Subject>Negation>Auxiliary>Low Adverb>Main Verb>Direct Object.
(Taras) ne bude švydko čytaty knyžku.
(Taras) not will quickly read book.ACC
'Taras will not read a book quickly.'

(35) Subject>Negation>Auxiliary>Direct Object>Low Adverb>Main Verb
(Taras) ne bude knyžku švydko čytaty.
(Taras) not will book.ACC quickly read
'Taras will not read the book quickly.'

(36) Subject>Direct Object>Negation>Auxiliary>Low Adverb>Main Verb
(Taras) knyžku ne bude švydko čytaty.
(Taras) book.ACC not will quickly read
'Taras will not read the book quickly.'

We close this section with an important premise of our proposal concerning the non-specific object. If the object contains a [−specific] value (e.g., [*i*SPEC: −*specific*]), then the sub-feature EPP cannot be added to the *v* even after Agree between *v* and D.

[15] The auxiliary *bude* is a part of a verbal form which indicates the future tense. At this point, it is not clear to us where exactly the auxiliary is generated. For the current paper, we stipulate that it is base-generated within the *v*P domain, probably where aspect phrases are normally generated. It should also be noted that we do not propose a new theory of the relative ordering between negation and various types of low adverbs on the vP edge. Given that negation can precede or follow the low adverb, we expect that the vP-edge should be an extended domain (just like the IP-domain) that can host a low-adverb, an auxiliary, and negation.

We argue that this is because the [−specific] value is incompatible with the EPP feature. Based on this assumption, we derive the fact that there is no scrambling of non-specific object in Ukrainian.

3.2.4 On the Optionality of Scrambling

We note that our proposal for non-specific objects raises a more fundamental question of why the EPP feature is incompatible with the [−specific] value. This question has been a long standing puzzle in the scrambling literature for other languages as well (e.g., Scandinavian Object Shift and scrambling in German and Dutch). We will briefly sketch the issues that are related to this puzzle.

First, if object scrambling (related to interpretational differences) is optional, it is puzzling what distinguishes languages that allow this operation obligatorily (e.g., Dutch) or optionally (e.g., Ukrainian) from languages that do not allow it at all (e.g., English). As for object movement (i.e., object shift for Scandinavian languages), Chomsky (2001: 35) proposed the following principles:

(37) a. v* is assigned an EPP-feature only if that has an effect on outcome.
b. The EPP position of v* is assigned Int.
c. At the phonological border of v*P, XP is assigned Int'.

Descriptively speaking, we may assume that the association between EPP and specificity is obligatory in languages like Dutch, so that post-verbal objects must be interpreted as non-specific (see also Footnote 8 for Russian). For languages like Ukrainian, we assume that the EPP feature is available, but not obligatorily so that a specific object may undergo movement or stay in-situ. Crucially, however, the object must receive Int (i.e. specific interpretation) at the *v*P edge when it undergoes object scrambling (37b).

According to this view, however, the problem as to why the EPP feature is optional in Ukrainian still remains. This problem has been recognized in a number of studies (see Diesing 1992 and Thrainsson 2001 among others), but there has not been a satisfactory solution offered so far. In this chapter, we claim that optional movement can be best understood by optional insertion of the EPP feature in the Minimalist Program, and that is the view we adapt to Ukrainian optional scrambling (see more on the optionality of the feature in Grewendorf and Sabel 1999 and Ko 2005).

Despite the puzzling nature of scrambling in general, the most important fact for the current research is clear:

(38) Non-specific objects do not undergo scrambling in Ukrainian.

This is also true for other languages exhibiting similar movement (e.g., Scandinavian OS and scrambling in German and Dutch). As Thrainsson

(2001: 193) points out, the generalization seems to be that a weak/existential reading is incompatible with Object Shift (or scrambling), but objects with a strong/quantificational/specific reading do not necessarily have to shift or scramble. The exact nature of this optionality in object movement deserves further research. We leave this important question open.

To sum up, our account of object scrambling links the availability of syntactic movement to the semantic feature of specificity. Adults are able to establish the connection between the EPP-feature and the specific semantic feature, and prefer scrambled structures. In the next section, we turn to the predictions for child scrambling under the current proposal.

4 Predictions for Acquisition of Ukrainian Object Scrambling

Given our proposals of scrambling in adult Ukrainian, several questions arise regarding the status of scrambling in child grammar. First, do children understand the concept of specificity at all? If so, then do they scramble specific objects? Is child grammar constrained by the same rule as adult grammar? In particular, do children know that non-specific objects cannot undergo scrambling?

In this chapter, we address these questions with bilingual children whose primary language is English and secondary language is Ukrainian. We adopt the premise that children acquire language with the aid of Universal Grammar (UG) and that they are able to overcome the *poverty of the stimulus* in the input. We also adopt the claim that bilingual children have full access to principles, parameters, and features available in UG in acquiring both languages (Schwartz 2003).

Since English lacks scrambling, knowledge of specificity effects on object movement cannot be transferred from English to Ukrainian, the specificity effects are not a topic of classroom instruction, and crucially, bilingual children receive a limited input for scrambling in their language environment. Therefore, if English-Ukrainian children demonstrate understanding of scrambling constraints, it cannot be attributed to a high frequency of explicit input either (as would be assumed under Usage-based approaches maintained by Tomasello 2003, Newport and Aslin 2004, Reali and Christiansen 2005 and Matthews et al. 2005 among others). Thus, by choosing bilingual children as our main participants, we can test the effect of specificity in scrambling in child grammar and the role of UG in language acquisition *simultaneously*.

Based on language acquisition theories put forward by Schwartz (2003), White (2003), and others, coupled with our syntactic analysis of Ukrainian scrambling, we hypothesize the following:

(39) a. Scrambling is a consequence of syntax-semantics mapping (i.e., association between EPP on *v* and a [+specific] feature on D).

b. (Bilingual) children have knowledge of specificity from an early stage due to full access to UG, regardless of their L1.

c. Children may have difficulty in understanding the mapping between syntax (the EPP feature) and semantics (specificity).

Our hypotheses (39) make various predictions concerning possible and impossible patterns of word order in bilingual children's grammar. First, if children have knowledge of specificity, they should be able to utter sentences with the scrambled object, in principle. On this view, we crucially diverge from the view that young children may lack knowledge of specificity and consequently would scramble optionally in all contexts (cf. a pragmatic approach of Schaeffer 2000b). Second, if children have difficulty in associating the EPP-feature (a pure syntactic feature) with a [+specific] feature (a semantic feature), we expect that children may apply less scrambling to specific objects than adults. Thirdly, we expect that children will not scramble objects randomly. If children can make a distinction between specific objects and non-specific objects (based on their knowledge of specificity), they would not wrongly scramble non-specific objects, just like specific objects. What we predict is that children may *undergenerate* scrambling with specific objects, but that they would not *overgenerate* scrambling with non-specific objects (cf. Avrutin and Brun 2001). When children utter scrambled sentences, they know that it is due to the presence of [+specific]. Given full access to UG in L2A, our predictions will hold for bilingual English-Ukrainian children despite the lack of scrambling in their primary language, English.[16]

Our predictions are summarized in (40):

(40) a. Children will use scrambling with specific objects.
b. Children may apply less scrambling than adults.
c. Children will not randomly scramble non-specific objects.
d. The predictions concerning scrambling hold for bilingual children despite the lack of scrambling in their L1.

[16] We assume that UG contains all the possible inventory of semantic and syntactic features, and that the task of language learners is to find the correct value and association of the features in the target language. If English learners of Ukrainian can associate the [+specific] feature with scrambling despite the fact that English has no direct evidence for the connection between the two, we take this as evidence for the claim that the learners can access to the feature inventory of UG and use it correctly. As a reviewer notes, however, it may be open whether the UG access is direct or indirect. One may argue that children have direct UG access to specificity, but others may argue that children's knowledge of specificity comes from some indirect evidence instantiated in English – such as referential *this* and partitive expressions such as *one of the*. In this paper, we take the former view which requires no further explanations on how children get to know the notion of specificity, and we leave the latter view as a possibility. We believe that the latter view would require an explicit theory of how children subtract information on specificity from English and connects it to scrambling in Ukrainian.

5 Experimental Study

5.1 Subjects

The experimental study was conducted with 41 bilingual children and a control group of 4 adult Ukrainian speakers. The age range of the children was from 2;10 to 7;11 (mean age 6;2) (6 children from age 2;10 to 3;8 (mean 3;3), 16 children from age 4;6 to 5;11 (mean 5), and 19 children from age 6 to 7;11 (mean 6;7)). The bilingual English-Ukrainian children were selected because their speech is a valuable testing ground for our proposals. Since English does not exhibit scrambling, and all the children live in a predominantly English-speaking environment, they should be able to overcome the poverty-of-the-stimulus in the input in order to acquire scrambling in Ukrainian. The children's proficiency in Ukrainian was first evaluated indirectly through a questionnaire designed for parents and then directly through a conversation session between the child and the investigator. Children younger than 3 years of age had significant difficulties understanding Ukrainian, and were not selected as participants. All the children were recruited and tested in two Ukrainian Saturday schools – in Uniondale, NY and in the city of New York. Most of the children were born in the USA and have parents who are Ukrainian speakers. A few children were born in the Ukraine and arrived in the USA before the age of 2. According to the parents, some of the children can also understand other languages: Polish (4 children), Russian (3 children), Lithuanian (1 child), and German (1 child).[17] There were 14 males and 27 females in the study.

The adult control group consisted of 2 females (18 and 49 years old) and 2 males (40 and 42 years old). They were recruited and tested at Stony Brook University, NY. All of the adult participants are native speakers of Ukrainian, fluent in Russian, and second language learners of English.

5.2 Procedure

The experiments started with a short training session conducted with a group of children to familiarize them with the task, and then each subject was invited to a separate room for an individual experiment. Two scenarios were specifically used as a Ukrainian proficiency test (for the children only). If a child was able to name all the puppets used in the experiment in Ukrainian, and answer questions after having watched two puppet shows, the experimenter proceeded with the main task.[18] The full session took no longer than 15–20 min

[17] The experimental data from these children did not differ from the other subjects' data, and are therefore included in the results (see Section 6.2)

[18] Only listening skills, knowledge of the necessary vocabulary, and the ability to build a full sentence in Ukrainian were taken into account when defining the proficiency level.

and consisted of 10 scenarios: 4 with different adverbs, 4 with negation, and 2 fillers. All 10 tokens were randomized so that each of four lists was presented in different orders. Children were tested at school and were rewarded for the participation with a small gift (a pen or a drawing board). The adult subjects were tested with the same scenarios as the children, but without breaking them into 4 groups. That is, each adult received all 32 test items and 8 fillers presented in a randomized order. Adult subjects were rewarded monetarily for their participation.

5.3 *Method*

The main goal of the experimental study was to determine whether children are aware of the correlation between specificity and scrambling in Ukrainian. The task is a modified version of Schaeffer's (2000b) experiment, which is a combination of a truth value judgment task and an elicited production task.[19] Each subject was presented with a short puppet show with two characters and a number of props (pictures or toys).

First, one puppet (either Winnie the Pooh, Piglet, or Roo) presented his story, and then, another puppet who was described as silly and did not know Ukrainian well (Tigger), either made a comment or asked for clarification. The subject, then, was asked to help by saying whether Tigger's comment was true or false, and if it was false, to correct it. The puppet comments and questions were designed in such a way that in responding to them, children would produce a sentence with a scrambled or non-scrambled word order, and either with an adverb or negation. The choice of word order was dependent on the context.

Four conditions were tested in the experiment: definite specific (as in (41)), indefinite specific (as in (42)), indefinite non-specific (as in (43)) and definite pronominal (as in (44)). The pronominal condition had the same context as the definite specific, but additional questions were included to trigger production of a personal pronoun as the direct object. The stimuli used in the study are exemplified below:

---

[19] High adverbs were not used in the stimuli because they take various positions in Ukrainian and thus do not serve the same role as in Dutch (see Footnote 12). Proper names as direct objects were also excluded from the experiment simply to limit the time to an amount that is appropriate even for the youngest children. The characters were changed to some that Ukrainian children are more familiar with. Indefinite contexts were modified based on Unsworth (2005). It is interesting to note that although Schaeffer and Unsworth define specificity in different terms (referentiality and partitivity, respectively), they both use the same stimuli. This means that they tested partitivity effects instead of specificity 'as speaker intent to refer'.

(41) Definite specific DP with an adverb

Roo: Look, what a nice butterfly. I have a new net, and I am going to catch it QUICKLY.

Tigger: Roo is going to catch the butterfly SLOWLY.

Exp: What is really happening?

Child:

Kenhuru	metelyka	ŠVYDKO	zlovyt'.
Roo	butterfly	quickly	will.catch
Kenhuru	švydko	zlovyt'	metelyka.
Roo	quickly	will.catch	butterfly

'Roo is going to catch the butterfly QUICKLY.'

(42) Indefinite specific DP with an adverb

Piglet: Look, two cats: 1, 2. I am going to draw one of them. And I'm going to do it NICELY!

Tigger: Piglet is going to draw one cat IN AN UGLY WAY!

Exp: What is really happening?

Child:

Porosjatko	odnoho kotyka	HARNO	namaljuje.	
Piglet	one	cat	nicely	will.draw
Porosjatko	harno	namaljuje	odnoho kotyka.	
Piglet	nicely	will.draw	one	cat

'Piglet is going to draw one cat NICELY.'

(43) Indefinite non-specific DP with an adverb

Winnie: I feel like catching something big. What can I catch? I can catch a whale, a shark, or a crocodile. [Child response . . .]. OK! And I am not going to do that CAREFULLY!

Tigger: Oh, I haven't understood it very well. What is Winnie going to do carefully?

Child:

	Winnie	oberežno	bude	lovyty	(akulu).
	Winnie	carefully	will	catch	shark
[#]	Winnie	(akulu)	oberežno	bude	lovyty.
	Winnie	shark	carefully	will	catch

'Winnie will catch a shark carefully.'

(44) Definite pronominal DP with negation

Winnie: Look, a boot is in the pond. I have a good fishing rod, but you cannot catch boots. So, I am not going to catch it.

Tigger: Winnie is going to catch it.

Exp: What is Winnie really going to do with the boot?

Child:

Winnie	joho	NE	BUDE	lovyty.
Winnie	him	not	will	catch

[*] Winnie ne bude lovyty joho.
Winnie not will catch him
'Winnie will not catch it.'

In (41) and (42), scrambled and non-scrambled word orders are both grammatical for adult speakers (although scrambled order is preferred). In (43), however, the use of the scrambled order (i.e., SO (Neg/Adv)V structure) is not acceptable. In (44), a scrambled structure is strongly preferred in adult speech, and all things being equal, it is expected to prevail in child production as well.

In order to ensure the presence of the direct object in child responses, only telic verbs were selected: *zlovyty* 'to catch up', *namaljuvaty* 'to draw', *vyrizaty* 'to cut out', *vykydaty* 'to throw out'.[20] Following Schaeffer (2000b), adverbs or negation were used in order to mark the landing site of a scrambled object and to control for the object being focused by stressing an adverb or negation instead. Focus movement of direct objects could affect object movement. To avoid these complications, we emphasized adverbs and negation when the test structures were produced. In half of the stimuli, negation was contrasted with affirmation. In the other half, antonymous pairs of low adverbs were used: *svydko/povil'no* 'quickly/slowly', *harno/pohano* 'nicely/wrongly', *pravyl'no/ nepravyl'no* 'well/wrongly', *oxajno/neoxajno* 'neatly/messily'. There were 32 tokens altogether, which were interspersed with 8 fillers designed similarly, but always triggering a 'yes' response from a subject. Fillers were necessary to test if the children were paying attention, and to prevent them from forming strategies in answering the questions.

6 Results

6.1 Group Results

The data are analyzed in terms of the percentage rate of scrambling in four tested conditions (number of responses with scrambled objects relative to the total number of tokens per condition). Word orders with pre-adverbial or pre-negation objects, such as S-O-Adv-V and S-O-Neg-V, were considered clear cases of scrambling. There was, however, more variation in scrambling types. We consider all preverbal objects indicated in Table 5 as examples of scrambling.

[20] Since only future events were discussed in the dialogs, subjects could use any of two forms of future tense. For example, for 3sg these forms are: *zlovyt'/bude lovyty* 'will catch'; *namaljuje/ bude maljuvaty* 'will draw', *vyriže/bude vyrizaty* 'will cut out', *vykyne/bude vykydaty* 'will throw out'. Although the distribution of telic verbs can interact with the specificity of the direct object (Slabakova 1999), the current study did not focus on this issue.

Table 5 Types of structures

	Adults	Children
SOAdvV	35.4% (23/65)	40.74% (55/135)
SONegV	**55.4% (36/65)**	**45.19% (61/135)**
SNegAuxOV	6.15% (4/65)	8.9% (12/135)
SAdvOV	3.10% (2/65)	3.7% (5/135)
OSV		1.48% (2/135)

Scrambling over negation (SONegV) was used at the highest rate, especially by adults. However, since all scenarios triggered responses about a future event and future tense can be expressed in Ukrainian either with or without a future auxiliary, subjects could use either of the structures: SNegAuxOV or SONegAuxV. When the auxiliary was used, some subjects preferred 'shorter' scrambling – SNegAuxOV over 'longer' scrambling – SONegAuxV. These responses were still coded as scrambling because they showed object movement to a higher situated pre-verbal position which can be associated with specificity in Ukrainian. Scrambling over adverbs (SOAdvV) was less productive for different reasons. Some subjects (mostly adults) focused on adverbs and changed the word order to emphasize the adverb and not the object, while others (mostly young children) had difficulty using adverbs at all (as was noticed in Schaeffer (2000a), too) and produced them with a delay at the end of the utterance. Thus, the structure SVOAdv was used by adults and children, but was considered as unscrambled.[21]

The overall experimental results for the two groups (child subjects and adult controls) are summarized in Table 6.

Table 6 Group results for scrambling across condition

Group	n	Definite specific	Indefinite specific	Indefinite non-specific	Definite pronominal
Children	41	45% (36/80)	65% (52/80)	**9%** (7/80)	45.45% (40/88)
Adults	4	53% (17/32)	69% (22/32)	**0%** (0/32)	81.25% (26/32)

First, the results show that both adult Ukrainian speakers and bilingual English-Ukrainian children employ object scrambling in three specific contexts, and exhibit knowledge of the correlation between scrambling and semantic interpretation.

Next, overall, the children use scrambling less than adults: 41.16% (135/328) vs. 50.78% (65/128). However, scrambling rates per condition indicate important similarities between child and adult group data, as presented in Fig. 1.

[21] SVOAdv structure could also be analyzed to be derived by vP movement. However, since adverbs in such sentences were always focused, we assume a different, non-scrambling, analysis for these structures.

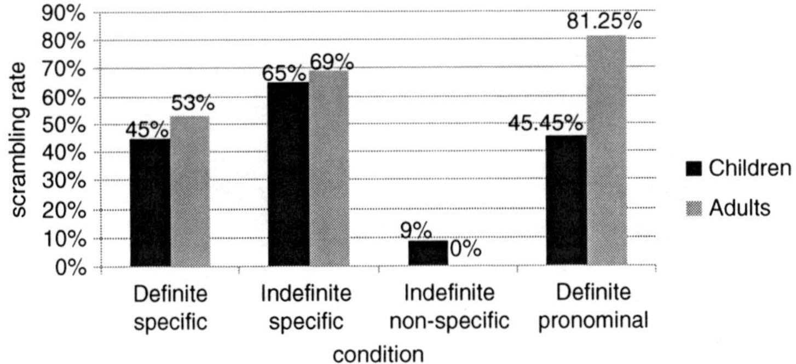

Fig. 1 Scrambling rate: children vs. adults

Adults consistently scramble pronominal direct objects (81.25%), but never scramble in a non-specific indefinite condition. Their group data also show optional scrambling in definite specific (53%) and indefinite specific (69%) conditions. Although the rate is not very high, there is no difference among subjects if the extreme outliers are excluded (this will be discussed in individual results in 6.2). Child data from the same conditions show the same tendency: they scramble 45% in definite specific contexts and 65% in indefinite specific contexts, but they rarely allow object scrambling in non-specific contexts (9%).

As for the pronominal direct object scrambling in the definite pronominal condition, children show less scrambling than the adults: 28.41% of the time (children) vs. 68.75% (adults) (Table 7).

Table 7 Percentage of scrambling in the Definite Pronominal condition

Group	Pronominal scrambling (%)	Total scrambling (%)
Children	28.41	45.45
Adults	68.75	81.25

However, even though the stimuli triggered use of pronouns in this condition, full DPs could also be used. So, if we count scrambling rates including pronouns and DPs that were used for pronouns, the total rate of scrambling of children amounts to 45%, as shown in Table 7. This rate is very similar to the scrambling rate obtained in the definite specific context (45%), which suggests that children follow the same rules in both cases, but might have difficulty with pronominal production.

Finally, a statistical analysis of the child data also supports the prediction about the non-random nature of scrambling in language learners' grammar. The direction of the means (presented in Fig. 2) indicates that the indefinite specific condition and the two definite conditions trigger scrambling much more often than the indefinite non-specific condition out of 8 tokens.

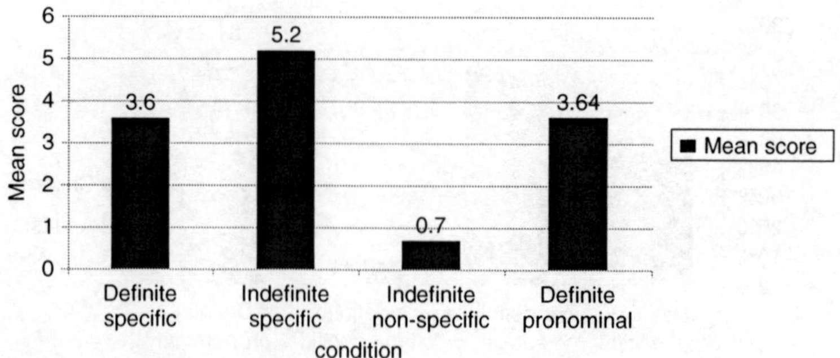

Fig. 2 Mean rate of scrambling: child data

The univariate analyses of variance (ANOVAs) show that there is a significant main effect of specificity on the word order choice in child production [F(3;41) = 9.992, $p < 0.0001$]. Contrast results confirm that the difference between the indefinite specific and the indefinite non-specific condition is highly significant ($p < 0.0001$). The difference between the definite specific and the indefinite non-specific condition is also significant ($p = 0.001$) as well as the difference between the definite pronominal and the indefinite non-specific condition ($p = 0.001$). Furthermore, the results also show that there is no significant difference between the definite specific and the indefinite specific conditions ($p = 0.065$) and the definite specific and the definite pronominal ($p = 0.965$). This suggests that specificity, instead of definiteness, significantly contributes to object scrambling by the learners.

6.2 *Individual Results*

The individual results for the adult controls are summarized below.

As can be seen from Table 8, no adult subjects scrambled in the indefinite non-specific condition. The rate of scrambling for the other conditions varies from 25% in a definite specific context (AS-3) to 100% in an indefinite specific context (AS-2). As expected, all of the subjects scrambled pronominal direct

Table 8 Adults: individual results for scrambling across condition

Subject	Total (%)	Definite specific	Indefinite specific	Indefinite non-specific	Definite pronominal
AS-1 (F)	56.25	62.5% (5/8)	87.5% (7/8)	**0% (0/8)**	75% (6/8)
AS-2 (M)	62.5	75% (6/8)	100% (8/8)	**0% (0/8)**	75% (6/8)
AS-3 (F)	34.38	25% (2/8)	37.5% (3/8)	**0% (0/8)**	75% (6/8)
AS-4 (M)	50	50% (4/8)	50% (4/8)	**0% (0/8)**	100% (8/8)

objects at a very high rate: from 75 to 100%. Overall, as shown in Fig. 4, none of the subjects scrambled obligatorily, which confirms that object scrambling in Ukrainian is optional even in adult grammar. That is, for AS-2 it is a preferred response in specific conditions, while AS-3 produces mostly unscrambled structures in all conditions except for the pronominal condition.

The individual grammar of AS-4 requires special attention. This subject consistently scrambled direct objects over negation, but, in definite specific and indefinite specific contexts that required the use of adverbials, he produced unscrambled structures – SVOAdv (which occurred in AS-3′s data). Although this structure differs from the base structure (SAdvVO), it is not considered an instance of object scrambling, but rather a adverbial focusing. Since other responses given by AS-4 show consistent scrambling, this result could be triggered by other factors to which we return below.

The children's individual responses confirm the group results. None of the subjects scrambled obligatorily in definite specific contexts. Only one subject scrambled 100% in the indefinite specific condition. Crucially, however, none of the child subjects used scrambled order more than twice in the indefinite non-specific condition. This again confirms the sporadic nature of scrambling in non-specific contexts. Moreover, four children never scrambled in non-specific conditions, showing adult-like performance. Most of the children scrambled at a high rate in the indefinite specific condition (i.e., three subjects produced 7 (out of 8) tokens with object scrambling in this context). Children who were claimed by their parents to be trilingual showed similar results, as indicated below (Table 9).

Table 9 Overall scrambling rate: bilingual (English-Ukrainian) vs. trilingual children

Children	Languages	No. of children	Total (%)
Bilingual	English-Ukrainian	32	40.63
Trilingual	+ Russian	3	41.7
	+ Polish	4	46.88
	+ Lithuanian	1	62.5
	+ German	1	12.5

A majority of the subjects were English-Ukrainian bilinguals, but some children grew up in families where other languages were spoken. It seems, though, that the general pattern of scrambling by bilingual and trilingual children does not differ: they scramble at a similar rate in all contexts. It should be noted that the child speaking German showed only 12.5% scrambling because the tokens received from her represented only indefinite/non-specific contexts, and, thus, such a result was expected.

On the other hand, child performance with pronominal direct objects was poorer than expected for all subjects mainly because very few pronominals were used. However, when they were used, they were always placed correctly above the adverb or negation.

Surprisingly, the child's age was not the main factor in pronoun usage: the youngest subject (2;10 year-old) had two responses with a scrambled pronoun, while the oldest child in this group (7;3 years old) had none.[22] Although it was not the goal of this study to establish developmental stages in the acquisition of scrambling, it seems that, in general, there was no strong correlation between the child's age and the ability to scramble in the specific condition.[23]

To summarize, our results demonstrate that the effect of specificity on scrambling established for adult speakers is significant for children as well. Children acquiring Ukrainian do not perform at random and appear to be aware of interpretative constraints on scrambling.

Table 10 Percentage of scrambling in different age groups

Mean age	*n*	Definite specific	Indefinite specific	Indefinite non-specific	Definite pronominal
3;3	6	56% (9/16)	62.5% (10/16)	**12.5% (1/8)**	50% (4/8)
5	16	50% (16/32)	75% (12/16)	**7.5% (3/40)**	42.5% (17/40)
6;7	19	34.4% (11/32)	62.5% (30/48)	**9.4% (3/32)**	47.5% (19/40)

7 Discussion

Our experimental results confirm the predictions presented in (40). First, our data clearly show that specificity interacts with object scrambling in child Ukrainian. Specific objects optionally occurred in a pre-verbal position via scrambling in the children's utterances. Moreover, the children uttered scrambled sentences significantly more often in specific contexts than in non-specific contexts. This result provides further arguments for the view that children do have the knowledge of specificity in their grammar from a very early stage (Avrutin and Brun 2001, Ilić and Deen 2004).

Second, our data demonstrate that children apply less scrambling than adults, as predicted in (40). Adults are able to establish an association between syntactic knowledge (EPP on *v*) and semantic knowledge (SPEC on D) and freely use scrambling in order to convey a specific interpretation of the direct

[22] This subject's performance on the test was rather out of the ordinary. The pronominal condition was the only one in which no scrambled structures were used. However, this child has a high level of proficiency in Ukrainian, and her spontaneous speech contained both pronominals and scrambled direct objects.

[23] Our results in Table 10 indicate that there is no correlation between syntactic development and children's pragmatic maturity. If it were the case, we would expect to see a gradual increase in the scrambling rate from younger to older children, contrary to facts reported in Table 10. As a reviewer notes, however, these results cannot be taken as direct counter-evidence against Schaeffer's claims. Schaeffer's arguments on pragmatic immaturity are based on data from children younger than 3, but our data come mostly from older children. We wish to investigate the scrambling rates of younger children (age below 3) in future research. We thank the reviewer for clarifying this point.

object. Children, on the other hand, may have difficulty correlating the [SPEC] and the EPP features. We suggest that a low rate of scrambling in child Ukrainian can be due to an unstable mapping between syntax and semantics. Our data can be taken as further support for a syntactic-semantic approach to the acquisition of scrambling proposed by Unsworth (2004, 2005). These results might also provide support for the proposals that L2-learners may have problems with mapping issues at the interface (see Prevost and White (2000) for mismapping between syntax and morphology and White (2003: 205) for the lack of mapping from the lexicon to the syntax).

Third, it has been shown that the children scramble optionally, but not randomly. When children scrambled an object, they scrambled the [+specific] object, as predicted in (40). This indicates that children can distinguish between specific and non-specific objects, reflecting their semantic knowledge of specificity. When they scramble direct objects, they know that it applies only to specific objects. There were infrequent instances of scrambling in non-specific contexts, but since the group scrambling rate in non-specific contexts was only 9%, we take those data as performance errors.

These results suggest that a pragmatic approach is unlikely to account for the optionality in scrambling observed in the study. The pragmatic approach to the acquisition of specificity was originally proposed by Maratsos (1976) to explain errors in article usage by children, and later widely adapted to explain errors in scrambling (e.g., Avrutin and Brun 2001, Schaeffer 2000b). Our data, however, suggest that the pragmatic approach to scrambling fails to account for the acquisition of scrambling in Ukrainian. On the pragmatic analyses, children might mark a [−specific] object as specific/definite according to their own beliefs, which in turn would trigger more scrambling of non-specific objects. Under Avrutin and Brun's view, for instance, the egocentricity of children could lead to obligatory scrambling everywhere. For Schaeffer, on the other hand, specificity can be underspecified, so random scrambling is expected across all contexts. The obtained experimental data, however, show that this was not the case: optional scrambling in child Ukrainian did not exhibit a significant overuse of object movement in the non-specific condition at any age group (Table 10), and, thus, the pragmatic approach is not supported by our data. As noted above (Footnote 23), however, further research with younger monolingual children is needed to directly compare our results with previous pragmatic approaches on specificity.

Finally, the Full Access to UG in child L2 hypothesis was confirmed by our results. In particular, our data show that English-Ukrainian bilingual children can understand constraints on scrambling despite the absence of scrambling in their primary language. Child learners of Ukrainian produce scrambled structures in specific contexts although they receive a reduced amount of input for scrambling. This suggests that the frequency in the input plays minimal role at the earlier stages of acquisition (cf. Usage-based approaches) and further supports the premise that child L2 learners have access to the specificity feature in UG.

8 Conclusion

In this chapter, we have seen that specificity effects are obtained in early child grammar. In particular, we have shown that bilingual children acquiring Ukrainian along with English have full access to the specificity feature, and that they apply scrambling to specific objects, but not to non-specific objects. Our study provides some empirical evidence that bilingual children have full access to principles and features in UG. It also supports the view that word order variation in Ukrainian syntax is tied to the semantic notion of specificity both in adult and child grammar.

Acknowledgments We wish to thank John Bailyn, Dan Finer, Richard Larson, Tania Ionin, audiences at GLOW XXX, FASL 16 and Gasla 9, and the reviewers of this volume for helpful comments and questions. This chapter was developed from our short papers that appeared in *FASL 16 proceedings* and *Gasla 9 proceedings*. This research was supported by a FAHSS Individual Grant awarded to Heejeong Ko by Stony Brook University. All errors are ours.

References

Adger, David. 2003. *Core syntax. A minimalist approach*. New York: Oxford University Press.

Avrutin, Sergey, and Dina Brun. 2001. The expression of specificity in a language without determiners: Evidence from child Russian. In *Proceedings of BUCLD 25*, ed. Anna H.-J. Do, Laura Dominguez and Aimee Johansen, 70–81. Somerville: Cascadilla Press.

Brown, Sue. 1999. *The syntax of negation in Russian: A minimalist approach*. Stanford: CSLI Publications.

Brun, Dina. 2005. What children definitely know about definiteness: Evidence from Russian. In *Formal approaches to Slavic Linguistics 13*, ed. Steven Franks, Frank Y. Gladney, and Mila Tasseva-Kurktchieva, 68–79. Ann Arbor: Michigan Slavic Publications.

Chomsky, Noam. 2001. Derivation by phase. In *Ken Hale: A life in language*, ed. Michael Kenstowicz. Cambridge: MIT Press.

Cinque, Guglielmo. 1999. *Adverbs and functional heads*. Oxford: Oxford University Press.

Clahsen, Harald, and Pieter Muysken. 1986. The availability of Universal Grammar to adult and child learners – a study of the acquisition of German word order. *Second Language Research* 2: 93–119.

Cummins, George. 1998. Indefiniteness in Czech. *Journal of Slavic Linguistics* 6(2): 171–203.

Deen, Kamil Ud. 2006. Object agreement and specificity in early Swahili. *Journal of Child Language* 33: 223–246.

Diesing, Molly. 1992. *Indefinites*. Cambridge: MIT Press.

Dyakonova, Marina. 2004. Information structure development: Evidence from acquisition of word order in Russian and English. In *Nordlyd: Tromso Working Papers on Language and Linguistics* 32: 1.

Enç, Murvet. 1991. The semantics of specificity. *Linguistic Inquiry* 22: 1–25.

Fodor, Janet, and Ivan Sag. 1982. Referential and quantificational indefinites. *Linguistics and Philosophy* 5: 355–398.

Grewendorf, Gunther, and Joachim Sabel. 1999. Scrambling in German and Japanese: Adjunction versus multiple specifiers. *Natural language and Linguistic Theory* 17: 1–65.

Heim, Irene. 1991. On the projection problem for presuppositions. In *Pragmatics*, ed. Steven Davis, 397–405. Oxford: Oxford University Press.

Holmberg, Anders. 1999. Remarks on Holmberg's generalization. *Studia Linguistica* 53(1): 1–39.

Hoop De, Helen. 1992. *Case configuration and noun phrase interpretation*. Doctoral dissertation, University of Groeningen.

Hopp, Holger. 2005. Constraining second language word order optionality: Scrambling in advanced English-German and Japanese-German interlanguage. *Second Language Research* 21: 34–71.

Ilić, Tatjana, and Kamil Ud Deen. 2004. Object raising and cliticization in Serbo-Croatian child language. In *Proceedings to the 2003 GALA conference*, eds. Jacqueline van Kampen and Sergio Baauw. Utrecht, Netherlands: LOT.

Ionin, Tania. 2003. *Article semantics in second language acquisition*. Doctoral dissertation, IT, Distributed by MITWPL.

Ionin, Tania, Heejeong Ko, and Ken Wexler. 2004. Article semantics in L2 acquisition: The role of specificity. *Language Acquisition* 12(1): 3–69.

Josefsson, Gunlög. 1996. The acquisition of object shift in Swedish child language. In *Children's Language* 9, eds. Carolyn E. Johnson and John H.V. Gilbert, 153–165. Mahwah: Lawrence Erlbaum.

Ko, Heejeong. 2005. *Syntactic edges and linearization*. Doctoral dissertation, MIT.

Ko, Heejeong, Tania Ionin, and Ken Wexler. 2007. Adult L2-learners lack *the* maximality presupposition, too. In *The Proceedings of the Inaugural Conference on GALANA*, University of Connecticut Occasional Papers in Linguistics 4: 171–182.

Koopman, Hilda. 1998. The internal and external distribution of pronominal DPs. In *Papers in Memory of Osvaldo Jaeggli*, eds. Kyle Johnson and Ian Roberts. Dordrecht: Reidel.

Krämer, Irene. 2000. *Interpreting indefinites. An experimental study of children's language comprehension*, Doctoral dissertation, Utrecht University.

Maratsos, Michael M. 1976. *The use of definite and indefinite reference in young children*. Cambridge: Cambridge University Press.

Matthews, Danielle, Elena Lieven, Anna Theakston, and Michael Tomasello. 2005. The role of frequency in the acquisition of English word order. *Cognitive Development* 20: 121–136.

Newport, Elissa L., and Richard N. Aslin. (2004). Learning at a distance: I. Statistical learning of non-adjacent dependencies. *Cognitive Psychology, 48*, 127–162.

Otsu, Yukio. 1994. Early acquisition of scrambling in Japanese. In *Language acquisition studies in generative grammar*, eds. Teun Hoekstra and Bonnie D. Schwartz. Amsterdam: John Benjamins.

Penner, Zvi, Rosemarie Tracy, and Jurgen Weissenborn. 2000. Where scrambling begins: Triggering object scrambling at the early stage in German and Bernese Swiss German. In *The acquisition of scrambling and cliticization*, eds. Susan M. Powers and Cornelia Hamann, 127–165. Dordrecht/Boston/London: Kluwer.

Pesetsky, David, and Esther Torrego. 2001. T-to-C: Causes and consequences. In *Ken Hale: A life in language*, ed. Michael Kenstowicz. Cambridge: MIT Press.

Pollock, Jean-Yves. 1989. Verb movement, UG and the structure of IP. *Linguistic Inquiry* 20: 365–424.

Powers, Susan M. 2000. Scrambling in the acquisition of English? In *The acquisition of scrambling and cliticization*, eds. Susan M. Powers and Cornelia Hamann, 95–127. Dordrecht/Boston/London: Kluwer.

Prevost, Philippe, and Lydia White. 2000. Missing surface inflection or impairment in second language acquisition? Evidence from tense and agreement. *Second Language Research* 16 (2): 103–133.

Reali, Florencia, and Morten H. Christiansen. 2005. Uncovering the richness of the stimulus: Structure dependence and indirect statistical evidence. *Cognitive Science: A Multidisciplinary Journal*, 29(6): 1007–1028

Schaeffer, Jeannette. 2000a. Object scrambling and specificity in Dutch child language. In *The acquisition of scrambling and cliticization*, eds. Susan M. Powers and Cornelia Hamann, 71–95. Dordrecht/Boston/London: Kluwer.

Schaeffer, Jeannette. 2000b. *The acquisition of direct object scrambling and clitic placement.* Amsterdam/Philadelphia: John Benjamins.

Schwartz, Bonnie D. 2003. Child L2 acquisition: Paving the way. In *Proceedings of BUCLD 27*, B. Beachley, eds. Amanda Brown and Frances Conlin, 26–50. Somerville: Cascadilla Press, Somerville.

Shevelov, George. 1993. The Ukrainian language. In *The Slavonic languages*, eds. Bernard Comrie and Greville G. Corbett. London/New York: Routledge.

Slabakova, Roumyana. 1999. The parameter of aspect in second language acquisition. *Second Language Research* 15(3): 283–317.

Thrainsson, Höskuldur 2001. Object shift and scrambling. In *The handbook of contemporary syntactic theory*, eds. M. Baltin and C. Collins. Oxford: Blackwell Publishing.

Tomasello, Michael. 2003. *Constructing a language: A usage-based theory of language acquisition.* Cambridge: Harvard University Press.

Unsworth, Sharon. 2004. On the syntax-semantics interface in Dutch: Adult and child L2 acquisition compared. *IRAL* 42: 173–187.

Unsworth, Sharon. 2005. *Child L1, child L2 and adult L2 acquisition: Differences and similarities. A study on the acquisition of direct object scrambling in Dutch.* Doctoral dissertation, Utrecht University.

Westergaard, Marit R. 2008. Verb movement and subject placement in the acquisition of word order: Pragmatics or structural economy? In *First language acquisition of morphology and syntax: Perspectives across languages and learners*, eds. Pedro Guijarro-Fuentes, Maria Pilar Larranaga and John Clibbens. Amsterdam: John Benjamins.

White, Lydia. 2003. *Second language acquisition and Universal grammar*. Cambridge: Cambridge University Press.

Yokoyama, Olga. 1986. *Discourse and word order*. Amsterdam: John Benjamins.

Zeijlstra, Hedde. 2004. Sentential negation and negative concord. Utrecht: LOT.

The Acquisition of Apparent Optionality: Word Order in Subject and Object Shift Constructions in Norwegian

Merete Anderssen, Kristine Bentzen, Yulia Rodina, and Marit Westergaard

Abstract This chapter discusses the word order of object shift and so-called subject shift constructions in Norwegian child language. Corpus data from young children (up to the age of approximately 3) show that they produce non-target-consistent word order in these contexts, failing to move pronominal subjects and objects across negation or sentence adverbs. Furthermore, the findings show that target-like word order in subject shift constructions falls into place relatively early (around age 2;6–3;0), while the delay is more persistent in object shift constructions. The paper also provides results of experimental data from somewhat older children which confirm these findings. In order to explain these child data, various factors are considered, e.g. pragmatic principles, prosody, syntactic economy and effects of frequency in the input. The paper concludes that the delay in movement can best be explained by a principle of economy, while the difference between the two constructions is accounted for by reference to input frequency.

Keywords Optionality · Input · Object shift · Subject placement · Acquisition

1 Introduction

Language-internal optionality has recently become a topic of great interest for language acquisition research. Word order variation is a highly relevant area, as natural languages exhibit numerous examples of this phenomenon. In this chapter we address this topic by focussing on the acquisition of the position of subjects and objects in clauses with negation by Norwegian-speaking children. These are so-called subject and object shift constructions, in which the position of subjects and objects may vary depending on whether they are pronouns or full DPs. Weak pronominal subjects and objects are obligatorily shifted to a position preceding negation in both constructions, as shown in (1a)

M. Anderssen (✉)
University of Tromsø, Tromsø, Norway
e-mail: merete.anderssen@uit.no

M. Anderssen et al. (eds.), *Variation in the Input*, Studies in Theoretical Psycholinguistics 39, DOI 10.1007/978-90-481-9207-6_10,

and (2a) respectively. Full DPs, on the other hand, occur in the position following negation. This word order is optional for the subject shift construction and obligatory for object shift, as shown in (1b-c) and (2b) respectively.

(1) a. Igår leste **han** ikke boka. **SS**
yesterday read.PAST he not book.DEF
'Yesterday he didn't read the book.'
b. Igår leste ikke **Jon** boka.
yesterday read.PAST not Jon book.DEF
c. Igår leste **Jon** ikke boka.
yesterday read.PAST Jon not book.DEF
'Yesterday Jon didn't read the book.'

(2) a. Jon leste **den** ikke. **OS**
Jon read.PAST it not
'Jon didn't read it.'
b. Jon leste ikke **boka**.
Jon read.PAST not book.DEF
'Jon didn't read the book.'

In this chapter we explore how children deal with such word order variation in the input and consider which factors influence the acquisition process. Our study aims to answer the following questions: (1) Is the distribution of variable word order an unproblematic aspect in language acquisition or do children experience problems acquiring the various word order options? (2) Are there developmental delays in the form of non-target-like subject or object placement? And (3), are both constructions acquired more or less at the same time or is there a discrepancy between the two?

In order to answer these questions we have investigated spontaneous child language in a corpus of three children from the age of 1;9 to 3;3. In addition we have performed a pilot elicitation experiment with four children in the age group 3;8–5;8. Both types of data reveal a certain delay in the acquisition of both subject and object shift, as both pronominal and full DP elements tend to occur in the non-shifted position at an early stage. More importantly, both types of data converge in showing that the object shift construction is acquired later than the subject shift construction. Several factors are considered in order to account for the children's non-target-consistent placement of pronominal subjects and objects as well as for the delay in the acquisition of object shift as compared to subject shift. With regard to the former, a pragmatic account is rejected in favor of an explanation in terms of structural economy. Input frequency is also argued to play a role for the extended delay in object shift constructions.

The chapter is organized as follows. Section 2 describes the positions of subjects and objects in Norwegian in more detail. In Section 3 some previous research on the acquisition of similar constructions in other languages is considered. Section 4 presents the analysis of the corpus data. Section 5 considers certain methodological issues and presents the results of the experimentation. In Section 6 the results are discussed in the context of prosody, pragmatics, clitic movement, syntactic economy, and frequency effects in the input. Finally section 7 provides a summary and conclusion.

2 The Positions of Subjects and Objects in the Target Language

As illustrated in examples (1) and (2) above, subjects and objects may either precede or follow negation in Norwegian. Object shift is well-known in the literature as an operation that moves a pronominal object across an adverb or negation in certain contexts (Holmberg 1986). Pronominal subjects also typically precede an adverb or negation, and this phenomenon has been referred to as subject shift (Westergaard 2008). However, there are certain differences between these two phenomena. In this section we briefly outline the target patterns of subject and object shift in Norwegian.

Although the term subject shift is not well established, the existence of multiple subject positions in Scandinavian has been extensively discussed in the literature (Holmberg 1993, Bobaljik and Jonas 1996, Bobaljik and Thráinsson 1998). Norwegian is an SVO language that displays verb second (V2) word order in finite main clauses. Subject shift is observed in non-subject-initial main clauses, as we saw in (1) above. Full DP subjects may either precede or follow negation, (1b–c), whereas unstressed pronominal subjects obligatorily precede negation, (1a).

The various subject positions have often been linked to interpretation. In Nilsen (1997), Svenonius (2002), and Bentzen (2009), it is observed that subjects with a strong, specific reading tend to precede negation and adverbs, whereas subjects with a weak, non-specific reading tend to follow these elements. In a similar vein, Westergaard and Vangsnes (2005) have linked the position of subjects to information structure. According to them, informationally given subjects (typically pronouns) precede negation and adverbs, whereas informationally new or focussed subjects tend to follow these elements. This is supported by the observation that, unlike unstressed pronominal subjects, pronominal subjects with contrastive focus follow negation, as shown in (3).

(3) Igår leste ikke **HAN** boka.
yesterday read.PAST not he book.DEF
'Yesterday *he* didn't read the book.'

Assuming that adverbs and negation occur in relatively fixed positions (e.g. along the lines of the hierarchy in Cinque 1999), one may refer to the observed subject positions as high(er) and low(er). From a theoretical perspective the exact location of these positions is an important issue. A central question concerns whether the high and low positions are in the same domain or not. One view maintains that both high and low subjects occur in the IP domain (cf. Cardinaletti 2004, Westergaard and Vangsnes 2005), while another argues that the higher position is either between the IP and the CP domain (Kiss 1996, Mohr 2005) or in the CP domain of the clause (Wiklund et al. 2007, Bentzen 2009). For the current study, the precise location of the various subjects is not crucial, and the two positions will simply be referred to as high and low.

Now let us turn to object shift. Whereas full DP objects obligatorily follow negation and adverbs (2b), unstressed pronominal objects have to precede these elements (2a). However, the shifting of objects across negation and adverbs can only occur in conjunction with verb movement of the lexical verb. This is known as *Holmberg's Generalization* (Holmberg 1986). As a consequence, object shift is not permitted in embedded clauses (which lack verb movement) or in main clauses where the moved verb is an auxiliary, as illustrated in (4a) and (4b), respectively.[1]

(4) a. De spurte om Jon {***den**} ikke likte {**den**}. (Norw.)
they ask.PAST whether Jon it not liked it
'They asked whether Jon didn't like it.'

b. Jon har {***den**} ikke lest {**den**}.
Jon have.PRES it not read it
'Jon hasn't read it.'

Various proposals have been made to account for what triggers object shift. One view argues that it is related to case assignment. According to this view, only elements that have been morphologically marked for case may undergo object shift (cf. Holmberg 1986, Vikner 1994, Holmberg and Platzack 1995). Alternatively, object shift may be associated with interpretation. Recall that subject shift appears to be closely related to information structure. In a similar way, informationally given objects precede negation and adverbs, while informationally new objects follow these elements. A further indication that objects, like subjects, are sensitive to information structure is illustrated by the fact that contrastively focussed object pronouns follow negation, as in (5a), which is parallel to (3) above. This can also be seen in the behaviour of non-specific

[1] Subject shift, in contrast, is not dependent on movement of the lexical verb. Subject shift across negation and adverbs occurs in non-subject-initial main clauses. Recall that Norwegian obligatorily displays V2 in main clauses, independently of whether this is ensured by an auxiliary or a lexical verb. Furthermore, subject shift across negation and adverbs is also found in embedded clauses, which generally lack verb movement in Norwegian. As we will not discuss embedded clauses in the current paper, we will not go further into this here.

indefinite object pronouns, which, unlike other non-focussed pronouns, cannot undergo object shift, as in (5b) (cf. Diesing 1996: 76, Vikner 1997: 11–12, 2006: 424).

(5) a. Jon leste ikke **DEN**.
Jon read.PAST not it
'Jon didn't read it.'
b. Jeg skulle gjerne ha gitt deg en sjokolade,
I should gladly have given you a chocolate
men jeg har {***en**} ikke {**en**}.
but I have.PRES one not one
'I would gladly give you a bar of chocolate, but I haven't got one.'

With respect to the landing site of the object in object shift constructions, several analyses have been proposed. In some of the earlier accounts, shifted objects are taken to appear in an adjoined position, for example adjoined to (the highest) VP (Holmberg and Platzack 1988, Vikner 1989, 1994). More recent approaches, on the other hand, assume that the object shifts into the specifier of some higher functional projection above VP/vP. This landing site has been associated with various projections: AgrOP (Déprez 1989, Chomsky 1993, Bobaljik 1995), TP (Bobaljik and Jonas 1996, Bošković 2004), or some IP-internal TopicP (Jayaseelan 2001, Josefsson 2001). As with the question of the position of shifted subjects, the exact landing site of pronominal objects is not crucial for the current study, and we will again simply refer to the two positions as high and low.

The leftward movement of objects is fairly common cross-linguistically. West Germanic languages such as Dutch and German exhibit leftward movement of various types of elements, including objects, as illustrated in (6) ((6a) is from Schaeffer 2000: 3; (6b) is from Vikner 2006: 403, our emphasis).

(6) a. Jan heeft **het boek**$_i$ niet t$_i$ gelezen. (Dutch)
Jan has the book not book read
'John didn't read the book.'
b. Ich habe **für das Buch**$_i$ nicht t$_i$ bezahlt. (German)
I have for the book not paid

This phenomenon is referred to as scrambling and is often compared to object shift. The two phenomena share the characteristic that they involve leftward movement of objects, and in both cases, the choice of position seems to be governed by properties of the object DP. However, there are also differences between the two phenomena, as object shift is a more restricted operation than scrambling. First, unlike object shift, scrambling is not limited to objects, as seen in (6b). Second, scrambling has several possible landing sites, whereas object shift is argued to have a fixed landing site (cf. e.g. Haider 2000, Vikner 2006).[2] Furthermore, as discussed above, object shift is dependent on movement of the finite main verb, and as illustrated in (6a–b); this is not the case for scrambling.

In the next section, we briefly outline some previous research on the acquisition of SS and OS-like phenomena, before we turn to our own investigations.

3 Some Previous Acquisition Research

From an acquisition perspective, the questions that need to be considered with respect to phenomena such as subject and object shift and scrambling are to what extent children exhibit target-like placement of the pronominal elements, and if not, how this can be accounted for. In this section, we review some studies that have addressed these issues. As the acquisition of scrambling in German and Dutch has been investigated much more extensively than the acquisition of subject and object shift, we start by considering some of these studies.

In a study of child Dutch, Barbier (2000) discusses object shift and scrambling as separate phenomena in the target language. The former involves negation, and shifting of the object is obligatory to ensure a wide scope interpretation of the negation as sentential rather than constituent negation. The latter involves leftward movement past an adverb. Barbier (2000) argues that object shift, which is claimed to be triggered by the need to check a Case feature, is in place at a very early stage, while scrambling, which is motivated by the presence of a [+focus] feature, lags behind. As the example in (7) illustrates, the constructions that Barbier refers to as object shift are not equivalent to object shift in the Scandinavian languages, because these constructions occur independently of the movement of the lexical verb (Barbier 2000: 41).

(7) ik wil **dat boek** niet lezen. (Dutch)
I will that book not read
'I do not want to read that book.'

In another study on the acquisition of scrambling, Schaeffer (2000) claims that in Dutch, referential DPs obligatorily have to move past negation, while

[2] One exception is the adverb *der* (there), which may undergo object shift in Icelandic and must do so in Danish when it is unstressed and defocussed (cf. Vikner 2006: 422). In Norwegian, however, this is not the case.

non-referential noun phrases have to stay low. Schaeffer (2000) carries out an experimental study of direct object scrambling, showing that before the age of three, Dutch children prefer to have negation preceding definite direct objects (names and common nouns). A relevant example is given in (8).

(8) Ernie gaat niet **die banaan** opeten. (M 2;4) (Dutch)
Ernie goes not the banana up-eat
'Ernie is not going to eat the banana.'
Target form: Ernie gaat **die banaan** niet opeten.

Similar results are obtained for indefinite DPs: children younger than three move indefinites past negation 33% less than the adult controls.[3] Thus, Schaeffer argues that Dutch children below the age of three optionally scramble direct objects in contexts where scrambling is obligatory in the target language. The reason for this optionality in child language is that referentiality, which Schaeffer claims drives object scrambling, is optionally marked in child language.[4] This is a reflection of an inability to consistently distinguish the knowledge of the interlocutor from that of the child. Schaeffer argues for the existence of a pragmatic principle referred to as the Concept of Non-Shared Knowledge, which states that speaker and hearer knowledge are independent of each other. The observed failure in young children to scramble indefinites is argued to be a reflection of this concept not being part of their grammars. In a more recent study of object scrambling, Mykhaylyk and Ko ('Optional Scrambling is not Random: Evidence from Ukrainian Acquisition', this volume) consider this phenomenon with regard to English-Ukrainian bilingual children. They argue that object scrambling in adult Ukrainian is optional with specific objects, but not acceptable with non-specific objects. Consequently, specific objects may or may not scramble, while non-specific objects must remain in situ. The child language study reveals that English-Ukrainian bilingual children, like their Dutch peers, scramble objects less frequently than adult speakers. However, Mykhaylyk and Ko argue against a pragmatic account of the lower rate of scrambling in child language. This is based on the observation that, while the children do not scramble specific objects as often as adult speakers, they never illegitimately scramble non-specific objects, which would be expected if the underlying problem were pragmatic in nature. Instead, Mykhaylyk and Ko

---

[3] In fact, Schaeffer tries to provide both referential and non-referential contexts for indefinites in her experiments to test whether the children are sensitive to this distinction. However, it turns out that even the adults struggle to determine whether indefinites are referential or not, so in the end, referential and non-referential indefinites are collapsed into one category for both children and adults. Nevertheless, the results clearly reveal that adults scramble more than children.

[4] However, this conclusion seems to be problematic given that Schaeffer actually collapses referential and non-referential indefinites.

suggest that the under-application of scrambling is the expression of a failure to consistently associate a syntactic EPP feature with the semantic notion of specificity.

As far as we know, there is only one study of the acquisition of object shift proper in Scandinavian languages, Josefsson (1996). According to Josefsson, only sporadic examples of object shift are found in corpora of Swedish child language. This made her question whether the lack of these structures in child corpora could be the result of an avoidance strategy. In order to test this, Josefsson (1996) carried out an elicited imitation experiment, in which children were supposed to repeat eight examples of object shift. In the study, which involved 15 children between the ages of 2;5 and 7;4, only two of the participants were able to correctly imitate all eight examples. Six of the children produced between four and seven target-like structures, while the remaining seven managed to successfully repeat between zero and three instances of object shift. The non-target structures were of several different kinds, including unshifted pronouns (9a), doubling of negation (9b), and deletion of the pronoun or the negation (9c, d) (Josefsson 1996: 159–160).

(9) a. Adult: Ser du **mej inte**? (Swedish)
see you me not
'Can you not see me?'
Child: Ser du **inte mej**? (Pia, 2;5)
see you not me

b. Adult: Hör du **mej inte**?
hear you me not
'Can you not hear me?'
Child: Hör du **inte mei in .... te**? (Fanny, 3;3)
hear you not me not

c. Adult: Jag vågar **det inte**.
I dare it not
'I don't dare.'
Child: Jag vågar **inte.** (Anna, 5;2)
I dare no

d. Adult: Jag ser **dej inte**.
I see you not
'I can't see you.'
Child: Jag ser **dej.** (Josef, 4;3)
I see you

Hamann and Belletti (2006) have discussed a similar kind of avoidance of object clitic constructions in French child language, observing that clitic objects are partly replaced by lexical objects. Similarly, it has been found that children acquiring Italian frequently omit and hence use a low proportion of object clitics (see e.g. Guasti 1994, Schaeffer 2000).

To our knowledge, there are no previous studies of the acquisition of subject shift. Josefsson (1996) very briefly comments on the acquisition of subject positions by stating that all the Swedish children except one in Söderbergh's naturalistic corpus (Söderbergh 1973) seem to display the adult pattern at once. However, the use of low as opposed to high subjects in German child language has been used as evidence for both the weak continuity/structure building approach (Clahsen et al. 1993/1994) and the strong continuity/full clause hypothesis (Poeppel and Wexler 1993), as illustrated in (10a) and (10b) respectively:

(10) a. darf **nich Julia** haben. (Mathias, stage II) (German)
may not Julia have
'Julia may not have that.'
Target form: Das darf Julia nicht haben.

b. den tiegt **a nich** wieda. (Andreas, age 2;1)
that.ACC gets he not again
'He won't get that back.'
Target form: Den kriegt er nicht wieder.

In (10a), the subject DP follows negation in the topicalized structure. Clahsen et al. (1993/1994) argue that this is a consequence of the clause structure in child language being smaller than in adult language at this stage, i.e. it contains IP but not CP. Thus, the presence of a topic makes it impossible for the subject to precede negation, as there is no landing site available. Poeppel and Wexler (1993), on the other hand, claim that the target-like topicalized structure in (10b) provides evidence that the full clause structure is available to children at an early stage, as the example has both a topic and a subject preceding negation, indicating that there are two specifier positions above the VP (i.e. both IP and CP are present).

As we have seen in this section, there is very little research into the acquisition of subject and object shift. The results of the one study of object shift suggest that this is a very problematic area in acquisition, and it was proposed that the construction is produced in a non-target-like manner for a prolonged period (Josefsson 1996). In Italian, children also omit or avoid object clitics, which, like pronominal objects in the Scandinavian languages, are found in a higher position in the clause. In Dutch, children younger than the age of three tend not to scramble direct objects in contexts where this is obligatory in the adult language, and it has been suggested that this is because they lack a pragmatic principle which enables them to distinguish speaker and hearer knowledge.

Thus, at the outset of the current study, there are several open questions with respect to the acquisition of object and subject shift. For example, will a study of Norwegian reveal the same as the Swedish study in the sense that object shift is a problematic area in acquisition? If so, what kinds of non-target-like patterns can be observed and when do target-like patterns emerge? Does the acquisition of object and subject shift develop at the same rate or is subject shift acquired earlier, as indicated in Josefsson (1996)? To address these questions, the next two sections present the results from a study of the acquisition of subject and object shift by Norwegian-speaking children.

4 The Norwegian Corpus Data

The corpus that has been used to investigate Norwegian children's early acquisition of subject and object shift consists of 70 files of three normally developing monolingual children, two girls and one boy, in spontaneous conversation with an investigator and to some extent also their parents.[5] The children are acquiring the Tromsø dialect of Norwegian. Recordings started around the age of 1;9, when the children were just beginning to produce multi-word utterances, and were carried out approximately every 2 weeks until the children were around 3 years of age (slightly longer for one of the children). Table 1 gives an overview of the corpus, providing information about the age span for each child, the number of recordings and the total number of child utterances.

Table 1 Overview of the Norwegian corpus of child language, Tromsø dialect (Anderssen 2006)

Name of child	Age	Files	Child Utterances
Ina	1;8.20–3;3.18	Ina.01-27	20,071
Ann	1;8.20–3;0.1	Ann.01-21	13,129
Ole	1;9.10–2;11.23	Ole.01-22	13,485
Total			46,685

The next two subsections investigate the three children's spontaneous production of the subject and object shift constructions found in the corpus. The data on subject shift have also been published in Westergaard (2008).

4.1 Subject Shift

As mentioned above, the context for subject shift is found in all non-subject-initial declaratives, all *yes/no*-questions as well as those *wh*-questions that appear with V2 word order.[6] The sentence must also contain negation or an adverb, so that the relevant structures are the following:

[5] Each file corresponds to approximately 1 h of recording.

[6] The children are growing up in Tromsø and are acquiring the local dialect. This variety of Norwegian shares with many other dialects the feature that certain *wh*-questions also allow non-V2 word order, see e.g. Vangsnes (2005) and Westergaard (2003, 2009a).

(11) (XP/*wh*) V_{fin} SUBJECT Neg/Adv
(XP/*wh*) V_{fin} Neg/Adv SUBJECT

There are altogether 213 such contexts found in the corpus, 43 produced by the child Ann, 69 produced by Ole, and as many as 101 produced by Ina. Table 2 gives an overview of the children's production of these clauses, with a specification of type of subject (pronoun or full DP) appearing with the two word orders, Neg-S for unshifted subjects, S-Neg for subjects that have been shifted to the higher position.

Table 2 Overview of the number of full DP and pronominal subjects in questions/non-subject-initial declaratives with negation, with Neg-S and S-Neg word order

	Neg-S		S-Neg		
Child/Word order:	DPs	Pronouns	DPs	Pronouns	Total
Ina.01-27	7	29	0	65	101
Ann.01-21	9	10	0	24	43
Ole.01-22	6	28	0	35	69
Total	22	67	0	124	213

The first striking observation that can be made about the data in Table 2 is the uneven proportion of pronouns vs. full DP subjects. There are 22 full DPs, making up only 10.3% of the total number of subjects involved in this construction (22/213). Furthermore, none of these DPs appear in the high subject position, but always follow negation in a target-consistent way. This is illustrated in examples (12) and (13), one from a relatively early file, the other from a relatively late file.

(12) der snakke **ikkje mannen.**[7] (Ina.09, age 2;2.12) **Neg-S**
*there speak.*PRES *not man.*DEF
'There the man doesn't speak.'

(13) komte **ikke reven** med mæ # i senga mi? (Ina.18, age 2;8.12)
*come.*PAST *not fox.*DEF *with me in bed.*DEF *mine*
'Didn't the fox come with me in my bed?'

[7] The children in the corpus use two different forms of the negation, *ikke* and *ikkje*. The latter is the original regional form, while the former represents the standard form, which is increasingly taking over for the regional form in the dialect. The children in the corpus are relatively young and probably influenced by the parents' language. In addition, the recordings for the Tromsø corpus were made between March 1997 and November 1998, and as such represents the Tromsø dialect from that time. This is relevant here because, as we will see in the experimental study carried out at the end of 2007, the (slightly older) children in this study consistently use the standard form, *ikke*.

Of the 191 pronominal subjects, 67 follow negation, while 124 have been shifted to the higher position. Examples of both word orders produced by all three children are provided in (14)–(19).

(14) har **ikkje han** fota her? (Ina.13, age 2;5.25) **Neg-S_{PRO}**
have.PRES not he feet here
'Doesn't he have feet here?'

(15) no kan **ikke han** sove mer. (Ann.10, age 2;3.9)
now can not he sleep more
'Now he can't sleep any more.'

(16) det får **ikke æ** lov til. (Ole.12, 2;5.18)
that get.PRES not I allowance to
'That I am not allowed to do.'

(17) nei, nå må **han ikke** røre. (Ina.21, age 2;9.18) **S_{PRO}-Neg**
no now must he not touch
'No, now he mustn't touch (it).'

(18) nei det kan **dem ikke**. (Ann.17, age 2;8.4)
no that can they not
'No, that they can't do.'

(19) korfor ser **æ ikke** skoan? (Ole.17, 2;8.24)
why see.PRES I not shoe.DEF/PL
'Why don't I see the shoes?'

A closer investigation of these 191 examples shows that both word orders are available from early on. Furthermore, the ones with unshifted word order generally appear in early files, while the examples with shifted subjects become more frequent at a later stage. Thus, there seems to be a clear development from non-target-consistent to target-consistent word order during the time of data collection. In Table 3, the child data have been divided into five periods based on the age of the three children. In Period 1, up to the age of 2;3, there are very few relevant examples in the data. In Period 2, all three children produce more of the non-target-consistent word order than the target-like shifted one. This changes for two of the children in Period 3 (Ann and Ole), and for the third child

Table 3 Overview of Neg-S_{PRO}/S_{PRO}-Neg word order in non-subject-initial declaratives and questions with negation/adverbs in the Norwegian child language corpus

Child	Period 1 (age 1;9–2;3)	Period 2 (age 2,3–2;6)	Period 3 (age 2;6–2;8)	Period 4 (age 2;8–3;0)	Period 5 (age 3;0–3;3)
Ina	0/0	7/4	7/4	10/**36**	5/**21**
Ann	0/2	9/7	1/**3**	0/**12**	
Ole	1/1	21/3	0/**13**	6/**18**	

in Period 4 (Ina), when the shifted word order is produced in the majority of cases. Note that once the target-consistent word order takes over, this situation seems to be stable, lasting into the next time period for all three children.

Thus, we have attested a certain delay in the acquisition of subject shift in the Norwegian child data: young children have an early preference for the low subject position both for full DP and pronominal subjects. However, this construction seems to fall into place around the age of 2;6–2;8 for two of the children, and only slightly later for the third child.

4.2 *Object Shift*

In this section we investigate the spontaneous production of object shift in the Norwegian child language corpus. Recall from Section 2 that the context for object shift is a sentence with a single finite (transitive) verb plus negation or an adverb, i.e. the following structures:

(20) ... V_{fin} Neg/Adv OBJECT or:
... V_{fin} OBJECT Neg/Adv

There are altogether 259 examples of such contexts in the corpus, again most of them produced by the child Ina, 141 examples, while Ann and Ole produce 51 and 67 examples respectively. Table 4 provides an overview of the types of objects found in this construction with the two relevant word orders, i.e. an object preceding or following negation.

Table 4 Overview of full DP and pronominal objects in sentences with a single finite verb and negation (259 examples in total)

	Neg-O		O-Neg		
Child/word order	DPs/*det*	Pronoun	DPs	Pronoun	Total
Ina.11-27	121	16	0	4	141
Ann.11-21	46	2	0	3	51
Ole.11-22	57	7	0	3	67
Total	224	25	0	10	259

As much as 86.5% (224/259) of the examples have objects that are either full DPs or demonstrative/expletive *det*, which is exactly the opposite of the situation for subject shift contexts, where the majority of subjects were pronouns (89.7%, 191/213). Again, all these elements occur in the low object position, i.e. they follow negation in a target-consistent way. Examples are provided in (21) and (22).

(21) æ har **ikkje smykke(t).** (Ina.12, age 2;4.28) **Neg-O**
I have.PRES not necklace(.DEF)
'I don't have (the) necklace.'

(22) æ trur **ikkje det** (Ina.25, age 3;1.8)
I think.PRES not it
'I don't think so.'

Only 35 of the 259 objects are pronouns (including referential *det* 'it'). Out of these, 25 follow negation, while there are only 10 target-consistent examples where the pronominal object has shifted to the higher position. In order to check whether there is any development, the data were again divided into five time periods, as illustrated in Table 5. Because there are so few examples overall, data from the earliest files were not checked. In Period 2, all three children produce a few examples, all with non-target-consistent word order. In Period 3, a few target-consistent examples of object shift appear, and this is the situation also in Periods 4 and 5, but two of the children still produce more examples of the unshifted word order even at this stage.[8] Some examples of both word orders are provided in (23)–(28).

Table 5 Overview of sentences with Neg-O$_{PRO}$/O$_{PRO}$-Neg word order in the Norwegian child language corpus

Child	Period 1 (age 1;9–2;4)	Period 2 (age 2,4–2;6)	Period 3 (age 2;6–2;8)	Period 4 (age 2;8–3;0)	Period 5 (age 3;0–3;3)
Ina	Not checked	2/0	6/2	3/2	5/0
Ann	Not checked	2/0	0/0	0/3	
Ole	Not checked	3/0	1/1	3/2	

(23) eg finn **<ikkje han>** [>]. (Ina.13, age 2;5.25) **Neg-O$_{PRO}$**
I find.PRES not him
'I can't find him.'
Target form: Eg finn han ikkje.

(24) æ [/] æ får **ikke den** løs. (Ann.13, age 2;5.10)
I I get.PRES not it loose
'I can't get it off.'
Target form: Æ får den ikke løs.

[8] Note that the child Ann produces three target-consistent examples in Period 4, and no unshifted ones. This child's production is extremely target-consistent also with respect to other aspects of the grammar at an early age (see e.g. Westergaard 2009b), and it could therefore be the case that the object shift construction is in place already at this stage. However, there are so few examples in the corpus that it is impossible to draw any firm conclusions.

(25) åh æ klare **ikke det**. (Ole.12, age 2;5.18)
*oh I manage.*PRES *not it*
'Oh, I can't do it.'
Target form: Æ klare det ikke.

(26) ho har **den ikkje** på sæ. (Ina.24, age 2;11.26) **O$_{PRO}$-Neg**
*she have.*PRES *it not on* REFL
'She doesn't have it on.'

(27) æ kom **meg ikke** ut. (Ann.19, age 2;9.17)
*I come.*PAST *me not out*
'I couldn't get out.'

(28) æ hold **mæ ikke** fast! (Ole.22, age 2;11.23)
*I hold.*PRES REFL *not tight*
'I am not holding on (to it).'

This means that a certain delay is also attested in the acquisition of object shift. However, unlike the situation for the subject shift construction, object shift does not seem to be in place by the end of data collection (around the age of three) – at least for two of the children. Furthermore, object shift is also extremely infrequent in the child data, as only 10 target-consistent examples are attested, compared to 124 for subject shift. This is similar to Josefsson's (1996) findings from Swedish child language. Nevertheless, many questions remain.

The dearth of relevant examples in young children's spontaneous production therefore makes it necessary to elicit experimental data from somewhat older children in order to determine the following issues: (1) is there a real difference between subject and object shift constructions?, (2) when does the object shift construction fall into place?, and (3) are young children avoiding the object shift construction, producing full DPs instead of pronominal objects? In the next section we turn to the experimental data.

5 The Experimental Data

In this section we examine data from two experiments conducted with four normally developing children, one boy and three girls: Are (3;8.7), Linn (4;5.21), Gry (4;6.15), and Mia (5;8.14). The children are monolingual speakers acquiring the Tromsø dialect of Norwegian. Although the data sets from the two experiments are not very large, there are some clear tendencies. Importantly, the results of the experimentation are in general consistent with the findings from the spontaneous production in the corpus, and the answers to the above questions seem to be: (1) Subject and object shift appear to be different in that the former is acquired somewhat earlier than the latter; (2)

object shift is not fully acquired until the age of approximately five, considerably later than subject shift; and (3) the children are not trying to avoid the object shift construction.

Two elicited production tasks were designed by the authors to elicit subject and object shift constructions. The tasks were carried out in one session with a break in between. In both tasks the children were shown pictures on a computer screen. In the subject shift task, the pictures were used to elicit *why*-questions containing negation and a non-clause-initial subject, whereas the object shift test intended to elicit transitive declarative clauses with negation and a pronominal object. The subject shift task preceded the object shift task for all the children. Two experimenters were engaged in each task, and their roles are specified below. The tasks were carried out in the home of one of the children. The materials (colored pictures of children and objects) were obtained at Microsoft Office Online (http://office.microsoft.com/en-au/clipart/default.aspx) and modified in accordance with the purpose of each task. Before the actual experiments took place, they were piloted with two older children (aged 5;10 and 8;8), who showed target-consistent behaviour in both tasks. The results of the pilot test thus confirmed that the experimental set-up triggered the appropriate kind of responses.

5.1 *Subject Shift: The Experiment and Results*

The first task was designed to elicit *wh*-questions, more specifically, *why*-questions containing a non-clause-initial subject and negation. One of the experimenters conducted the procedure and the other played the role of a puppet called Elmo, whose task was to provide funny answers to the *why*-questions asked by the child. To encourage children to ask questions, Elmo was described as a shy creature who refused to talk to adults.

The task was divided into two conditions. Each condition had 12 test contexts (two initial trial items and 10 test items) and four fillers (follow-up *wh*-questions without negation). In the first condition, pronominal subjects were elicited. In the introduction the experimenter explained the task to the child and presented the two trial items. The first picture shown on the computer screen portrayed two children, a boy and a girl. They were introduced without names in order to ensure pronominal subjects in the children's responses. Then each character was shown separately. First, the child was shown a picture on the screen of a boy performing some action, e.g. playing with a ball. Next, an identical picture which was crossed out was added on the screen. The experimenter then explained to the child that the crossed-out picture indicated that the action did not happen. Specifically, in the preamble, the experimenter showing the pictures proceeded as follows: *Her ser vi at han leke med ballen sin. Han lekte med ballen i dag, men ikke i går. Så han lekte ikke med ballen sin i går.* [Here we see him playing with his ball. Today he played with the ball (pointing at the non-crossed-out picture), but not yesterday (pointing at the crossed-out picture). So he didn't play with his ball yesterday.] Then the experimenter showed only the crossed-out picture and asked the following elicitation question: *Kan du spørre han Elmo korfor det?* [Can you ask Elmo why?] The intended response was as follows: *Korfor lekte* ***han ikke*** *med ballen i går?* [Why didn't he play with the ball yesterday?] Each time Elmo provided a funny answer to the child's question.

In the second condition, two new characters were introduced. This time, however, the characters were given names, and the child was asked to remember and use their names, since Elmo, who could not see the screen, would otherwise not know who the question was about. Thus we attempted to make the child produce full DP subjects. Apart from this, the second test condition was identical to the first one.

The results for all four children are presented in Table 6. Recall that there were twelve relevant contexts in each condition: two trials and ten test items. The former are included in the table to enlarge the data set. In the test condition eliciting pronominal subjects, both Gry and Mia gave appropriate responses for each test context. Linn produced one irrelevant response (leaving out the subject) and Are produced four irrelevant responses (two instances with missing subjects and two instances of the word order *wh*-S-V-Neg). In the second test condition, none of the children provided appropriate responses with negation and full DPs for all 12 test contexts. Instead, they tended to substitute the proper names of the characters with pronouns. In fact, all the children produced some structures with negation and a pronominal rather than a full DP subject in this condition: Are and Linn four each, Gry and Mia two each. These responses are not included in the table, but it should be noted that they all displayed the target-consistent word order for such structures: S_{PRO}-Neg. In addition, Are produced six other responses in this condition, one which was irrelevant and another five which we return to below.

Table 6 The children's placement of pronominal and full DP subjects in *why*-questions with negation

Condition	Condition I: pronominal subjects			Condition II: DP subjects		
Child/Word order:	Neg-S_{PRO}	S_{PRO}-Neg	Total	Neg-S_{DP}	S_{DP}-Neg	Total
Are (3;8.7)	1	7	8	1	1	2
Linn (4;5.21)	0	11	11	8	0	8
Gry (4;6.15)	0	12	12	10	0	10
Mia (5;8.14)	0	12	12	10	0	10
Total	1	42	43	29	1	30

With regard to pronominal subjects, it is clear from Table 6 that on the overall level, the children exhibit target-like behaviour, i.e. they tend to shift pronouns across negation. There was only one target-deviant structure with the pronoun following negation in the production of the youngest child, Are, illustrated in (29). The other seven structures in his production were target-consistent, i.e. pronominal subjects preceded negation, as in (30).

(29) korfor leke **ikke han** med ballen? (Are, 3;8.7) **Neg-S$_{PRO}$**
why play.PRES not he with ball. DEF
'Why does not he play with the ball?'
Target form: Korfor leke han ikke med ballen?

(30) korfor sykle **han ikke** der? (Are, 3;8.7) **S$_{PRO}$-Neg**
why bike.PRES he not there
'Why does not he bike there?'

With regard to full DP subjects, the children show a clear overall preference for the non-shifted position. A relevant example is provided in (31). Again there was only one counter-example to the preferred order, also from Are's production, illustrated in (32).

(31) korfor fiske **ikke ho Nora**?[9] (Gry, 4;6.15) **Neg-S$_{DP}$**
why fish.PRES not she Nora
'Why does not Nora fish?'

(32) korfor drikk **han Simon ikke** kakao? (Are, 3;8.7) **S$_{DP}$-Neg**
why drink.PRES he Simon not cocoa
'Why does not Simon drink cocoa?'

As mentioned above, Are produced five non-target-like responses, which merit special attention. In these five clauses a pronominal and a full DP subject cooccur in the same structure. In all these cases, the pronominal element appears to the left of negation, while the DP occurs to the right, as shown in (33). Importantly, the order of the elements in these subject-doubling structures is always appropriate in that pronouns precede and DPs follow negation.

(33) korfor klatra **han ikke han Simon** oppi treet? (Are, 3;8.7) **Neg-S$_{PRO}$**
why climb.PAST he not he Simon up.in tree.DEF
'Why does not he (Simon) climb a tree?'

The results of the experiment are thus consistent with the results obtained from the corpus study. The corpus data indicate that the subject shift

---

[9] In the Tromsø dialect of Norwegian, as in most varieties of North Norwegian, person names appear with pronominal determiners, i.e. the third person pronouns *ho* 'she' and *han* 'he' (e.g. *ho Nora*), also called proprial articles (Anderssen 2006).

construction is acquired between the ages of 2;6–3;0. As subject shift is unproblematic for these 3–5-year-olds, the experimental data confirm that this construction falls into place prior to the age of three. This is arguably true even for the youngest child, Are. Although he only produces two constructions with full DP subjects, one of which exhibits the non-target-consistent word order, his five utterances containing both a pronominal and a DP subject suggest that he also prefers the low position for full DP subjects. Thus, at this stage, all the four children participating in the experiment already have knowledge of the two different subject positions: pronominal subjects are placed in front of negation and full DP subjects follow negation.

5.2 Object Shift: The Experiment and Results

The second task was designed to elicit transitive declarative clauses with a pronominal object and negation. This task was presented as a guessing game. The children were introduced to an unfamiliar character called Bert Bert, and were invited to learn more about his habits. Then the experimenter presented pictures on the computer screen of Bert Bert together with some object, e.g. a toothbrush. The experimenter would then proceed as follows: *Her ser vi en tannborst. Kan du gjette om han treng den eller ikke?* [Here we see a toothbrush. Can you guess whether he needs it or not?]. There were 15 test contexts (three initial trial items and 12 test items) and four fillers (guessing contexts not involving negation). Initially the design was such that the child would make a guess, either responding *Han treng den* [He needs it] or *Han treng den ikke* [He doesn't need it]. This worked well with the oldest child, Mia, who produced 12 responses containing a pronominal object and negation. However, this design turned out to be problematic when we used it with the younger child Gry. She consistently made her guesses by responding with embedded clauses, e.g. *Æ trur han ikke har den* [I think he doesn't have it], i.e. a context that is irrelevant for object shift. It was not clear whether this was just an individual preference or whether this response pattern was a consequence of the design. In any case, we decided to modify the experiment by introducing a second experimenter who would make the guesses. The child's task now was to judge whether the experimenter's answer was correct or not. In case of a wrong answer, the child was to provide the correct answer. This design was used with Linn and Are. As before, there were fifteen test contexts (three initial trial items and 12 test items) and four fillers. Upon showing and explaining the pictures to the child, the first experimenter would tell the second experimenter to make a guess: *Treng han den eller ikke?* [Does he need it or not?]. The second experimenter would make a guess contained in an embedded clause, in order to be able to use negation without producing object shift: *Æ trur at han (ikke) treng den* [I think that he (does not) need(s) it]. When the second experimenter provided an incorrect answer (which she did most of the time), the screen went blank to indicate to the child that this was wrong. The child was then told to give the correct answer, the target being *Han treng den (ikke)* [He (does not) need(s) it]. Whenever the correct answer was given, Bert Bert appeared on the screen performing some action.

The results reported in Table 7 are from Mia, Linn, and Are, and again, the trial items are included in the table to enlarge the data set. Gry's data had to be excluded as she only produced embedded clauses, not yielding appropriate contexts for object shift. As mentioned above, Mia produced responses containing a pronominal object and negation in 12 out of the 15 test contexts. Of the remaining three responses, one simply contained the word *Riktig* [Correct] and two responses were positive answers not containing negation. Linn produced eleven responses with a pronominal object and negation. Of her remaining four contexts, one contained only the answer *Ja* [Yes], two were positive answers without negation, and one was an embedded clause with negation. Finally, Are produced five responses containing a pronominal object and negation. His remaining responses included four positive clauses, one clause lacking an object, one clause with the pronoun *noen* [someone/anyone] (see below for a comment on this), and four irrelevant responses.

Table 7 The children's placement of pronominal objects in sentences with negation

Condition	Pronominal objects		
Child/Word order	O_{PRO}-Neg	Neg-O_{PRO}	Total
Are (3;8.7)	1	4	5
Linn (4;5.21)	8	3	11
Mia (5;8.14)	12	0	12
Total	21	7	28

Even though the children shifted pronominal objects in a target-consistent way in the majority of cases (21/28), there were seven target-deviant structures where pronouns followed negation. Importantly, the errors occurred in the speech of the youngest children, Are and Linn. Recall also from Section 5.1 that Are made one error with pronominal subjects, while Linn's production was error-free. Some examples of the children's responses illustrating both word orders are provided in (34)–(35).

(34) han kjenne **ikke ho**. (Are, 3;8.7) **Neg-O_{PRO}**
he know.PRES not her
'He doesn't know her.'
Target form: Han kjenne ho ikke.

(35) han vanne **den ikke**. (Linn, 4;5.21) **O_{PRO}-Neg**
he water.PRES it not
'He doesn't water it.'

The children do not seem to be avoiding object shift constructions, as at least two of them (Mia and Linn) use pronominal objects with negation in the majority of the test contexts. Furthermore, in the two girls' production there are no instances of missing objects or pronominal objects substituted by full DPs. Are, who produced the fewest object shift structures of the three children, only left out the object once, illustrated in (36). In addition, he used one structure containing the pronominal object *noen* [someone/anyone], (37). This is an interesting case, as this pronoun cannot be interpreted as strong or specific in this context in the target language (yielding the reading 'there is someone such that he doesn't know that/those person(s)'). Rather, this pronoun is obligatorily weak or non-specific, yielding the reading 'he does not know anyone', and it has to remain in a low position. In (37), Are thus uses this pronoun in a target-like way.

(36) han mate ikke. (Are, 3;8.7)
*he feed.*PRES *not*
'He does not feed (him).'
Intended form: Han mate han ikke. (He does not feed him.)

(37) han kjenne ikke noen. (Are, 3;8.7)
*he know.*PRES *not someone*
'He does not know anyone.'
Intended form: Han kjenne dem ikke. (He does not know them.)

From the experimental data it can thus be concluded that the object shift construction remains problematic at a later stage, which is consistent with the findings from the children's spontaneous production, where unshifted word order persisted until the end of the investigated period, i.e. the age of 3–3;3. The experimental results indicate that this construction does not fall into place until approximately the age of five, as two of the children aged 3;8.7 and 4;5.21 sometimes failed to shift pronominal objects. The situation is only stable for the oldest child, who was 5;8.14 at the time of the experiment.

5.3 Summary of Findings

The two types of data examined in this study reveal a difference between the subject and object shift constructions. The results of the experiments are consistent with the results of the spontaneous production data in that it indicates that the object shift construction is acquired later than the subject shift construction. According to the spontaneous production data, the latter falls into place before the age of three. The former is not acquired until approximately the age of five, as indicated by the experimental data. It is thus clear that the initial delay in the acquisition of both constructions observed in the corpus is more persistent with object shift. Finally, even though the children in the corpus produced few object shift constructions, this does not appear to be the result of an avoidance strategy, because in the experimental situation, the children used pronominal objects consistently and did not tend to substitute them with full DPs.

6 Discussion

As we have seen, non-target-like behaviour is observed with respect to both subjects and objects. The corpus data show that both pronominal subjects and pronominal objects may remain in an unshifted position in early child Norwegian. Furthermore, the non-target-like pattern for object placement persists for an extended period, as illustrated by the results from the experimental study. Thus, we have demonstrated that there is a discrepancy in the acquisition of subject and object shift. In this section we discuss (i) why children produce these non-target-like patterns and (ii) why there is a developmental lag in the acquisition of object shift as compared to subject shift. We will first consider three possible explanations for the non-target production: prosody, clitic movement, and pragmatics. All three are rejected as they can only account for one of the observed behaviours. Instead we explain the developmental patterns in terms of an interaction between economy and input frequencies.

In the acquisition literature, it has been argued that children acquire full syllabic vowels before they acquire reduced schwas (see e.g. Kehoe and Lleó 2003). If we consider this in connection with the previously mentioned fact that stressed pronouns cannot shift past negation, one possible explanation for the existence of unshifted subjects and objects in child language is that it is a side effect of an inability to destress pronominal elements. However, this does not seem to be the case, as the recorded material reveals that the children do not stress their unshifted pronouns. On the contrary, both these pronouns and the shifted ones often occur in a rather destressed form, as illustrated in (38), where the pronoun *den* 'it' is reduced to *dn*. Consequently, destressing does not seem to be the problem, and this account can thus be rejected.

(38) han vask ikke **dn**.[10] (Linn 4;5.21)
he clean.PRES not it
'He doesn't clean it.'

[10] In the Tromsø dialect, the present tense of the verb *å vaske* (to clean) is *vaske* rather than *vask*, which is the form used in (38). This might make us wonder whether it is the final vowel of *vaske* or the initial vowel of *ikke* that is reduced, yielding *vaske'ke* with a clitic form of the negation. However, we feel convinced that it is the final vowel of the verb that is reduced, because we see the same reduction in other places, including when the verb is followed by a word with an initial consonant, as in *korfor* ***lek(e) han*** *ikke med ballen?* [why doesn't he play with the ball] and *korfor* ***hør(e) han*** *ikke på musikk her på bildet da?* [why isn't he listening to music in this picture then?].

Another possible explanation for the existence of unshifted pronouns in child language is that these occur as a result of the negation moving to the V2 position together with the finite verb. If we assume that negation can cliticize onto the verb and subsequently move along with it into a higher position, then both the verb and the negation will end up preceding the pronominal elements, regardless of whether these elements occur in a high or a low position, as in (39). However, there are reasons to reject this analysis as well. First, although the children in the study occasionally produce cliticized negation, it is not the case that they use negation as a clitic whenever they fail to shift pronominal objects across negation, as shown in (40).[11]

(39) Han så'ke den.
he see.PAST-NEG.CL it
'He didn't see it.'

(40) han like **ikke dn**. (Are 3;8.7)
he like.*PRES* not it
'He doesn't like it.'

Second, unshifted pronouns can also cooccur with adverbs, as illustrated in (41). The adverb *og* 'also' is prosodically prominent in the clause, despite being monosyllabic. Consequently it cannot be cliticized onto the verb and clitic movement can be ruled out as an explanation both for the order in (41) and unshifted pronominal elements in general.

(41) det må og æ vise ho Marit.
it must also I show she Marit
'I must also show this to Marit.'

Finally, as we have seen, subjects and objects do not behave in the same way, and it is unlikely that the children's grammars would permit negation to move along with the verb when a pronominal subject is involved, but not when a pronominal object is involved. A clitic movement operation of this kind, involving a verb and clitic negation, should not be sensitive to the other elements that may appear in the clause.

---

[11] In fact, the children generally produce the full form of the negation and only occasionally prosodify it as a clitic. This seems to happen only in specific contexts, such as after the feminine pronoun *ho*, yielding *ho'ke* [she not], or after the verb *er*, which is pronounced *e*, yielding *e'ke* [is not]. As the experiment included few examples with *be* but many third person pronouns, there were many more examples such as *ho'ke* [she not] than *e'ke* [is not] in the data. As a result, clitic negation mainly occurs in contexts where the pronoun has shifted past negation.

A third potential explanation of the non-target-like production of unshifted pronominal elements is that it is related to an immature pragmatic component. As already mentioned in Section 2, the subject and object shift patterns are related to information structure in the target language in the sense that given elements (such as pronouns) are shifted across negation, whereas new or focussed elements (such as full DPs or emphatic pronouns) tend to follow negation. It is therefore a possibility that children's errors stem from a lack of pragmatic competence. However, based on a detailed study of the acquisition of subject shift by the children in the current corpus, Westergaard (2008) argues that such an account of the error patterns is unlikely. For one thing, we see that the errors the children make are not random. Although they sometimes fail to shift pronominal elements across negation, they never shift full DPs to a non-target-like position preceding negation. This suggests that they do have some knowledge of information structure. Furthermore, if the non-target-like production were the result of a pragmatic deficit, one would expect subject and object shift to be equally affected. The same objection applies to Schaeffer's (2000) pragmatically based 'Concept of Non-Shared Knowledge' as an account of the data discussed here.

Having rejected prosody, clitic movement, and pragmatics as adequate explanations for the observed acquisition patterns, we now give an account in terms of economy and input frequency. The notion of economy has played an important role in linguistic theory in the last couple of decades (e.g. Chomsky 1995). Economy principles are taken to select one among several converging operatons. Several models of acquisition have also been proposed in which children are assumed to start out with the least costly grammar. One such approach is the 'Initial Hypothesis of Syntax' (IHS) of Platzack (1996). Platzack suggests that children start out with a grammar in which all features are weak, and consequently no movement operations are necessary. Movement will only gradually be acquired if there is substantial evidence for this in the input. Another approach with a similar outcome is a weak continuity/structure building model (Clahsen 1990, Clahsen et al. 1993/1994, Clahsen et al. 1996). Children are assumed to have access to a universal pool of functional categories, but they will only build as much structure as there are sufficient cues for in the input. According to an economy approach to language acquisition, one would therefore expect children to initially avoid costly operations like movement, and only acquire this if exposed to strong and consistent cues for such operations. Zuckerman (2001) and Zuckerman and Hulk (2001) take an economy approach to children's acquisition of structures involving optionality in the adult language. Using French *wh*-questions as examples, they argue that, when there is optional movement in the target language, children will prefer the option that involves no movement.

In Section 4 we saw that the children initially prefer not to shift both subjects and objects, something that is consistent with an economy explanation for the non-target behaviour. However, at the same time, both the corpus data and the experimental data clearly show that children start shifting subjects before they start shifting objects. Furthermore, as already mentioned, while pronominal subjects are consistently moved past negation early on, their object counterparts display an inconsistent behaviour for a prolonged period. Consequently, we can conclude that even though economy principles can explain the initial lack of leftward movement with pronominal subjects and objects, it is clear that economy alone cannot account for the developmental patterns observed here. If economy were the only constraint at play, we would expect subjects and objects to behave the same way. When they fail to do so, this indicates that we have to appeal to other factors in addition to economy to account for all the data.

A relevant question is whether input frequencies may have an effect on acquisition and possibly shed some light on the distinction found between subject and object shift constructions in the child data. In Westergaard (2008) a sample of adult data investigated for the frequency of subject shift constructions (INV, Ole.14) showed that, out of 42 contexts for subject shift, 35 subjects were realized as pronouns and 28 of these were shifted. An investigation of the same sample for object shift constructions shows that there are only 11 potential contexts for this construction, and only three objects are realized as pronouns, all of which are shifted. It thus seems like subject shift is more frequent (28 vs. 3) in the input, but it is necessary to confirm this by studying more examples of typical child-directed speech. In this chapter, therefore, a larger sample of adult data from the corpus has been studied, viz. the production of the investigator (INV) in the files Ina.02-12, 17, and 19, corresponding to approximately 13 h of recording.

In this sample there are altogether 187 examples of the context for subject shift, i.e. a structure containing an initial XP, the finite verb in second position, and then the subject and the negation *ikkje* 'not' in either order, XP-V-*ikkje*-S or XP-V-S-*ikkje*. By comparison there are only 93 examples of potential contexts for object shift, i.e. a single finite verb followed by an object or negation *ikkje* in either order, V-*ikkje*-O or V-O-*ikkje*. This means that the context for subject shift appears more than twice as frequently as the contexts for object shift in the adult data. This is illustrated in Table 8.

But the major difference between these constructions in the input is to be found in the actual number of examples of the two: In the potential contexts for subject shift, there are only 11 full DP subjects and as many as 176 pronouns. Out of these 176 pronouns, 157 are shifted up to the high position. The realization of objects, on the other hand, is very different: Most of the 93 objects are realized as clauses or full DPs, and only 4 are pronouns, 3 of which are shifted. This means that the number of subject shift constructions in the sample is approximately

Table 8 Subject and object shift constructions in a sample of child-directed speech, INV in Ina.02-12, 17, and 19

	Subject shift	Object shift
Potential contexts	187	93
Pronominal elements	176	4
Shifted pronominal element	157	3

50 times higher than the number of object shift constructions (157 vs. 3 examples). From this we can conclude that there is an extreme difference in frequency between subject and object shift constructions in the input. This indicates that the frequency difference between the two constructions in the corpus of child language is not due to an avoidance strategy on the part of the children. In fact, the proportions of the two constructions in the child data (124 vs. 10) more or less match that found in the adult sample, and the difference between the two data sets actually indicates that the children produce somewhat more object shift.

The frequency difference between the two constructions in both the child and adult data seems to be due to a conspiracy of factors. First of all, there are more subjects than objects overall. While all clauses have to have a subject, many lack an object, e.g. those that contain intransitive or unaccusative verbs. This presumably accounts for the difference between the two constructions with respect to the number of potential contexts (187 vs. 93). Furthermore, there seems to be a tendency for negation to appear with modals, both in child-directed speech and in child language, e.g. *will not, must not, cannot*, etc. This means that the context for object shift disappears in these cases, as the construction requires the presence of a single finite main verb only.

Nevertheless, the most important factor contributing to the frequency difference is the fact that subjects more often convey given information than objects do. Evidence for this is that subjects are predominantly realized as pronouns. Objects, on the other hand, more often convey new information and are thus predominantly realized as full DPs or clauses. In the adult sample investigated here, the 187 subjects in subject shift contexts are realized by pronouns 94% of the time (176/187), while objects in contexts for object shift are realized by personal pronouns only 4.3% of the time (4/93). These proportions are confirmed in another study of both Norwegian and English child-directed speech (Westergaard forthcoming/2010), where it is shown that subjects in general (not only in contexts for subject shift) are realized by pronouns between six and eleven times more often than as full DPs (with some variation across samples). In comparison, objects are generally realized by DPs or clauses 3–4 times more often than as pronouns.

Thus, it is not unlikely that input frequency plays a role with respect to the lack of object shift in the child data as well as the delay attested in target-consistent production of this construction, especially compared to the similar subject shift construction. However, note that we are not arguing that lack of frequency is the cause of the children's delay in target-consistent production. Rather, the error pattern is originally caused by a principle of economy, as outlined earlier in this section. But as also argued in previous work, e.g. Westergaard and Bentzen (2007), we would like to claim that an error pattern that is originally caused by economy or complexity may *persist* longer in children's I-language grammars if the relevant construction is infrequent in the input. Thus, while the subject and object shift constructions are both somewhat delayed due to economy, children's problems with object shift are more persistent because of relatively sparse evidence for it in the input.

7 Conclusion

In this chapter we have investigated how children deal with a particular kind of word order optionality in the input. The results of the study of object and subject shift constructions in Norwegian child language suggest that word order optionality is a challenging domain for first language learners. According to the spontaneous and elicited production data considered in this study, there is a developmental delay in the acquisition of subject and object shift constructions. We have found that Norwegian children initially have a preference for a non-shifted word order both with pronominal and full DP subjects and objects. Furthermore, we have found that subject shift is in place before the age of three and object shift not until around the age of five. The initial delay in the acquisition of these constructions has been accounted for in terms of structural economy. Specifically, we have argued that children's non-target behaviour is consistent with the assumption that children initially avoid costly operations like syntactic movement. We have also argued that this delay cannot be directly explained in terms of prosody, clitic movement or pragmatics.

The comparison of the children's spontaneous and elicited production data has allowed us to conclude that there is real difference between subject and object shift constructions. Object shift appears to be a more problematic area in acquisition than subject shift, as the object shift construction was produced in a non-target-like manner for a prolonged period of time. Based on the results of the empirical data, we have suggested that the children do not apply an avoidance strategy here. Evidence that supports this proposal includes the observation that the children in this study did not tend to omit pronominal objects or substitute them with full DPs. This impression is reinforced by the fact that object shift is infrequent in the adult data as well. Instead, the delay in the acquisition of object shift compared to subject shift is attributed to the former construction being much less frequent in the input.

References

Anderssen, Merete. 2006. *The acquisition of compositional definiteness in Norwegian*. Doctoral Dissertation, University of Tromsø.

Barbier, Isabella. 2000. An experimental study of scrambling and object shift in the acquisition of Dutch. In *The acquisition of scrambling and cliticization*, eds. Susan M. Powers and Cornelia Hamann, 41–69. Dordrecht: Kluwer Academic Publishers.

Bentzen, Kristine. 2009. Subject positions and their interaction with verb movement. *Studia Linguistica* 63(3): 1–31.

Bobaljik, Jonathan David. 1995. *Morphosyntax: The syntax of verbal inflection*. Ph.D. dissertation, MIT.

Bobaljik, Jonathan David, and Dianne Jonas. 1996. Subject positions and the roles of TP. *Linguistic Inquiry* 27(2): 195–236.

Bobaljik, Jonathan David, and Höskuldur Thráinsson. 1998. Two heads aren't always better than one. *Syntax* 1(1): 37–71.

Bošković, Željko. 2004. PF merger in stylistic fronting and object shift. In *Minimality effects in syntax*, eds. Arthur Stepanov, Gisbert Fanselow and Ralf Vogel, 37–71. Berlin: Mouton de Gruyter.
Cardinaletti, Anna. 2004. Towards a cartography of subject positions. In *The structure of CP and IP: The cartography of syntactic structures*, vol. 2, ed. Luigi Rizzi, 115–165. New York: Oxford University Press.
Chomsky, Noam. 1993. A minimalist program for linguistic theory. In *The view from building 20*, eds. Kenneth Hale and Samuel Keyser, 1–52. Cambridge, MA: MIT press.
Chomsky, Noam. 1995. *The minimalist program*. Cambridge: MIT Press.
Cinque, Guglielmo. 1999. *Adverbs and functional heads: A cross-linguistic perspective*. New York: Oxford University Press.
Clahsen, Harald. 1990. Constraints on parameter setting. A grammatical analysis of some stages in German child language. *Language Acquisition* 1: 361–391.
Clahsen, Harald, Martina Penke, and Teresa Parodi. 1993/1994. Functional categories in early child German. *Language Acquisition* 3: 395–429.
Clahsen, Harald, Sonja Eisenbeiss, and Martina Penke. 1996. Lexical learning in early syntactic development. In *Generative perspectives on language acquisition: Empirical findings, theoretical considerations and crosslinguistic comparison* [Language Acquisition and Language Disorders 14], ed. Harald Clahsen, 129–159. Amsterdam/Philadelphia: John Benjamins.
Déprez, Viviane. 1989. *On the typology of syntactic positions and the nature of chains: Move A to the specifier of functional projections*. Ph.D. dissertation, MIT.
Diesing, Molly. 1996. Semantic variables and object shift. In *Studies in comparative Germanic syntax II*, eds. Höskuldur Thráinsson, Samuel David Epstein and Steve Peter, 66–84. Dordrecht: Kluwer Academic Publishers.
Guasti, Maria Teresa. 1994. Verb syntax in Italian child grammar: Finite and non-finite verbs. *Language Acquisition* 3: 1–40.
Haider, Hubert. 2000. Scrambling: What's the state of the art? In *The acquisition of scrambling and cliticization*, eds. Susan M. Powers and Cornelia Hamann, 19–40. Dordrecht: Kluwer Academic Publishers.
Hamann, Cornelia, and Adriana Belletti. 2006. *Developmental patterns in the acquisition of French clitics: Comparing monolinguals, early and adult L2ers, bilingual children, and French children with specific language impairment*. Ms., University of Oldenburg and University of Siena.
Holmberg, Anders. 1986. *Word order and syntactic features in the Scandinavian languages and English*. Doctoral Dissertation, University of Stockholm.
Holmberg, Anders. 1993. Two subject positions in the IP in Mainland Scandinavian. *Working Papers in Scandinavian Syntax* 52: 29–41.
Holmberg, Anders, and Christer Platzack. 1988. On the role of inflection in Scandinavian syntax. *Working Papers in Scandinavian Syntax* 42: 23–42.
Holmberg, Anders, and Christer Platzack. 1995. *The role of inflection in Scandinavian syntax*. Oxford: Oxford University Press.
Jayaseelan, Karattuparambil. 2001. IP-internal topic and focus phrases. *Studia Linguistica* 55 (1): 39–75.
Josefsson, Gunlög. 1996. The acquisition of object shift in Swedish child language. In *Children's language* 9, eds. Carolyn E. Johnson and John H. V. Gilbert, 153–165. Mahwah: Lawrence Erlbaum.
Josefsson, Gunlög. 2001. The true nature of Holmberg's Generalization revisited – once again. *Working Papers in Scandinavian Syntax* 67: 85–102.
Kehoe, Margaret, and Conxita Lleó. 2003. A phonological analysis of schwa in German first language acquisition. *Canadian Journal of Linguistics* 48: 289–327.
Kiss, Katalin É. 1996. Two subject positions in English. *Linguistic Review* 13.2: 119–142.

Mohr, Sabine. 2005. *Clausal architecture and subject positions: Impersonal constructions in the Germanic languages*. Amsterdam: John Benjamins.

Nilsen, Øystein. 1997. Adverbs and A-shift. *Working Papers in Scandinavian Syntax* 59: 1–31.

Platzack, Christer. 1996. The initial hypothesis of syntax: A minimalist perspective on language acquisition and attrition. In *Generative perspectives on language acquisition: Empirical findings, theoretical considerations, crosslinguistic comparisons* [Language Acquisition and Language Disorders 14], ed. Harald Clahsen, 369–414. Amsterdam/Philadelphia: John Benjamins.

Poeppel, David, and Kenneth Wexler. 1993. The full competence hypothesis of clause structure in early German. *Language* 69: 1–33.

Schaeffer, Jeanette. 2000. *The acquisition of direct object scrambling and clitic placement: Syntax and pragmatics*. Amsterdam/Philadelphia: John Benjamins.

Söderbergh, Ragnhild. 1973. *Projektet Barnspråkssyntax* [Project Child Language Syntax]. Department of Scandinavian Languages, Stockholm University.

Svenonius, Peter. 2002. Subject positions and the placement of adverbials. In *Subjects, expletives, and the EPP*, ed. Peter Svenonius, 201–242. New York: Oxford University Press.

Vangsnes, Øystein Alexander. 2005. Microparameters for Norwegian *wh*-grammars. In *Linguistic variation yearbook* 5, eds. Pierre Pica, Johan Rooryck and Jereon van Craenenbroeck, 187–226. Amsterdam and Philadelphia: John Benjamins.

Vikner, Sten. 1989. Object shift and double objects in Danish. *Working Papers in Scandinavian Syntax* 44: 141–155.

Vikner, Sten. 1994. Scandinavian object shift and West Germanic scrambling. In *Studies on scrambling*, eds. Norbert Corver and Henk van Riemsdijk, 487–517. Berlin: Mouton de Gruyter.

Vikner, Sten. 1997. The interpretation of object shift, optimality theory and minimalism. *Working Papers in Scandinavian Syntax* 60: 1–24.

Vikner, Sten. 2006. Object Shift. In *The blackwell companion to syntax*, vol. III, eds. Martin Everaert and Henk van Riemsdijk, 392–436. Oxford: Blackwell.

Westergaard, Marit. 2003. Word order in *wh*-questions in a North Norwegian dialect: Some evidence from an acquisition study. *Nordic Journal of Linguistics* 26.1: 81–109.

Westergaard, Marit. 2008. Verb movement and subject placement in the acquisition of word order: Pragmatics or structural economy? In *First language acquisition of morphology and syntax: Perspectives across languages and learners* [Language Acquisition and Language Disorders], eds. Pedro Guijarro-Fuentes, Pilar Larranaga and John Clibbens. Amsterdam: John Benjamins.

Westergaard, Marit. 2009a. 'Microvariation as Diachrony: A View from Acquisition.' *Journal of Comparative Germanic Linguistics* 12(1): 49–79.

Westergaard, Marit. 2009b. *The acquisition of word order: Micro-cues, information structure and economy* [Linguistik Aktuell/Linguistics Today 145]. Amsterdam: John Benjamins.

Westergaard, Marit. Forthcoming/2010. 'Cue-based acquisition and information structure drift in diachronic language development.' In *Diachronic Studies on Information Structure: Language Acquisition and Change [Language, Context and Cognition 10]*, eds. Gisella Ferraresi and Rosemarie Lühr. Berlin: de Gruyter.

Westergaard, Marit, and Øystein Alexander Vangsnes. 2005. *Wh*-questions, V2, and the left periphery of three Norwegian dialect types. *Journal of Comparative Germanic Syntax* 8: 117–158.

Westergaard, Marit, and Kristine Bentzen. 2007. The (non-) effect of input frequency on the acquisition of word order in Norwegian embedded clauses. In *Frequency effects in language acquisition: Defining the limits of frequency as an explanatory concept* [Studies on Language Acquisition], eds. Insa Gülzow and Natalia Gagarina, 271–306. Berlin/New York: Mouton de Gruyter.

Wiklund, Anna-Lena, Gunnar Hrafn Hrafnbjargarson, Kristine Bentzen, and Thorbjörg Hróarsdóttir. 2007. Rethinking Scandinavian verb movement. *Journal of Comparative Germanic Linguistics* 10(3): 203–233.

Zuckerman, Shalom. 2001. *The acquisition of "optional" movement*. Ph.D. dissertation, Groningen University.

Zuckerman, Shalom, and Aafke Hulk. 2001. Acquiring optionality in French *wh*-questions: An experimental study. *Revue Québécoise de Linguistique* 30(2): 71–97.

Index

A

Aaron, D., 159–161, 173–174
Acquisition, 1–13, 20, 23, 29–30, 36, 53, 64–92, 95–125, 130–131, 134, 136–138, 140, 142–147, 150–155, 158, 161–162, 165, 167, 173–174, 179–181, 187, 193, 202–203, 207–238, 241–267
Acquisition of dative constructions, 130, 136–138
Adjectival ordering, 7, 65–92
Adjectives
  descriptive, 66–67, 72, 74–78, 86–89, 92
  determiner-like, 69, 71–72, 81–83
  individual-level, 90–91
  possessive, 66–67, 70–74, 78, 83–85, 92
  quantity (QA(P)), 69–71, 92
  stage-level, 76, 78, 89–91
Adverb, 3–4, 10, 34, 54, 56–59, 66–67, 159, 211–212, 214, 218–221, 223–224, 229–232, 235, 243–244, 246, 250, 252–253, 263
Agouraki, G., 185
Aguado-Orea, J., 189
Alexiadou, A., 183–184, 186
Ambiguity in English *to*, 131, 138, 151, 154
Ambiguous verb particle, 105
American Sign Language (ASL), 9, 12, 157–176
Anagnostopoulou, E., 183–184, 186
Anderssen, M., 1–13, 154, 203, 209, 241–267
Aspectual verb, 161–162, 167
Atelic verb particle, 117
Avrutin, S., 202, 207–210, 212–213, 215, 217, 227, 236–237

B

Bader, T., 34, 39–40, 46, 56
Barbier, I., 4, 246
Bayer, J., 34, 48–50, 51
Beck, S., 134
Behrend, D. A., 106, 124
Behrens, H., 96–97, 104, 110
Bel, A., 189, 193
Belletti, A., 92, 188, 248
Bentzen, K., 1–13, 30, 203, 241–267
Bernardini, P., 84, 87, 92
Bilingual, 10, 12, 108, 130–131, 138–140, 142–144, 146–155, 208–210, 226–228, 232, 235, 237–238, 247
Bilingual language acquisition, 130
Blackwell, A., 90–91
Bloom, L., 139, 181
Brandner, E., 48–51, 63
Brown, R., 107, 139, 181
Brow raise, 9, 159, 161, 165–166, 170–173, 175–176
Brun, D., 207–210, 212–213, 215, 217, 227, 236–237

C

Canonical word order, 9, 158, 164, 166–167, 175
Cantonese dative constructions, 131, 140, 146–150, 155
Cantonese-English bilingual children, 139, 142–143, 150
Carden, G., 26
Cardinaletti, A., 7, 11, 65–92, 188, 244
Carry-over effect, 61–62
Chan, W., 133–134, 138, 140–141, 152–154
Child-driven learning mechanism, 106

M. Anderssen et al. (eds.), *Variation in the Input*, Studies in Theoretical Psycholinguistics 39, DOI 10.1007/978-90-481-9207-6,

Child language/grammar, 12, 81–83, 87, 188–189, 196–198, 202–203, 208, 211–212, 215, 226, 236
Chomsky, N., 29, 33, 179, 185, 222–223, 225, 245, 264
Cinque, G., 7, 68, 74–76, 78, 87, 89–91, 218, 243
Clitic, 7, 43–47, 52, 54–55, 57, 186, 243, 248, 262–264, 267
Clitic movement, 243, 262–264, 267
Clitic object, 248
Comrie, B., 103
Concept of Non-Shared Knowledge, 208, 247, 264
Contrastive focus, 159–160, 174, 187, 243
Crain, S., 18, 20, 26, 29

D

De Cat, C., 202
Declarative, 49, 172, 250–252, 256, 259
Deen, K. U., 207, 215, 223, 236
Definite, 69, 81, 209, 211–212, 214–217, 229–230, 232–237, 247
Demonstratives, 5, 71, 216–217
Determiner, 47, 69, 71–74, 80–83, 85, 216–217, 221
Developmental lag (in dative constructions), 8, 31, 134, 137, 262
De Villiers, J., 21
Dialectal variation, 35, 38, 51, 62
Direct object, 1–2, 129–130, 208, 210, 215–226, 229, 231, 233, 247
Discourse, 2, 6, 9, 41, 66, 68–69, 78, 92, 159–160, 165, 174, 180, 184, 187–189, 193, 198, 200, 202–203, 208, 210–213, 223
D-linking, 41
Double object construction, 2, 8
Double object datives, 8, 130–134, 136–151, 153–155
Doubly-filled COMP (DFC), 7, 33–63
DP (Determiner Phrase), 1–2, 4, 7, 9–10, 69–70, 73, 79–82, 91, 129–130, 144, 179, 182–187, 189–191, 193, 196, 198–201, 207–208, 216–217, 221, 223, 230, 242, 244–245, 249, 251, 253, 257–259, 267
Dutch, 4, 7, 10, 23–24, 34, 208–211, 213–215, 221, 225, 229, 245–247, 249
Dyadic dative *to*, 151
Dyakonova, M., 207

E

Economy, 1, 3–4, 10, 12, 49, 243, 262, 264, 265–267
  principles, 1, 10, 264–265
Elicitation/elicited, 4, 7, 36, 52–53, 59–62, 210–211, 214, 229, 242, 256, 257, 267
Elicitation experiment, 242
Embedded clause, 3–4, 34, 36–37, 43, 52–53, 59, 61, 63, 185, 244, 259–260
Enç, M., 214, 216
Endstate-orientation, 106, 122, 124
English, 2, 6–12, 18, 23, 25–26, 30, 34, 58, 76, 90–91, 107–108, 121, 129–155, 181, 188, 203, 207–238, 247, 266
English-Ukrainian, 10–11, 207–238, 247
Environment-driven learning mechanism, 106–108, 124
EPP-feature, 225–226
Event type, 96, 104, 106
Experimental, 4, 7, 21, 24–25, 27, 208, 210–211, 214, 221, 228–232, 236–237, 247, 251, 255–262, 264
Extraposed/extraposition, 37, 100–101, 103

F

Finite, 37, 43, 49–50, 53, 56, 59–60, 97–99, 102, 181–182, 220, 224, 243, 246, 253, 263, 265–266
Fischer, S, 157–159, 161–162
Fixed word order strategy, 164
Focus, 7, 24, 26, 35, 47, 66, 80, 106, 108, 124, 133, 158–160, 171, 174, 184, 187–189, 195, 200–201, 208, 218, 223, 231, 243, 246
Focussed, 50, 73, 84, 243–245, 264

G

Gender, 6, 82, 139–140, 182, 217
Gene see, F., 130
Gennari, S., 24–25, 28
Gentner, D., 106, 108
Gil, D., 28
Giusti, G., 7, 11, 65–92
Given information, 51, 165, 266
Gleitman, L., 30
Glenberg, A., 21
Goal (thematic role), 132
Gordishevsky, G., 202
Greek, 5, 9, 11, 179–203

Grinstead, J., 188–189, 195–196, 202
Grodzinsky, Y., 19, 81
Gualmini, A., 7, 11, 17–30
Guasti, M. T., 79, 249

H
Handling verb, 162, 167, 169
Harley, H., 134
Harris, T., 169, 181
Hoffmeister, R., 163–167, 169, 175
Höhle, T. N., 99
Holmberg, A., 218, 243–245
Holmberg's Generalization, 244
Holton, D., 191
Hong Kong Bilingual Child Language Corpus, 139
Horn, L., 21, 25
Hulk, A., 3, 130, 264
Hulsey, S, 17, 22, 26

I
Ilić, T., 207, 215, 236
Indefinites, 18, 23–24, 26, 29, 70, 81, 103, 211–212, 214–215, 217, 221, 229–230, 232–236, 245, 247
Information
  focus, 174
  structure, 2–3, 11–13, 51, 183, 200–202, 243–244, 264
Informationally
  given, 3, 5, 243–244
  new, 3, 5, 243–244
Input ambiguity, 136, 155
Intrusive n, 43–44
Inverted double object dative constructions, 130–131, 140
Israeli Sign Language (ISL), 170–173, 175

J
Johnson, K., 134
Josefsson, G., 4, 208, 245, 248–250

K
Kabak, B., 44, 47, 63
Kapetangianni, K., 9, 11, 179–203
Kiss, K., 184, 186, 201, 244
Ko, H., 10–12, 207–238, 247

L
Labov, W., 26, 30
Ladusaw, W., 18, 29
Lakusta, L., 138
Landau, I., 132
Language acquisition, 2, 6, 12, 20, 23, 29–30, 81, 95–96, 109, 122, 130, 179–180, 187, 208, 210, 214, 226, 241–242, 264
Language-driven learning mechanism, 124
Larson, R. K., 134, 155, 238
Latent C-feature, 49–50
Lee, T., 139, 152, 155
Left sentence bracket, 99, 101–103, 113, 119–120, 123
Levinson, L., 135, 151
Lidz, J., 17, 25–26
Linking *n*, 43

M
MacDonald, M., 24–25, 28
MacWhinney, B., 137, 139, 190
Matthews, S., 130, 133, 139, 143, 226
Maxim of Charity, 26, 28
McKee, C., 18
Medial wh-construction, 37
Micro-variation, 3, 13
Mills, A. E., 56, 96, 104
Mismapping, 210, 215, 237
Modification
  direct, 74–78, 89–92
  indirect, 76–78, 89–92
Monosyllabic wh-phrase, 7, 35, 40–41, 43, 45–52, 54–56, 59–62
Musolino, J., 17–19, 21–22, 25–26

N
Naigles, L. R., 107, 121
Negation, 3–4, 7, 10, 18, 22–25, 27–33, 36, 185, 197–198, 200, 211–212, 214, 218–221, 224, 229–232, 235, 241–244, 246–254, 256–266
New information, 9, 11, 159–160, 173, 183, 186–187, 198–200, 266
Nominal expressions, 66, 68–69, 78, 91
Noncanonical word order, 158, 167
Non-focussed, 245
Non-monosyllabic wh-phrase, 35, 41, 43, 45, 47, 51–52, 54–56, 60–61
Non-referential, 247

Non-shifted (subjects/objects), 10, 242, 258
Non-specific, 10–11, 209, 212–215, 217, 224–227, 229–230, 232–238, 243–244, 247, 261
Non-specific reading, 209, 217, 243
Non-subject-initial clause, 4, 243–244, 250, 252
Norwegian, 1–6, 10–12, 34–35, 39, 48, 50–52, 62, 154, 202, 208–209, 241–267
Noun phrase, 5–6, 159, 171, 182, 247
Null subject languages, 2, 180–181, 187–188, 193, 195

O

Object (placement, shift, pronoun, DP), 1–2, 4, 10, 44, 58, 154, 167, 208–209, 211, 217–218, 225–226, 241–267, 262
  clitic, 44–45, 211, 248–249
  determiner phrase (DP), 216
  placement, 10, 242, 262
  pronoun, 2, 44, 58, 167, 244–245
  shift, 4, 10, 12, 154, 209, 217–218, 225–226, 241–267
Optionality, 1–7, 10, 29, 35–36, 39, 55, 62, 66–78, 91–92, 125, 129–130, 152, 154, 179, 181–187, 209–211, 213, 215, 223, 225–226, 237, 241–261, 263–265, 267
Optional verb movement, 35, 50–52
Order of emergence of Cantonese dative constructions, 148–149
Order of emergence of English dative constructions, 147, 150
Overt DP subject, 9, 187, 190–191, 193, 196, 198
OV word order, 175

P

Paradis, J., 130
Parental input, 96, 107, 109, 114–124
Particle shift, 1–2
Particle verb, 1, 8, 96–101, 104–106, 111–125
Partitive, 214, 216, 227
Penner, Z., 34, 39–40, 46, 52–53, 56, 59, 96, 104–106, 124, 208
Pesetsky, D., 41, 134, 223
Phase Theory, 222
Philippaki-Warburton, I., 182, 184–186
Pierce, A., 180
Pine, J. M., 189
Pinker, S., 30, 96
Pires, A., 186, 203
Poeppel, D., 12, 181, 249
Pollock, J.-Y., 181, 219
Possessors (pre-nominal, post-nominal), 5–6
Postverbal, 9, 11, 72, 158, 160, 180, 182–187, 190, 193–196, 198–200, 202, 212–213, 217
Pragmatic
  principles, 10, 182, 189, 198, 200, 202, 215
  word order variation, 176
Prepositional datives, 8, 130–132, 134–139, 141–146, 150–152, 154–155
Preverbal, 9, 72, 158, 162, 165, 167, 169, 175, 183–190, 194–201, 212–213, 217, 221, 231
Preverbal object, 158, 162, 165, 167, 175, 213, 231
Primary linguistic data (PLD), 179
Principles and Parameters, 29, 180
Production data, 3, 9, 36, 38, 53, 61–62, 180, 187, 189–190, 194, 261, 267
Pronominal
  object, 4, 6, 243–245, 249, 253, 255–256, 259–263, 267
  subject, 10, 43, 45, 241–243, 251, 252–253, 256–260, 262–263, 265
Prosodic
  break, 9, 170, 172–173, 175–176
  unit, 43, 45–47, 52
Prosody, 10, 35, 39, 43, 47–48, 50, 52, 62–63, 175, 243, 262, 264, 267
Pylkkänen, L., 134

Q

Quantifiers (QP), 27, 66, 69–71, 69–70, 80–81, 188, 220
Question under discussion, 26–28

R

Radford, A., 202
Referential, 71, 160, 210, 212, 214, 216, 227, 229, 246–247, 254
Register, 66–68, 72, 75, 80, 87, 89, 92
Regularize, 11, 36, 63
Reilly, J., 165–166, 170, 171, 176
Reinhart, T., 19
Reordering morphology, 9, 161–162, 167–169, 171, 175
Revithiadou, A., 186

Richards, N., 108, 121, 134
Right sentence bracket, 8, 99–103, 105, 113, 119–120, 123–124
Rivero, M. L., 182
Rizzi, L., 2, 51, 81, 184, 188
Rodina, Y., 4, 6, 10, 75, 241–267
Roeper, T., 2
Roussou, A., 186–187
Russian, 6, 202, 207–208, 210, 212–213, 215, 217, 228, 235

S
Saliency of sentence position, 108
Sandhofer, C. M., 107, 111, 121
Schaeffer, J., 4, 10, 208, 210–215, 219, 221, 227, 229, 231–232, 236–237, 245–247, 249, 264
Schick, B., 163–170, 175
Schiering, R., 44, 47
Schwarz, B., 29
Scope, 17–30, 68, 159, 171, 188, 201, 220, 246
Scrambling, 4, 6, 10, 12, 207–238, 245–248
Semantics, 12, 83, 104, 132, 151, 154, 216, 226–227, 237
Sentence final position, 95, 99–103, 108, 118–119, 122–124
Serial verb dative constructions, 131–132, 135, 138, 146–148, 153–155
Shifted (subjects/objects), 245, 251–252, 262
Simplex verb, 8, 11, 96–97, 101–107, 110–124
Snow, C., 139, 190
Snyder, W., 8, 12, 131, 137–141, 144–145
Spatial verb, 162, 167
Specificity, 10–12, 207–213, 215–217, 222–223, 225–227, 229, 231–232, 234, 236–238, 248
Specific reading, 7, 26, 30, 209, 217, 226, 243
Spontaneous production, 3, 38, 62, 66, 163, 250, 253, 255, 261
Spyropoulos, V., 184–186
Steedman, M., 20, 26, 28
Stephany, U., 190, 192, 194, 198–200
Stress/stressed, 27, 43–44, 46–47, 51–52, 185, 262
Stromswold, K., 8, 131, 137–141, 144–145
Subject
  -initial clause, 243–244
  placement, 198
  pronoun, 43–46
  subject (placement, shift, pronoun, DP), 5, 10, 43–46, 198, 242–244, 249–253, 255–259, 261–262, 264–267
  -verb order, 180–182, 196, 203
Subject Determiner Phrase (DP), 249
Swedish, 1, 4, 208, 248–249, 255
Syntactic
  development, 180, 189, 202, 236
  -semantic, 137, 207–210, 213–215, 218–226, 237
  word order variation, 175
Syntax, 2, 7, 11, 12–13, 62, 66–67, 78, 96, 132, 134, 151, 154, 189, 213, 215, 226–227, 237–238, 264
Szabolcsi, A., 18

T
Tager-Flusberg, H., 21
Tang, S., 131–134, 141, 155
Tardif, T., 97, 103, 107–108, 123
Telicity, 104, 106, 117
Telic verb particle, 96, 105, 114, 117, 122–124
Theme (thematic role), 129, 130, 133–134, 136, 141, 147–154, 162, 164, 167, 169
Theoretical Bilingualism Hypothesis, 2
Thornton, R., 18
Thrainsson H., 207, 218–219, 225
Token frequency, 8, 107, 111, 115–116, 118, 121
Tomasello, M., 96, 107, 164, 226
Topic, 6, 8–9, 69, 72, 159–161, 163, 165–166, 169–176, 183–184, 186–188, 198–200, 221, 226, 241, 249
  nonmanual, 159, 161, 163, 165–166, 169–173, 175
Topicalisation in ASL, 163
Topological field model, 99, 123
Tracy, R., 96, 105
Triadic dative *to*, 9, 144–146, 151, 155
Trochaic foot, 43, 47
Tromsø dialect, 3, 250–251, 255, 258, 262
Truth Value Judgement task, 18, 211, 229
Tsimpli, I. M., 182, 184, 186, 189, 193–194, 200–201
Type 1 topics, 173–174
Type frequency, 8, 97, 107, 111, 116, 121, 124
Type token ratio (TTR), 97, 107–109, 116–117, 121–122, 124

U
Ukrainian, 10–12, 207–238, 247
Universal Grammar (UG), 7, 12, 20, 78, 90, 154, 179, 188, 209, 226–227, 237
Unsworth, S., 23, 208, 210, 213–215, 221, 229, 237

V
V2, 3–4, 36–38, 41, 43, 50–51, 53–56, 60–62, 97–99, 112, 124, 181, 243–244, 250, 263
Vangsnes, Ø. A., 3, 5, 50–52, 243–244, 250
Variability, 5, 7–8, 11, 68–69, 74, 92, 95–125, 157–176, 180–181, 186–187, 196, 200, 202–203
Variation, 1–13, 20, 26, 28, 30, 35, 38–39, 51, 62–63, 66–68, 72, 78, 109, 118, 122–124, 130, 158, 161–162, 164–165, 167, 169–176, 181–182, 188, 193, 231, 241–242, 266
  learning, 2, 7, 28, 30
    model, 2, 230
Variation in the input, 2–3, 6, 10–13, 109, 124, 181, 242
Verb
  -final, 8, 35–36, 38, 40–41, 53–54, 59–60, 62, 157, 162
  island hypothesis, 164
  particle, 8, 95, 98–101, 105–106, 110–119, 121–124, 144, 146
    construction, 8, 144, 146
  placement, 3, 35, 38, 52, 57, 63
  -projection raising, 37
VIA, 3–4, 6, 10
Viau, J., 8, 131, 137–140, 142–143, 145

W
Wagner, L., 138
Wason, P., 21, 25
Westergaard, M., 1–13, 50–52, 202, 208–209, 241–267
Wexler, K., 2, 12, 180–181, 249
Wh-complement, 7, 33–63
Wh-operator, 49
Word frequency, 8, 95–125
Word order
  in dative constructions, 129–155
  variability, 8, 68, 95–125, 157–176, 202–203

Y
Yang, C., 2, 7, 17, 20, 23–24, 29
Yes-/no-question, 172, 250
Yip, V., 130, 133, 139, 143

Lightning Source UK Ltd.
Milton Keynes UK
30 September 2010

160603UK00007B/56/P